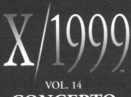

X/1999™

VOL. 14

CONCERTO

Shōjo Edition

STORY & ART BY CLAMP

ENGLISH ADAPTATION BY FRED BURKE

Translation/Lillian Olsen
Touch-Up Art & Lettering/Stephen Dutro
Cover and Interior Design/Yuki Ameda
Supervising Editor/Michelle Pangilinan
Editor/P. Duffield

Managing Editor/Annette Roman
Editor in Chief/Alvin Lu
Production Manager/Noboru Watanabe
Sr. Director of Licensing & Acquisitions/Rika Inouye
VP of Marketing/Liza Coppola
Sr. VP of Editorial/Hyoe Narita
Publisher/Seiji Horibuchi

X/1999 is rated "T+" for Older Teens. It may contain violence, language, alcohol or tobacco use, or suggestive situations.

Printed in Canada

Published by VIZ, LLC
P.O. Box 77010 • San Francisco, CA 94107

Shōjo Edition
10 9 8 7 6 5 4 3 2 1
First printing, April 2004

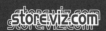

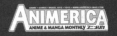

X/1999 ™

Vol. 14
CONCERTO

Shōjo Edition

Story and Art by
CLAMP

X/1999
THE STORY THUS FAR

The End of the World has been prophesied …and time is running out. Kamui Shiro is a young man who was born with a special power—the power to decide the fate of the Earth itself.

Kamui had grown up in Tokyo, but had fled with his mother after the suspicious death of a family friend. Six years later, his mother too, dies under suspicious circumstances, engulfed in flames. Her last words to him are that he should return to Tokyo…that his destiny awaits.

Kamui obeys his mother's words, but almost immediately upon his arrival, he's challenged to a psychic duel—a first warning that others know of his power, and of his return.

Kamui is also reunited with his childhood friends, Fuma and Kotori Monou. Although Kamui attempts to push his friends away, hoping to protect them, they too are soon drawn into the web of destiny that surrounds him.

Meanwhile, the two sides to the great conflict to come are being drawn. On one side is the dreamseer Hinoto, a blind princess who lives beneath Japan's seat of government, the Diet Building. On the other side is Kanoe, Hinoto's dark sister with similar powers, but a different vision of Earth's ultimate future. Around these two women gather the Dragons of Heaven and the Dragons of Earth, the forces that will fight to decide the fate of the planet. The only variable in the equation is Kamui, whose fate it will be to choose which side he will join.

And Kamui finally does make a choice. He chooses to defend the Earth as it stands now. But by making this choice, he pays a terrible price. For fate has chosen his oldest friend to be his "twin star"—the other "Kamui" who will fight against him. And in this first battle, the gentle Kotori is the first casualty.

Now Kamui must face the consequences of his decision…and try to come to terms with not only his ultimate fate, but that of the Earth….

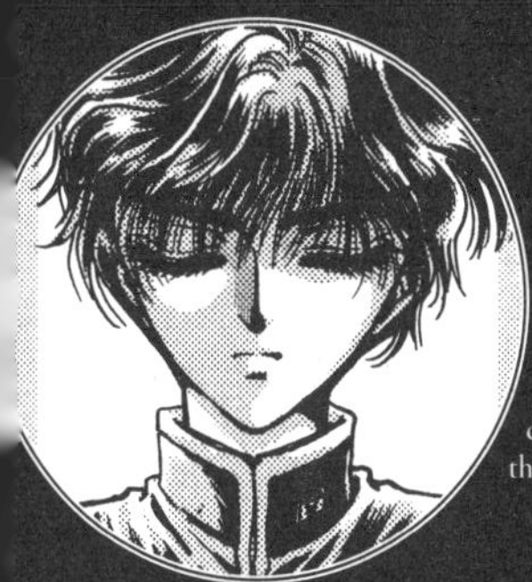

Kamui Shiro
A young man with psychic powers whose choice of destiny will decide the fate of the world.

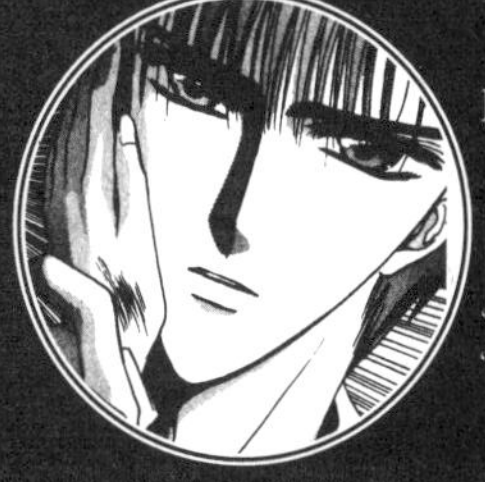

Fuma Monou
Kamui's childhood friend. When Kamui made his choice, Fuma was chosen by fate to become his "Twin Star"—the other "Kamui."

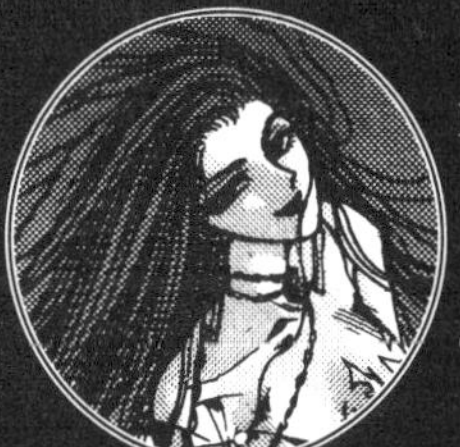

Kanoe
Hinoto's sister shares her ability to see the future… but Kanoe has predicted a different final result.

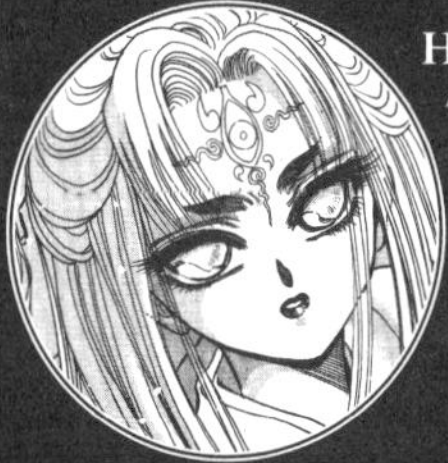

Hinoto
A powerful prophetess who communicates with the power of her mind alone. She lives in a secret shrine located beneath Tokyo's Diet Building.

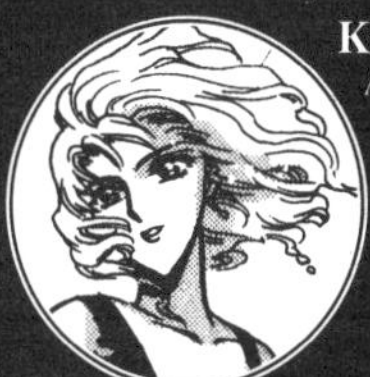

Karen Kasumi
A young woman who works in a Japanese bathhouse (massage parlor). She can control fire.

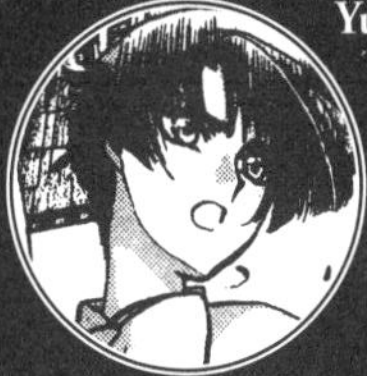

Yuziriha Nekoi
The youngest of the Dragons, she is always accompanied by a spirit dog named Inuki.

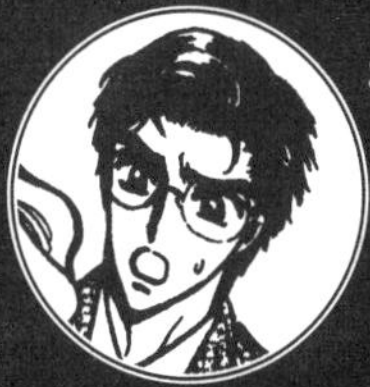

Seiichiro Aoki
A magazine editor, Seiichiro is a devoted family man. He can control the wind.

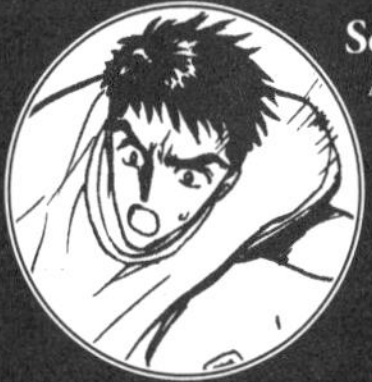

Sorata Arisugawa
A brash, but good-natured priest of the Mt. Koya shrine.

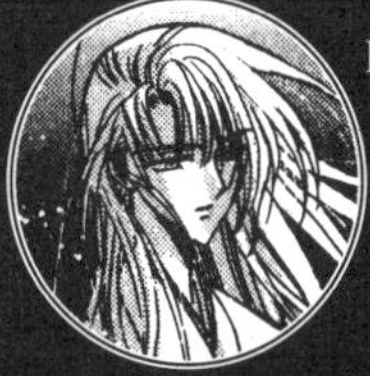

Kakyo Kuzuki
A dreamseer like Hinoto, Kakyo is a hospital-bound invalid kept alive by machines.

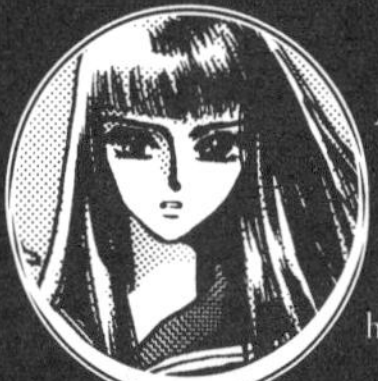

Arashi Kishu
Priestess of the Ise Shrine, Arashi can materialize a sword from the palm of her hand.

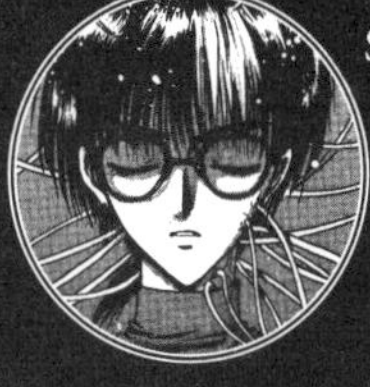

Satsuki Yatoji
A computer expert, Satsuki can interface directly with her personal machine, "The Beast."

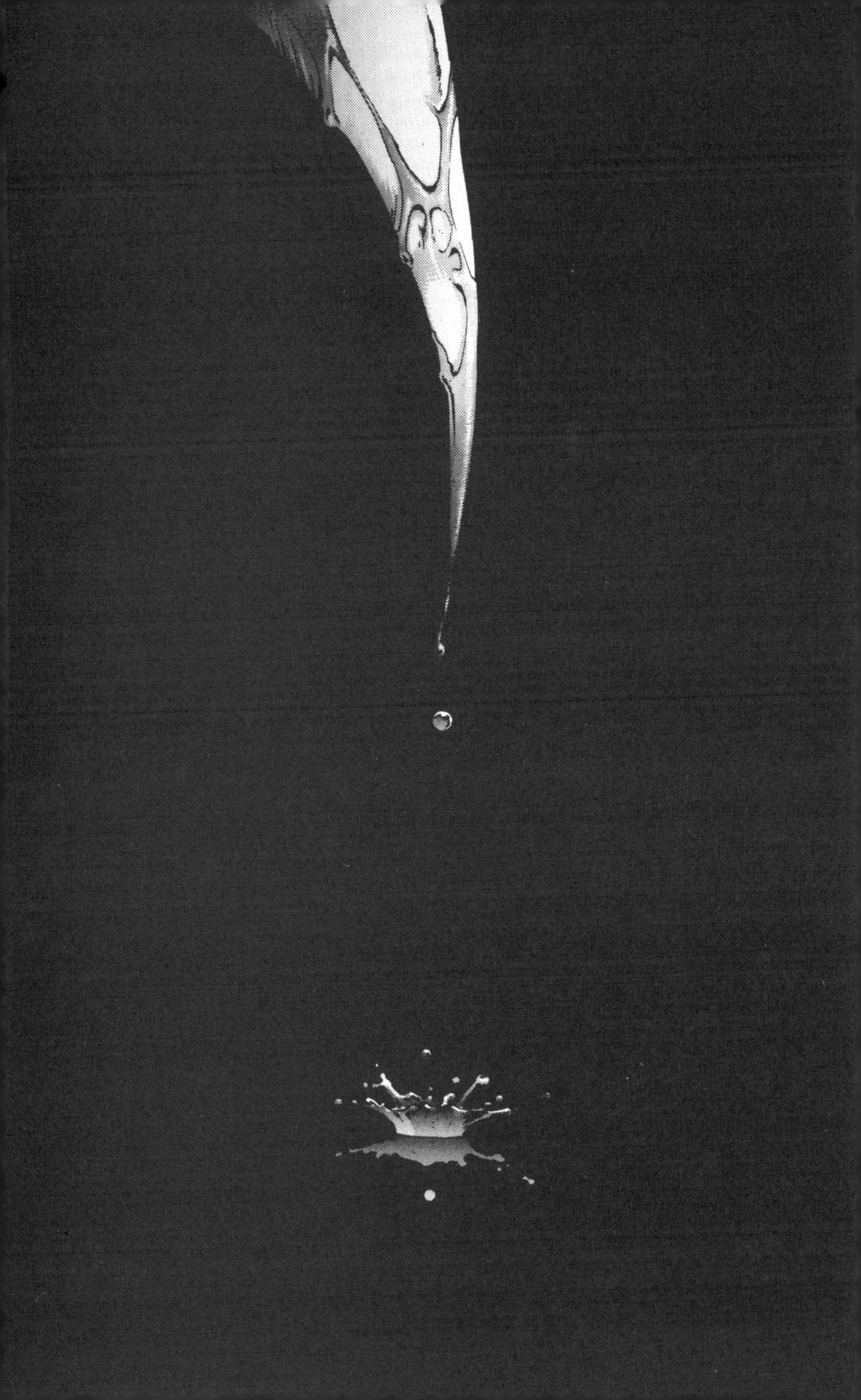

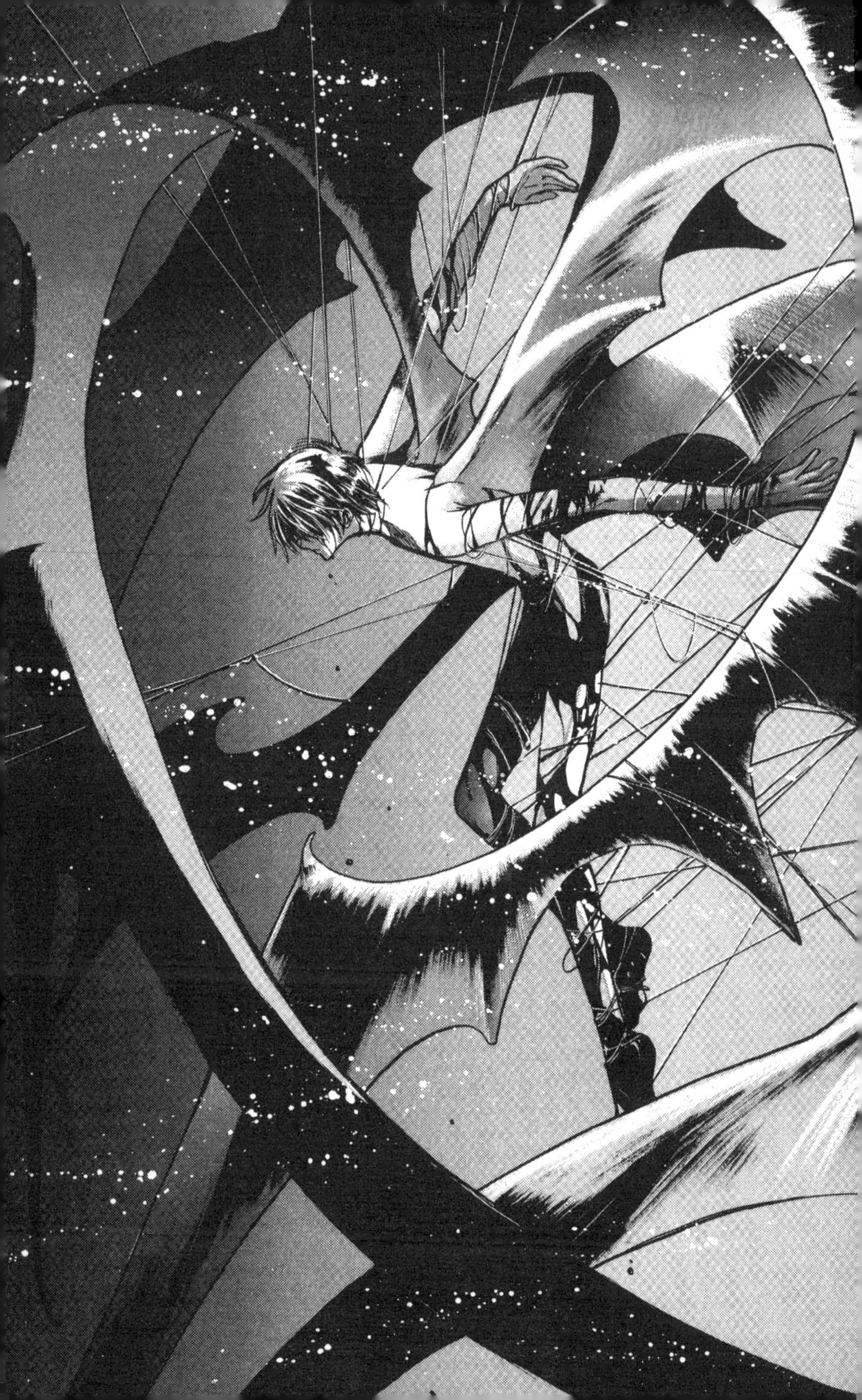

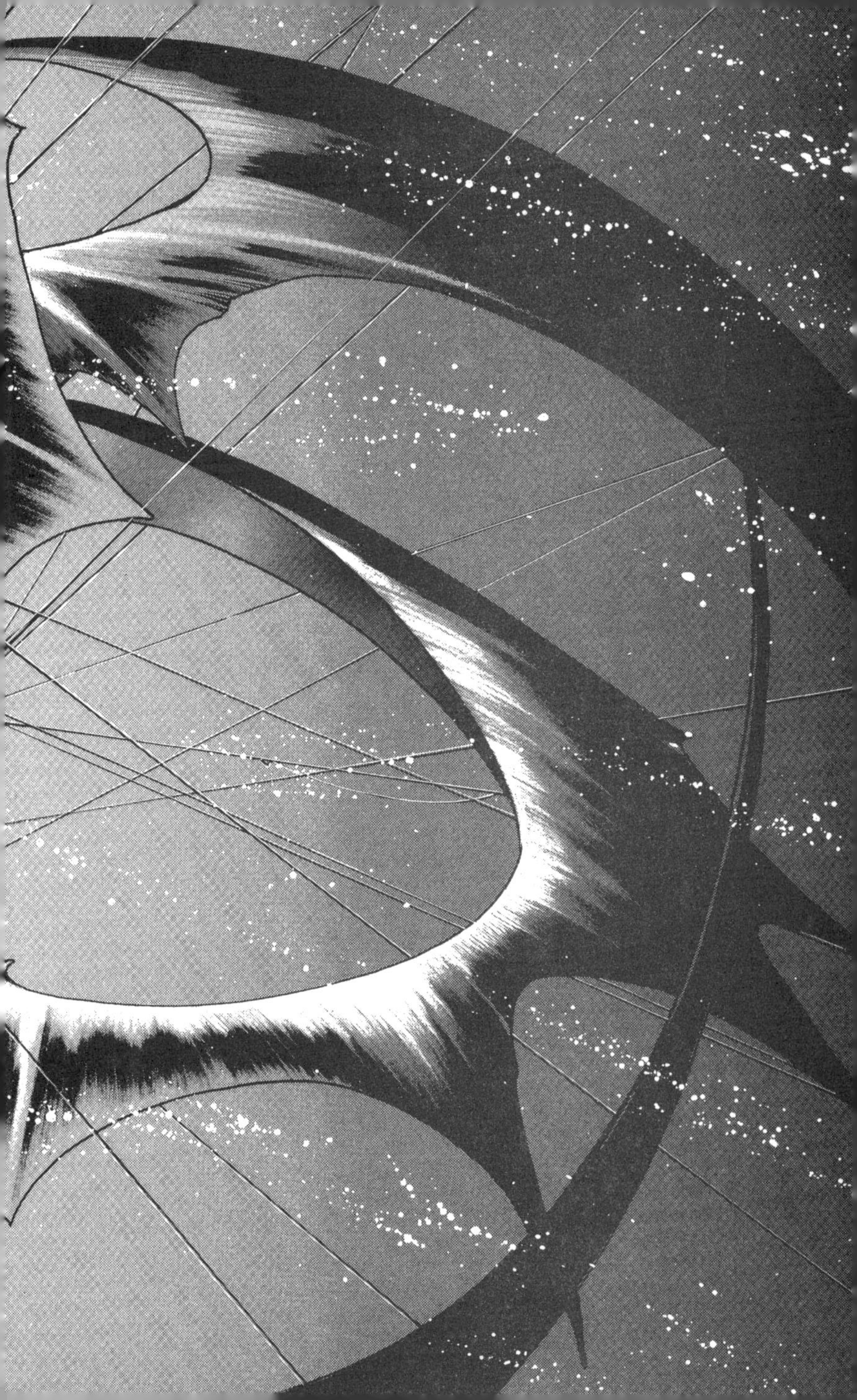

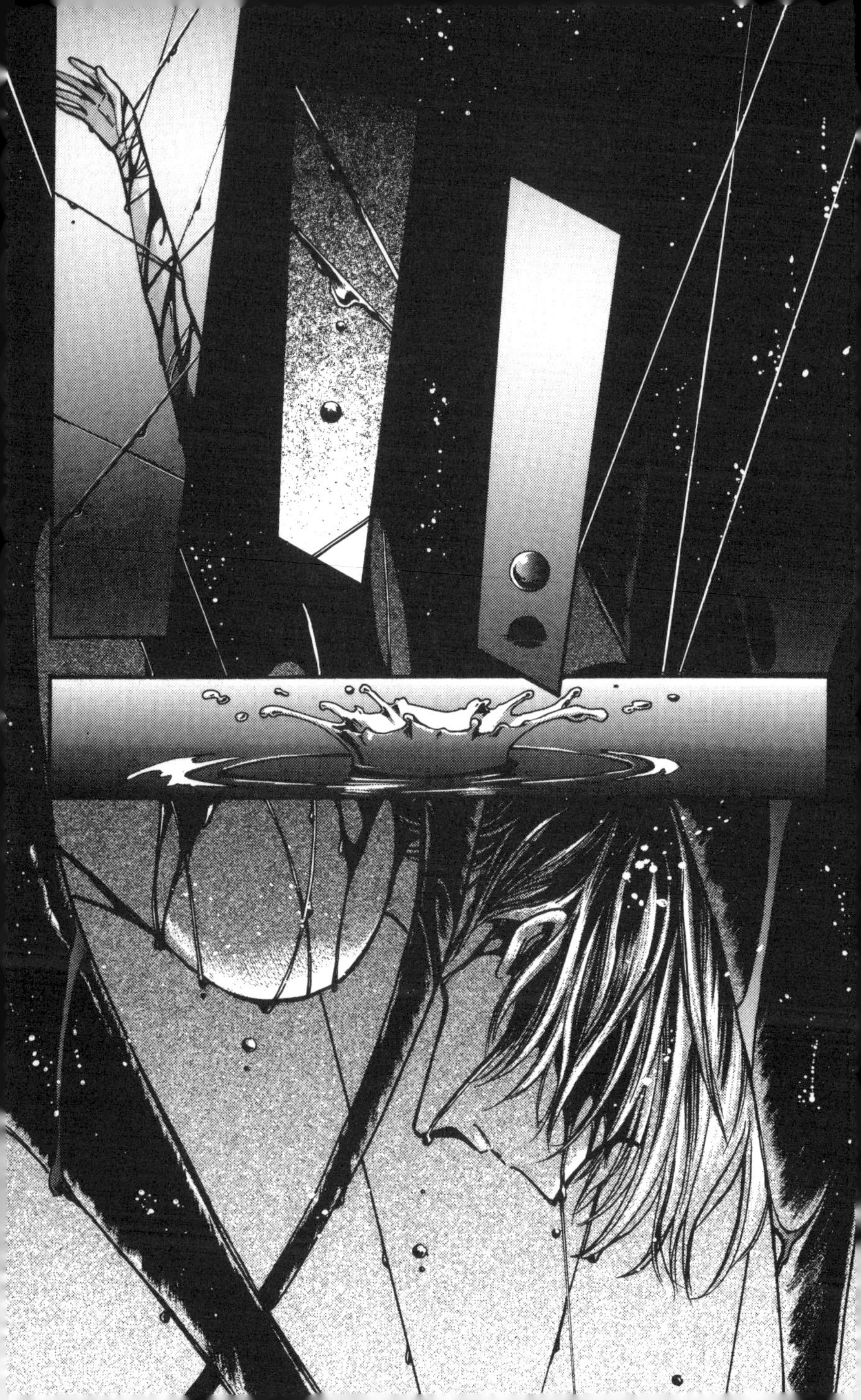

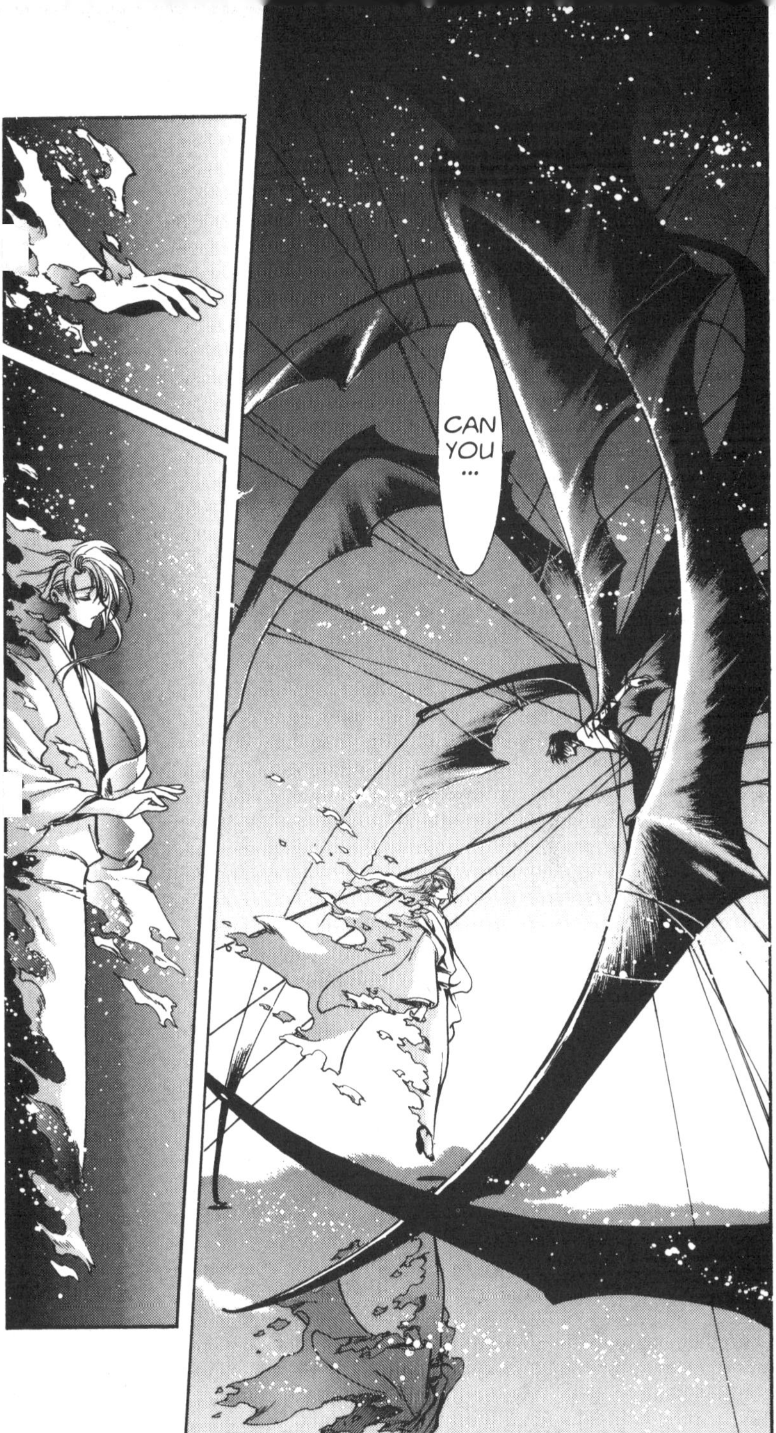
CAN YOU ...

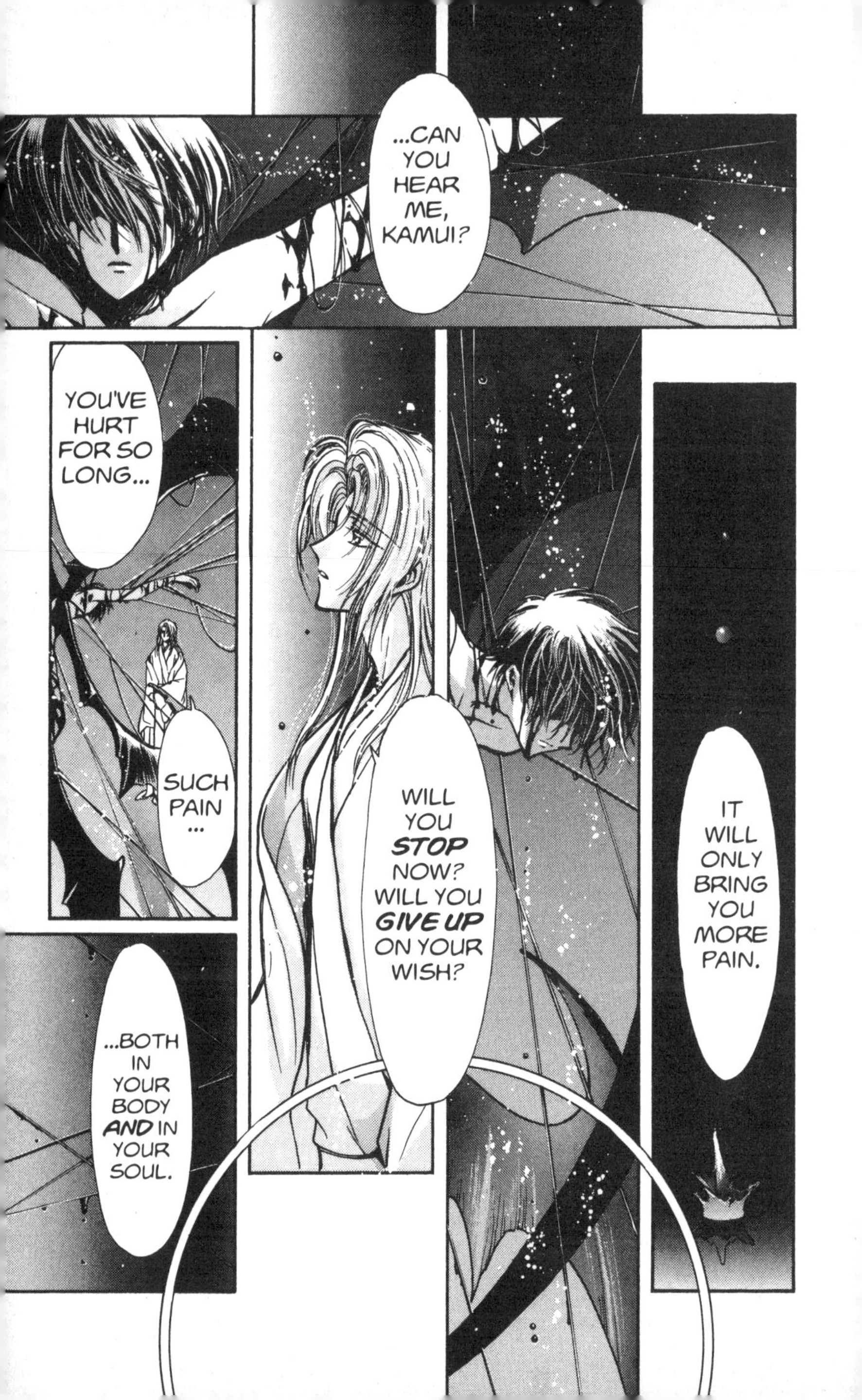
...CAN YOU HEAR ME, KAMUI?
IT WILL ONLY BRING YOU MORE PAIN.
WILL YOU STOP NOW? WILL YOU GIVE UP ON YOUR WISH?
YOU'VE HURT FOR SO LONG...
SUCH PAIN ...
...BOTH IN YOUR BODY AND IN YOUR SOUL.

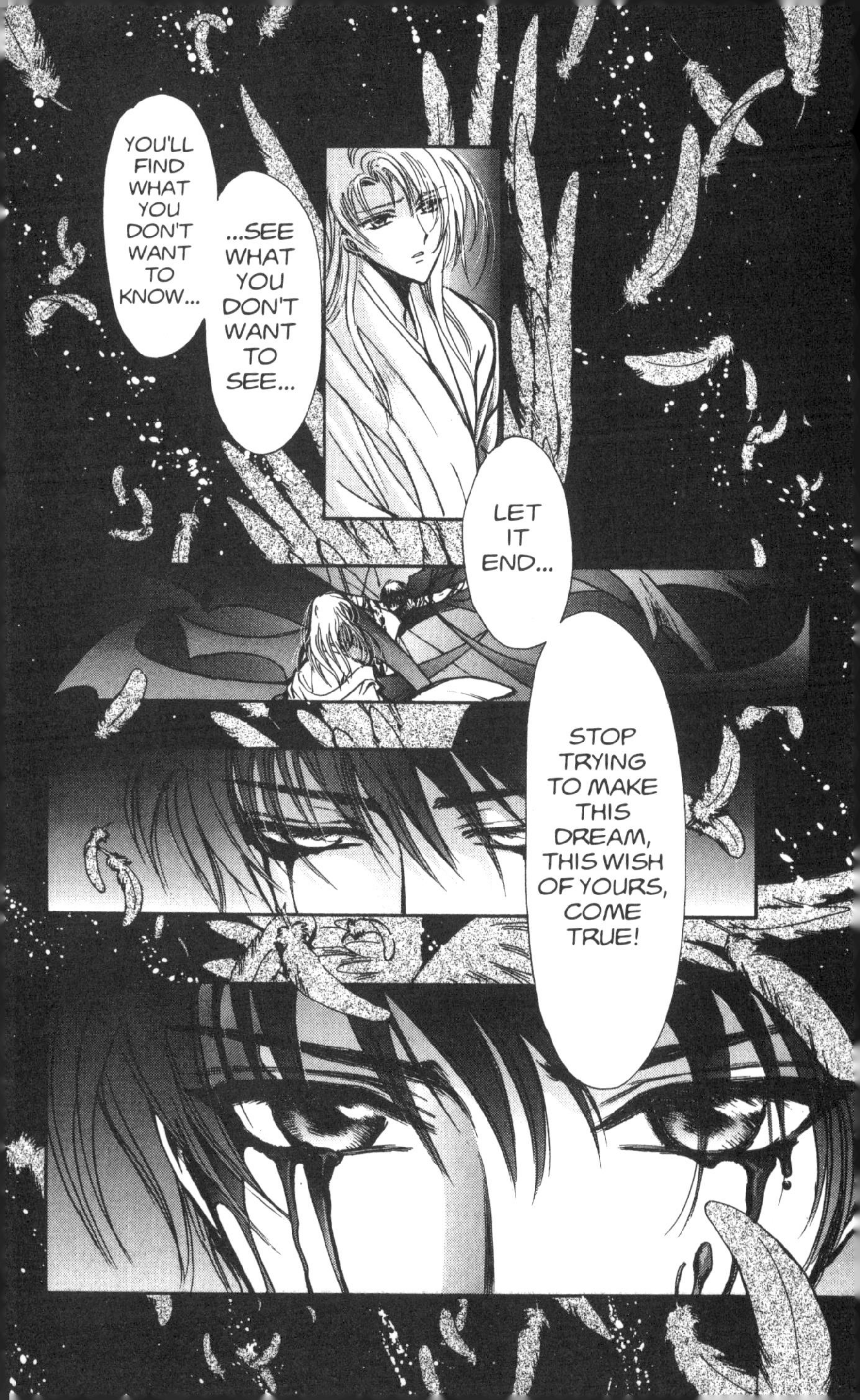
...SEE WHAT YOU DON'T WANT TO SEE...
YOU'LL FIND WHAT YOU DON'T WANT TO KNOW...
LET IT END...
STOP TRYING TO MAKE THIS DREAM, THIS WISH OF YOURS, COME TRUE!

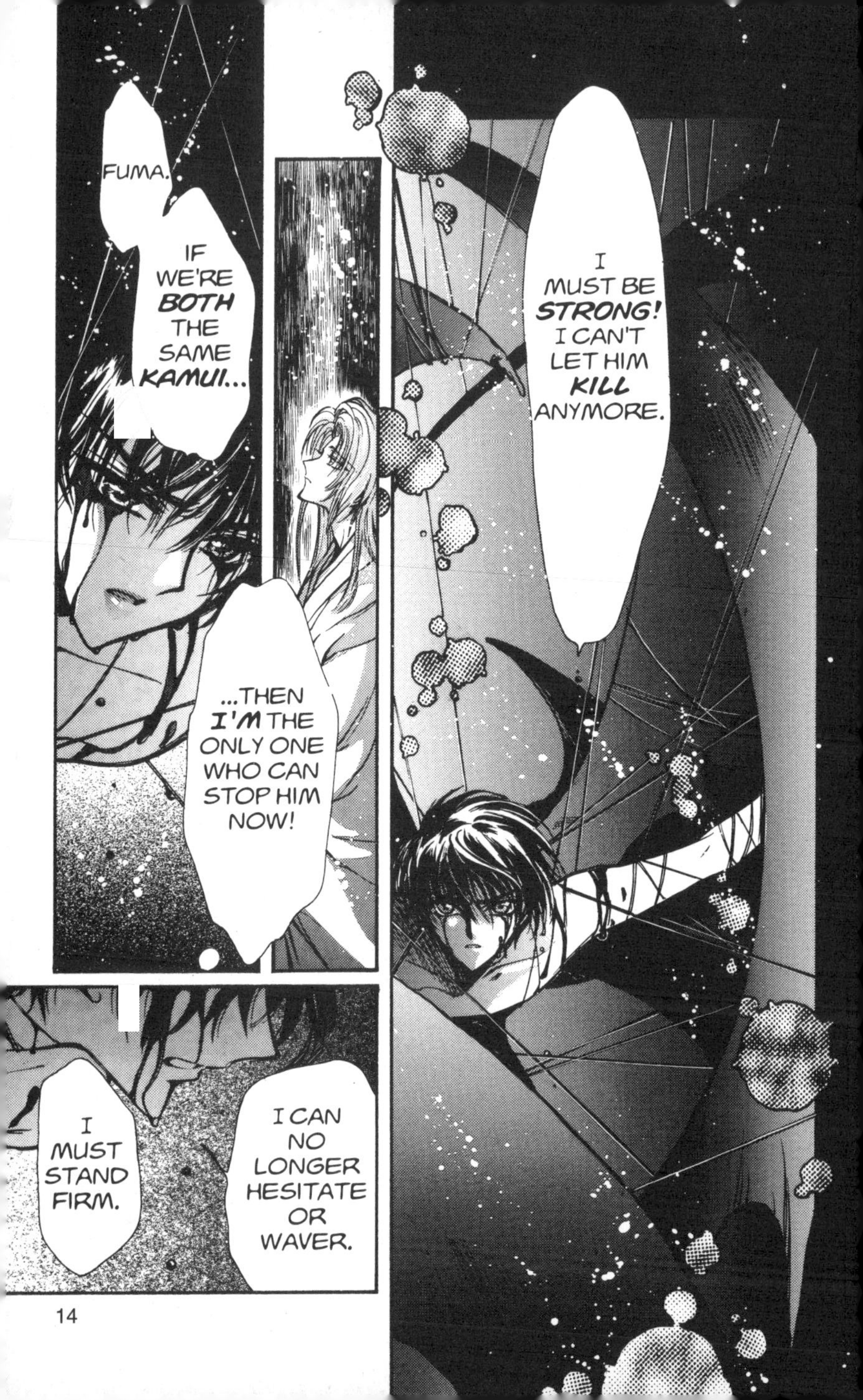
I MUST BE **STRONG!** I CAN'T LET HIM **KILL** ANYMORE.
FUMA.
IF WE'RE **BOTH** THE SAME **KAMUI...**
...THEN **I'M** THE ONLY ONE WHO CAN STOP HIM NOW!
I CAN NO LONGER HESITATE OR WAVER.
I MUST STAND FIRM.

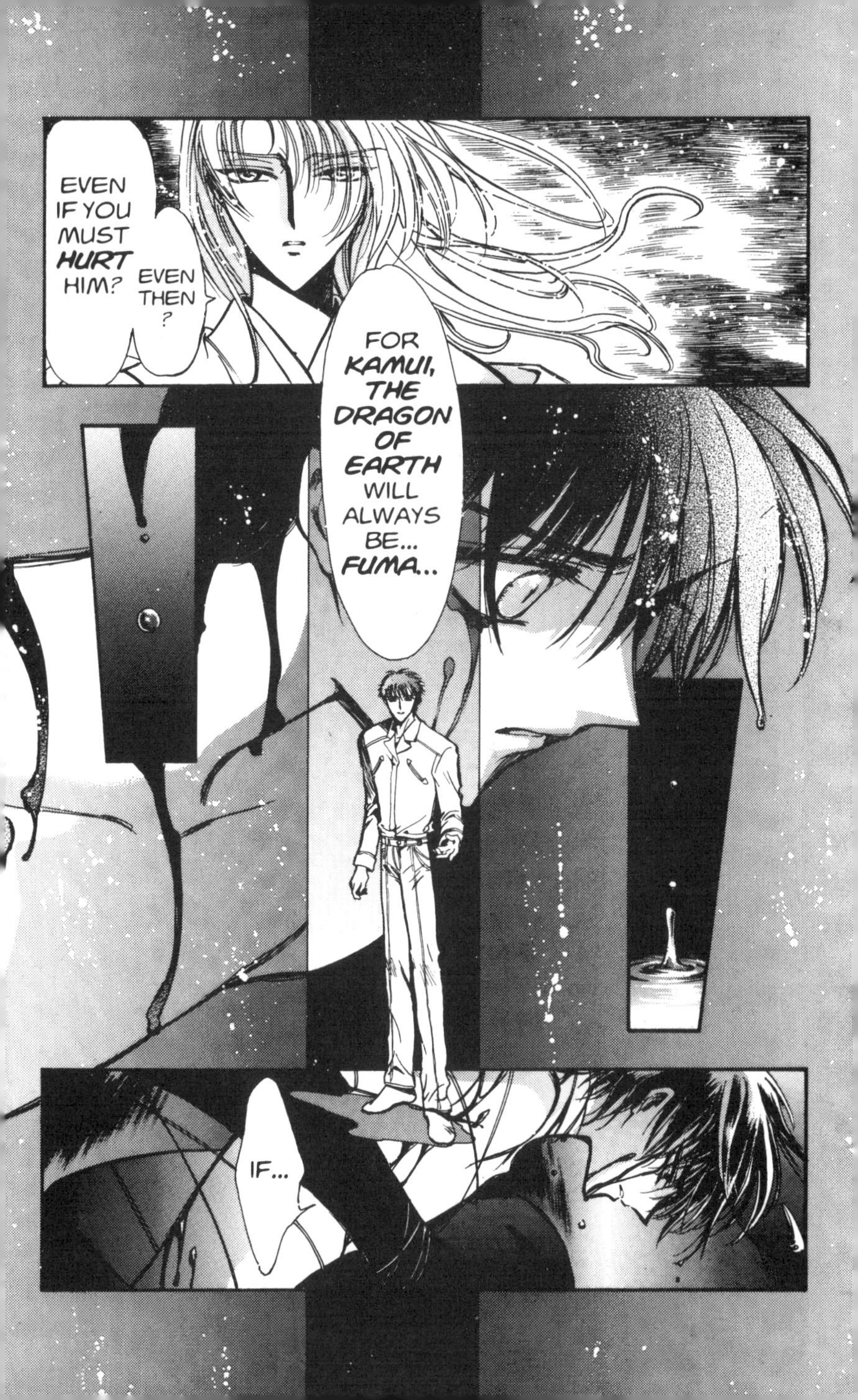
EVEN IF YOU MUST HURT HIM?
EVEN THEN ?
FOR KAMUI, THE DRAGON OF EARTH WILL ALWAYS BE... FUMA...
IF...

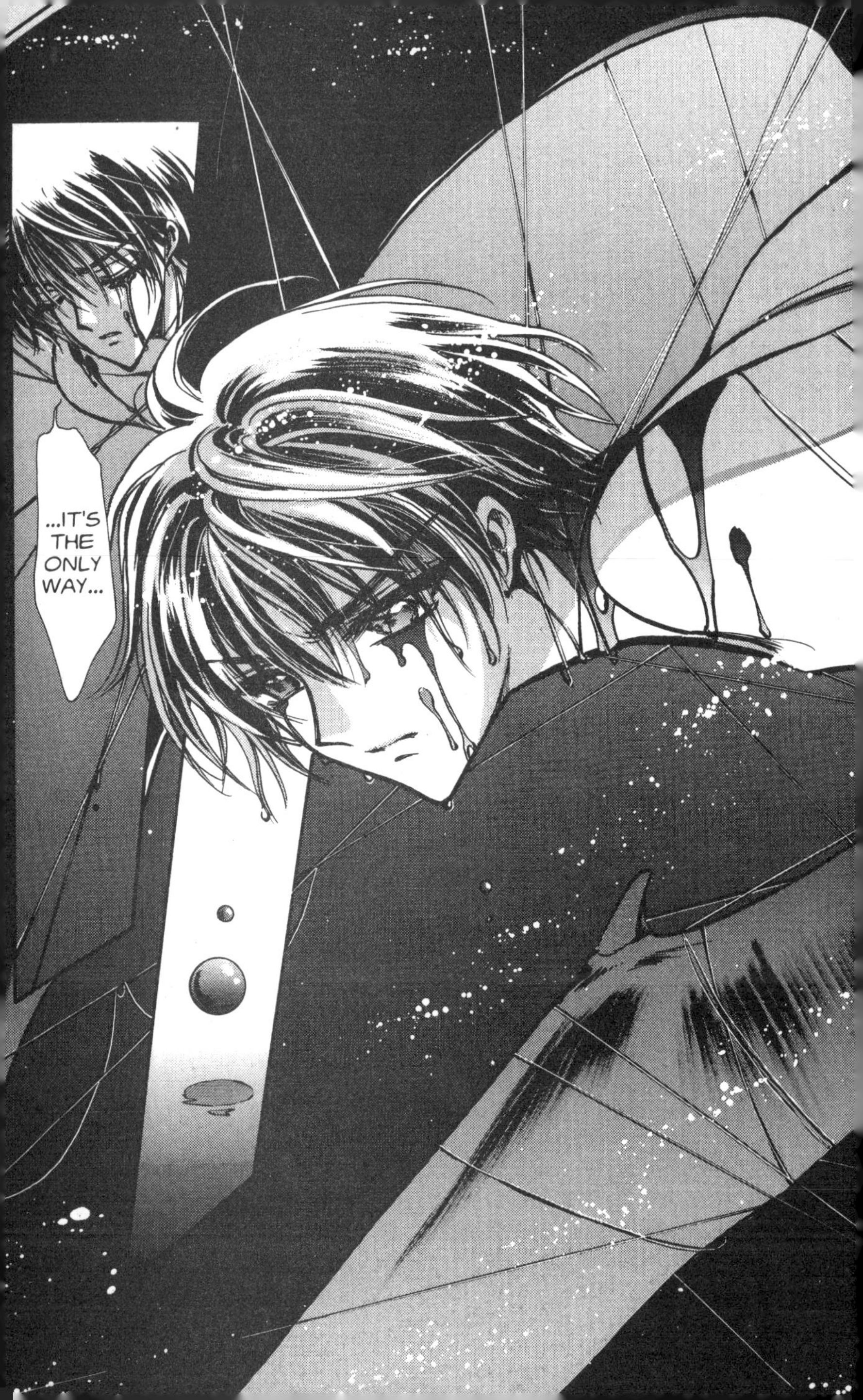
...IT'S THE ONLY WAY...

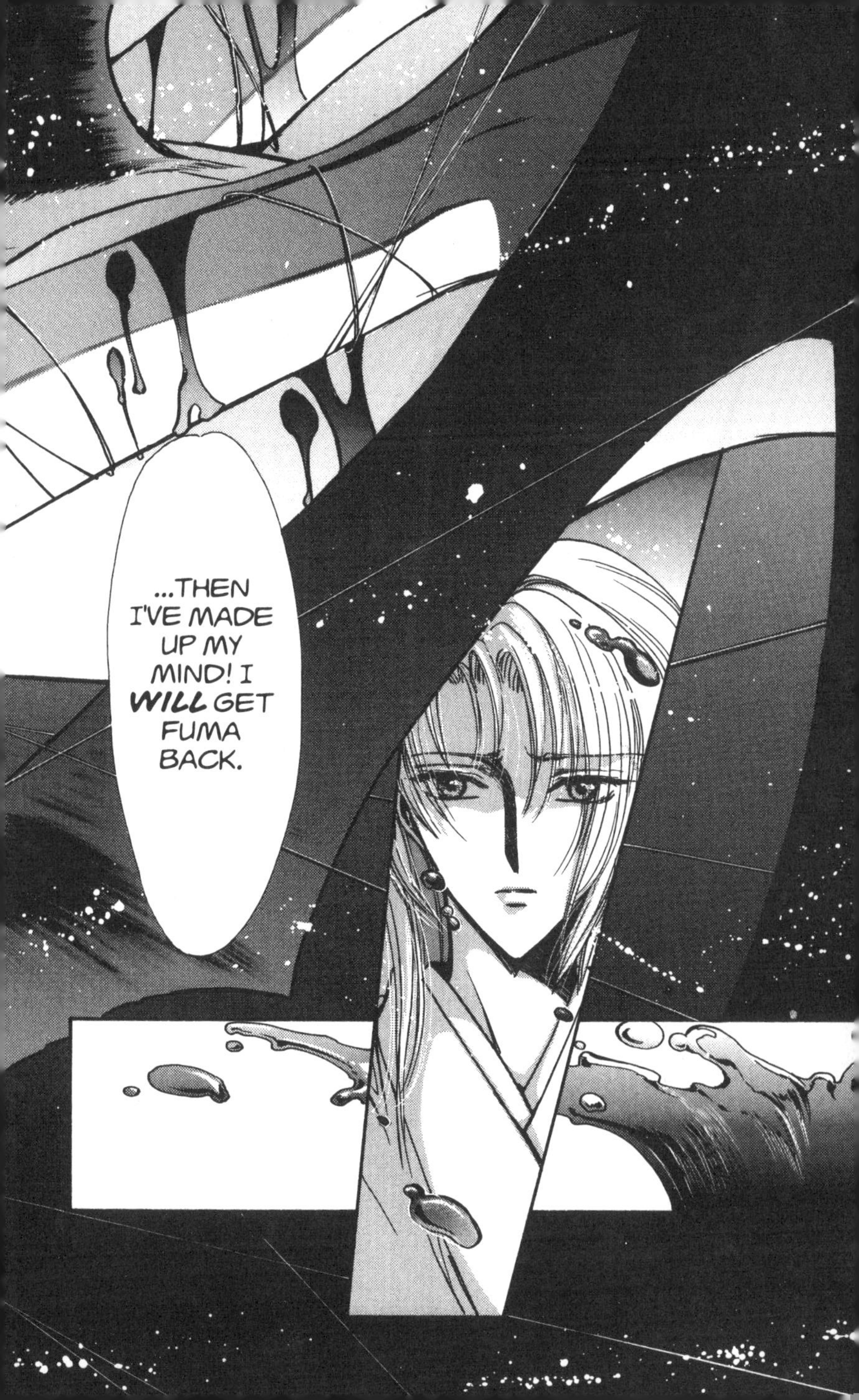
...THEN I'VE MADE UP MY MIND! I **WILL** GET FUMA BACK.

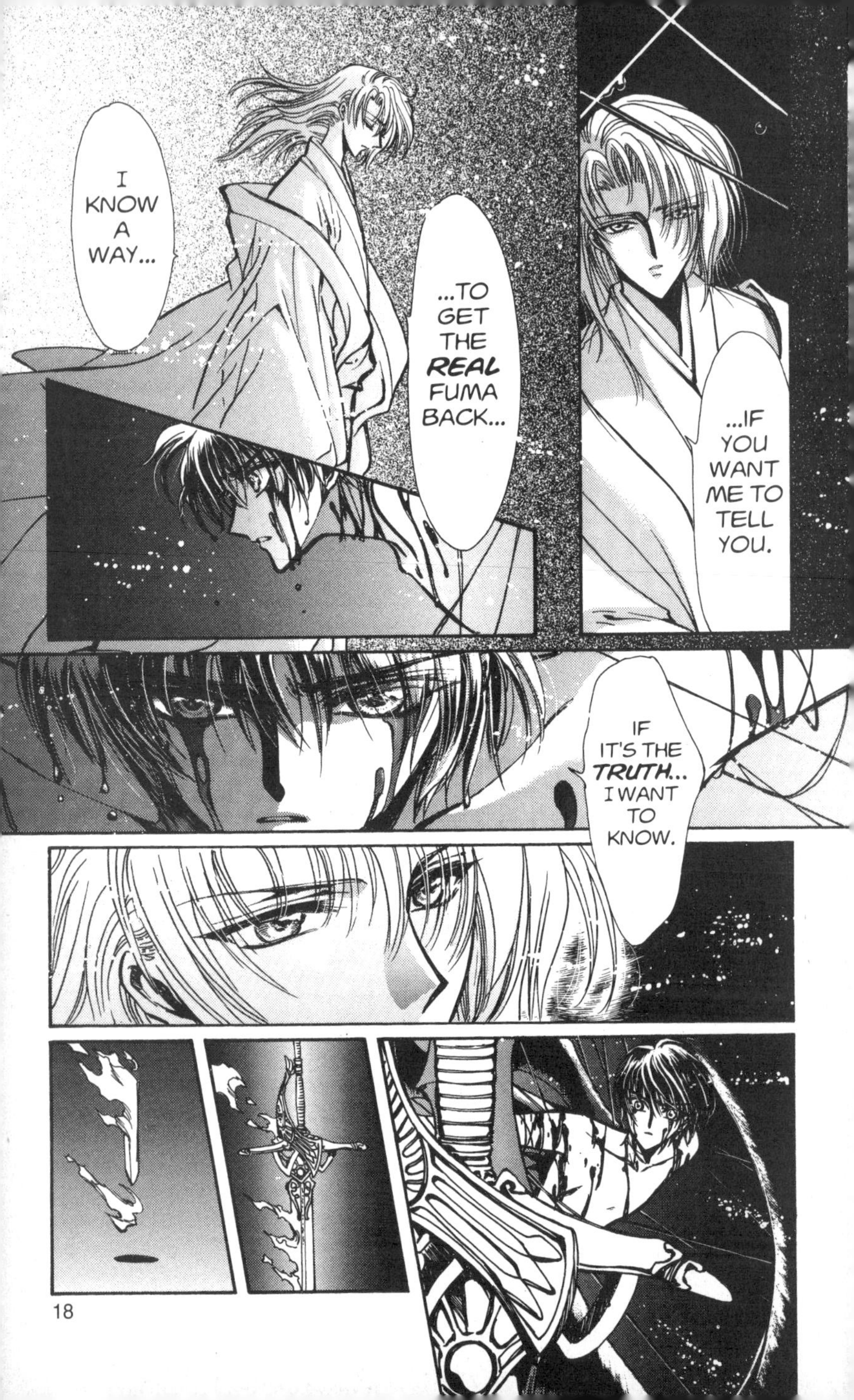
I KNOW A WAY...
...TO GET THE REAL FUMA BACK...
...IF YOU WANT ME TO TELL YOU.
IF IT'S THE TRUTH... I WANT TO KNOW.

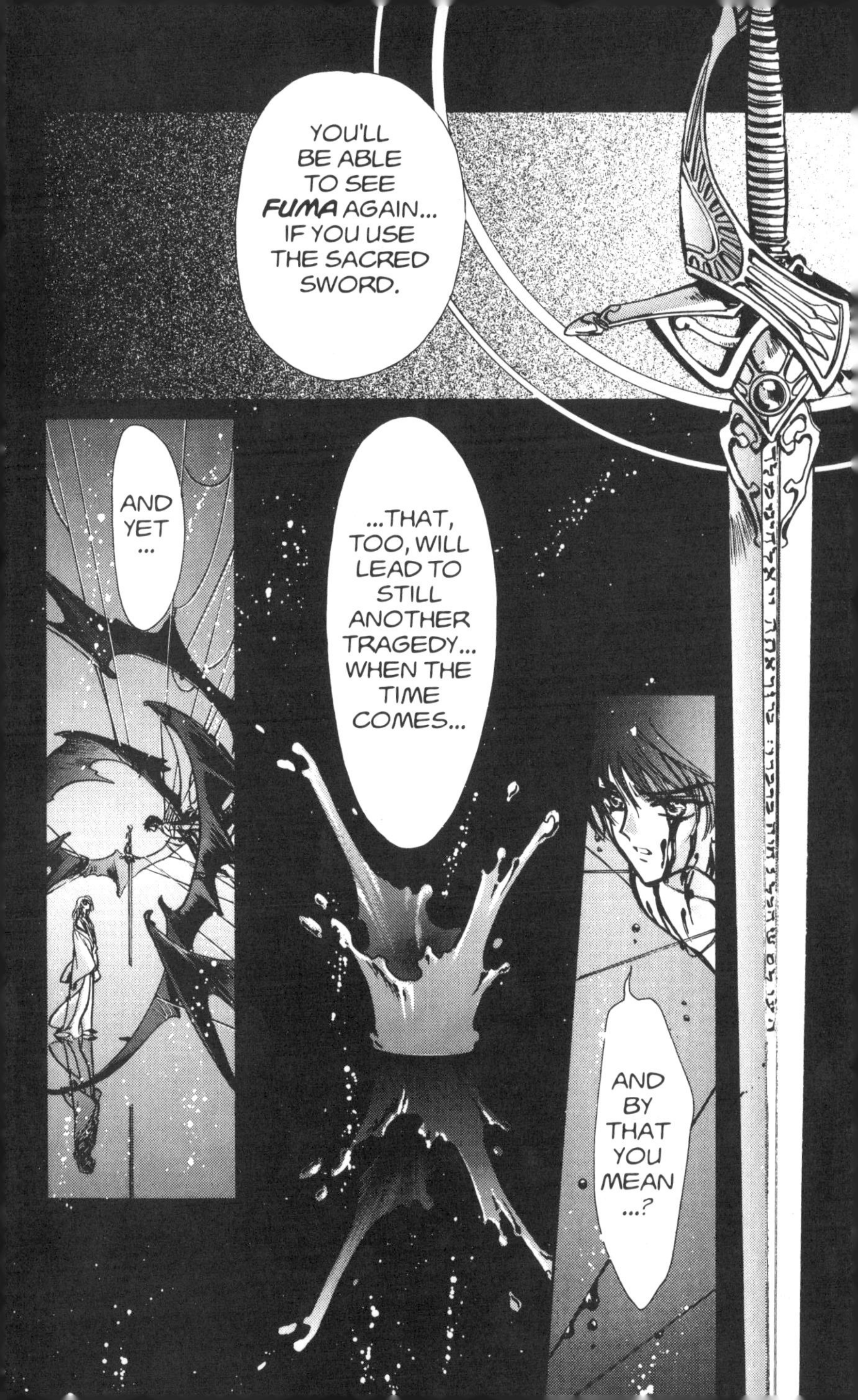
YOU'LL BE ABLE TO SEE FUMA AGAIN... IF YOU USE THE SACRED SWORD.
AND YET ...
...THAT, TOO, WILL LEAD TO STILL ANOTHER TRAGEDY... WHEN THE TIME COMES...
AND BY THAT YOU MEAN ...?

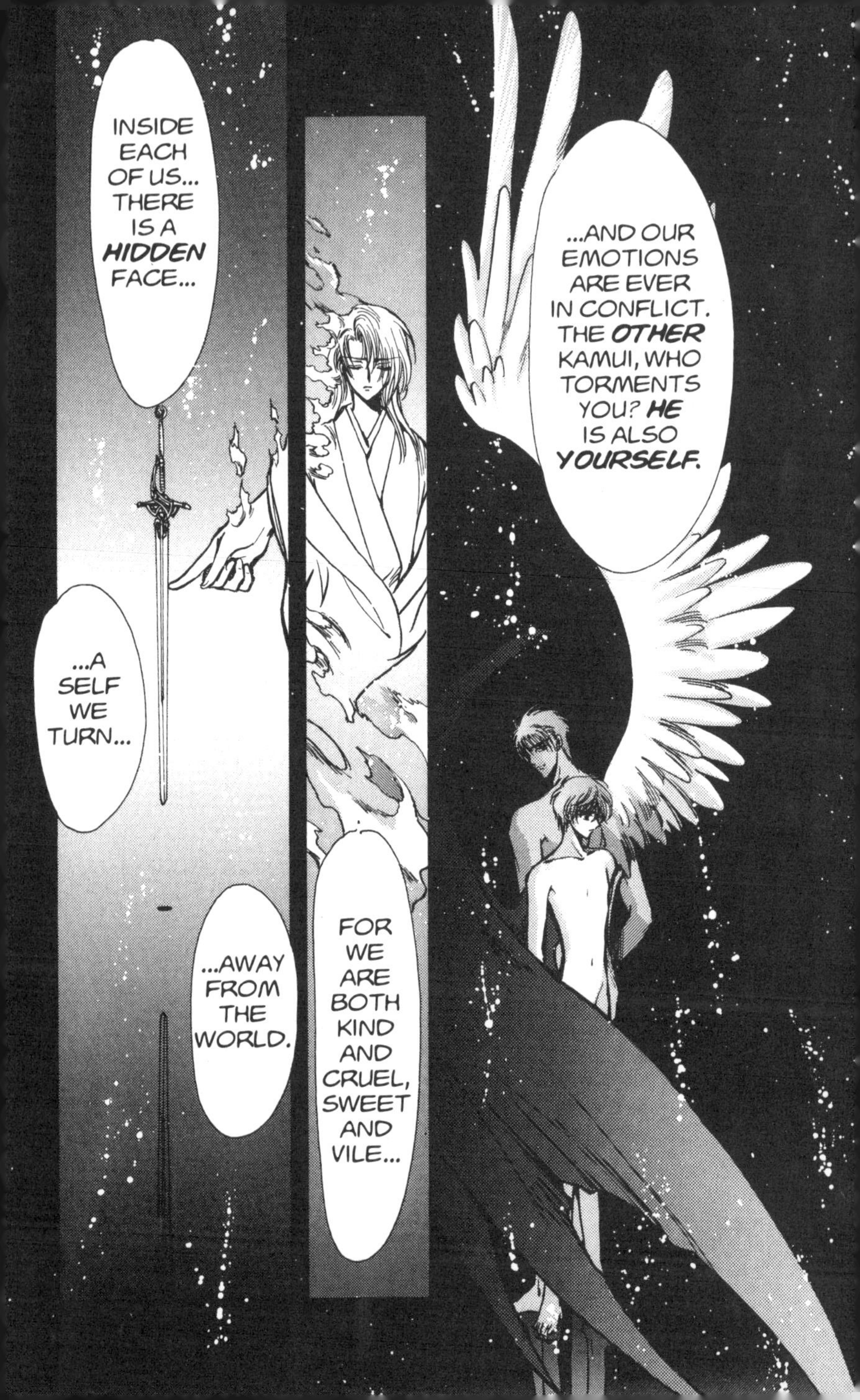
INSIDE EACH OF US... THERE IS A HIDDEN FACE...
...A SELF WE TURN...
...AWAY FROM THE WORLD.
FOR WE ARE BOTH KIND AND CRUEL, SWEET AND VILE...
...AND OUR EMOTIONS ARE EVER IN CONFLICT. THE OTHER KAMUI, WHO TORMENTS YOU? HE IS ALSO YOURSELF.

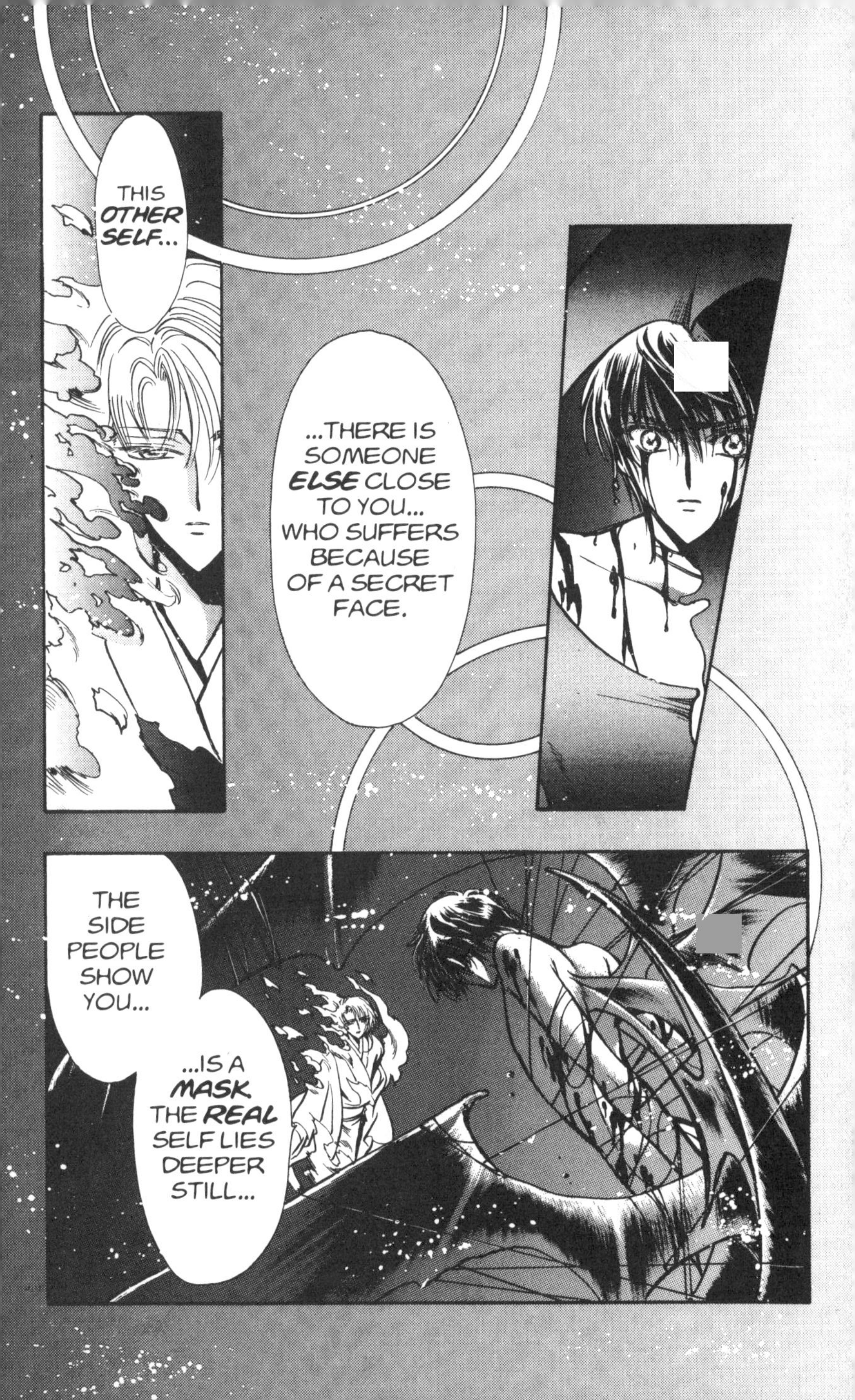
THIS OTHER SELF...
...THERE IS SOMEONE ELSE CLOSE TO YOU... WHO SUFFERS BECAUSE OF A SECRET FACE.
THE SIDE PEOPLE SHOW YOU...
...IS A MASK. THE REAL SELF LIES DEEPER STILL...

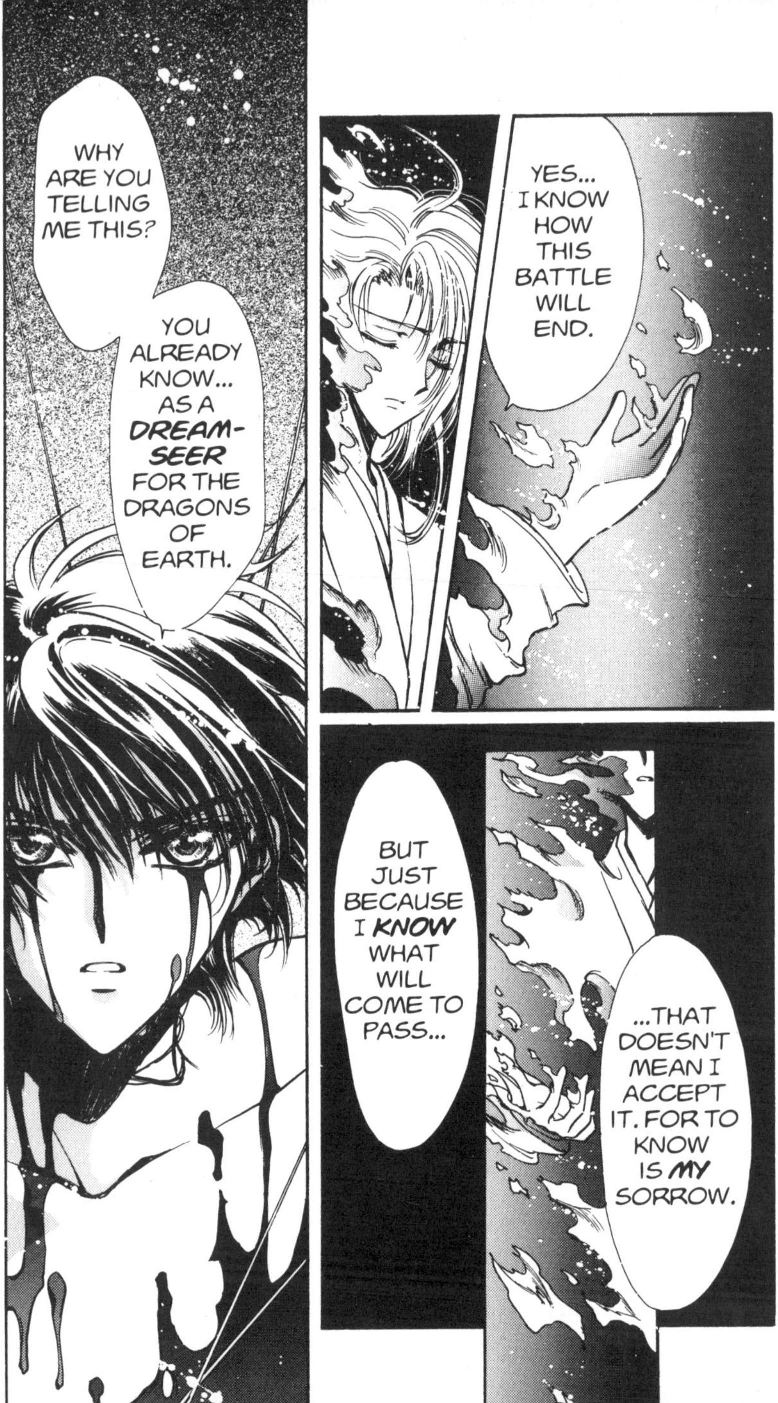
WHY ARE YOU TELLING ME THIS?
YOU ALREADY KNOW... AS A **DREAM-SEER** FOR THE DRAGONS OF EARTH.
YES... I KNOW HOW THIS BATTLE WILL END.
BUT JUST BECAUSE I **KNOW** WHAT WILL COME TO PASS...
...THAT DOESN'T MEAN I ACCEPT IT. FOR TO KNOW IS **MY** SORROW.

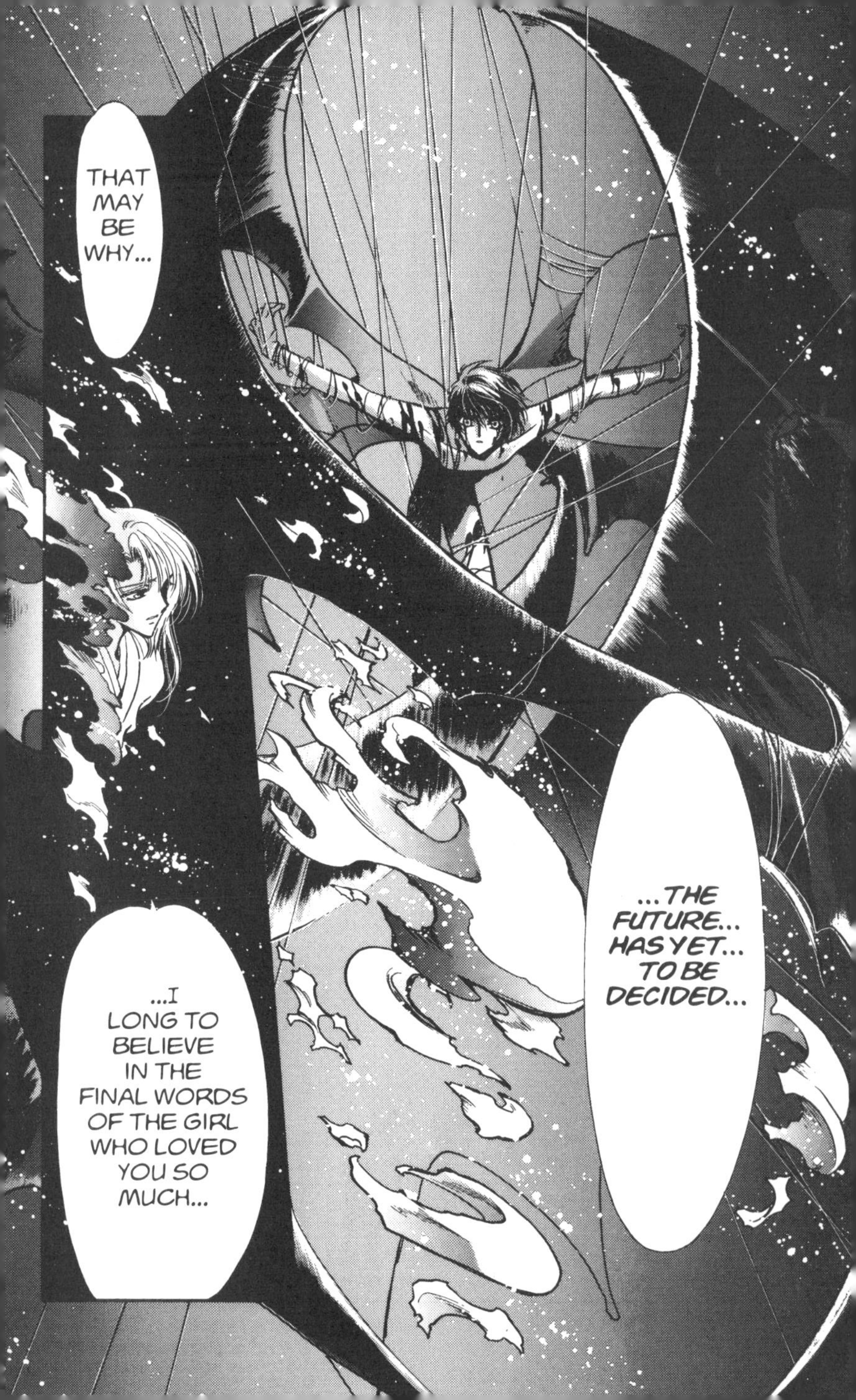
THAT MAY BE WHY...
...THE FUTURE... HAS YET... TO BE DECIDED...
...I LONG TO BELIEVE IN THE FINAL WORDS OF THE GIRL WHO LOVED YOU SO MUCH...

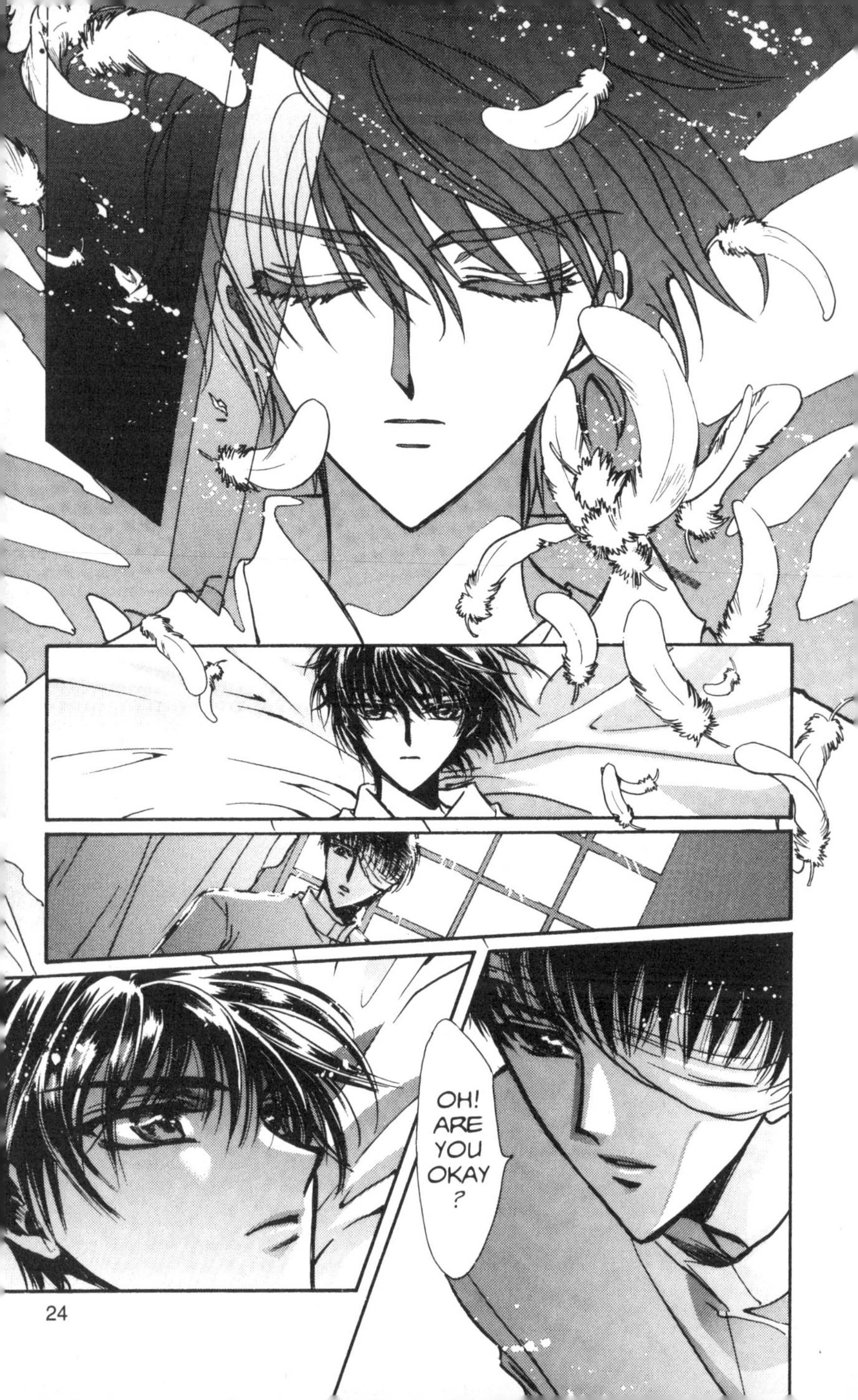
OH! ARE YOU OKAY ?

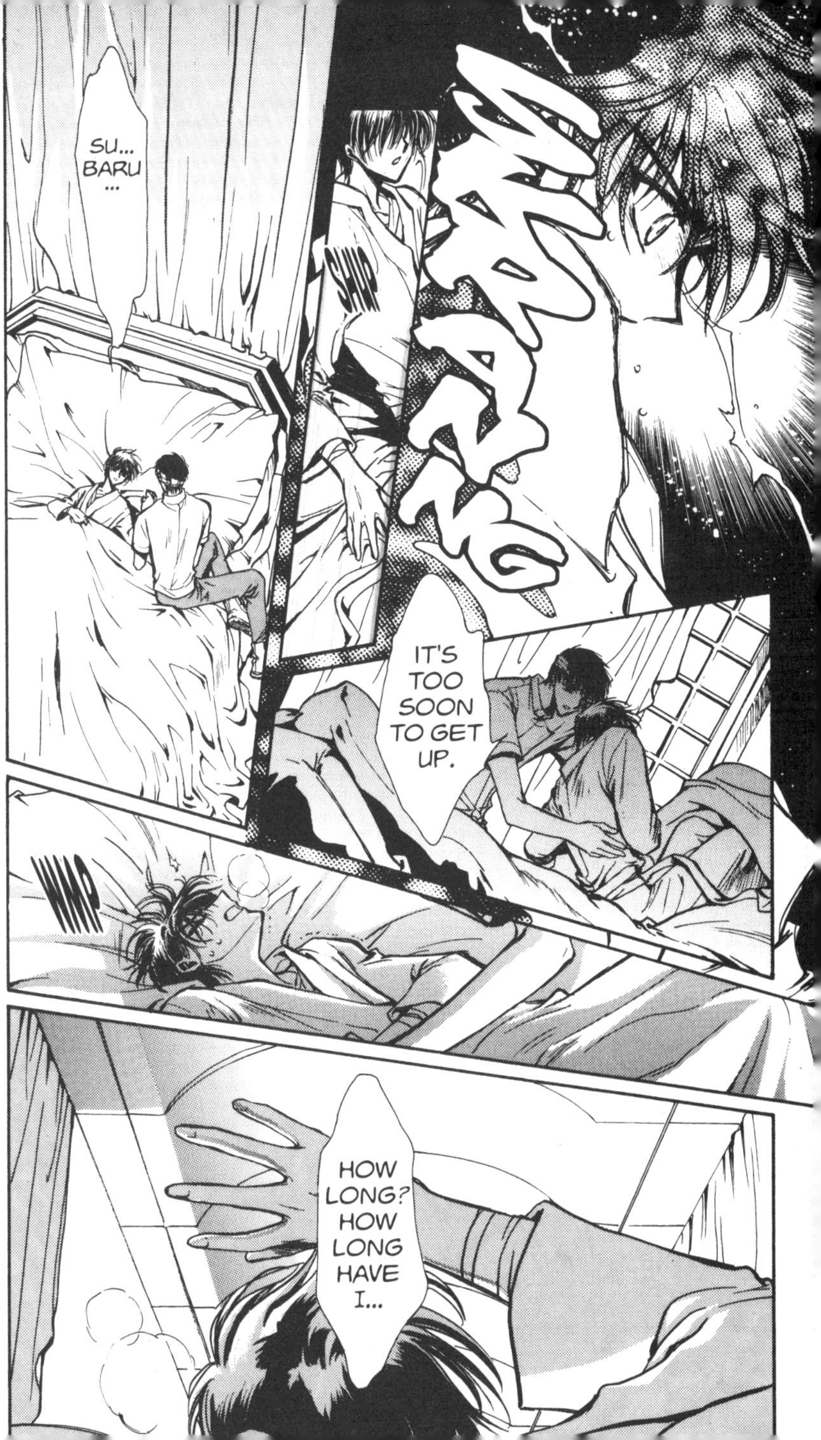
SHP
SU... BARU ...
IT'S TOO SOON TO GET UP.
HMP
HOW LONG? HOW LONG HAVE I...

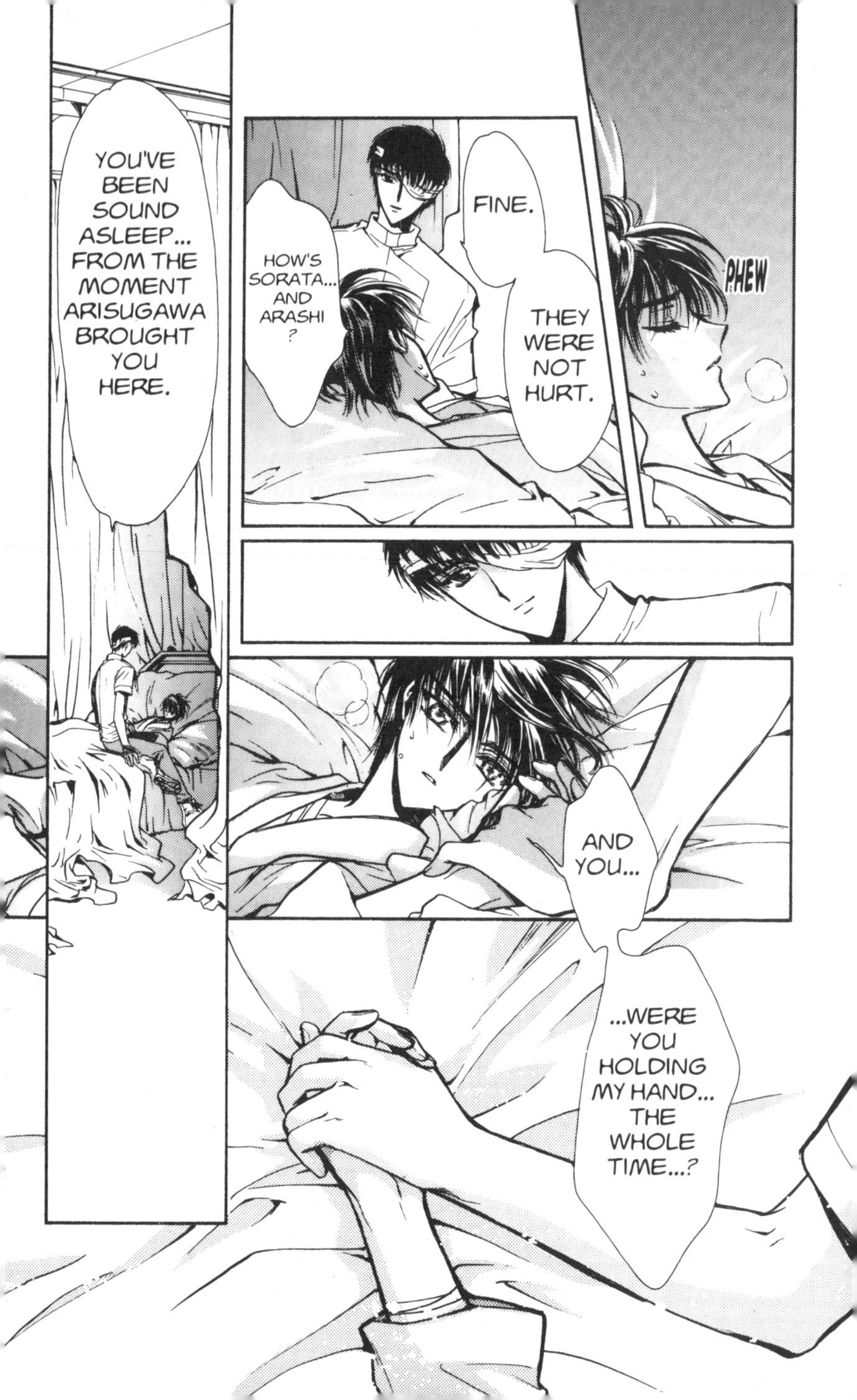
PHEW
HOW'S SORATA... AND ARASHI?
FINE.
THEY WERE NOT HURT.
YOU'VE BEEN SOUND ASLEEP... FROM THE MOMENT ARISUGAWA BROUGHT YOU HERE.
AND YOU...
...WERE YOU HOLDING MY HAND... THE WHOLE TIME...?

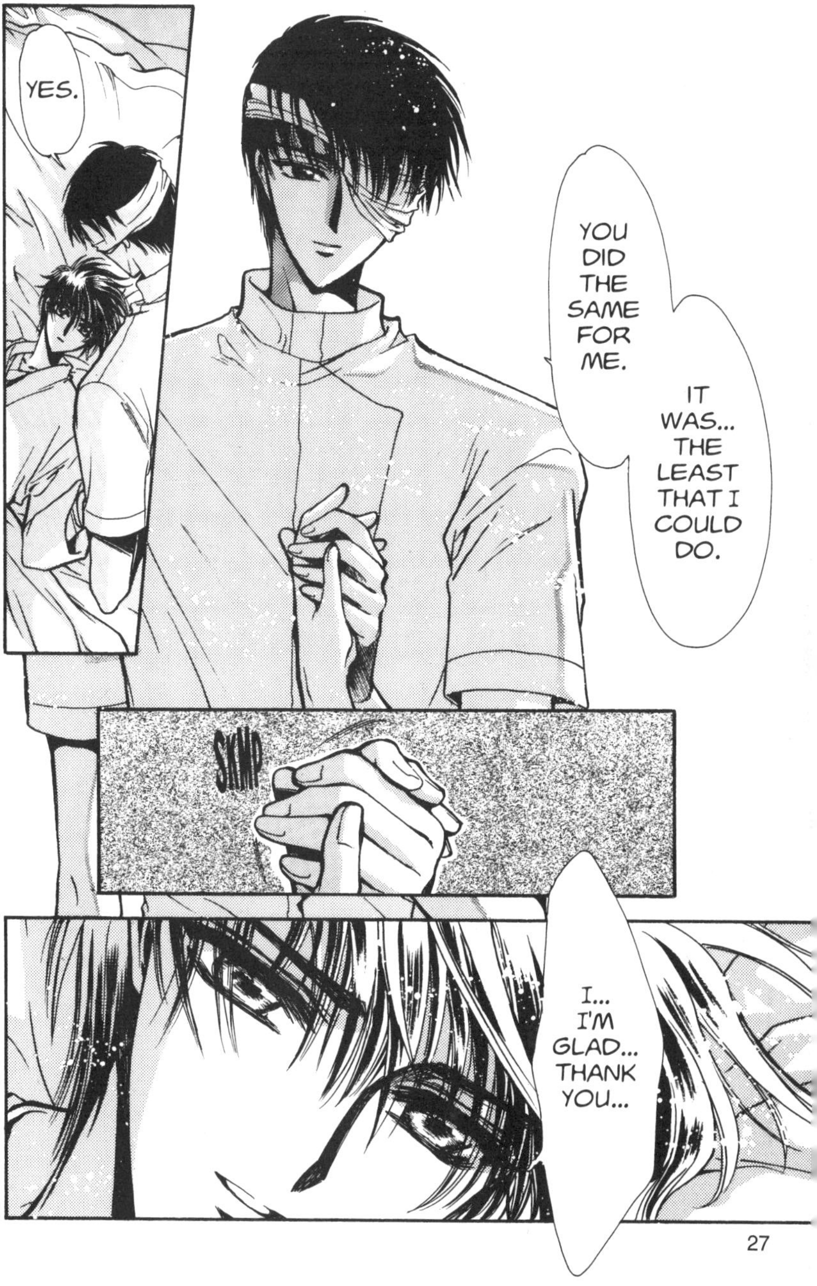
YOU DID THE SAME FOR ME.
IT WAS... THE LEAST THAT I COULD DO.
YES.
SKMP
I... I'M GLAD... THANK YOU...

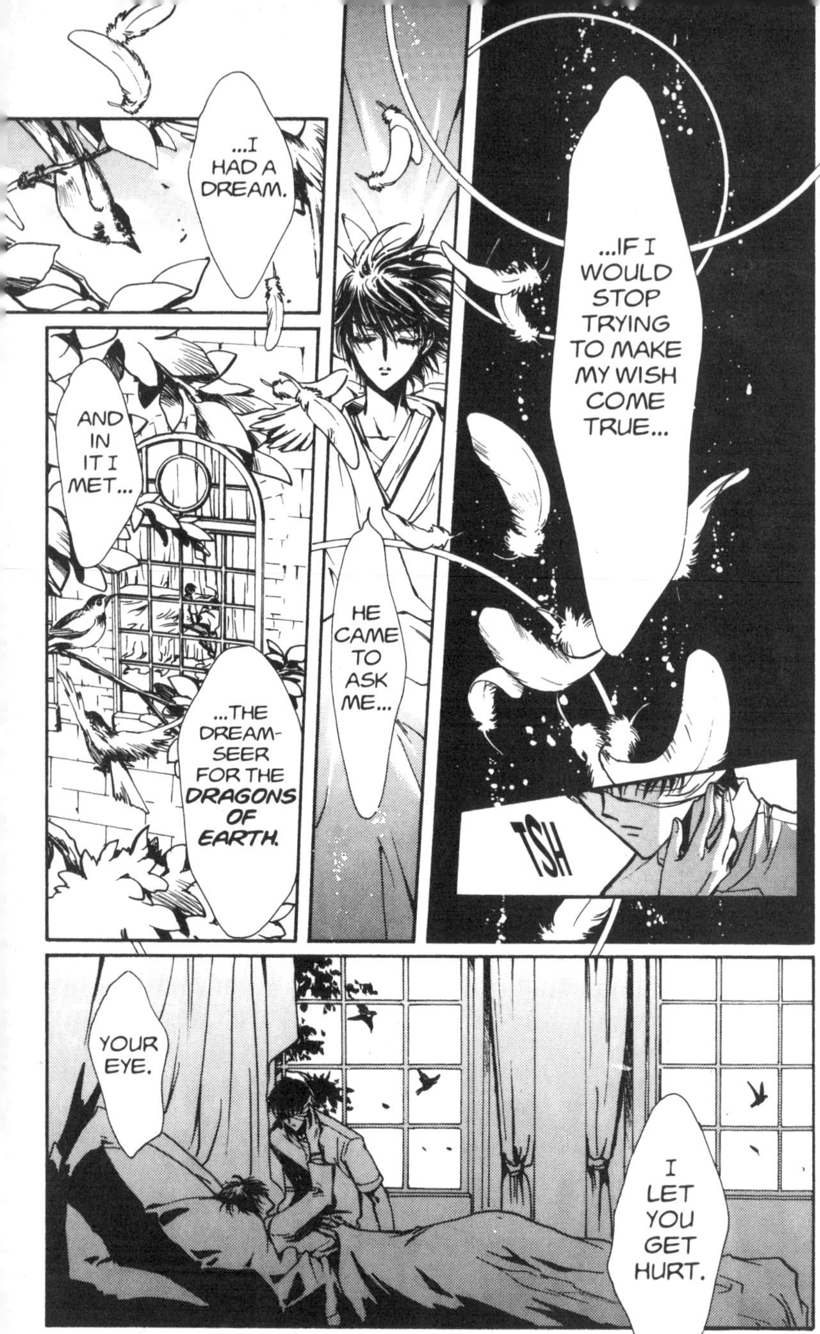
...I HAD A DREAM.
AND IN IT I MET...
...THE DREAM-SEER FOR THE DRAGONS OF EARTH.
HE CAME TO ASK ME...
...IF I WOULD STOP TRYING TO MAKE MY WISH COME TRUE...
TSH
YOUR EYE.
I LET YOU GET HURT.

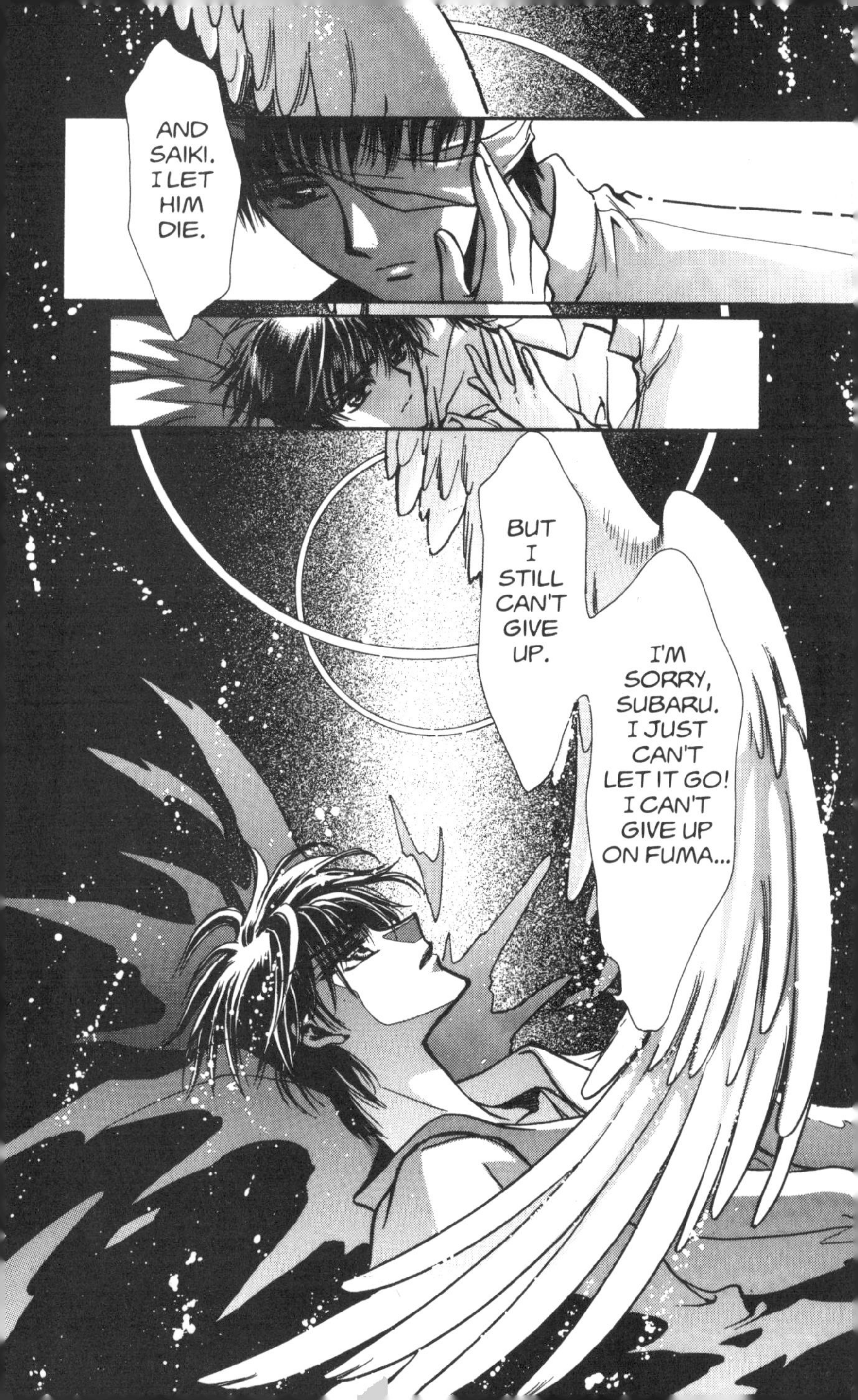
AND SAIKI. I LET HIM DIE.
BUT I STILL CAN'T GIVE UP.
I'M SORRY, SUBARU. I JUST CAN'T LET IT GO! I CAN'T GIVE UP ON FUMA...

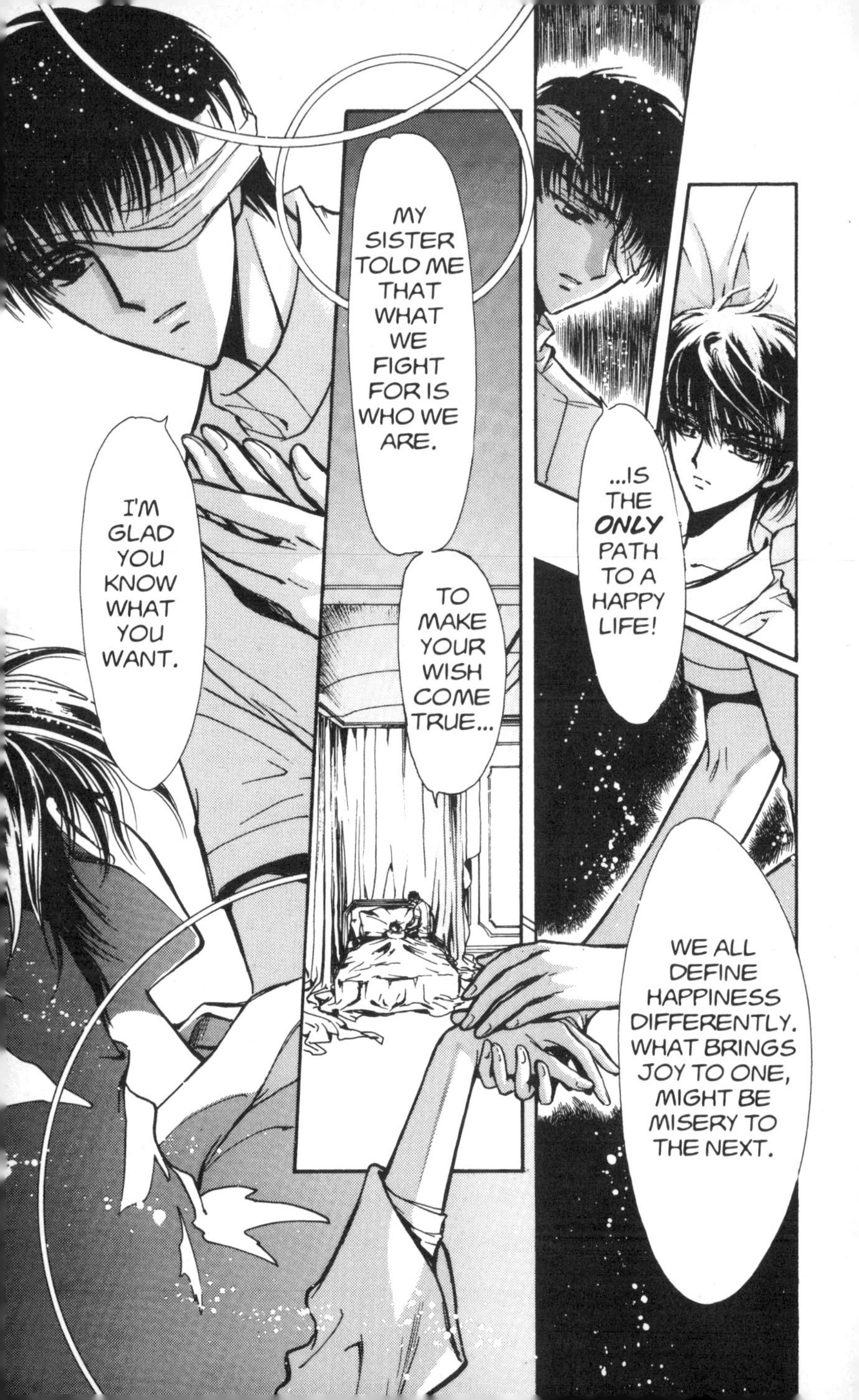

MY SISTER TOLD ME THAT WHAT WE FIGHT FOR IS WHO WE ARE.
TO MAKE YOUR WISH COME TRUE...
...IS THE ONLY PATH TO A HAPPY LIFE!
WE ALL DEFINE HAPPINESS DIFFERENTLY. WHAT BRINGS JOY TO ONE, MIGHT BE MISERY TO THE NEXT.
I'M GLAD YOU KNOW WHAT YOU WANT.

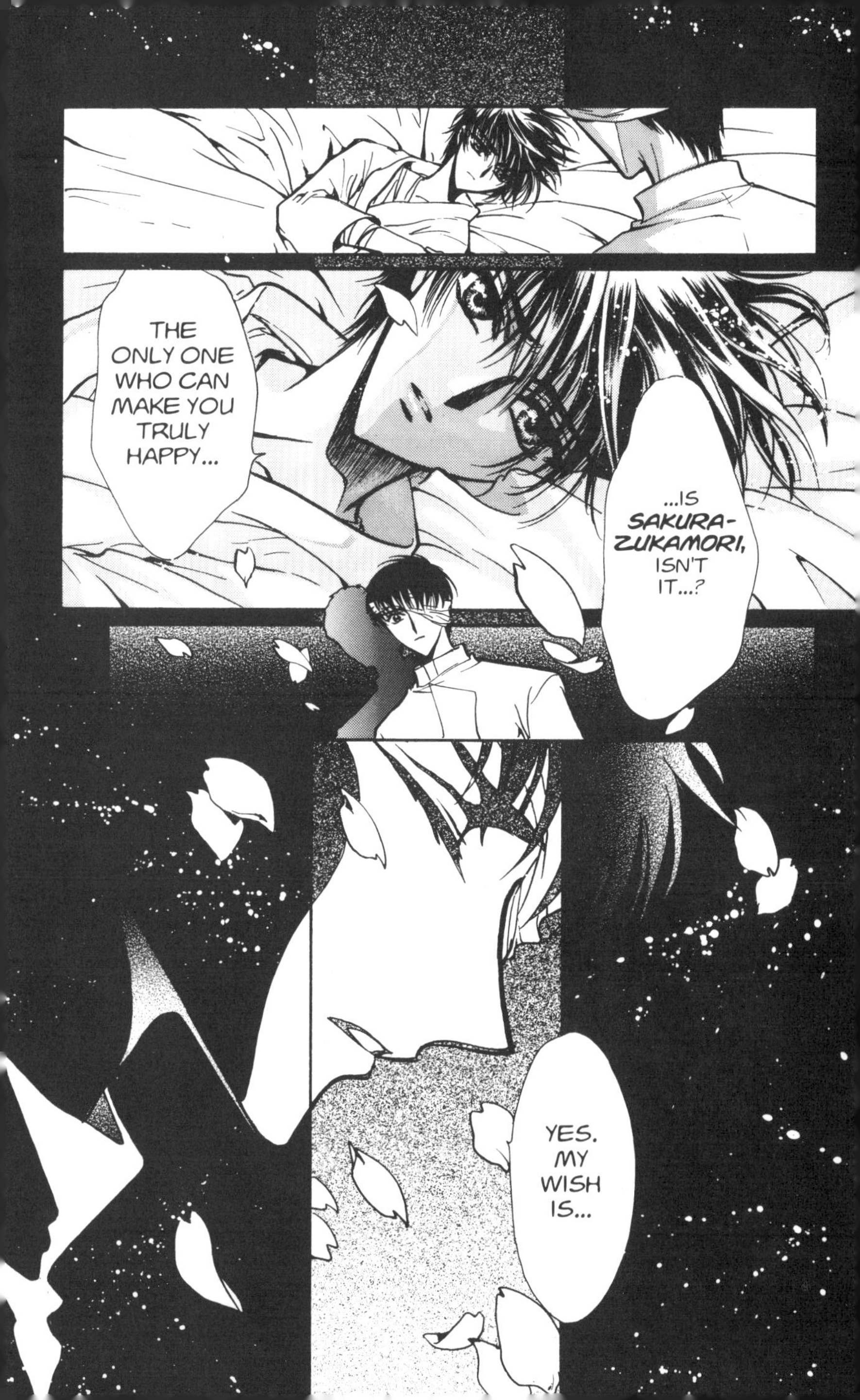
THE ONLY ONE WHO CAN MAKE YOU TRULY HAPPY...
...IS SAKURA-ZUKAMORI, ISN'T IT...?
YES. MY WISH IS...

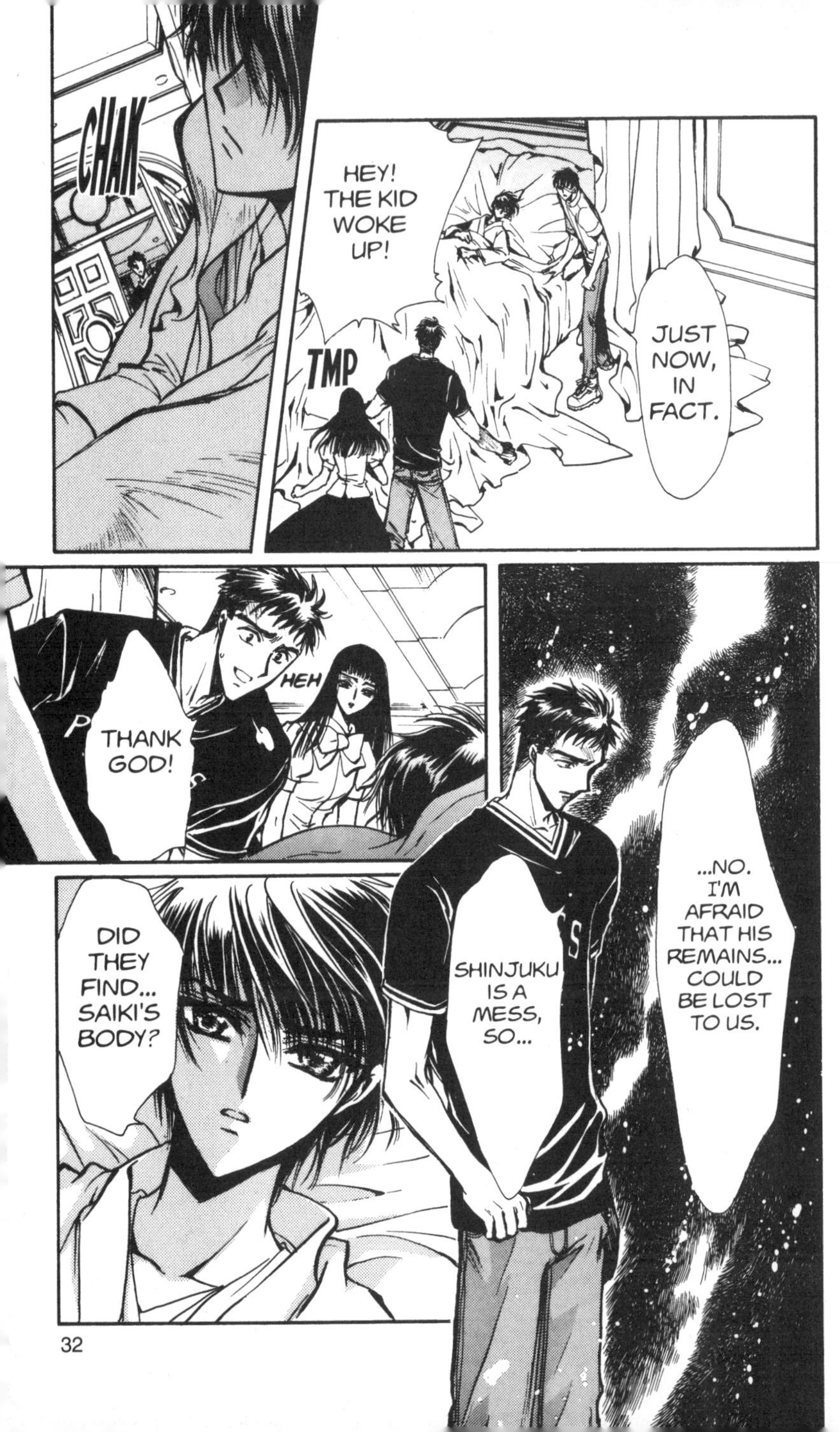
CHAK
HEY! THE KID WOKE UP!
TMP
JUST NOW, IN FACT.
THANK GOD!
HEH
DID THEY FIND... SAIKI'S BODY?
...NO. I'M AFRAID THAT HIS REMAINS... COULD BE LOST TO US.
SHINJUKU IS A MESS, SO...

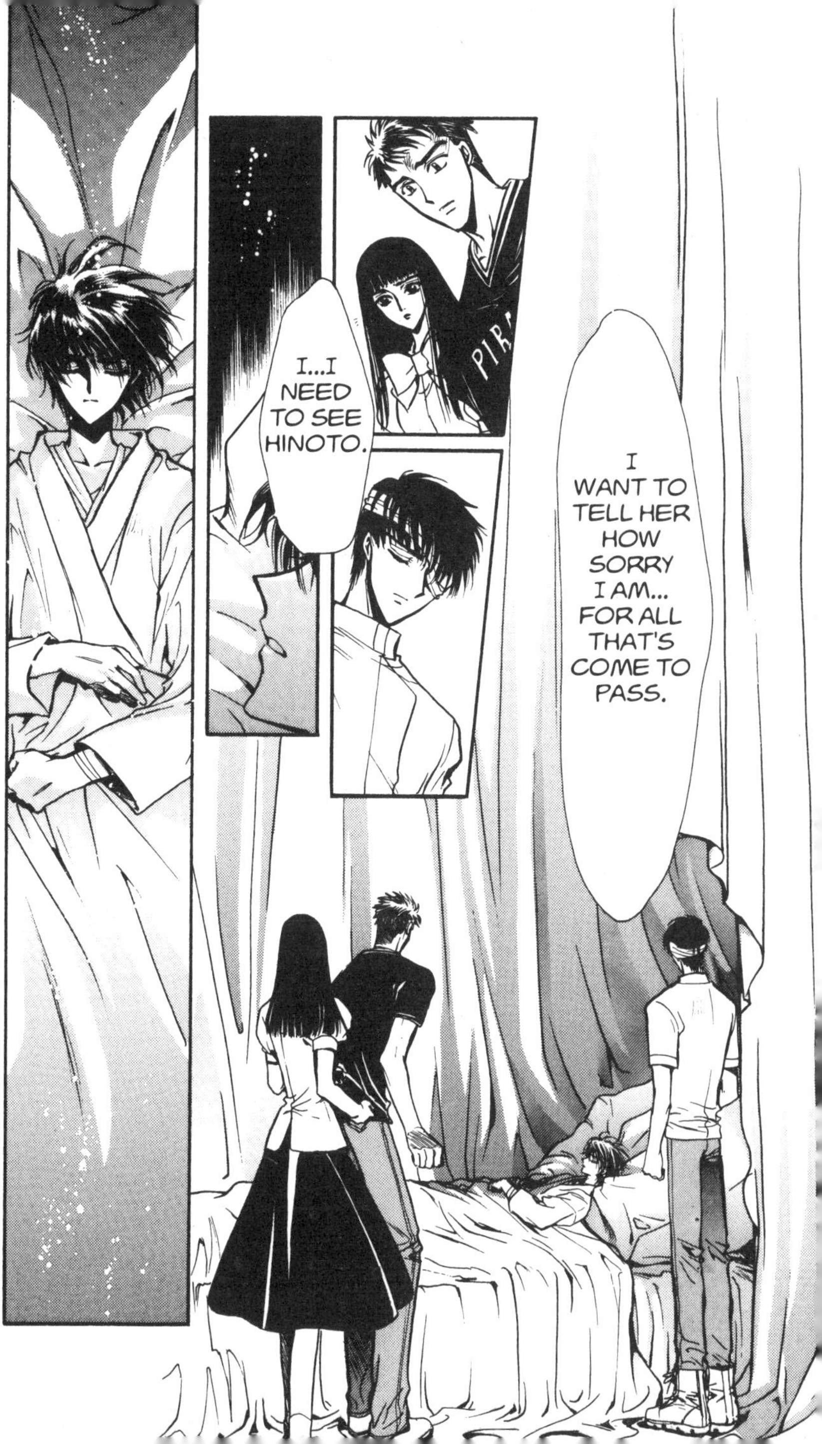
I...I NEED TO SEE HINOTO.
I WANT TO TELL HER HOW SORRY I AM... FOR ALL THAT'S COME TO PASS.

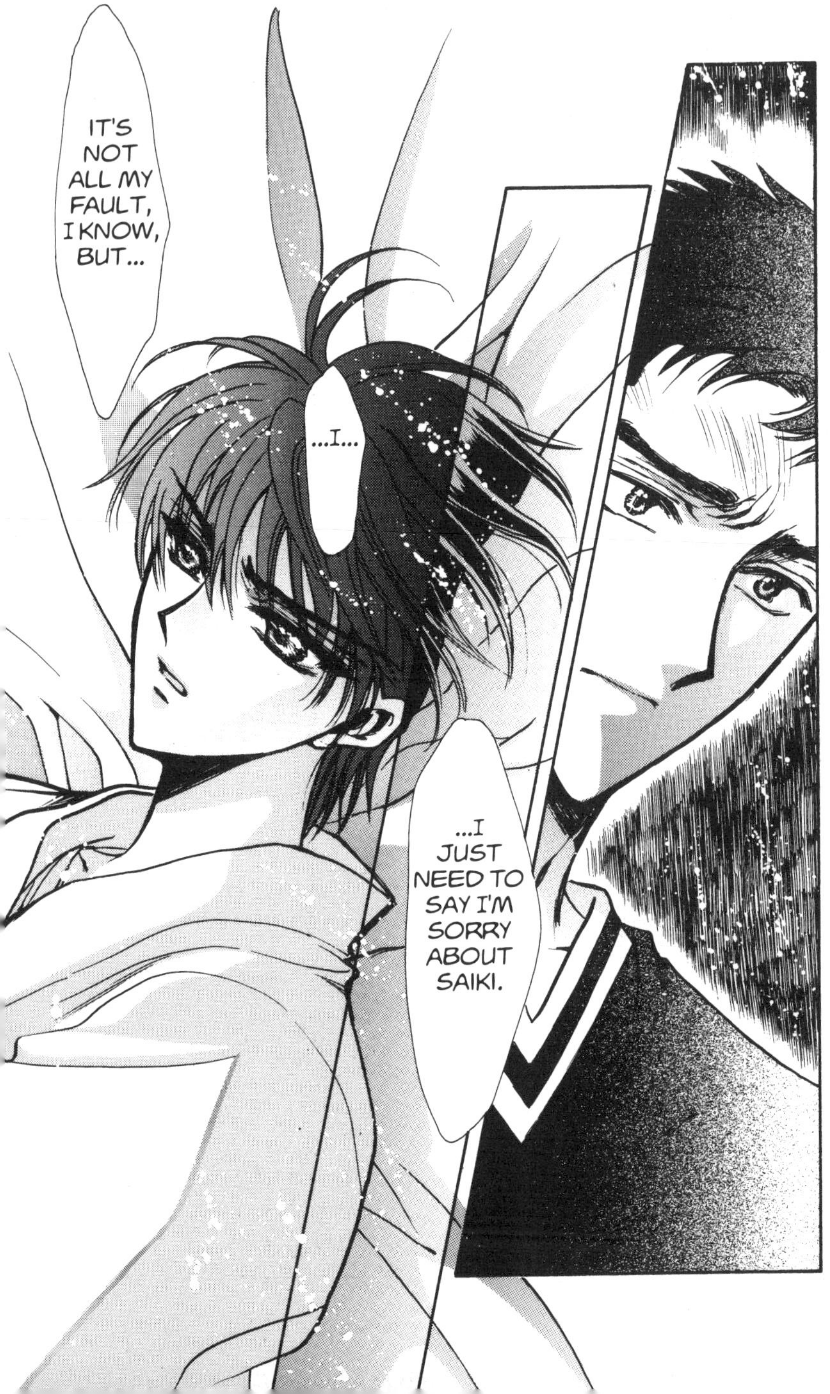
IT'S NOT ALL MY FAULT, I KNOW, BUT...
...I...
...I JUST NEED TO SAY I'M SORRY ABOUT SAIKI.

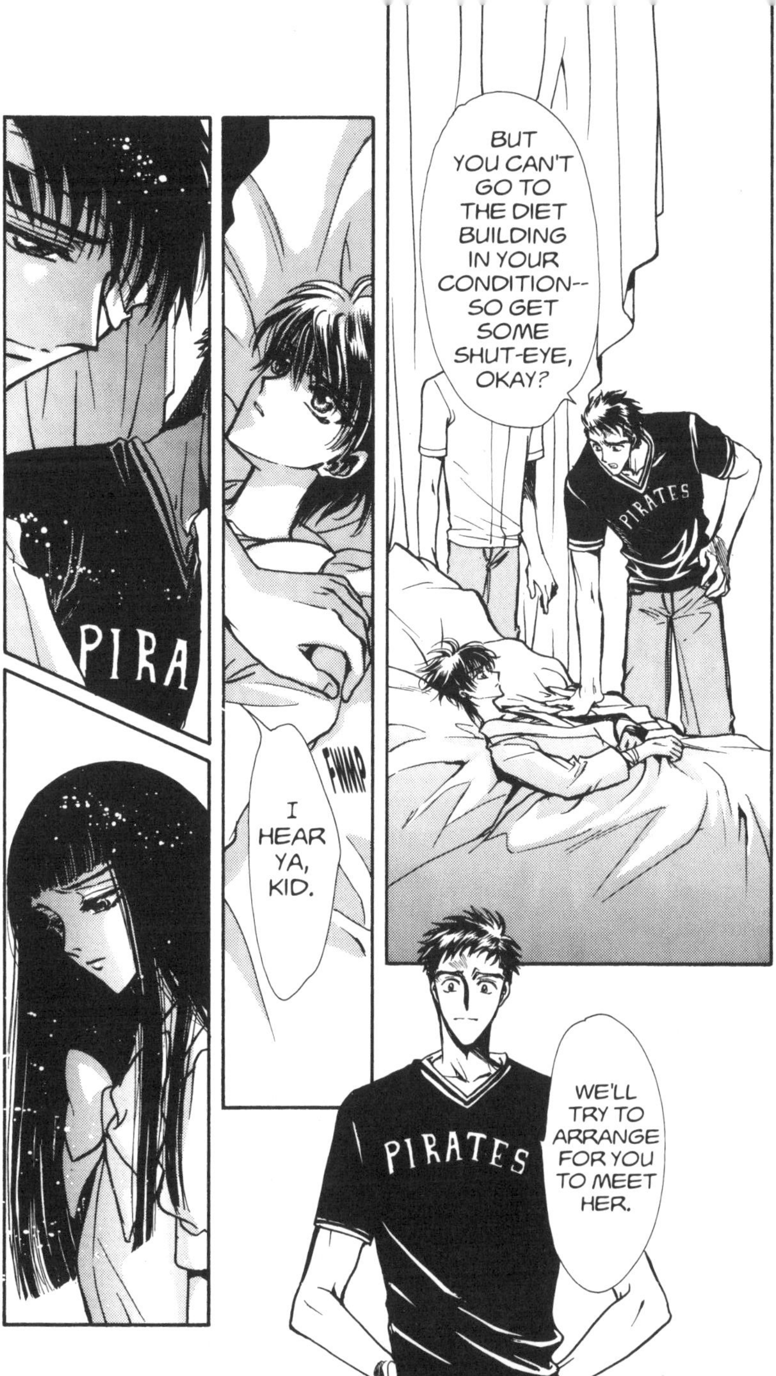
BUT YOU CAN'T GO TO THE DIET BUILDING IN YOUR CONDITION-- SO GET SOME SHUT-EYE, OKAY?
PIRATES
WE'LL TRY TO ARRANGE FOR YOU TO MEET HER.
PIRATES
FWMP
I HEAR YA, KID.
PIRA

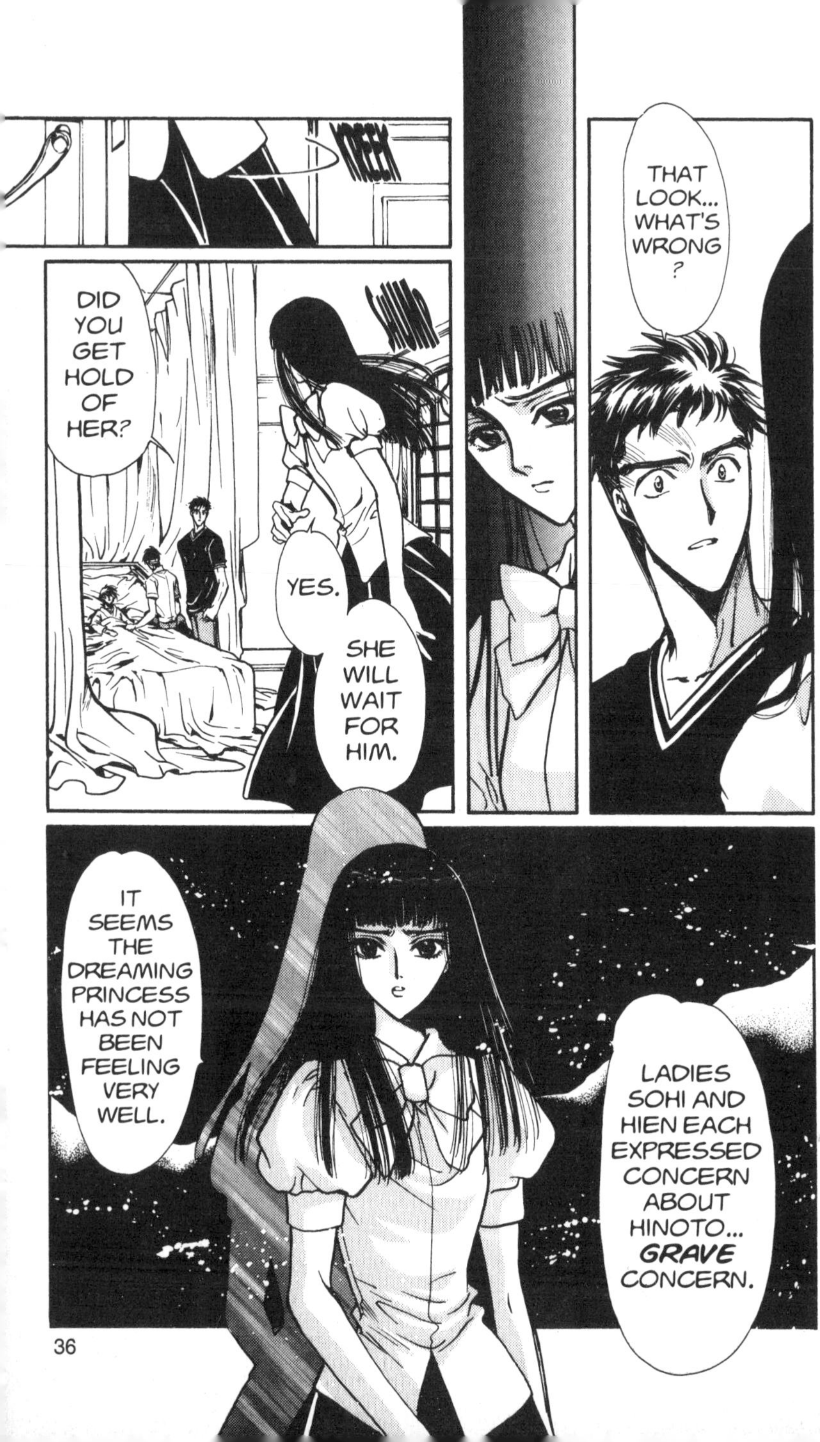
KREEK
DID YOU GET HOLD OF HER?
YES.
SHE WILL WAIT FOR HIM.
THAT LOOK... WHAT'S WRONG?
IT SEEMS THE DREAMING PRINCESS HAS NOT BEEN FEELING VERY WELL.
LADIES SOHI AND HIEN EACH EXPRESSED CONCERN ABOUT HINOTO... *GRAVE* CONCERN.

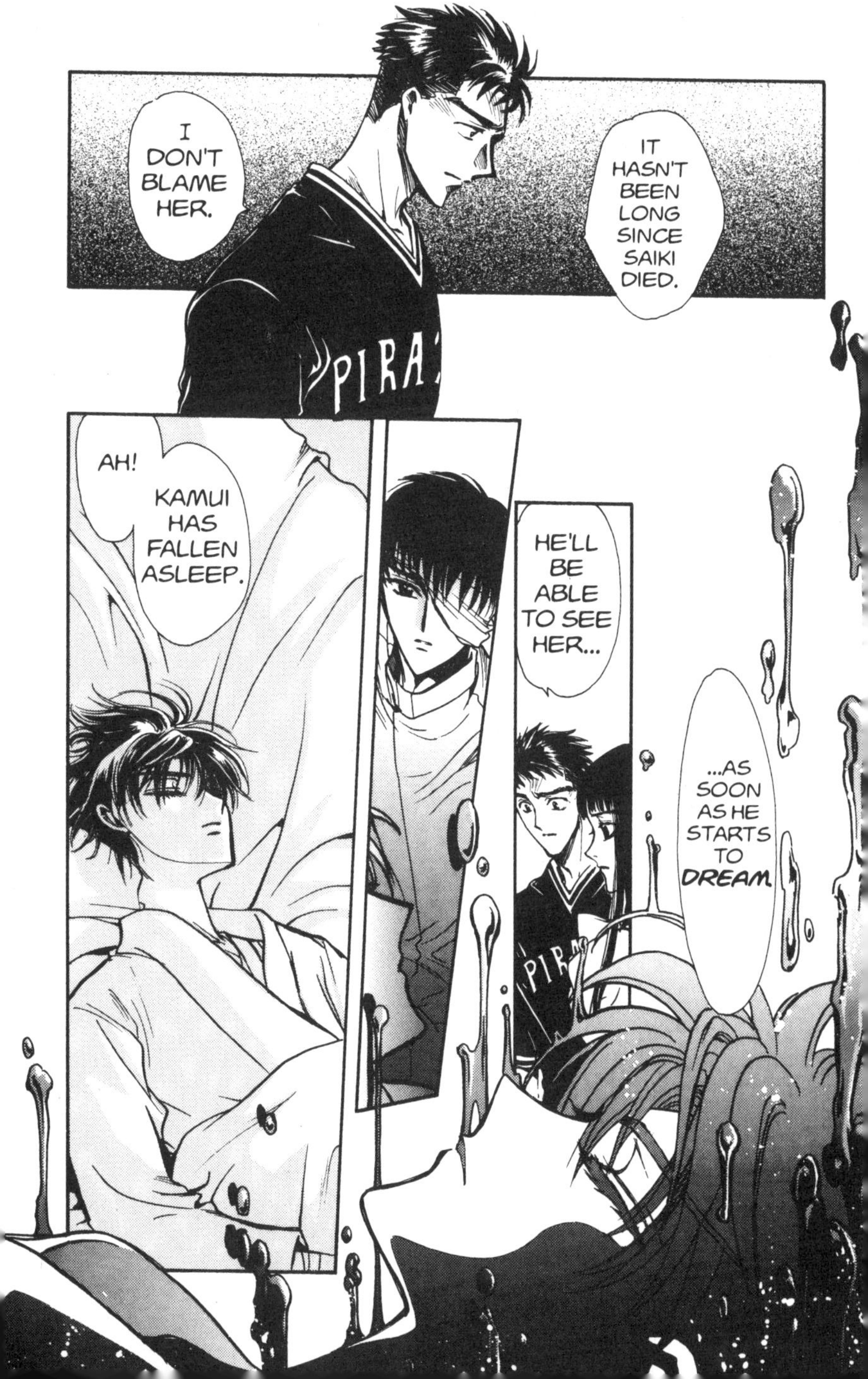
IT HASN'T BEEN LONG SINCE SAIKI DIED.
I DON'T BLAME HER.
HE'LL BE ABLE TO SEE HER...
...AS SOON AS HE STARTS TO DREAM.
AH! KAMUI HAS FALLEN ASLEEP.

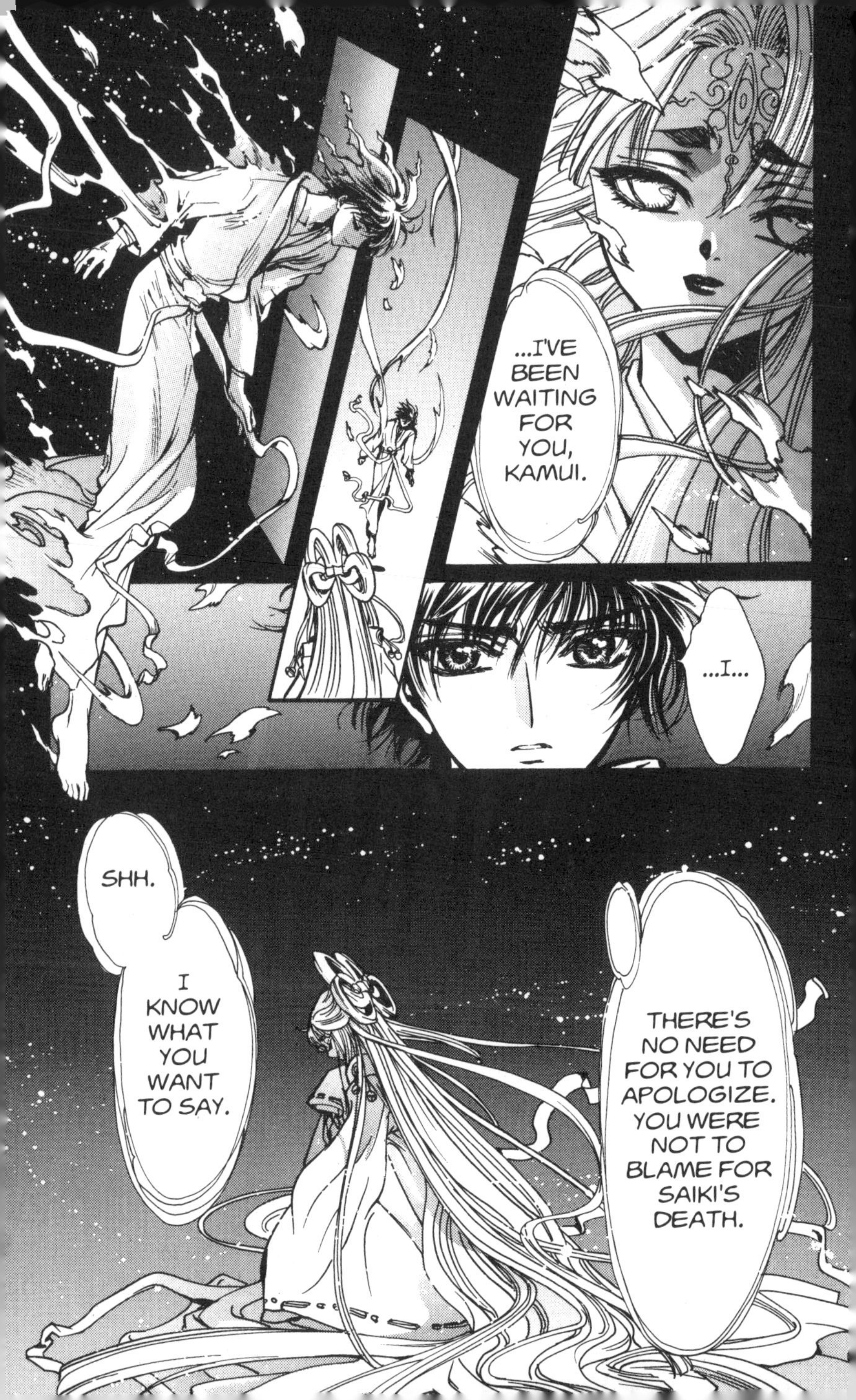
...I'VE BEEN WAITING FOR YOU, KAMUI.
...I...
THERE'S NO NEED FOR YOU TO APOLOGIZE. YOU WERE NOT TO BLAME FOR SAIKI'S DEATH.
SHH.
I KNOW WHAT YOU WANT TO SAY.

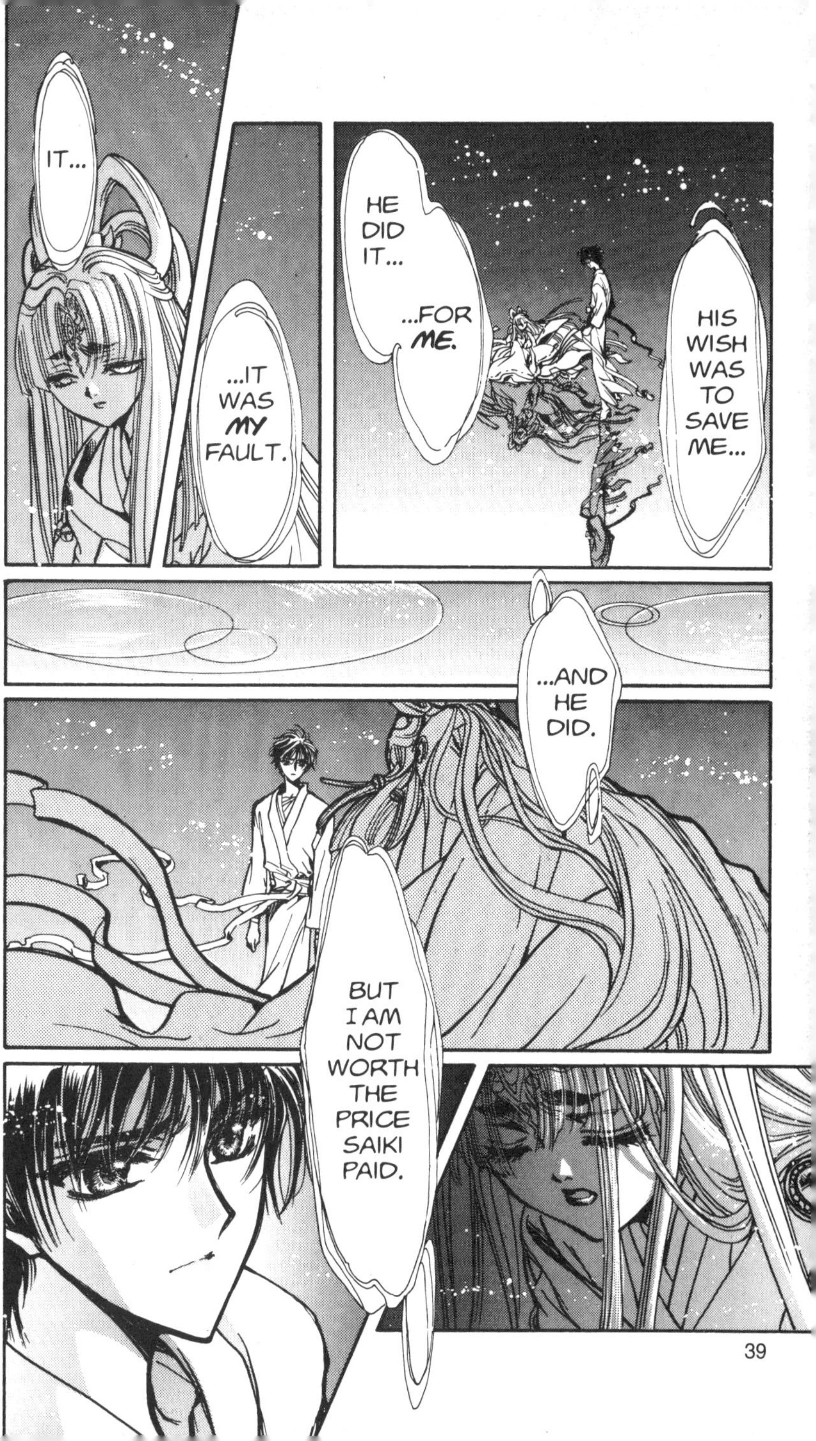
HE DID IT...
...FOR ME.
HIS WISH WAS TO SAVE ME...
IT...
...IT WAS MY FAULT.
...AND HE DID.
BUT I AM NOT WORTH THE PRICE SAIKI PAID.

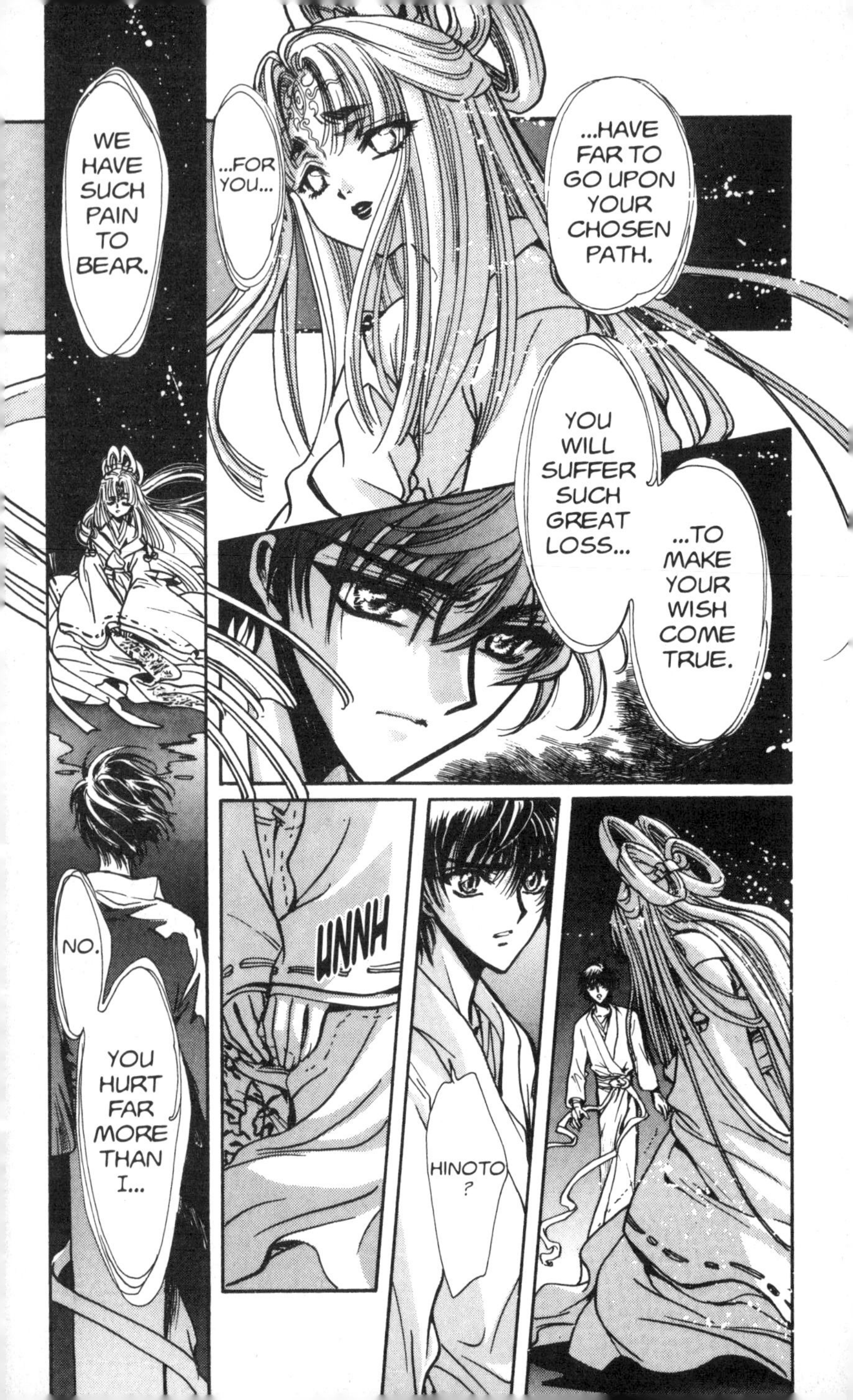
WE HAVE SUCH PAIN TO BEAR.
...FOR YOU...
...HAVE FAR TO GO UPON YOUR CHOSEN PATH.
YOU WILL SUFFER SUCH GREAT LOSS...
...TO MAKE YOUR WISH COME TRUE.
NO.
YOU HURT FAR MORE THAN I...
UNNH
HINOTO?

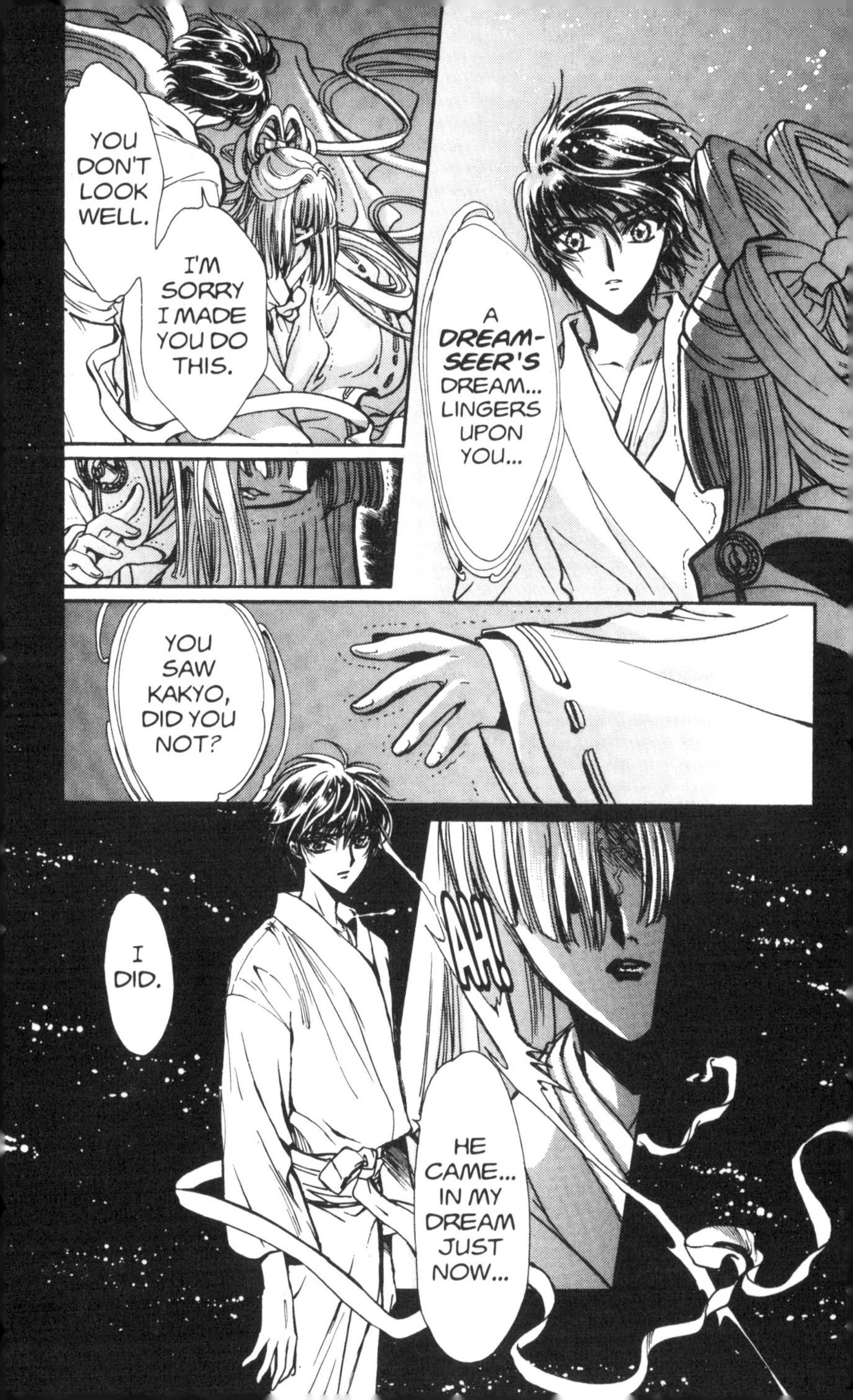
A DREAM-SEER'S DREAM... LINGERS UPON YOU...
YOU DON'T LOOK WELL.
I'M SORRY I MADE YOU DO THIS.
YOU SAW KAKYO, DID YOU NOT?
AH!
I DID.
HE CAME... IN MY DREAM JUST NOW...

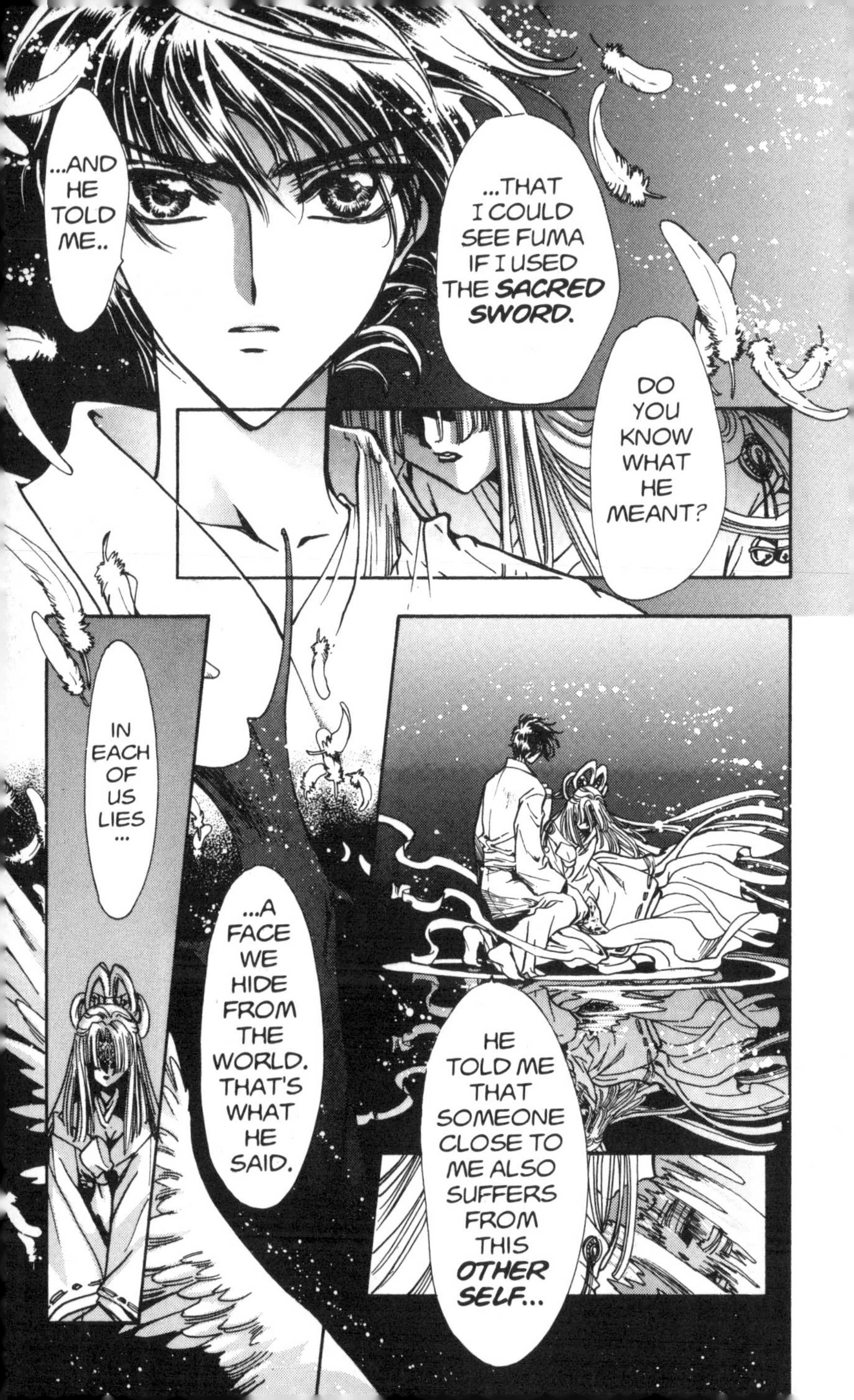
...AND HE TOLD ME..
...THAT I COULD SEE FUMA IF I USED THE **SACRED SWORD.**
DO YOU KNOW WHAT HE MEANT?
IN EACH OF US LIES ...
...A FACE WE HIDE FROM THE WORLD. THAT'S WHAT HE SAID.
HE TOLD ME THAT SOMEONE CLOSE TO ME ALSO SUFFERS FROM THIS **OTHER SELF...**

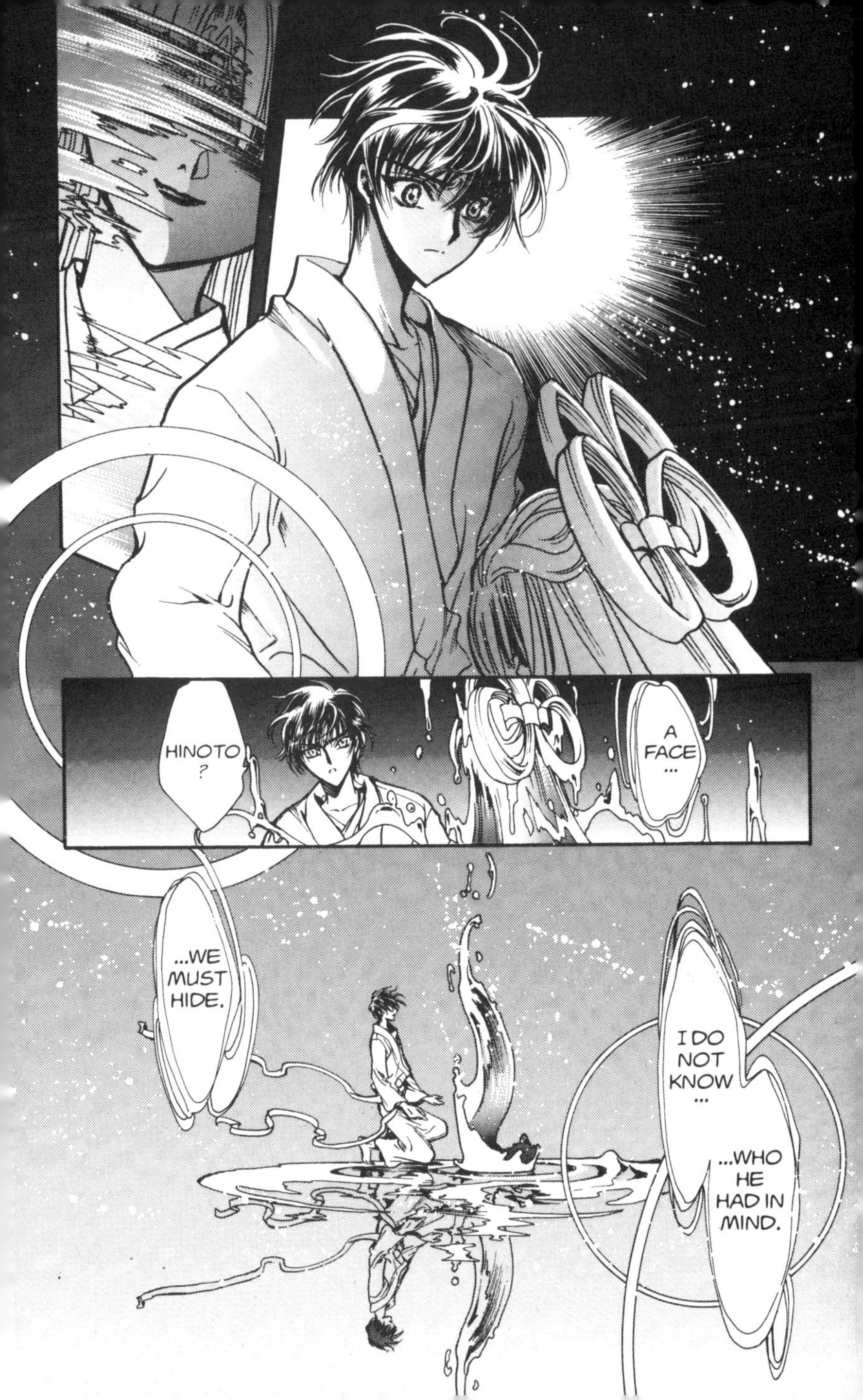
A FACE ...
HINOTO ?
I DO NOT KNOW ...
...WHO HE HAD IN MIND.
...WE MUST HIDE.

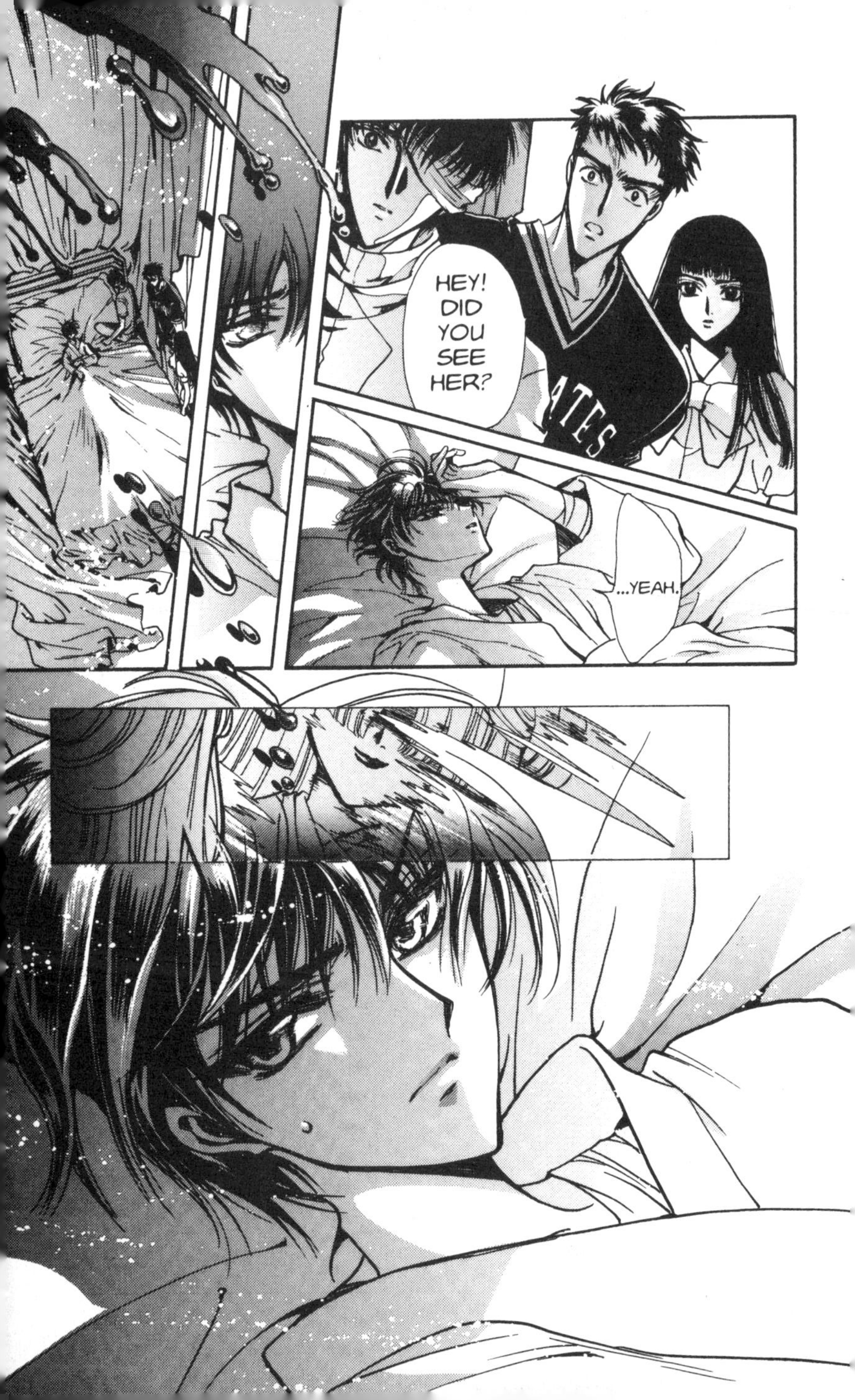
HEY! DID YOU SEE HER?
...YEAH.

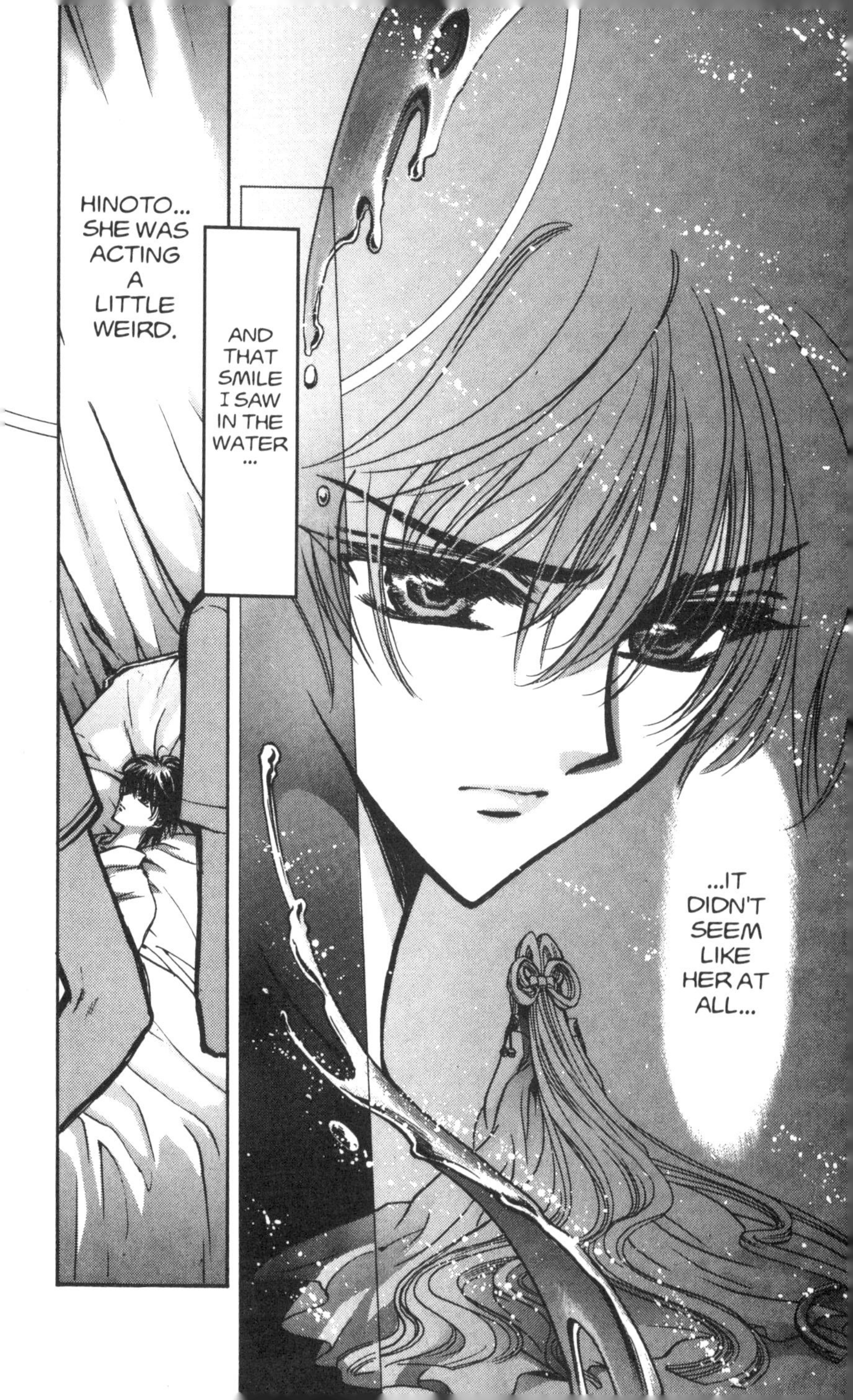
...IT DIDN'T SEEM LIKE HER AT ALL...
AND THAT SMILE I SAW IN THE WATER ...
HINOTO... SHE WAS ACTING A LITTLE WEIRD.

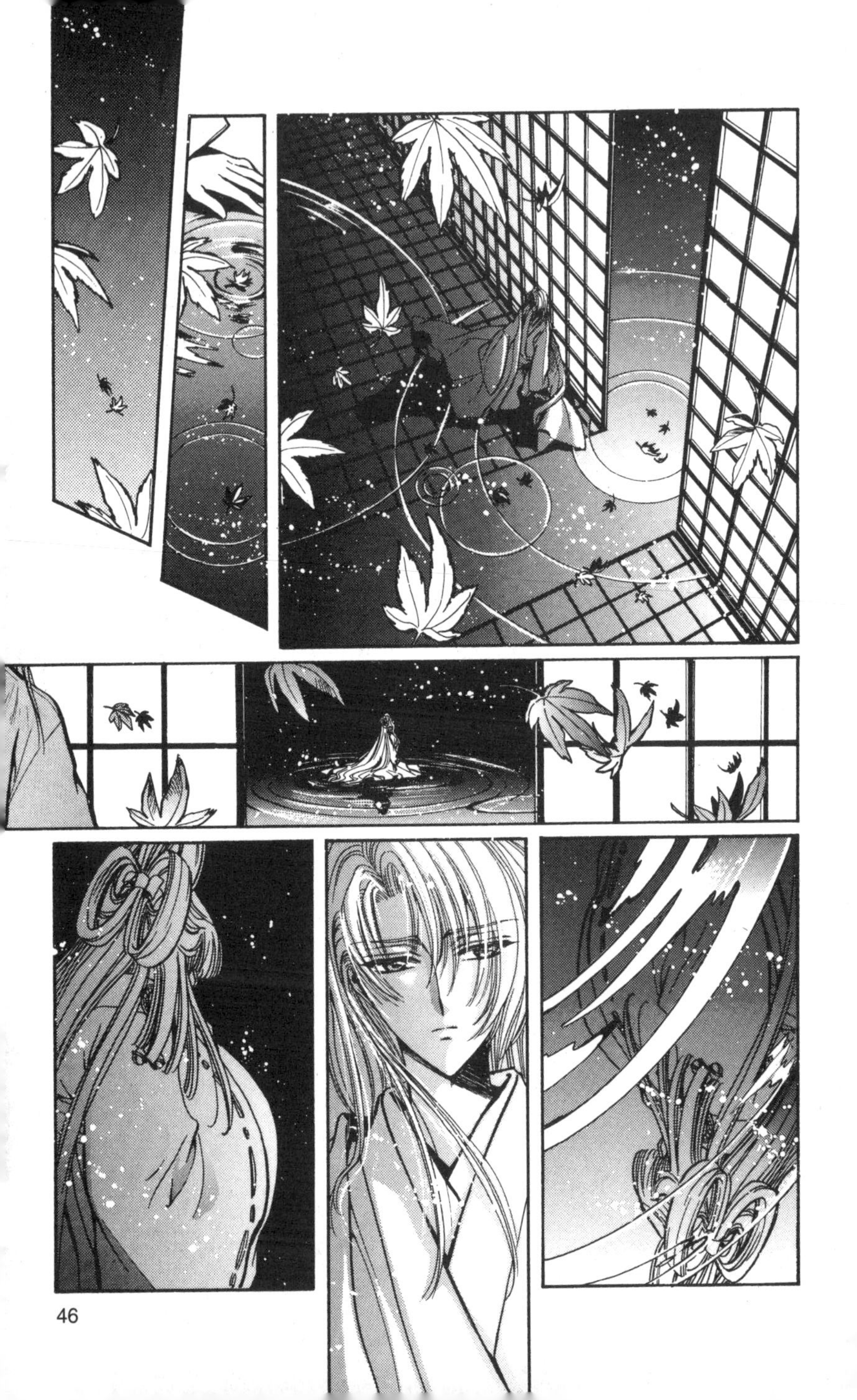

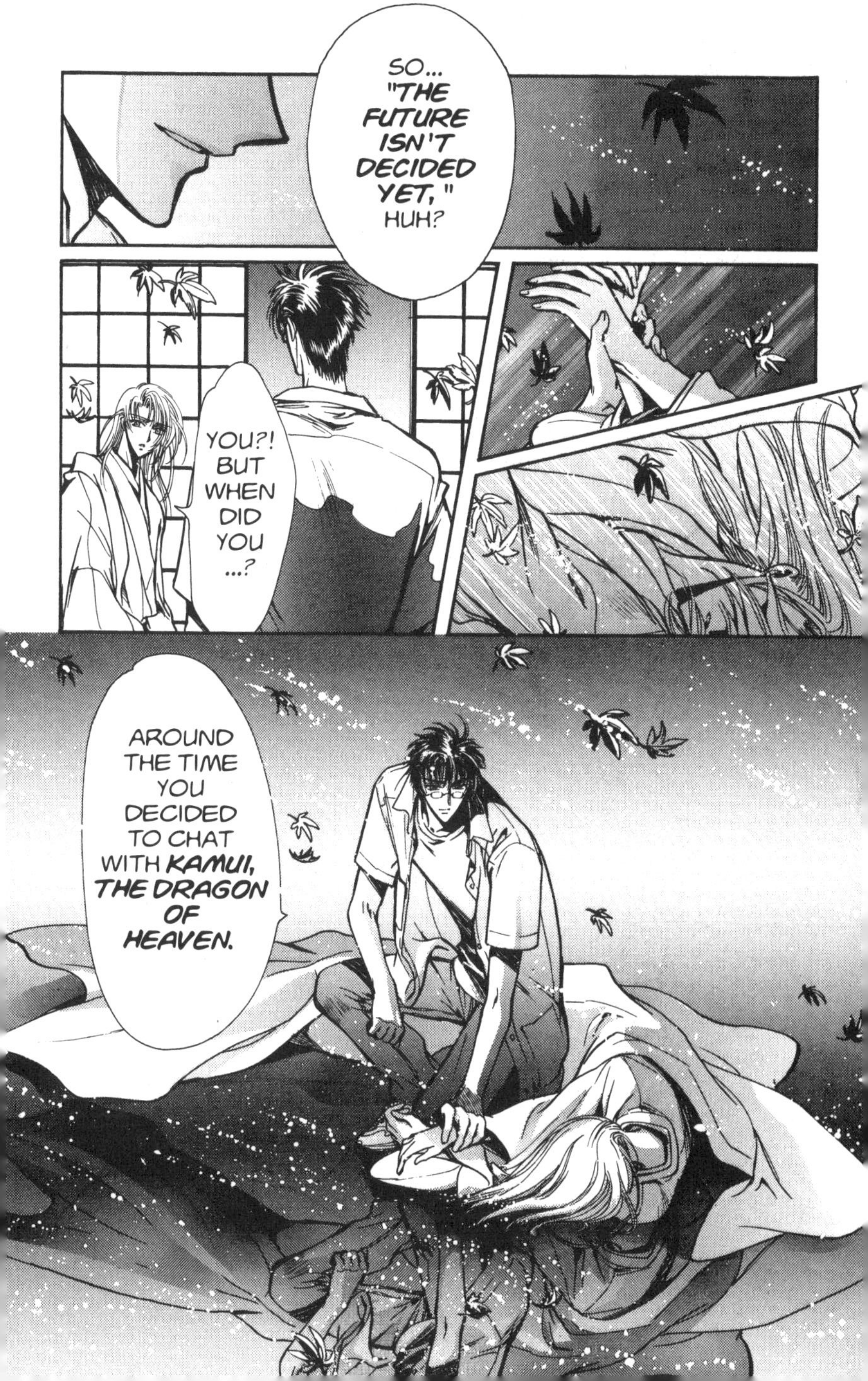
SO... "THE FUTURE ISN'T DECIDED YET," HUH?
YOU?! BUT WHEN DID YOU ...?
AROUND THE TIME YOU DECIDED TO CHAT WITH KAMUI, THE DRAGON OF HEAVEN.

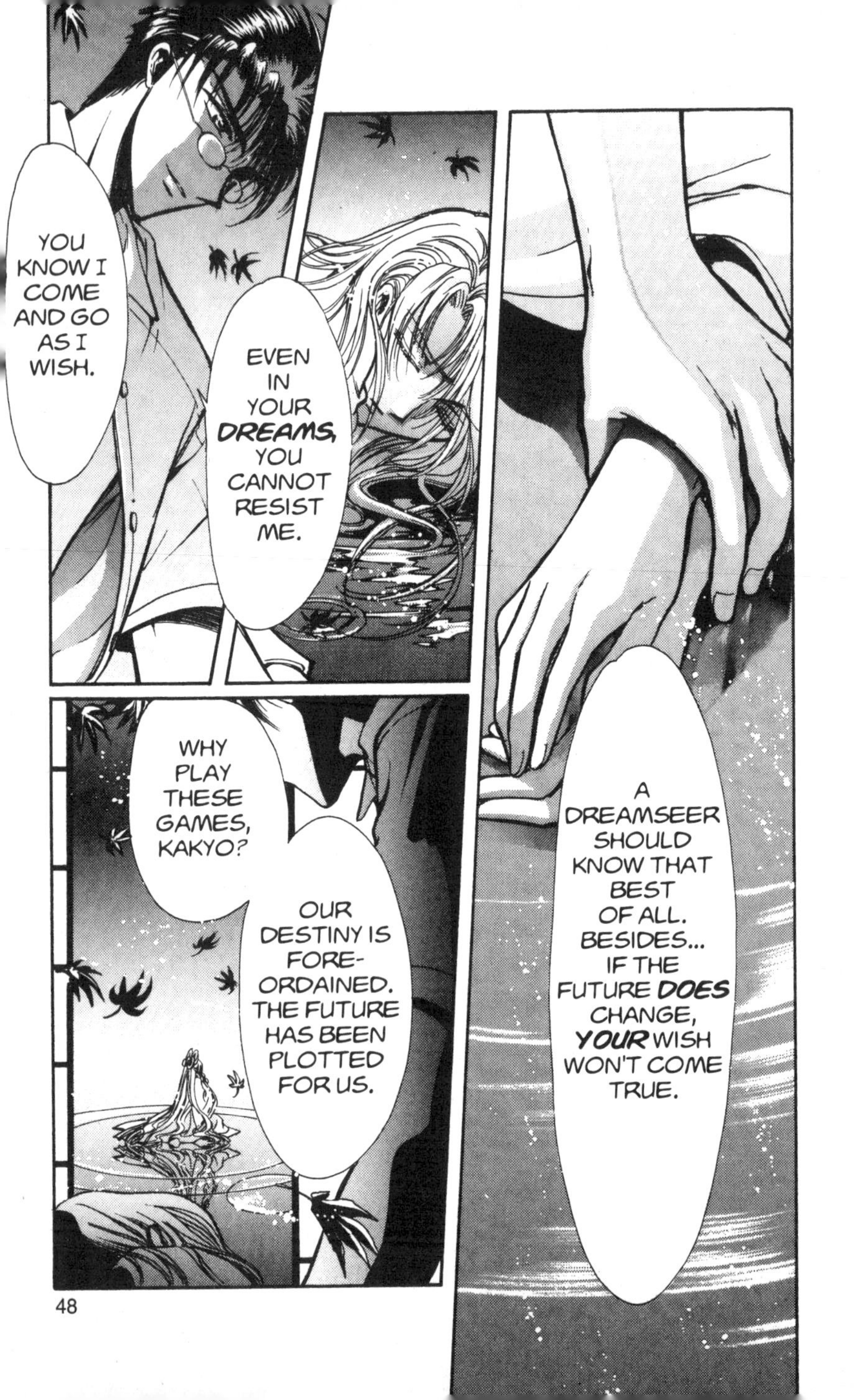
EVEN IN YOUR DREAMS, YOU CANNOT RESIST ME.
YOU KNOW I COME AND GO AS I WISH.
WHY PLAY THESE GAMES, KAKYO?
OUR DESTINY IS FORE-ORDAINED. THE FUTURE HAS BEEN PLOTTED FOR US.
A DREAMSEER SHOULD KNOW THAT BEST OF ALL. BESIDES... IF THE FUTURE DOES CHANGE, YOUR WISH WON'T COME TRUE.

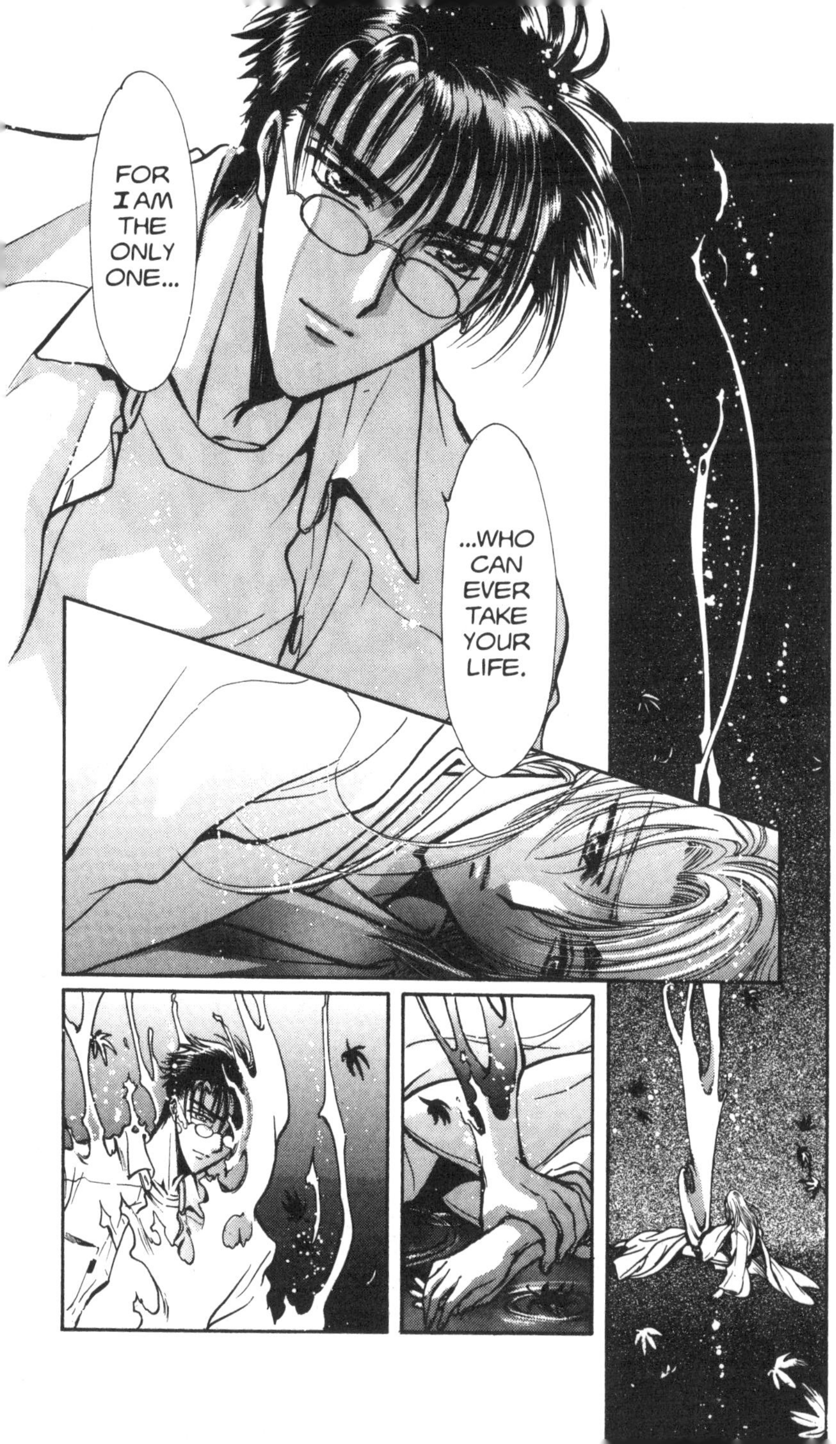
FOR I AM THE ONLY ONE...
...WHO CAN EVER TAKE YOUR LIFE.

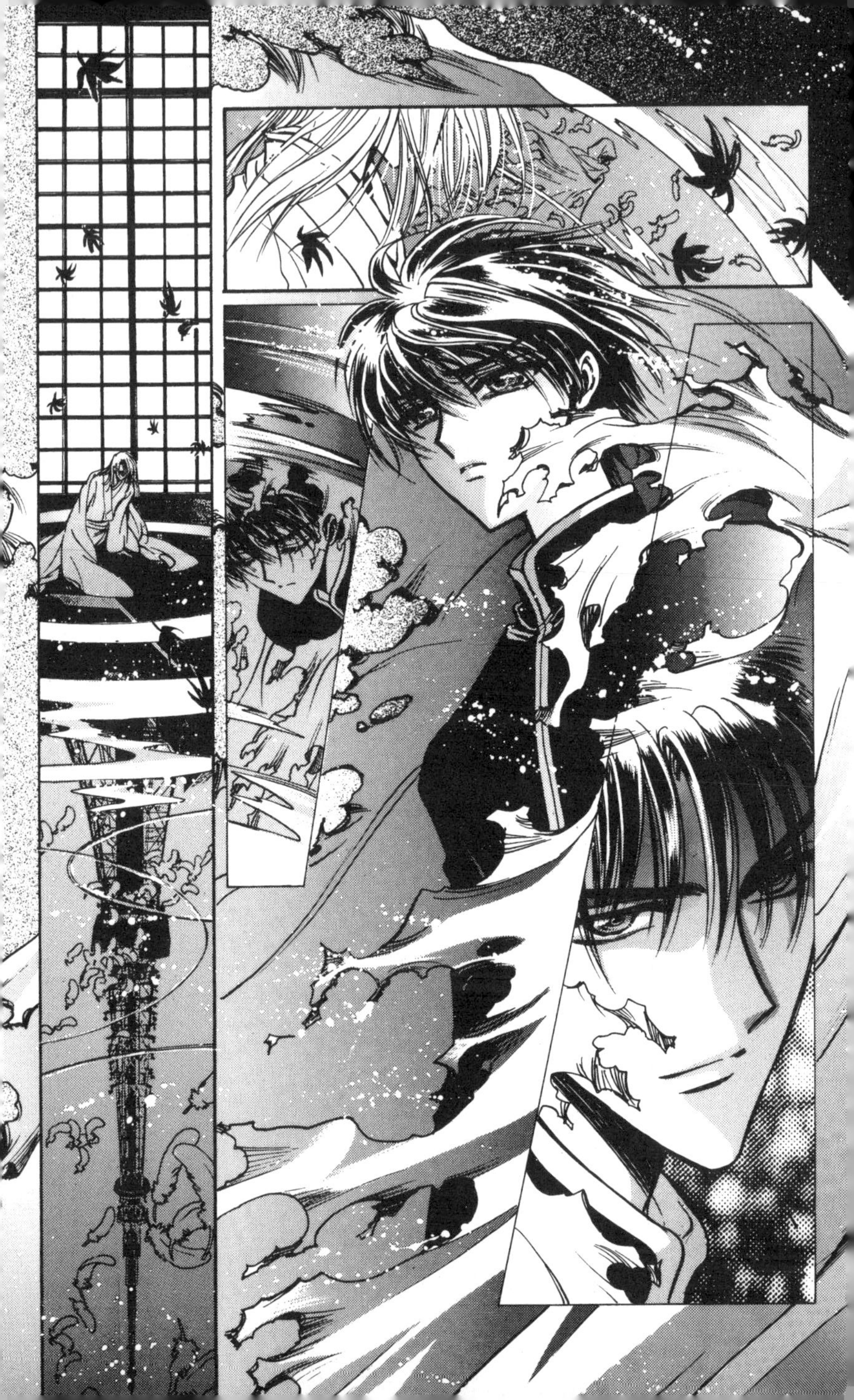

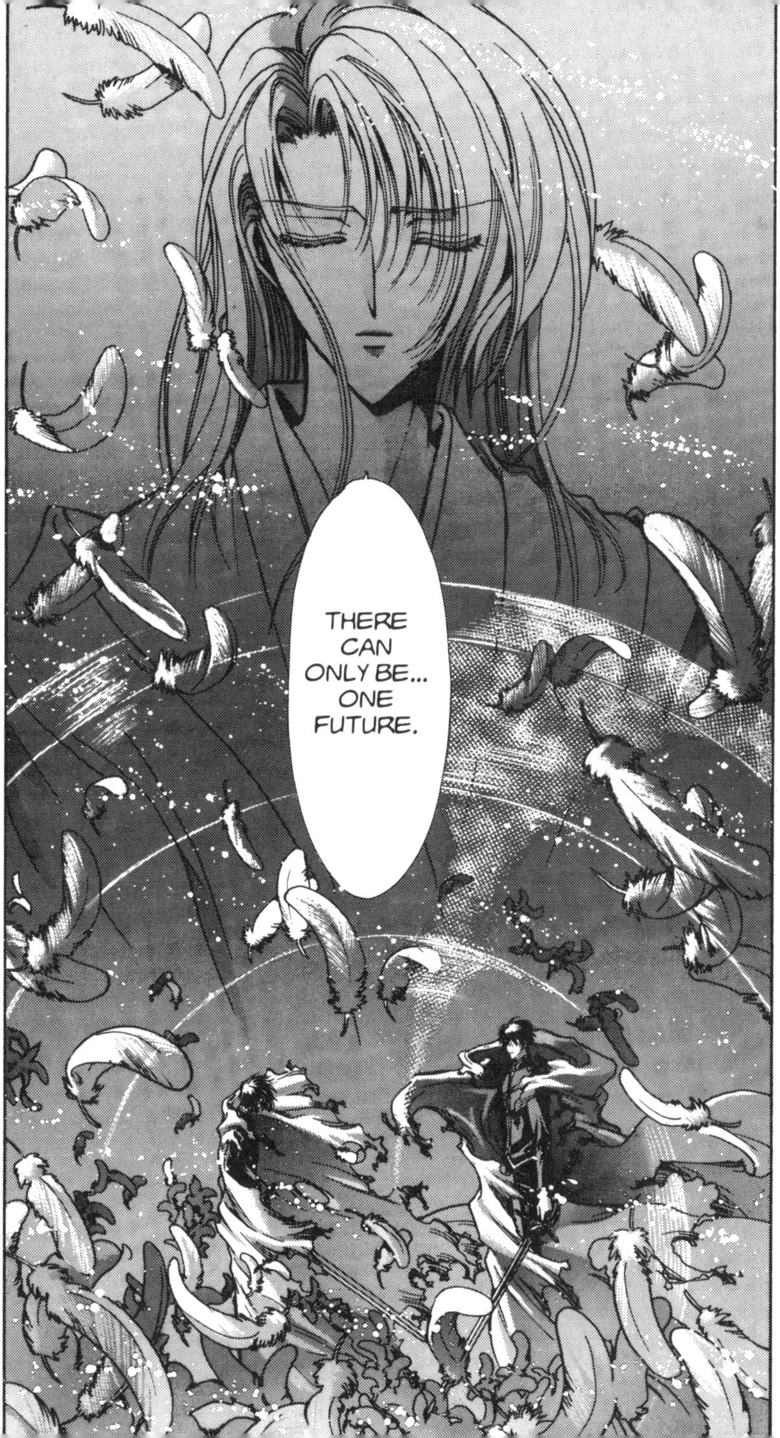
THERE CAN ONLY BE... ONE FUTURE.

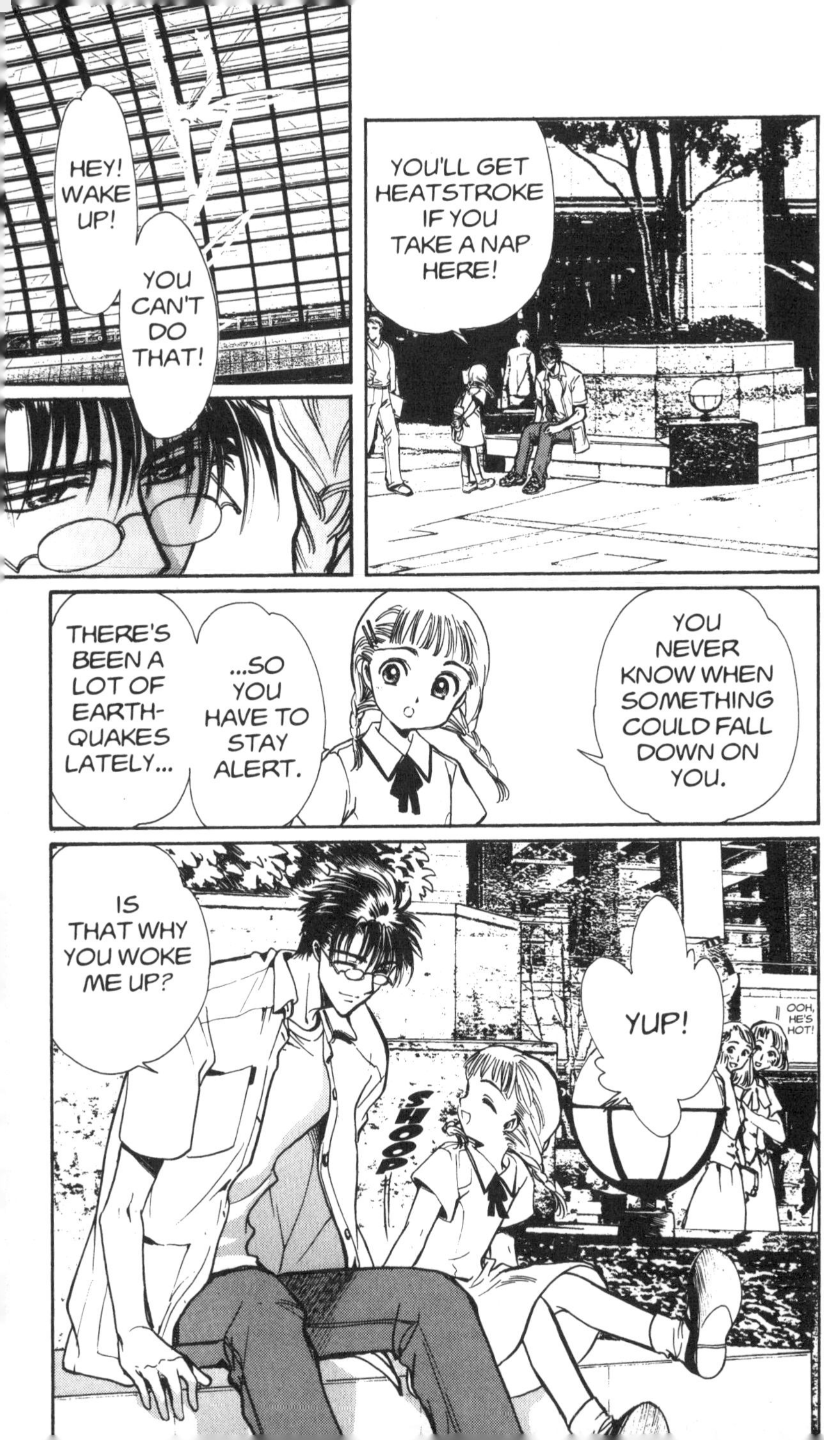
HEY! WAKE UP!
YOU CAN'T DO THAT!
YOU'LL GET HEATSTROKE IF YOU TAKE A NAP HERE!
THERE'S BEEN A LOT OF EARTHQUAKES LATELY...
...SO YOU HAVE TO STAY ALERT.
YOU NEVER KNOW WHEN SOMETHING COULD FALL DOWN ON YOU.
IS THAT WHY YOU WOKE ME UP?
SHOOOP
YUP!
OOH, HE'S HOT!

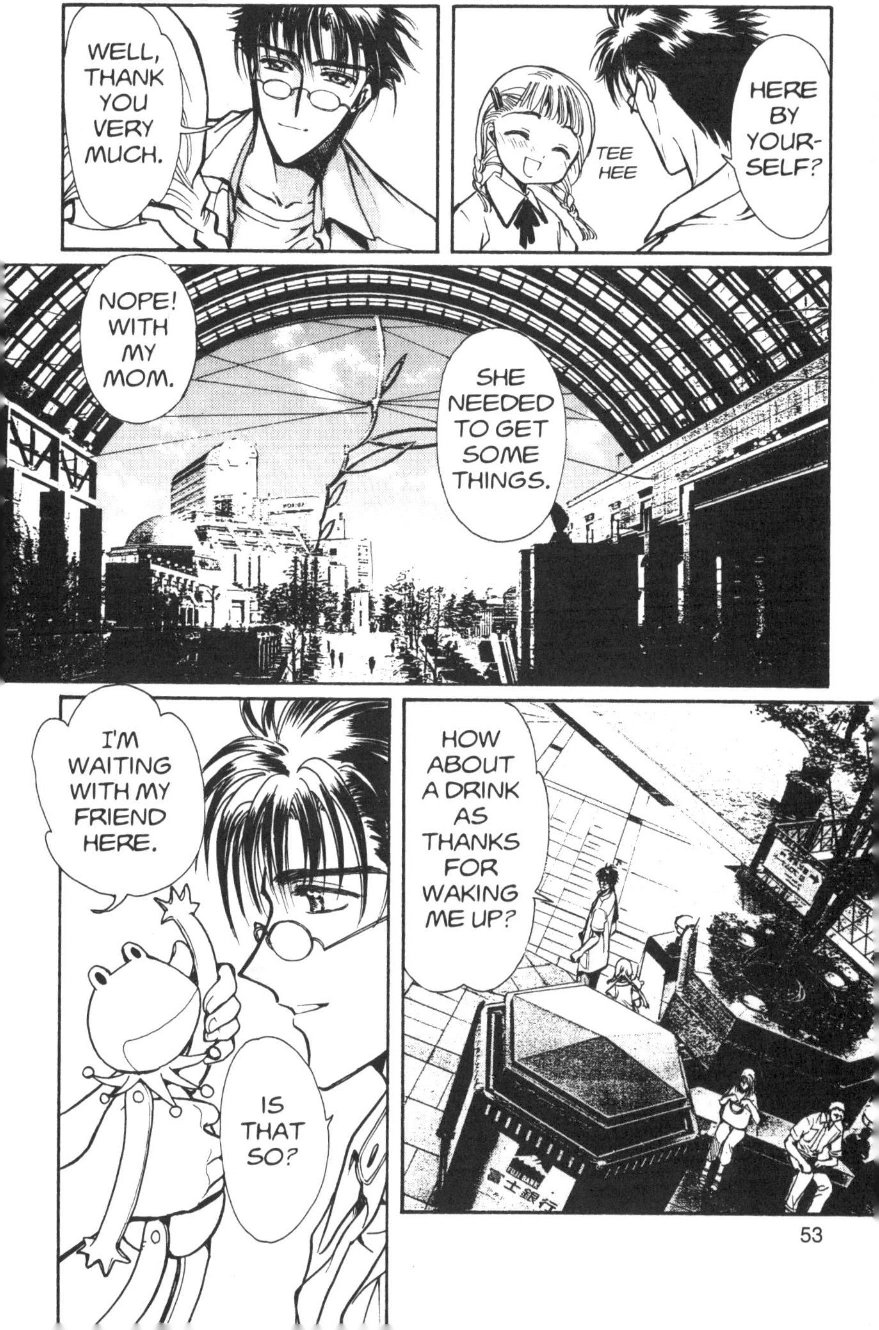
WELL, THANK YOU VERY MUCH.
HERE BY YOURSELF?
TEE HEE
NOPE! WITH MY MOM.
SHE NEEDED TO GET SOME THINGS.
I'M WAITING WITH MY FRIEND HERE.
IS THAT SO?
HOW ABOUT A DRINK AS THANKS FOR WAKING ME UP?

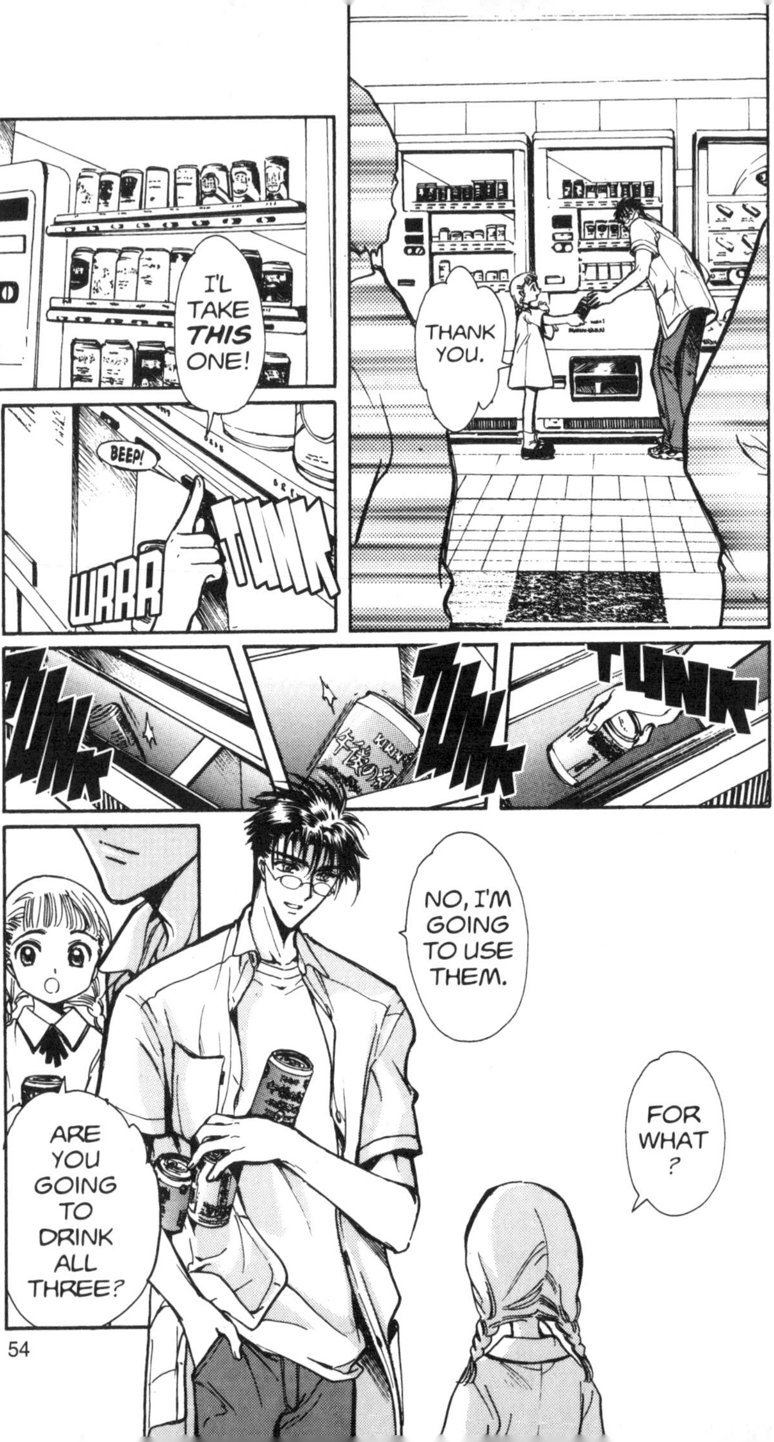
I'L TAKE **THIS** ONE!
BEEP!
WRRR
TUNK
THANK YOU.
TUNK
TUNK
TUNK
ARE YOU GOING TO DRINK ALL THREE?
NO, I'M GOING TO USE THEM.
FOR WHAT?

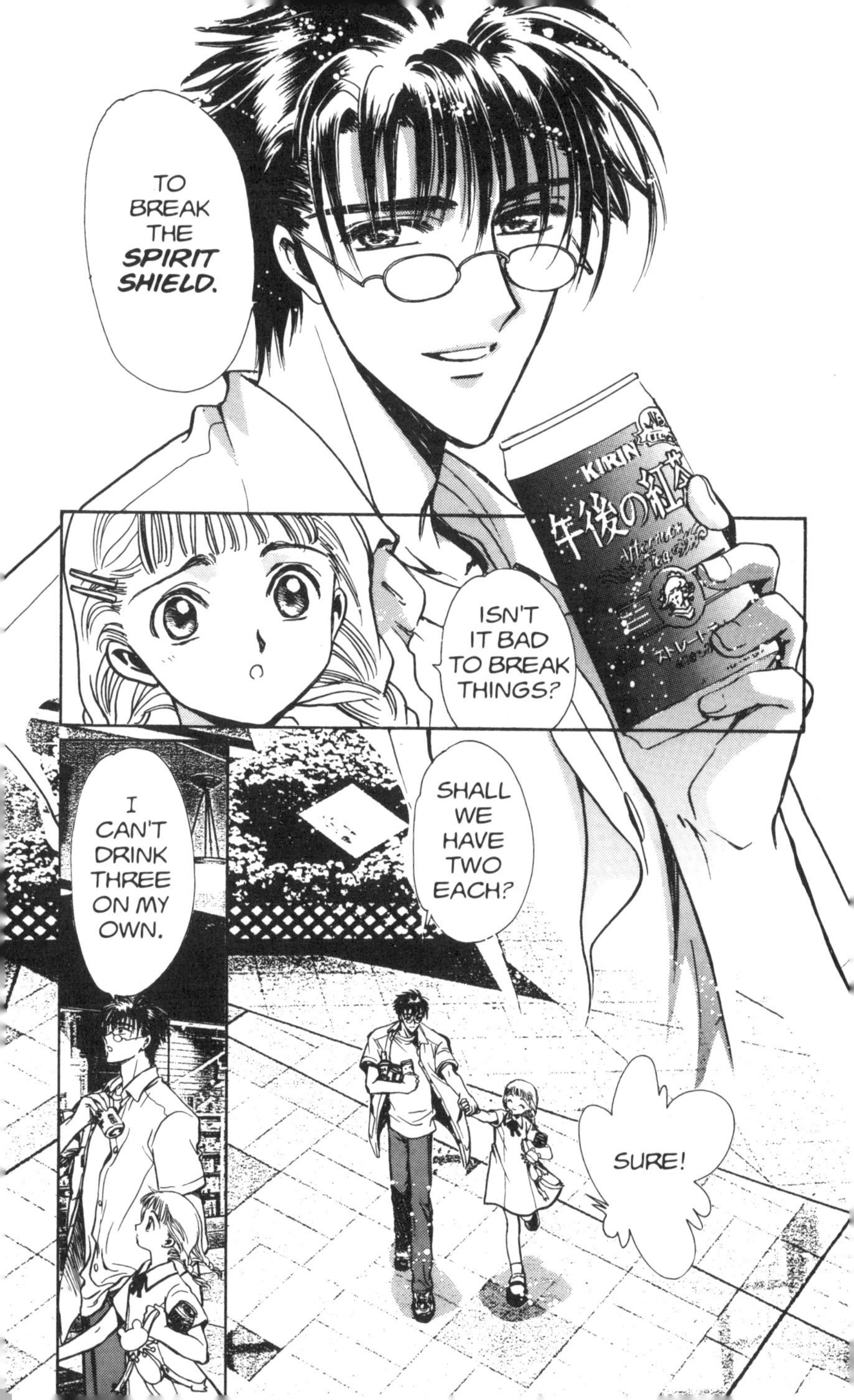
TO BREAK THE SPIRIT SHIELD.
KIRIN
ISN'T IT BAD TO BREAK THINGS?
I CAN'T DRINK THREE ON MY OWN.
SHALL WE HAVE TWO EACH?
SURE!

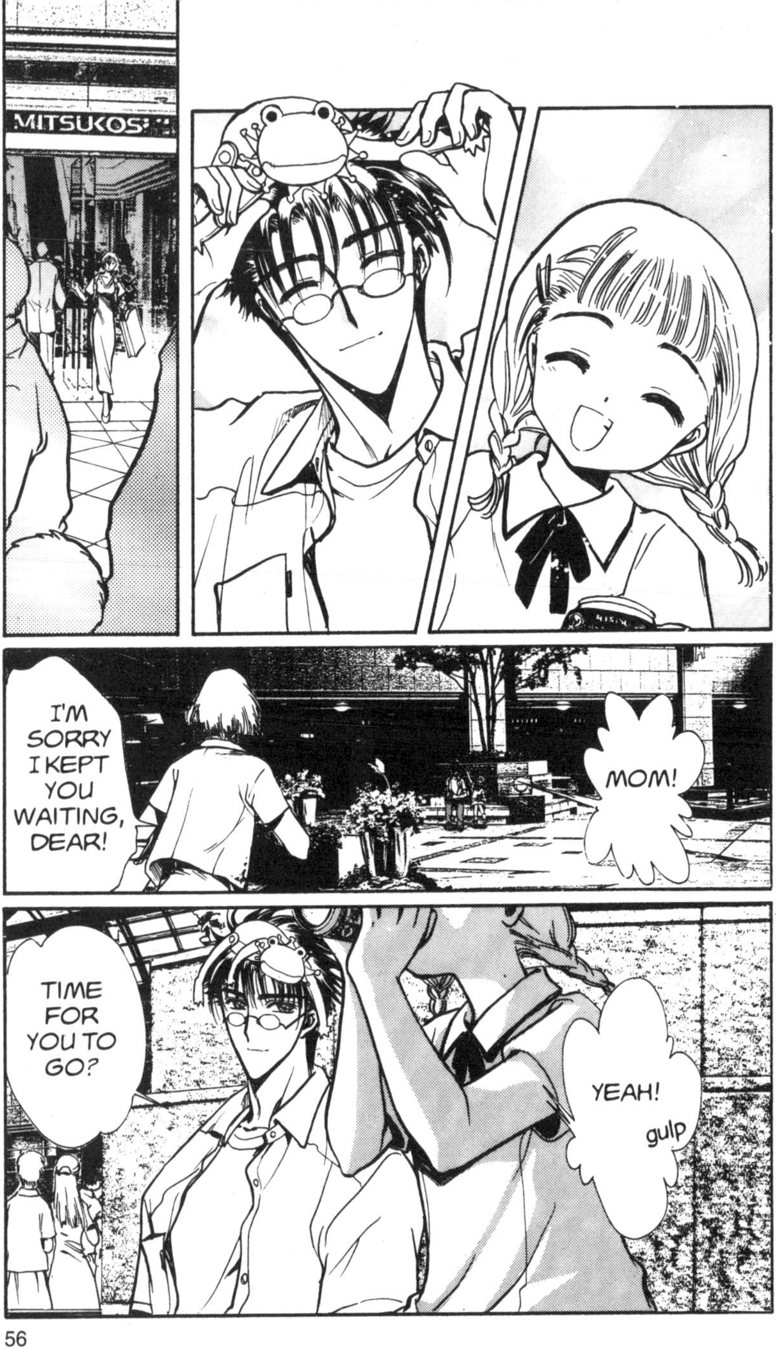
MITSUKOS
MOM!
I'M SORRY I KEPT YOU WAITING, DEAR!
TIME FOR YOU TO GO?
YEAH! gulp

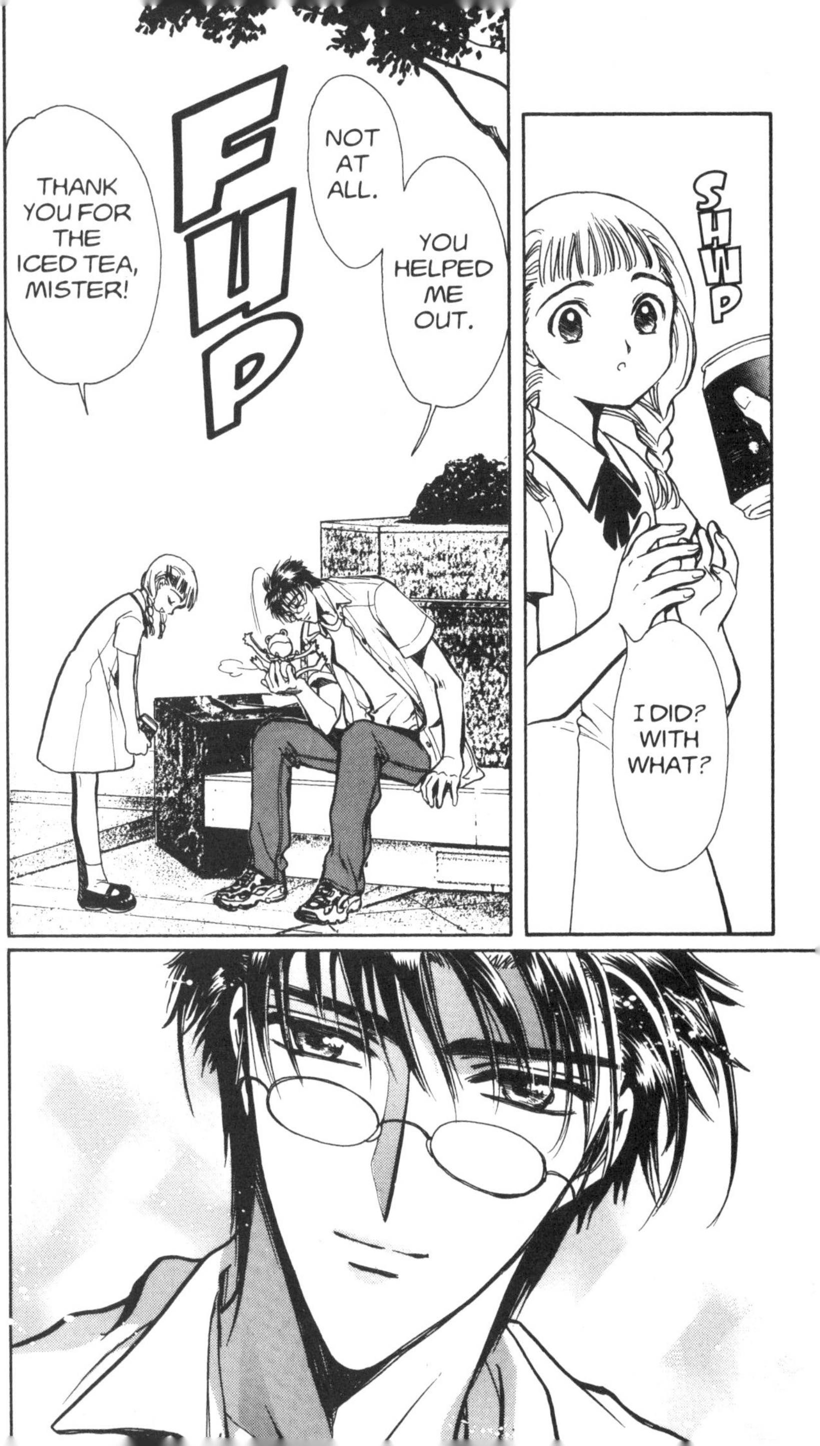
THANK YOU FOR THE ICED TEA, MISTER!
FUP
NOT AT ALL.
YOU HELPED ME OUT.
SHWP
I DID? WITH WHAT?

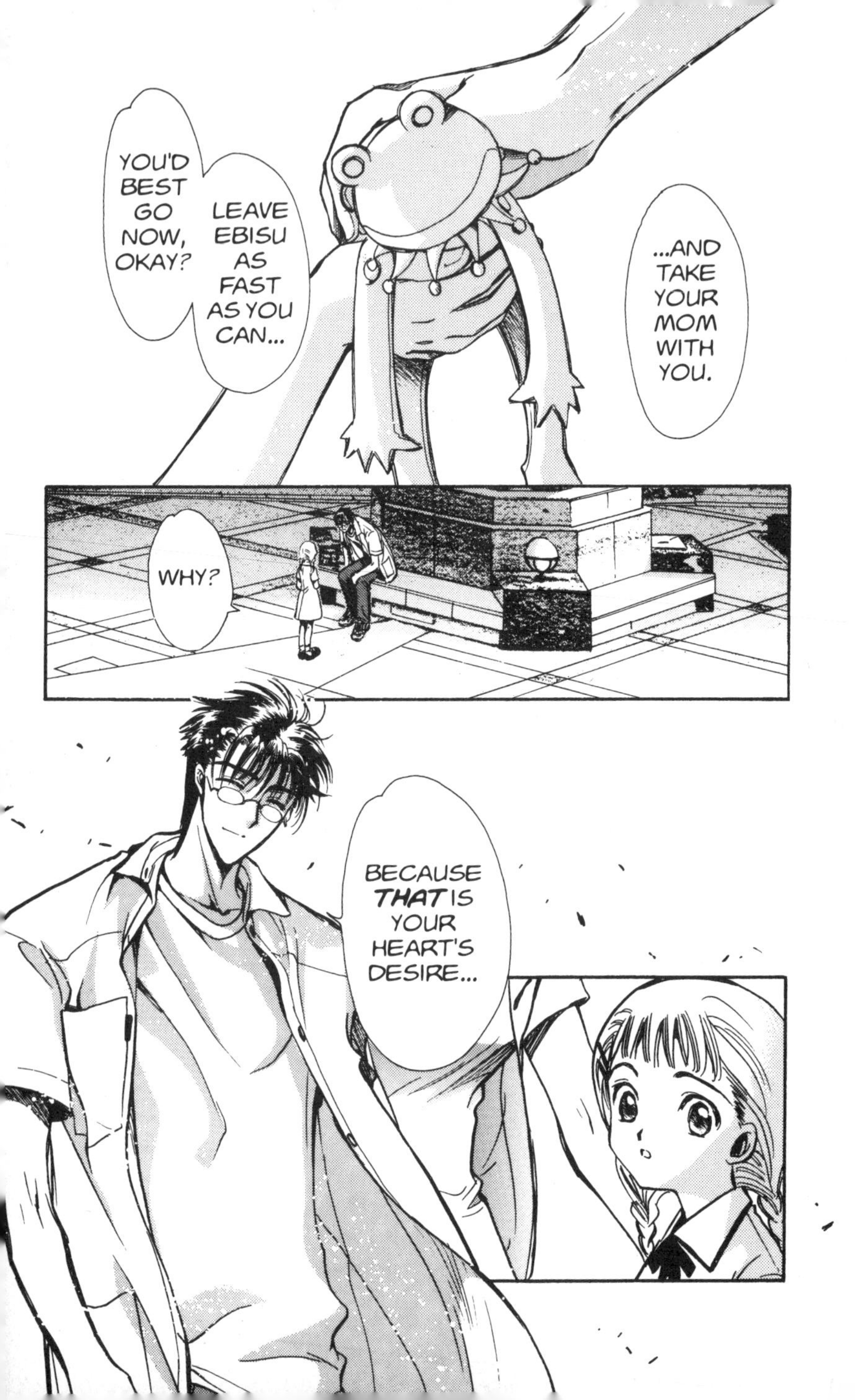
YOU'D BEST GO NOW, OKAY?
LEAVE EBISU AS FAST AS YOU CAN...
...AND TAKE YOUR MOM WITH YOU.
WHY?
BECAUSE ***THAT*** IS YOUR HEART'S DESIRE...

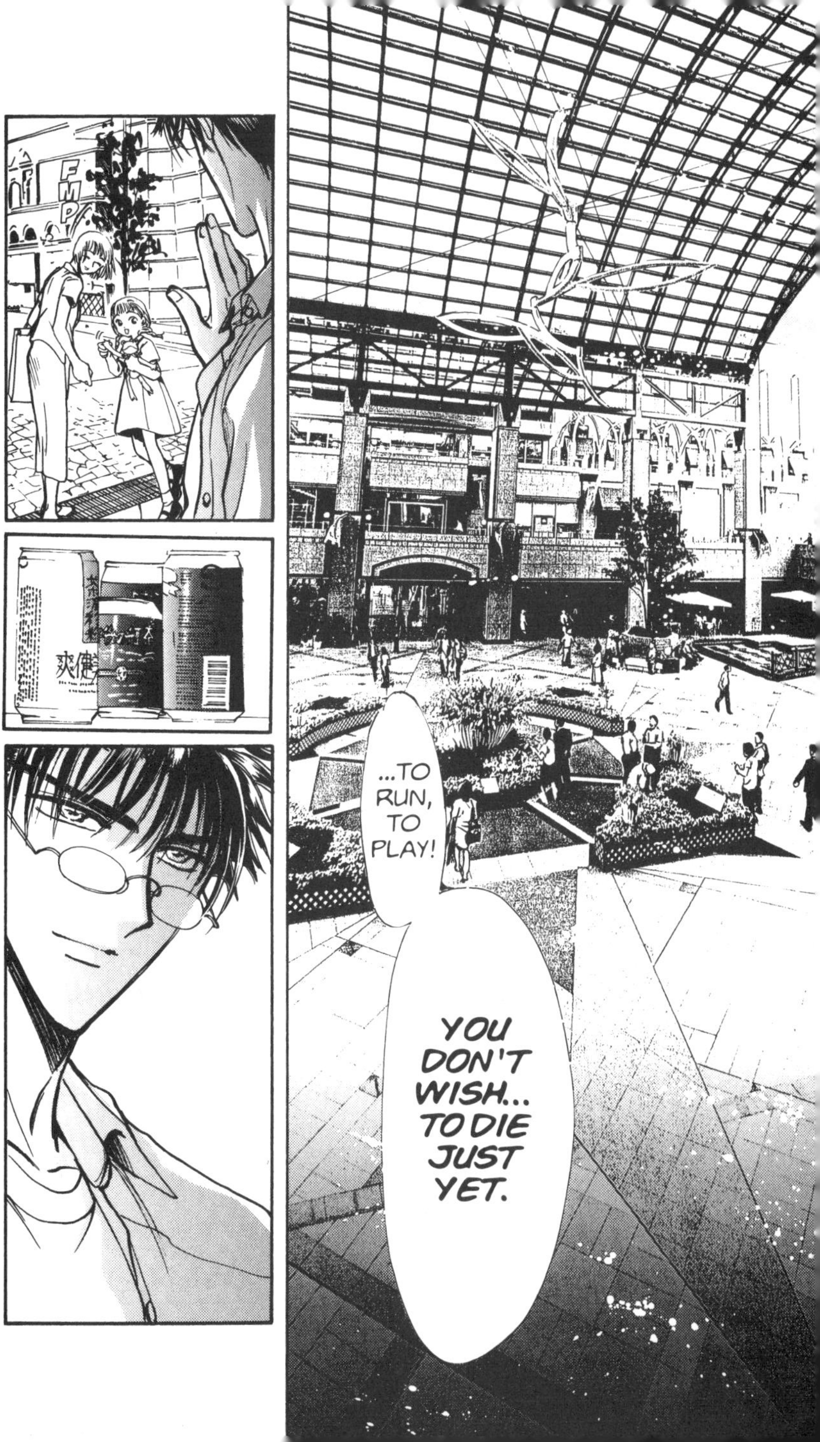
...TO RUN, TO PLAY!
YOU DON'T WISH... TO DIE JUST YET.
FMP

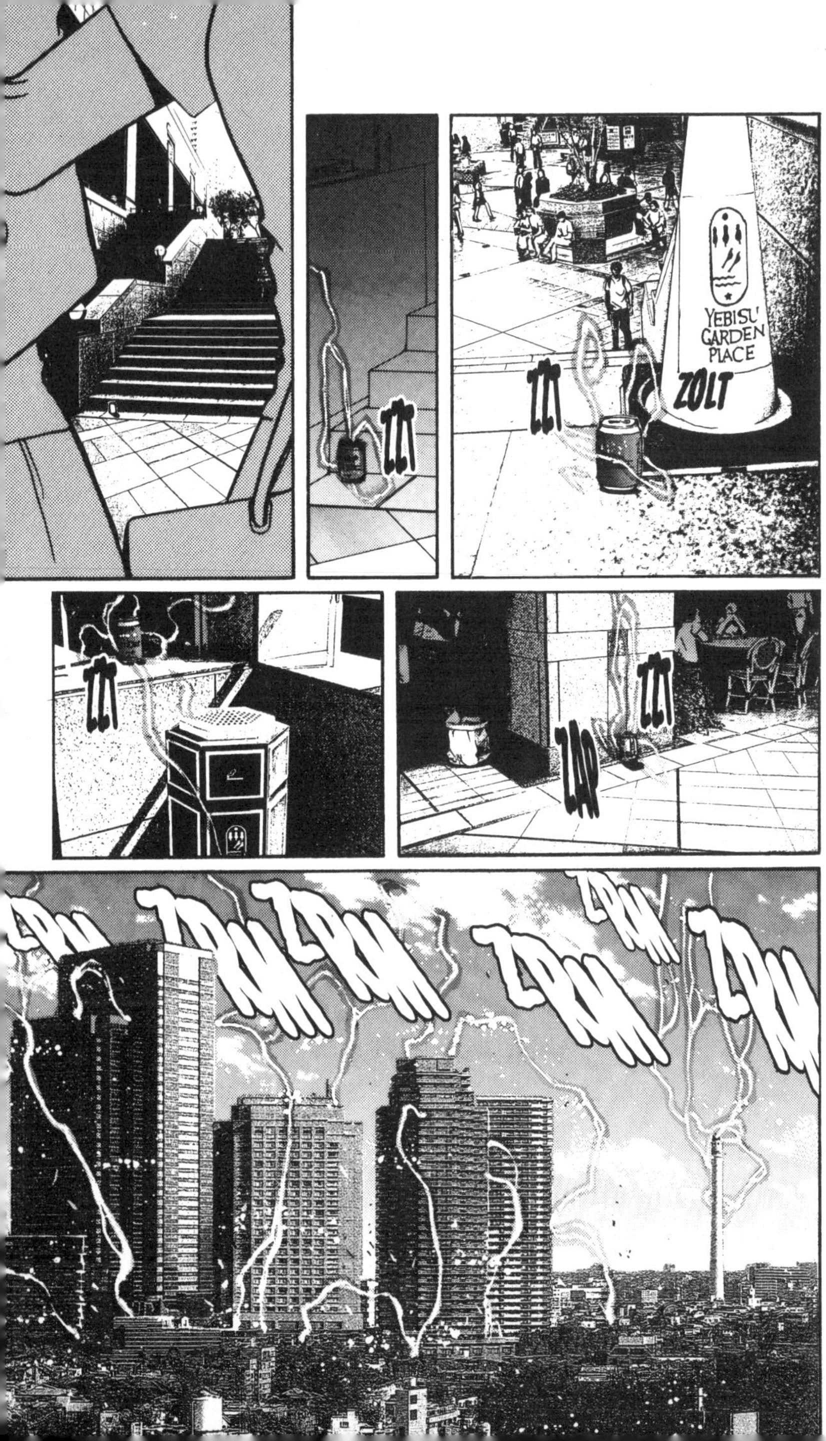
YEBISU GARDEN PLACE
ZOLT
ZZT
ZZT
ZZT
ZAP
ZZT

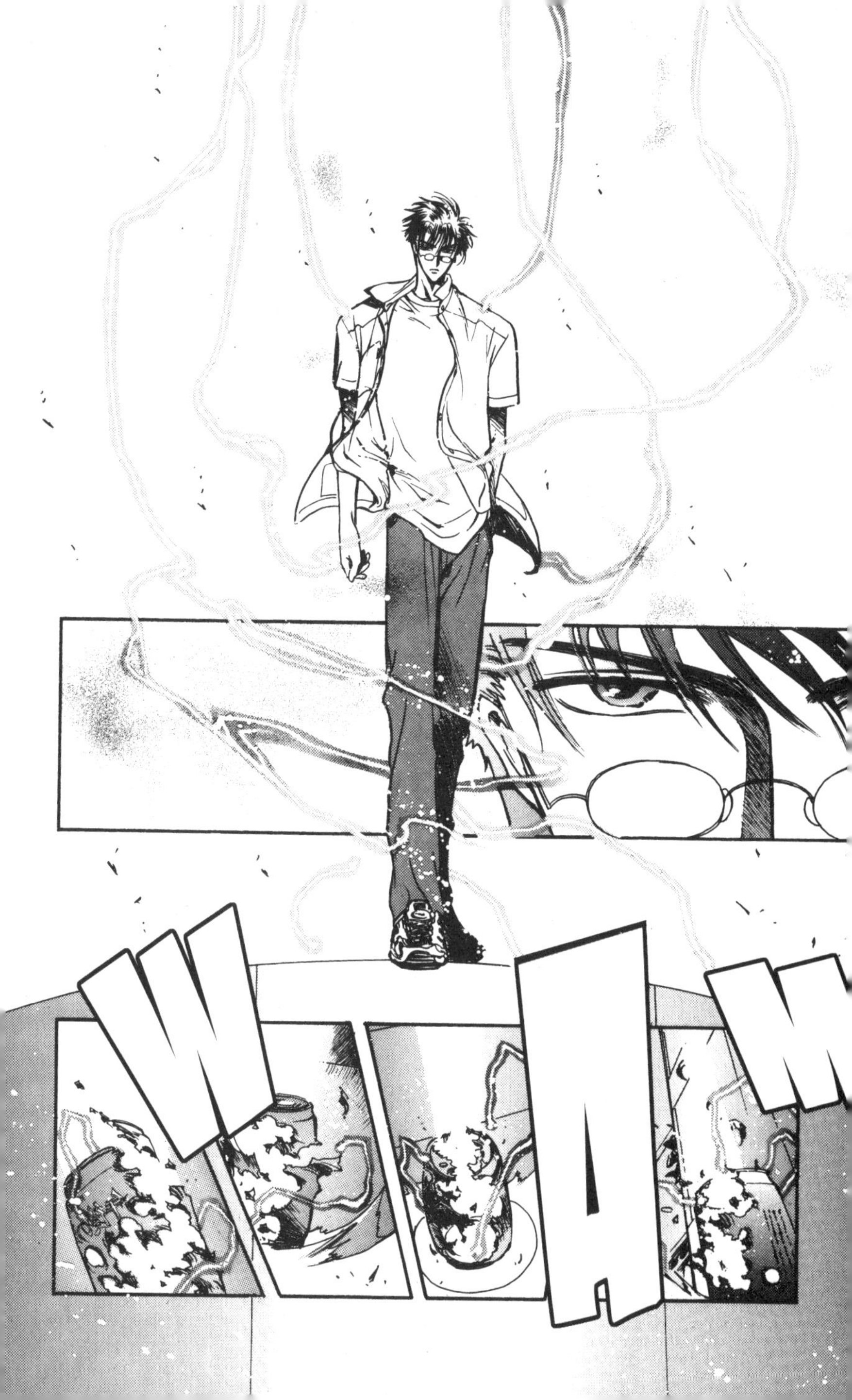
WAM

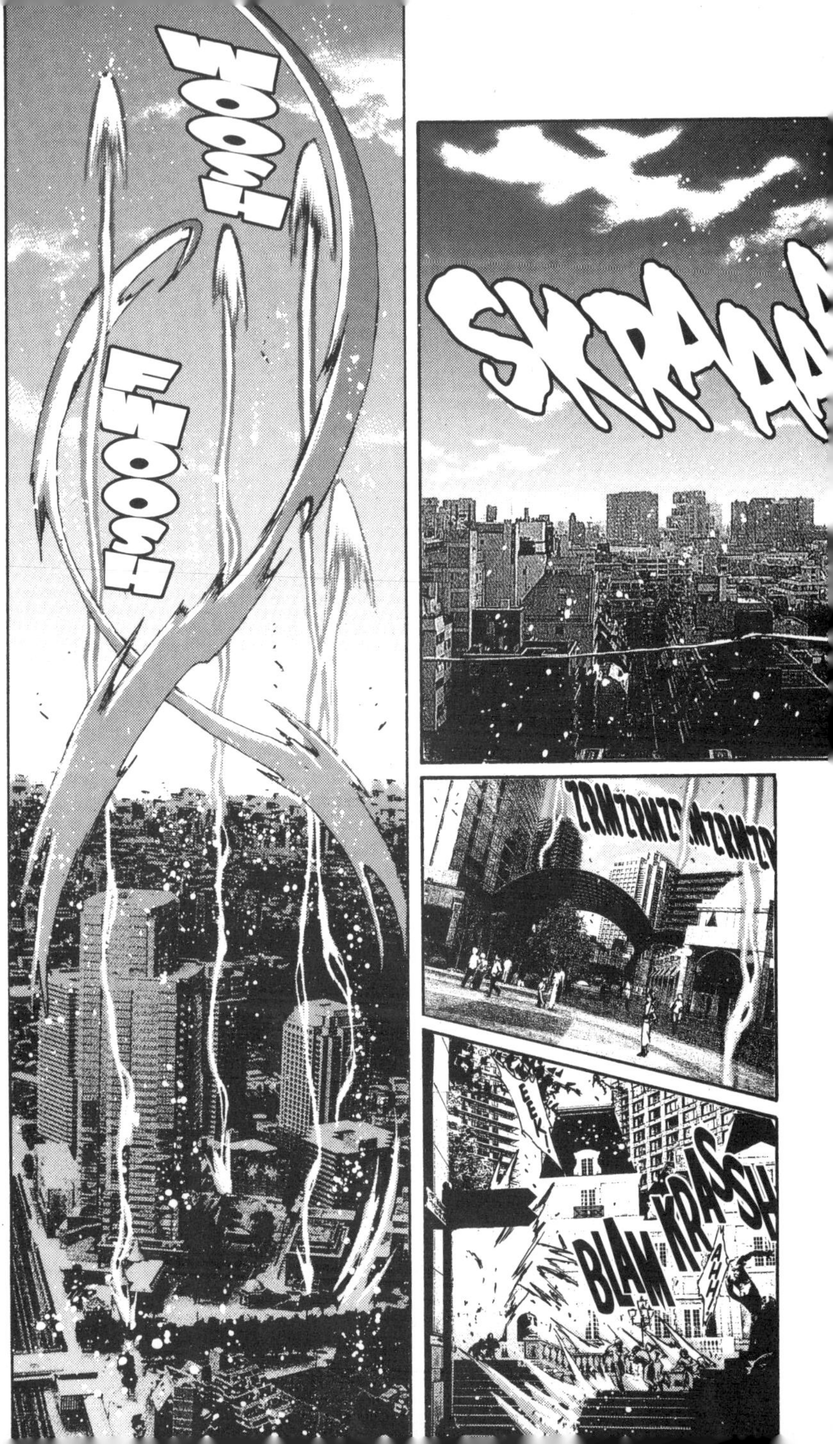
SKRAAA
EEEK!
KRASH
AHH
BLAM
WOOSH
FWOOSH

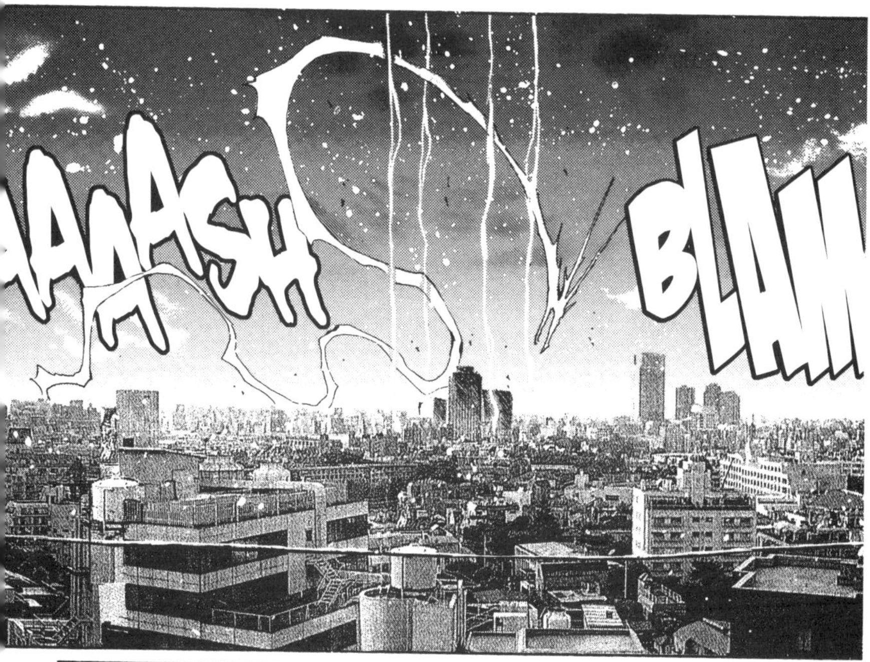
BLAMM
AAAASH

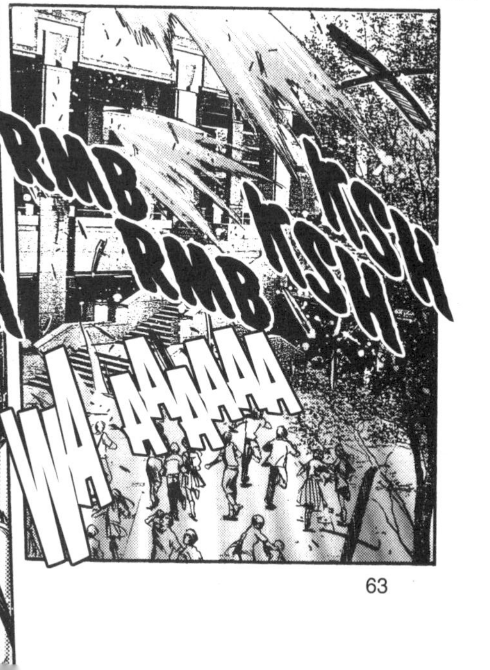
RMB
RMB
KRSH
KRSH
WAAAAAAA

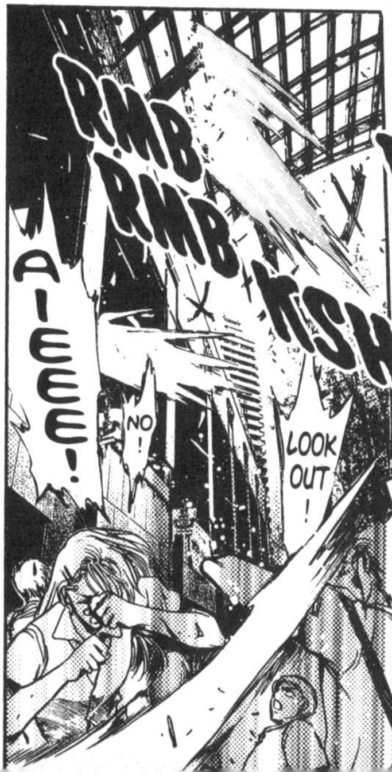
RMB
RMB
KRSH
LOOK OUT!
NO!
AIEEE!

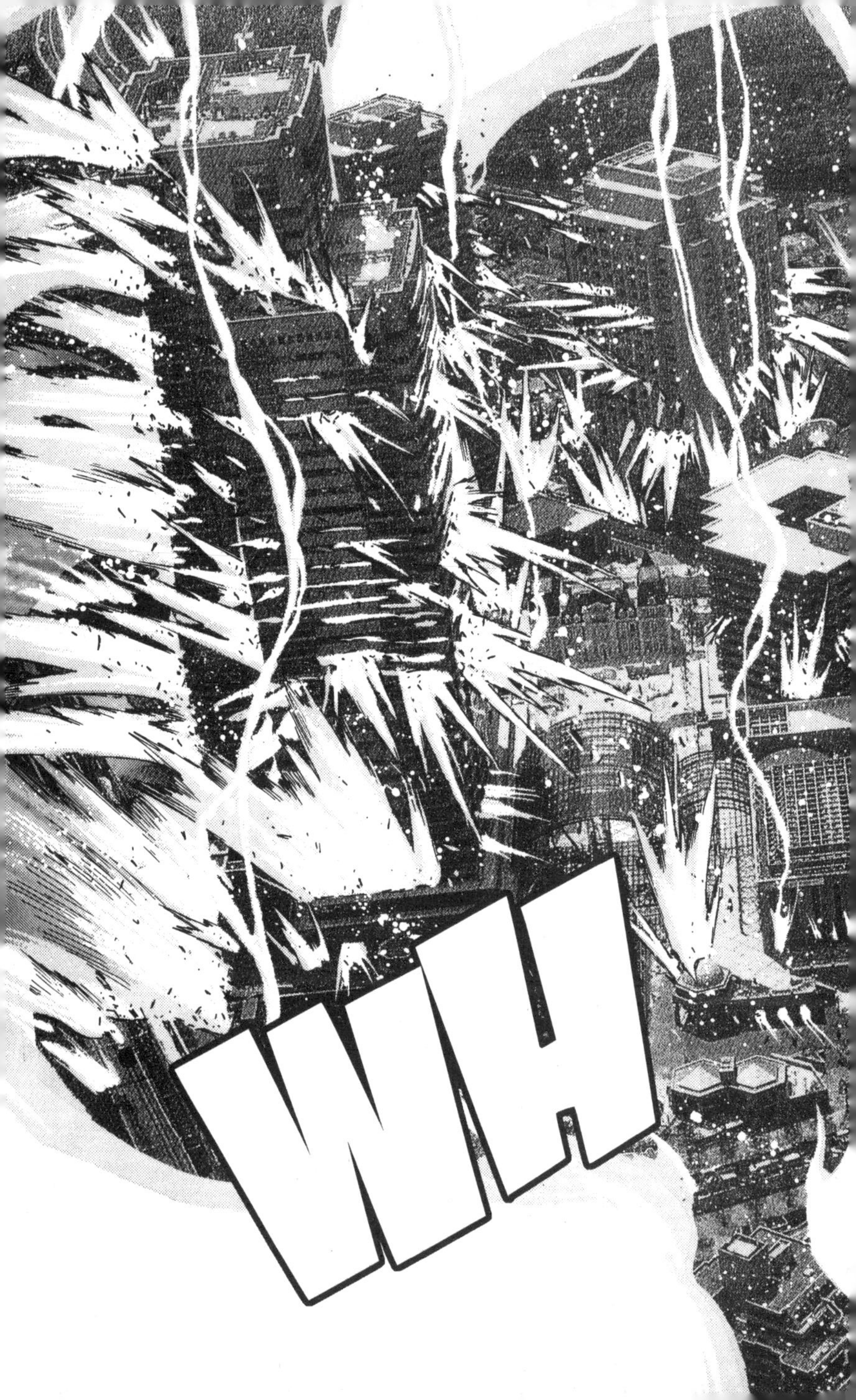
WH

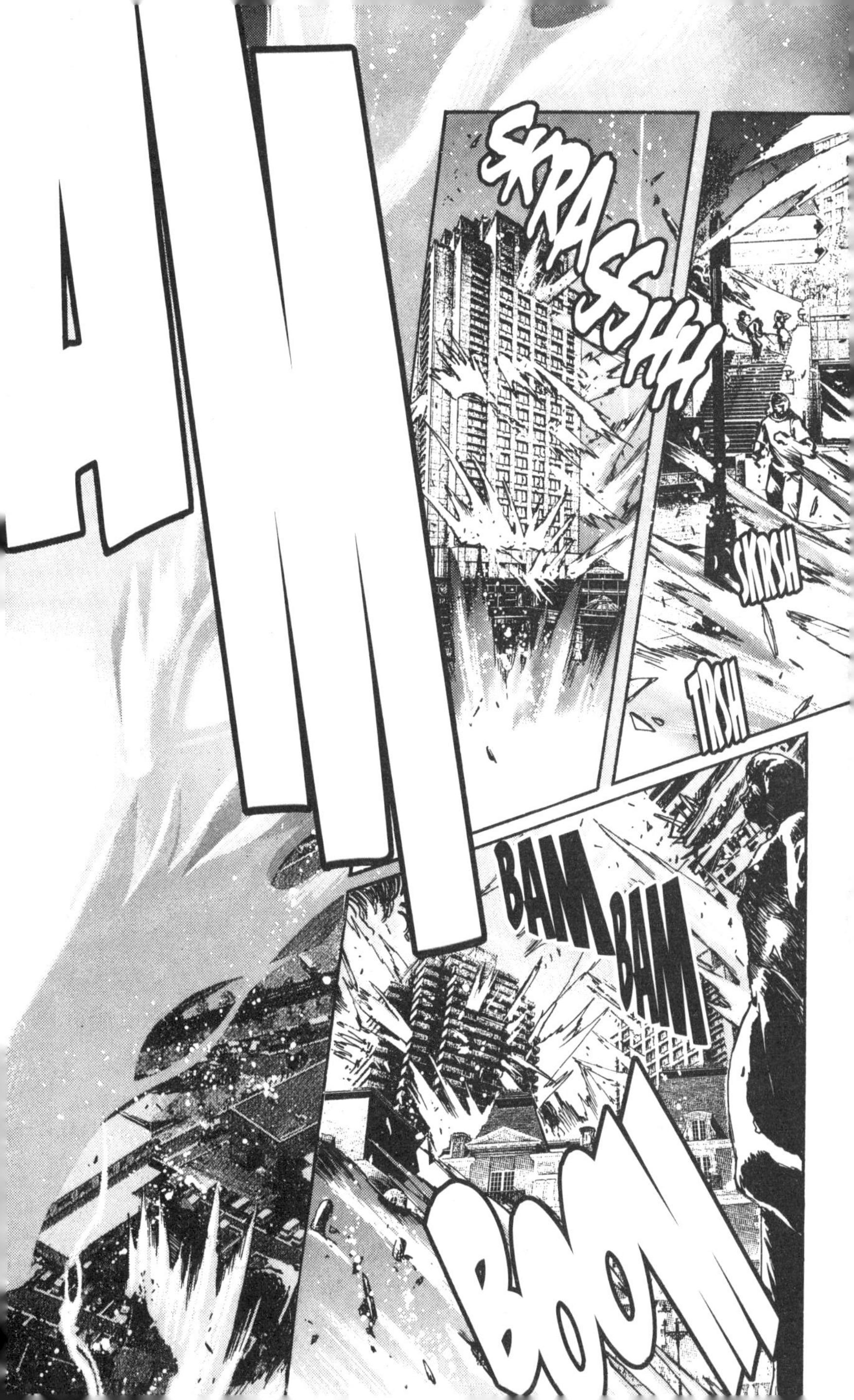
SKRASSHH!
SKRSH
TRSH
BAM
BAM
BOOM

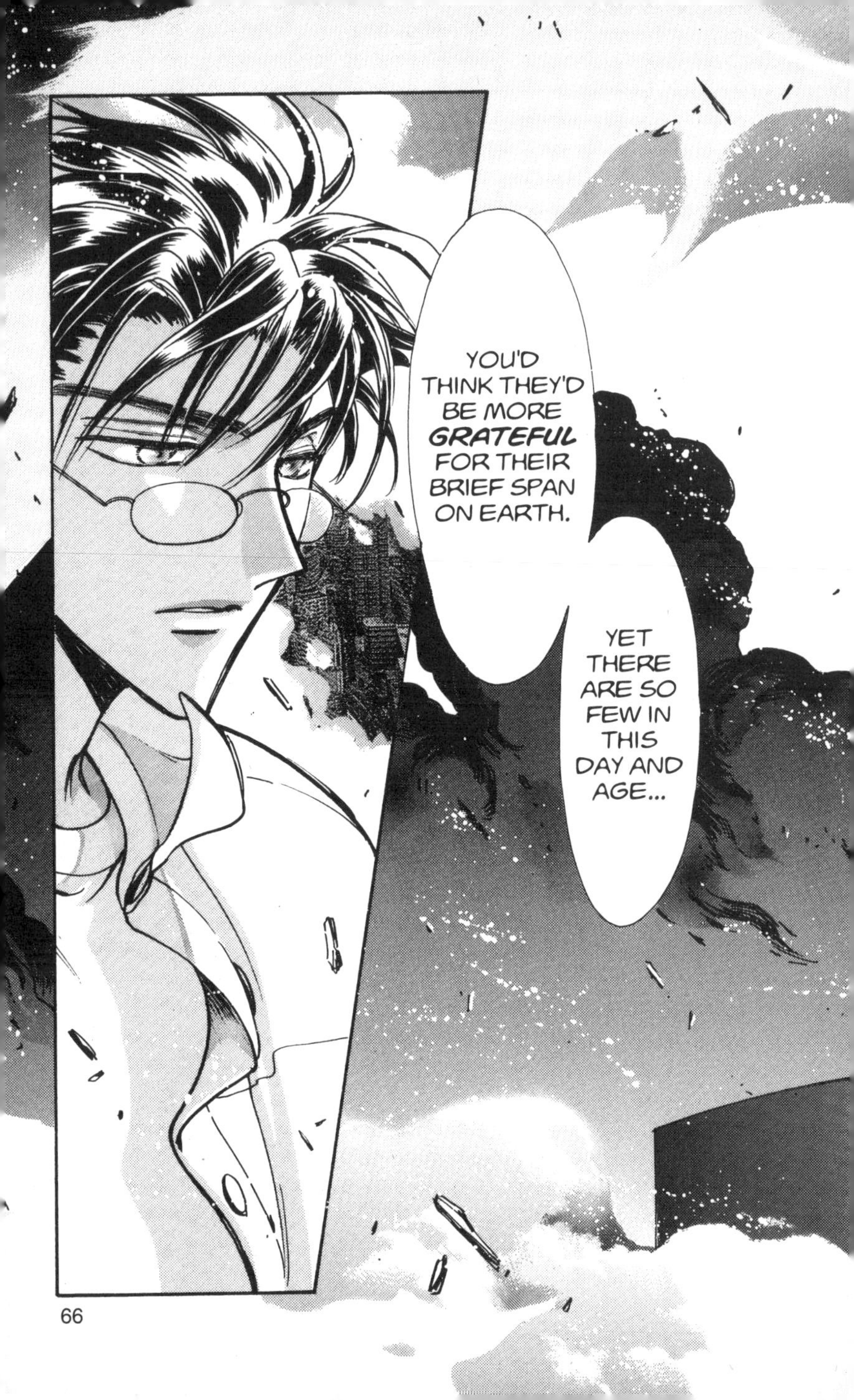
YOU'D THINK THEY'D BE MORE **GRATEFUL** FOR THEIR BRIEF SPAN ON EARTH.
YET THERE ARE SO FEW IN THIS DAY AND AGE...

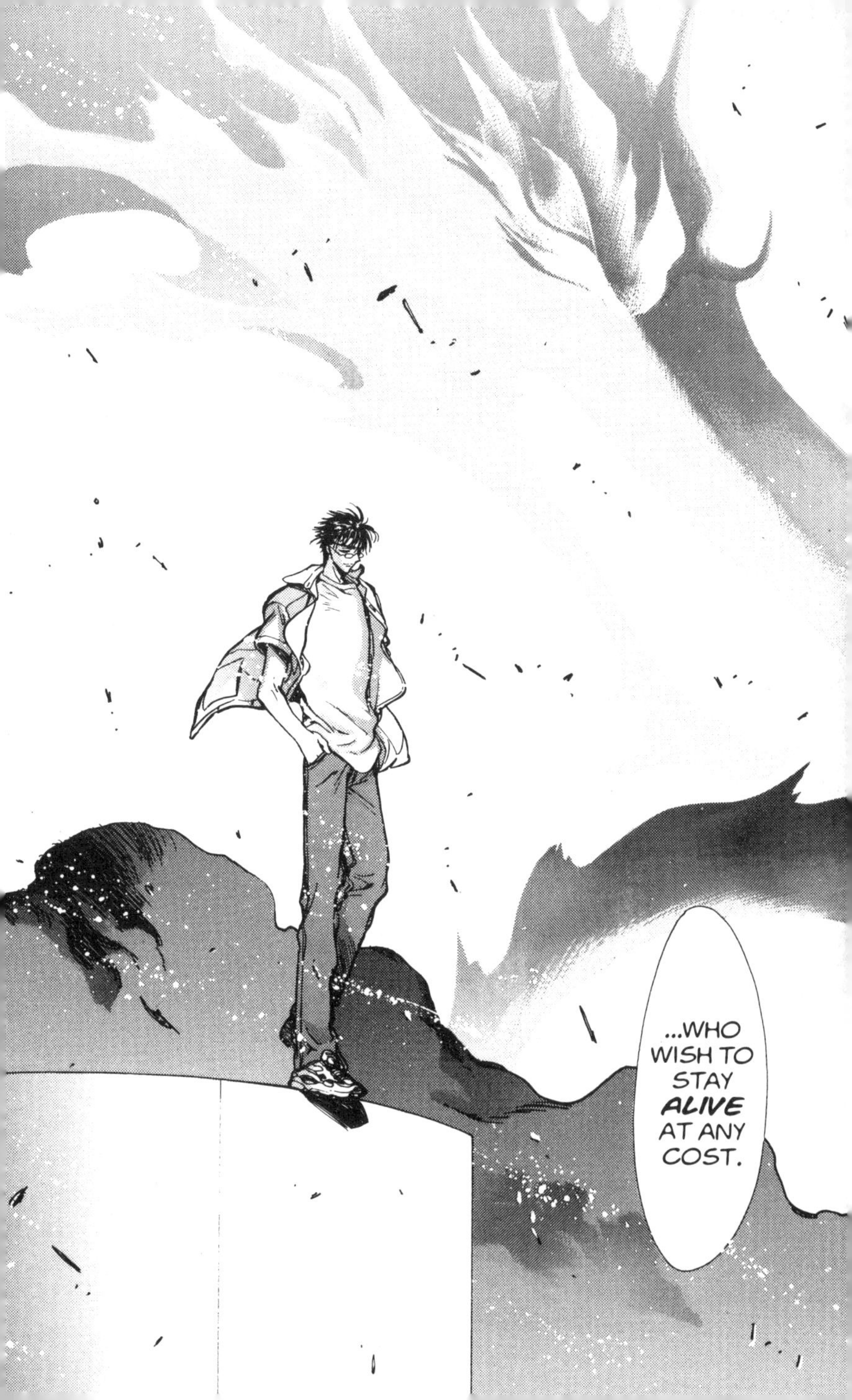
...WHO WISH TO STAY ALIVE AT ANY COST.

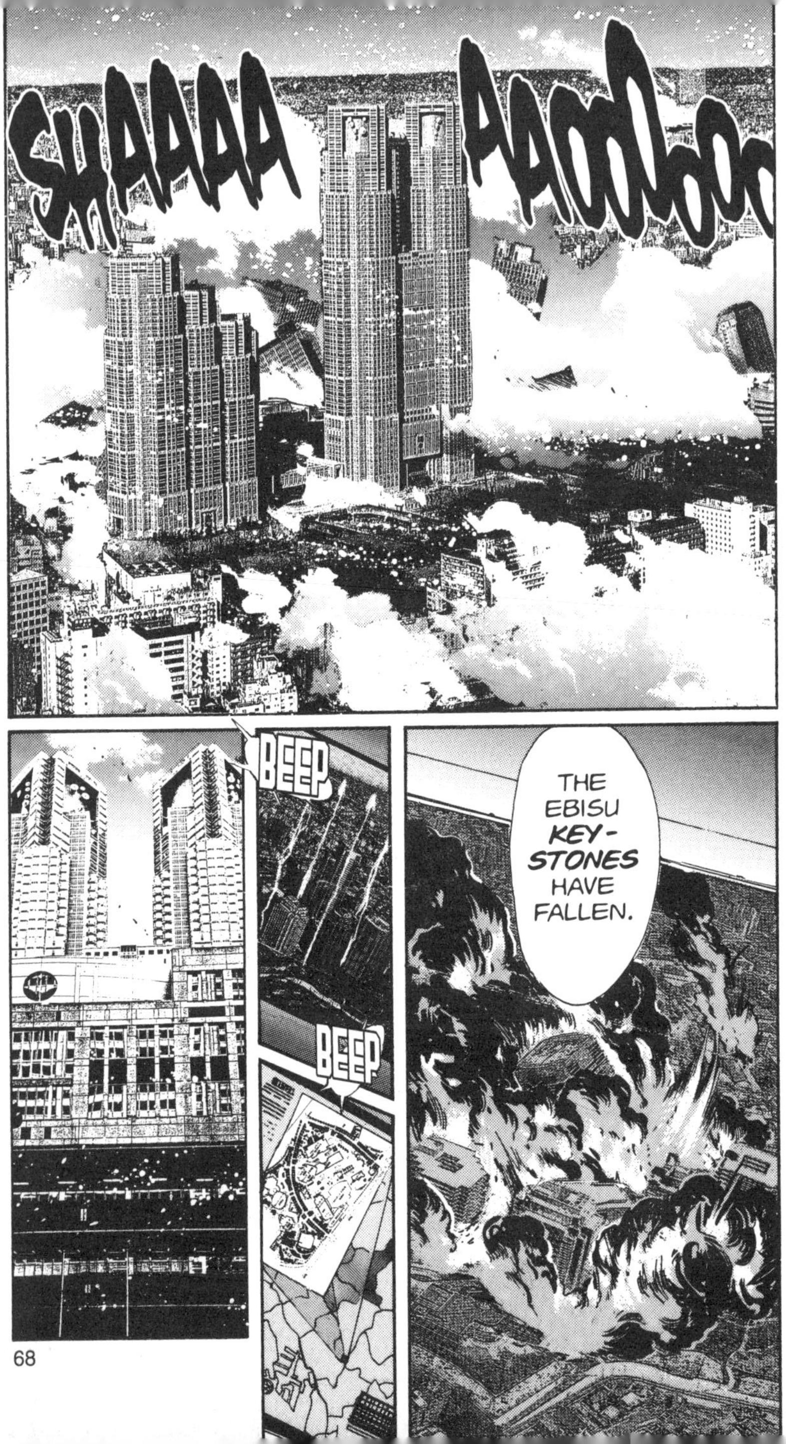
SHAAAA AAOOOooo
THE EBISU KEY-STONES HAVE FALLEN.
BEEP
BEEP

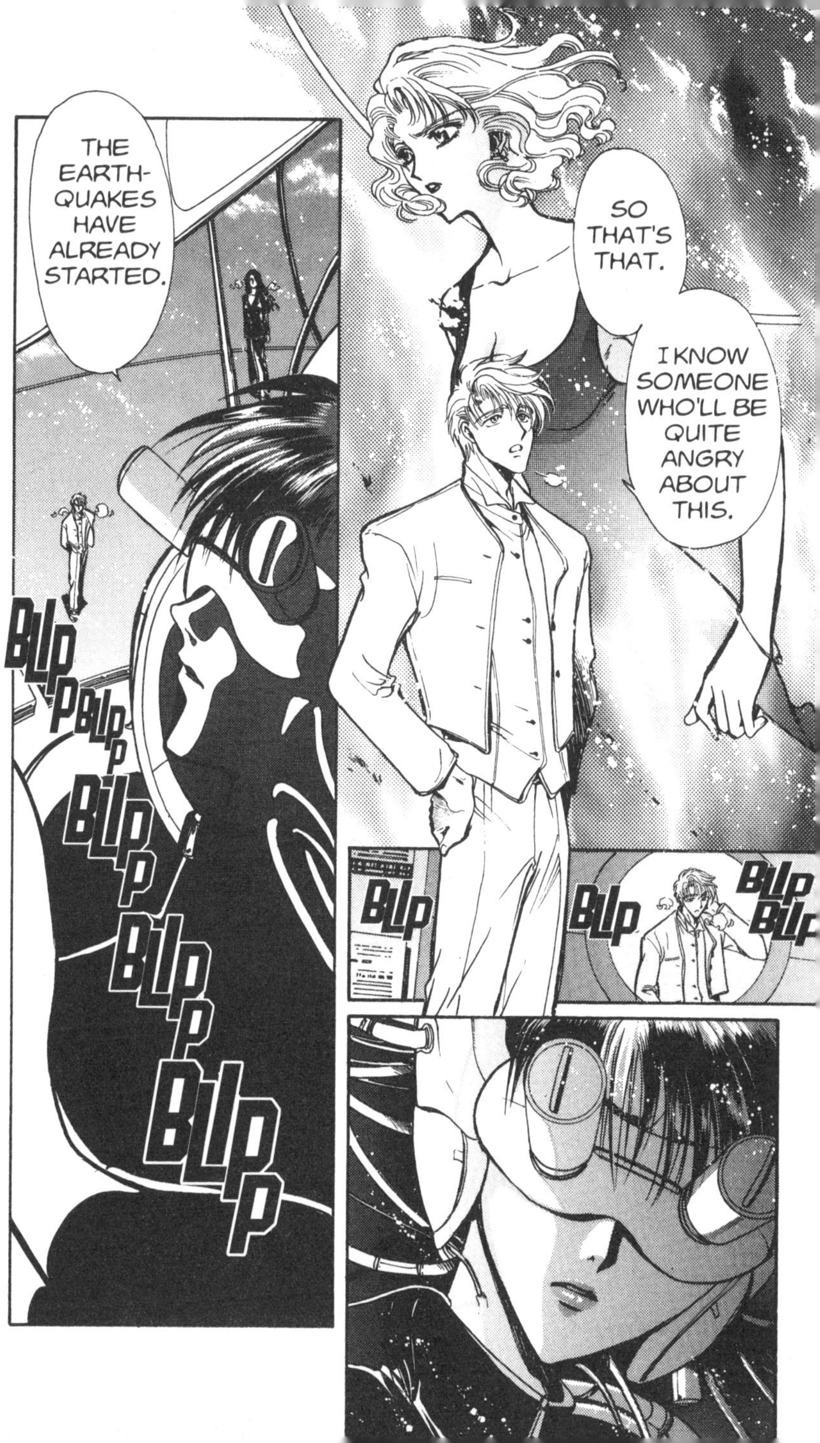
SO THAT'S THAT.
I KNOW SOMEONE WHO'LL BE QUITE ANGRY ABOUT THIS.
BLIP BLIP
BLIP
BLIP
THE EARTH-QUAKES HAVE ALREADY STARTED.
BLIPP BLIPP
BLIPP
BLIPP
BLIPP

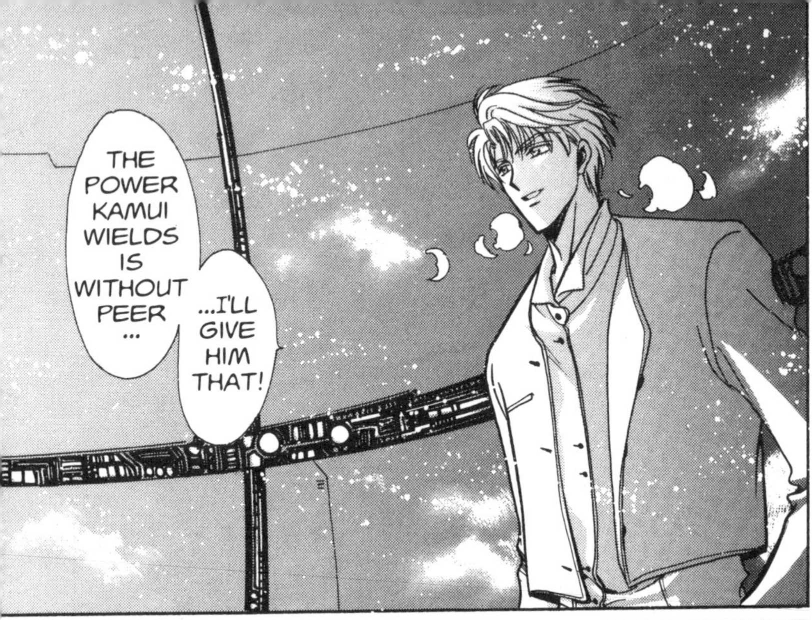
THE POWER KAMUI WIELDS IS WITHOUT PEER ...
...I'LL GIVE HIM THAT!

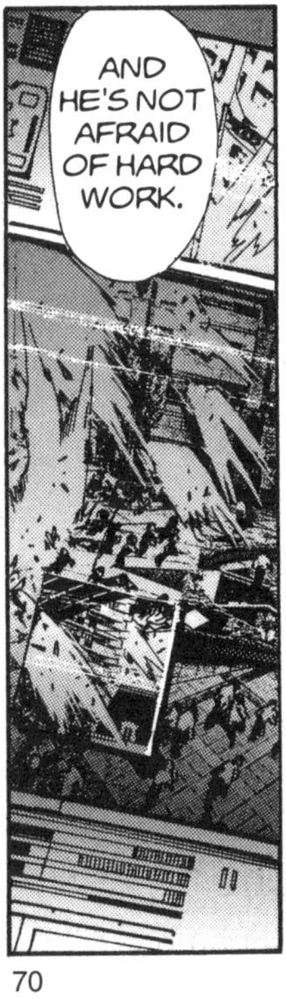
AND HE'S NOT AFRAID OF HARD WORK.

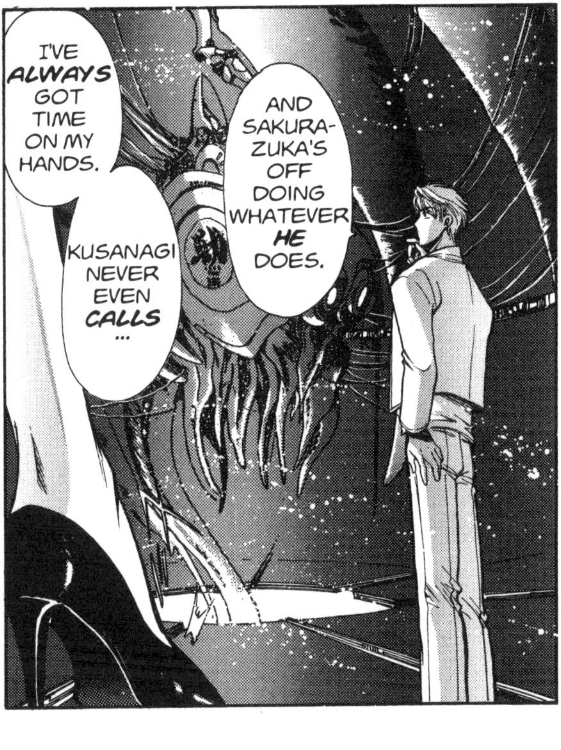
I'VE ALWAYS GOT TIME ON MY HANDS.
KUSANAGI NEVER EVEN CALLS ...
AND SAKURAZUKA'S OFF DOING WHATEVER HE DOES.

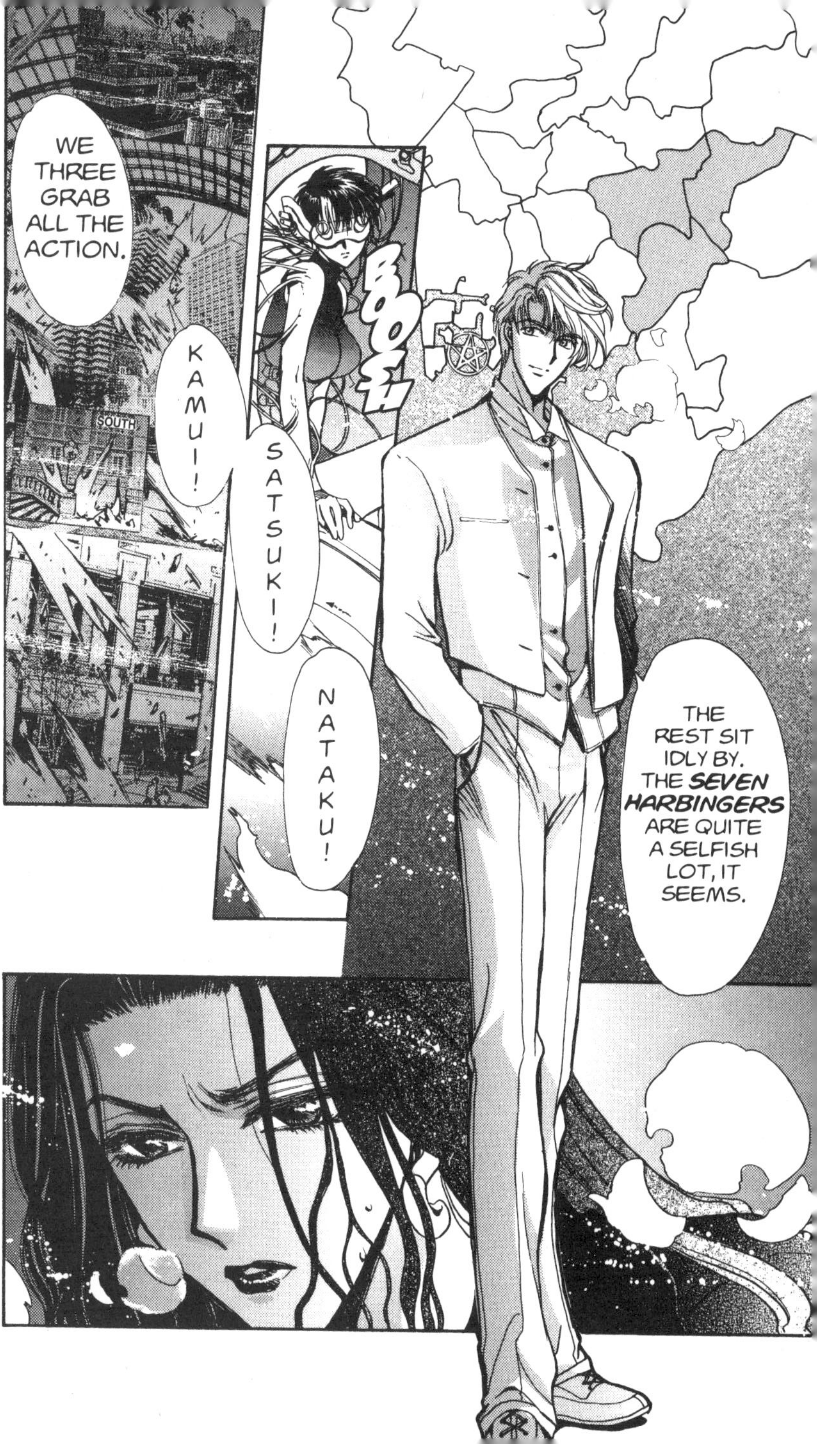

WE THREE GRAB ALL THE ACTION.
BOOSH
KAMUI!
SATSUKI!
NATAKU!
THE REST SIT IDLY BY. THE **SEVEN HARBINGERS** ARE QUITE A SELFISH LOT, IT SEEMS.
SOUTH

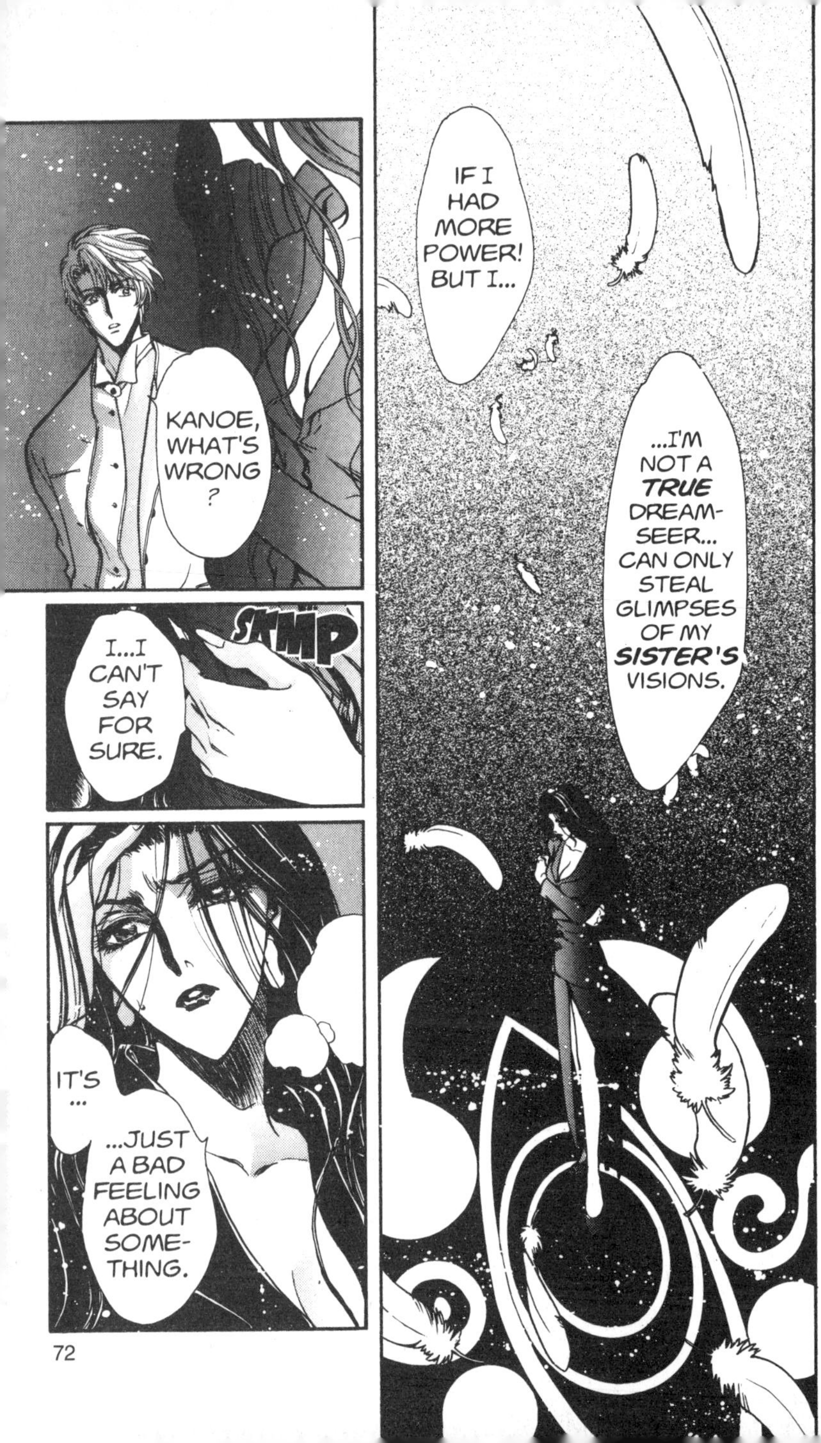
KANOE, WHAT'S WRONG?
SKMP
I...I CAN'T SAY FOR SURE.
IT'S...
...JUST A BAD FEELING ABOUT SOME-THING.
IF I HAD MORE POWER! BUT I...
...I'M NOT A TRUE DREAM-SEER... CAN ONLY STEAL GLIMPSES OF MY SISTER'S VISIONS.

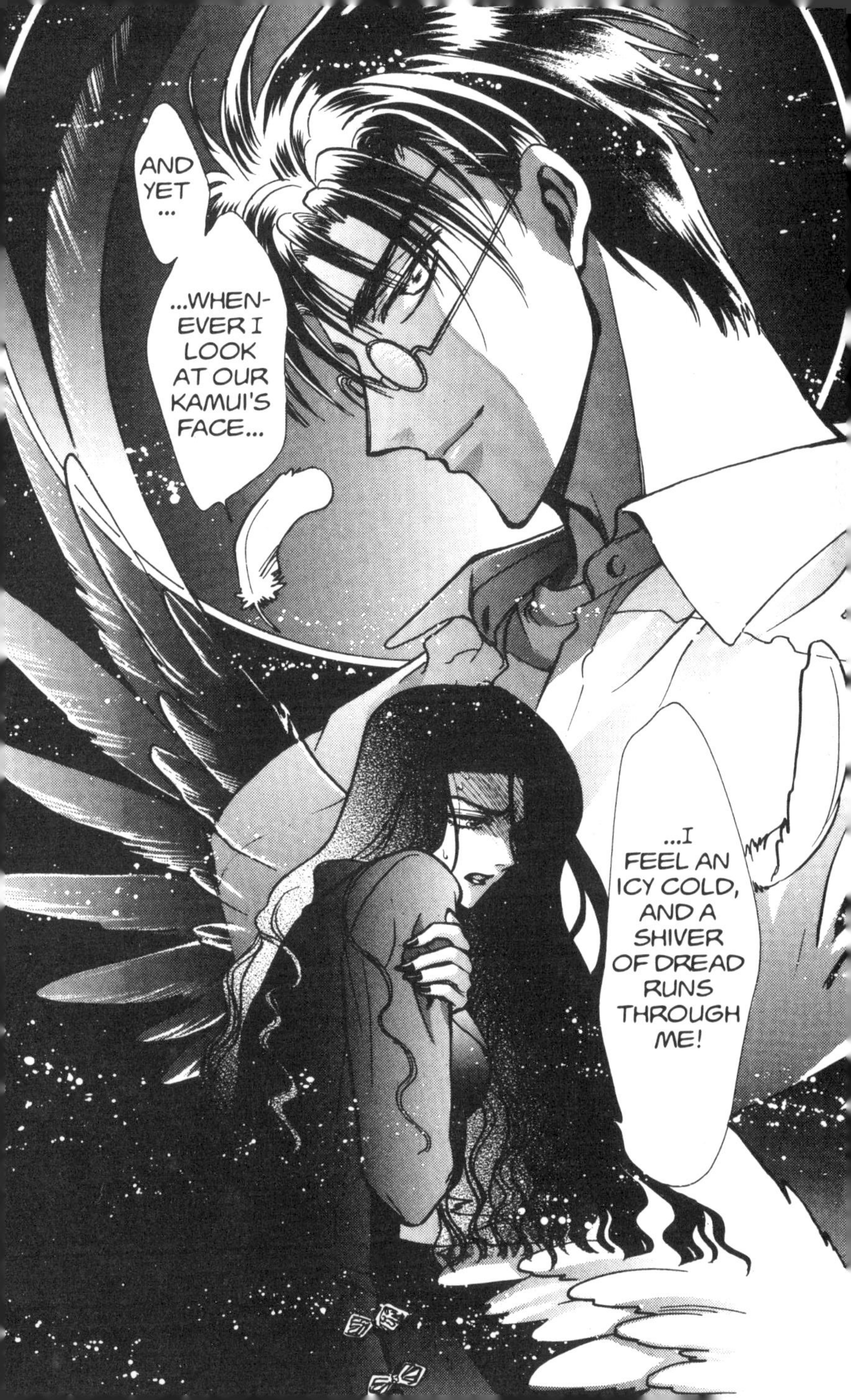
AND YET ...
...WHEN-EVER I LOOK AT OUR KAMUI'S FACE...
...I FEEL AN ICY COLD, AND A SHIVER OF DREAD RUNS THROUGH ME!

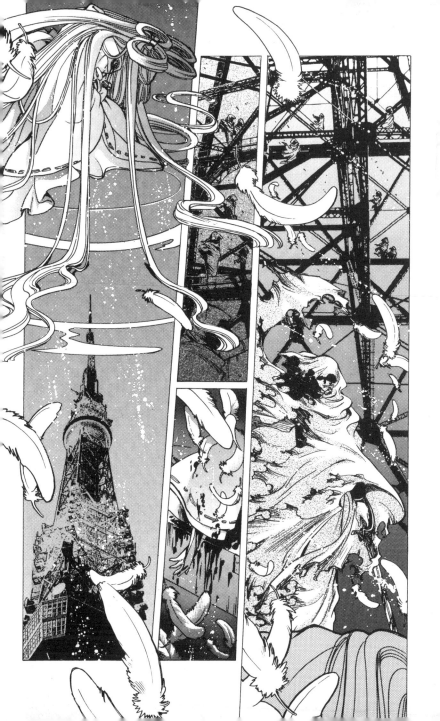

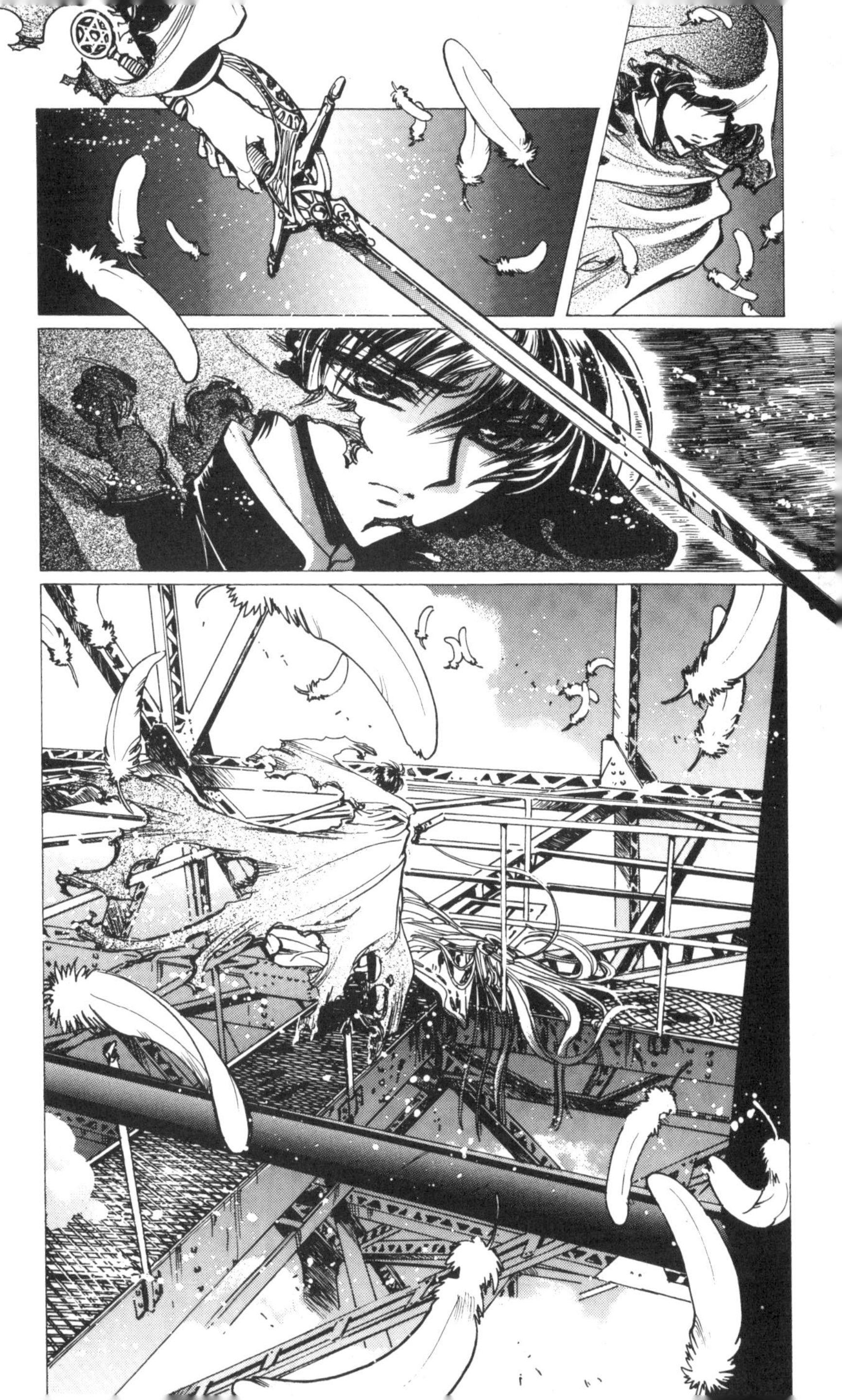

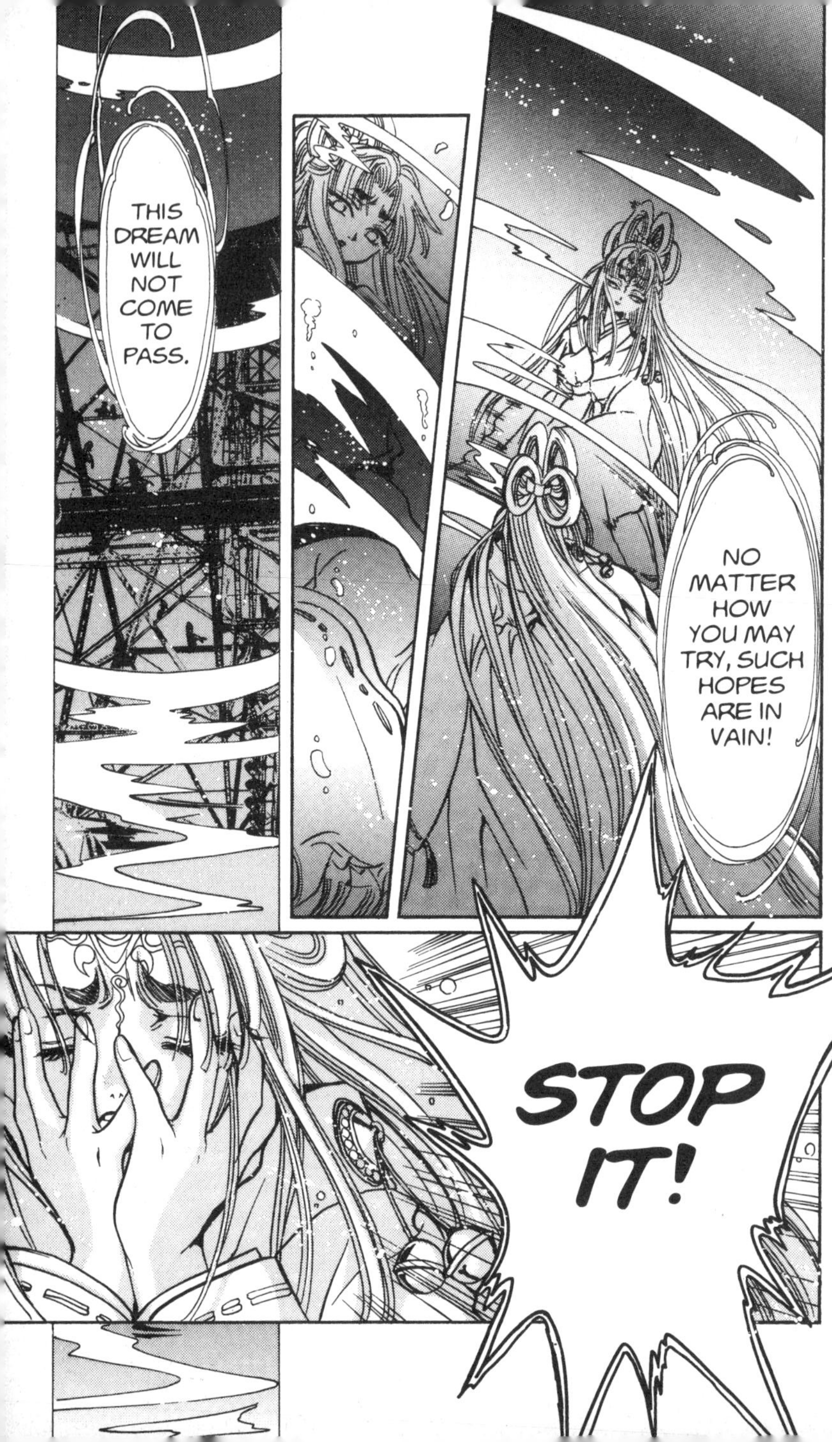
NO MATTER HOW YOU MAY TRY, SUCH HOPES ARE IN VAIN!
THIS DREAM WILL NOT COME TO PASS.
STOP IT!

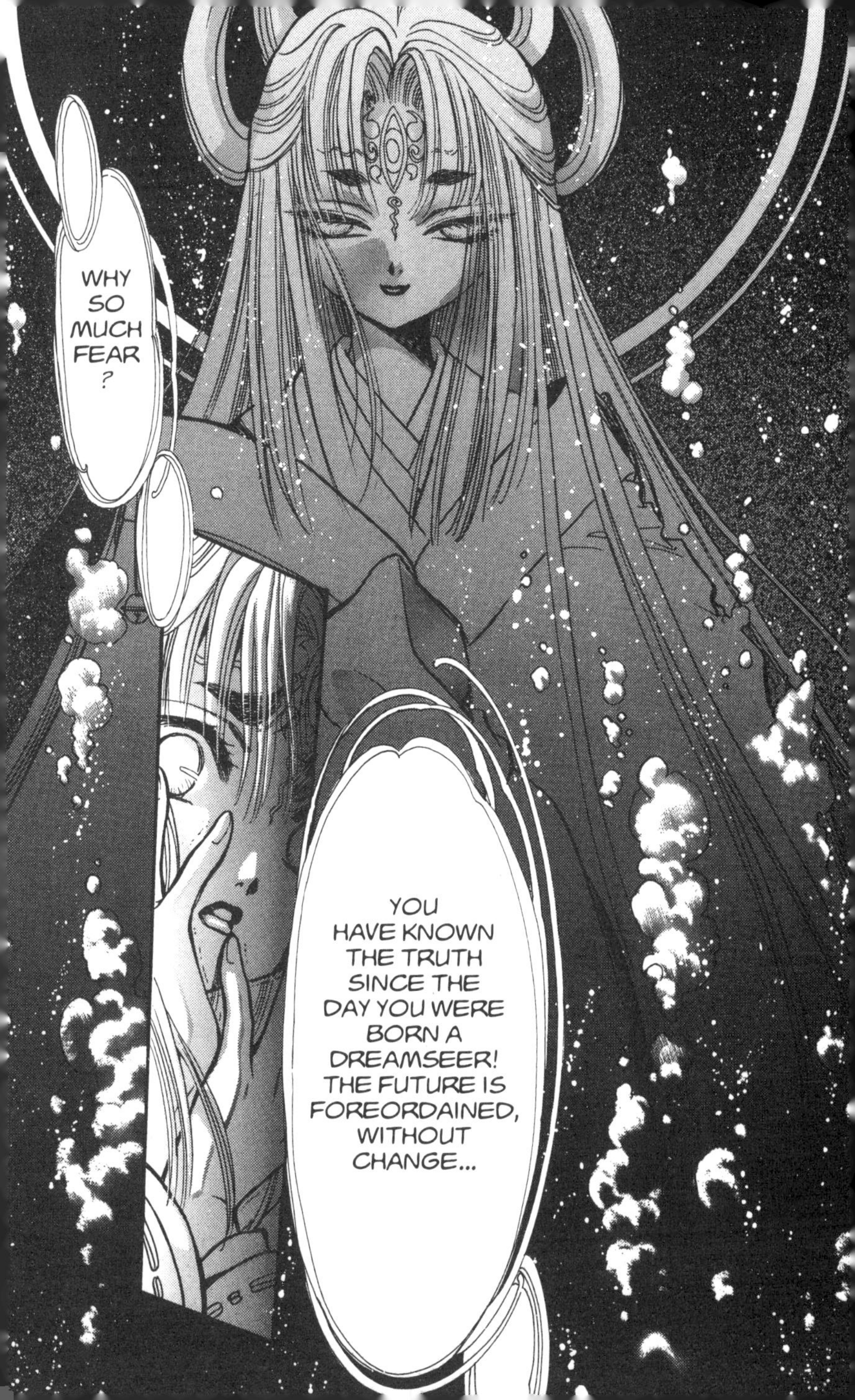
WHY SO MUCH FEAR?
YOU HAVE KNOWN THE TRUTH SINCE THE DAY YOU WERE BORN A DREAMSEER! THE FUTURE IS FOREORDAINED, WITHOUT CHANGE...

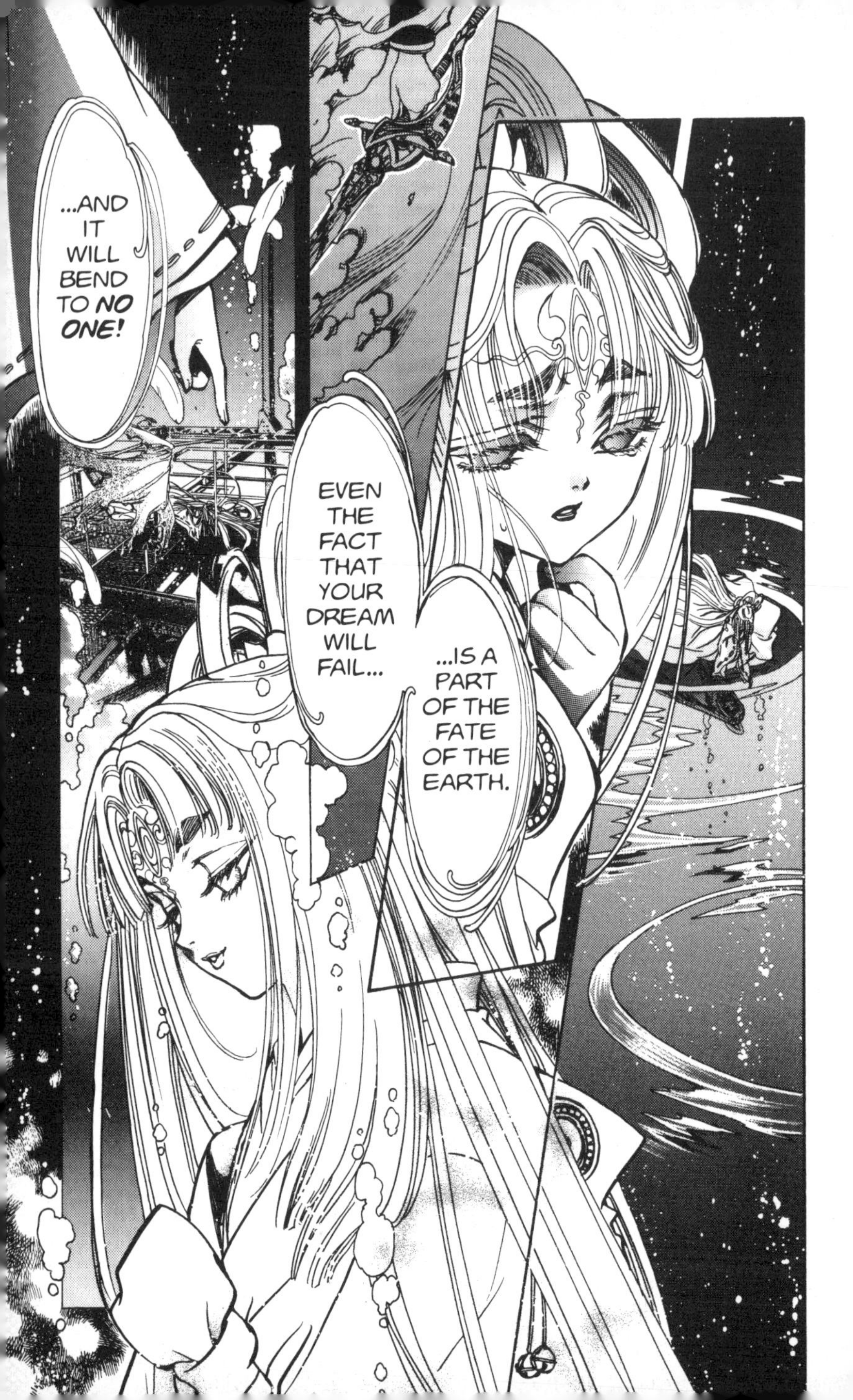
...AND IT WILL BEND TO NO ONE!
EVEN THE FACT THAT YOUR DREAM WILL FAIL...
...IS A PART OF THE FATE OF THE EARTH.

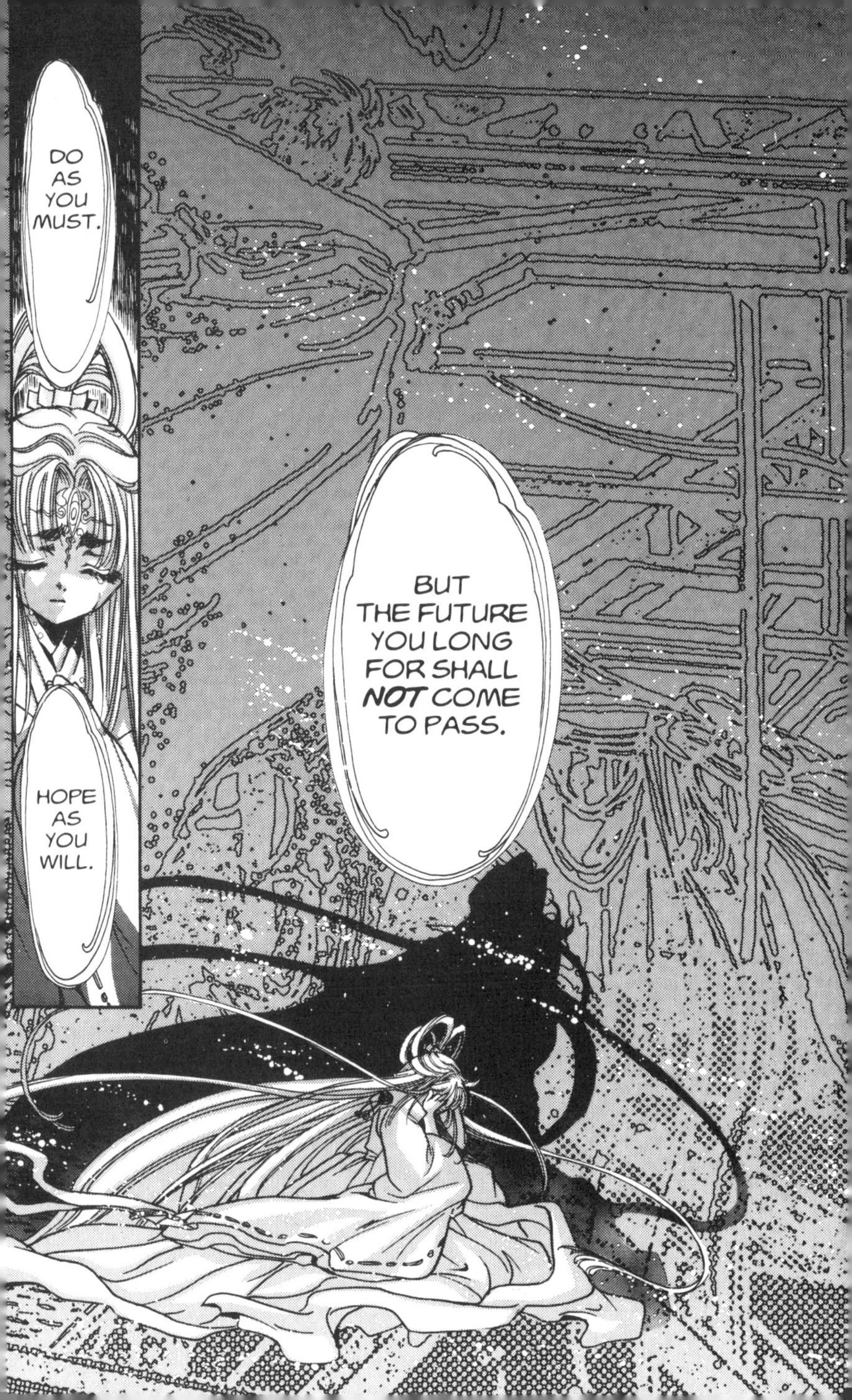
DO AS YOU MUST.
HOPE AS YOU WILL.
BUT THE FUTURE YOU LONG FOR SHALL NOT COME TO PASS.

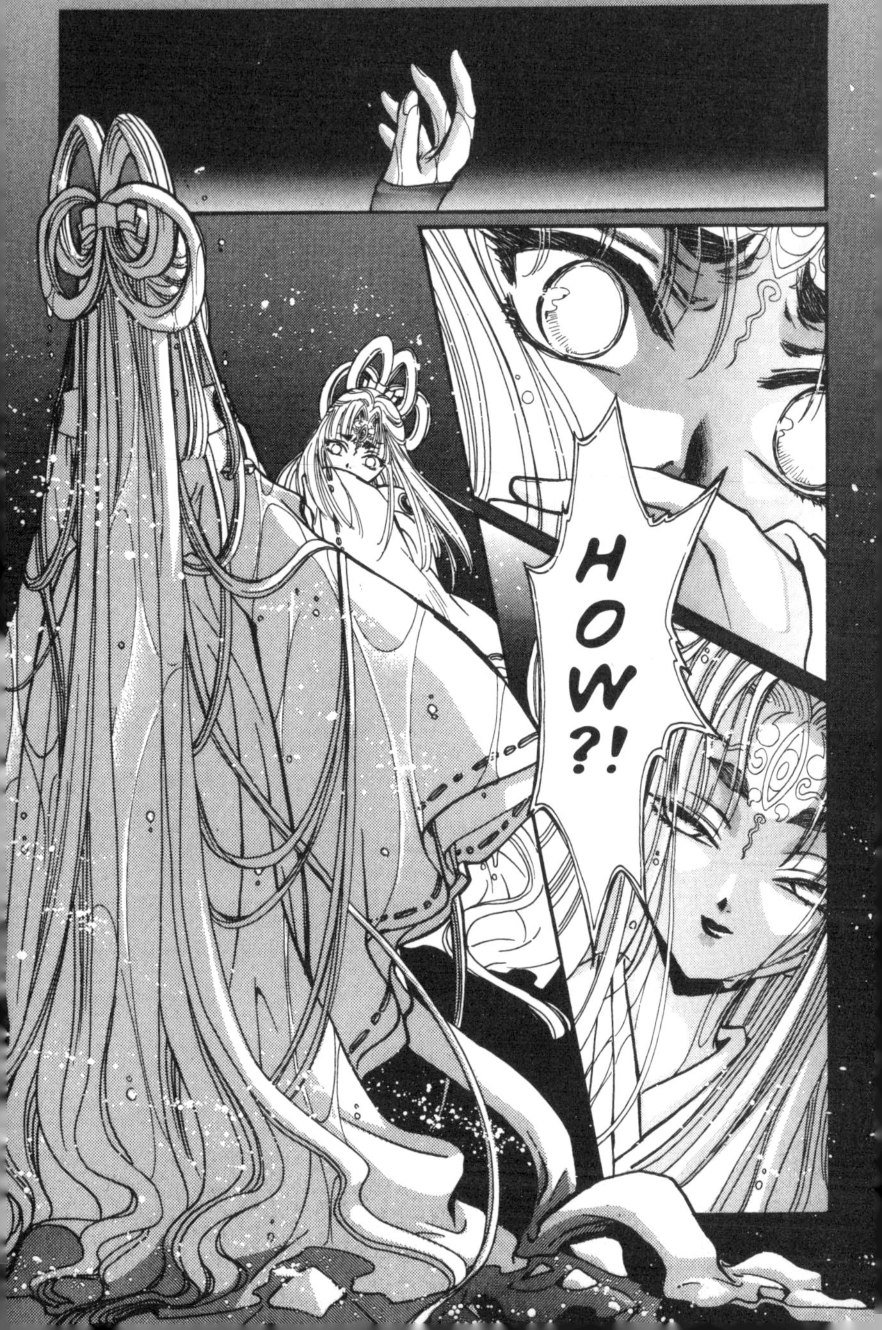
HOW?!

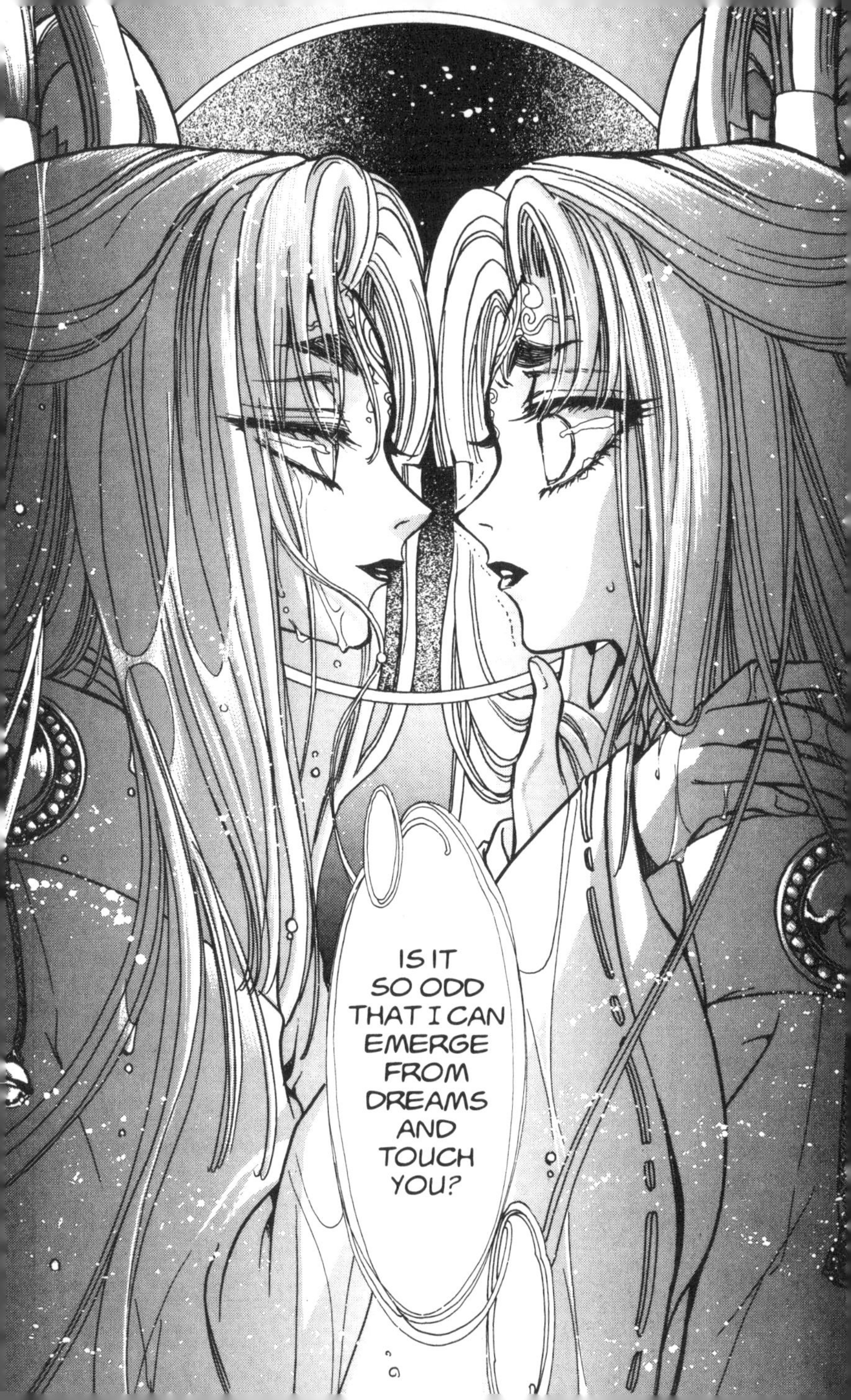
IS IT SO ODD THAT I CAN EMERGE FROM DREAMS AND TOUCH YOU?

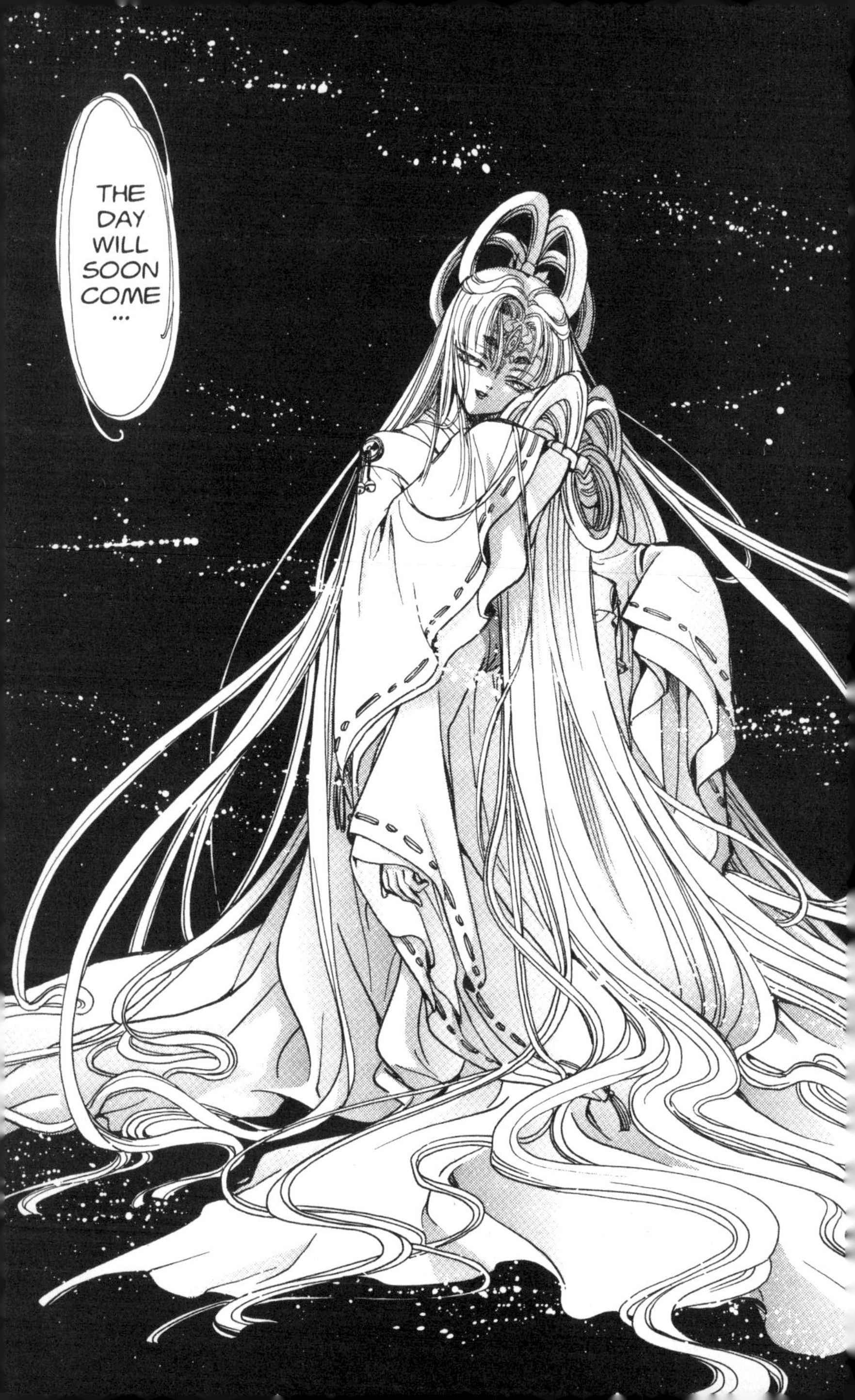
THE DAY WILL SOON COME ...

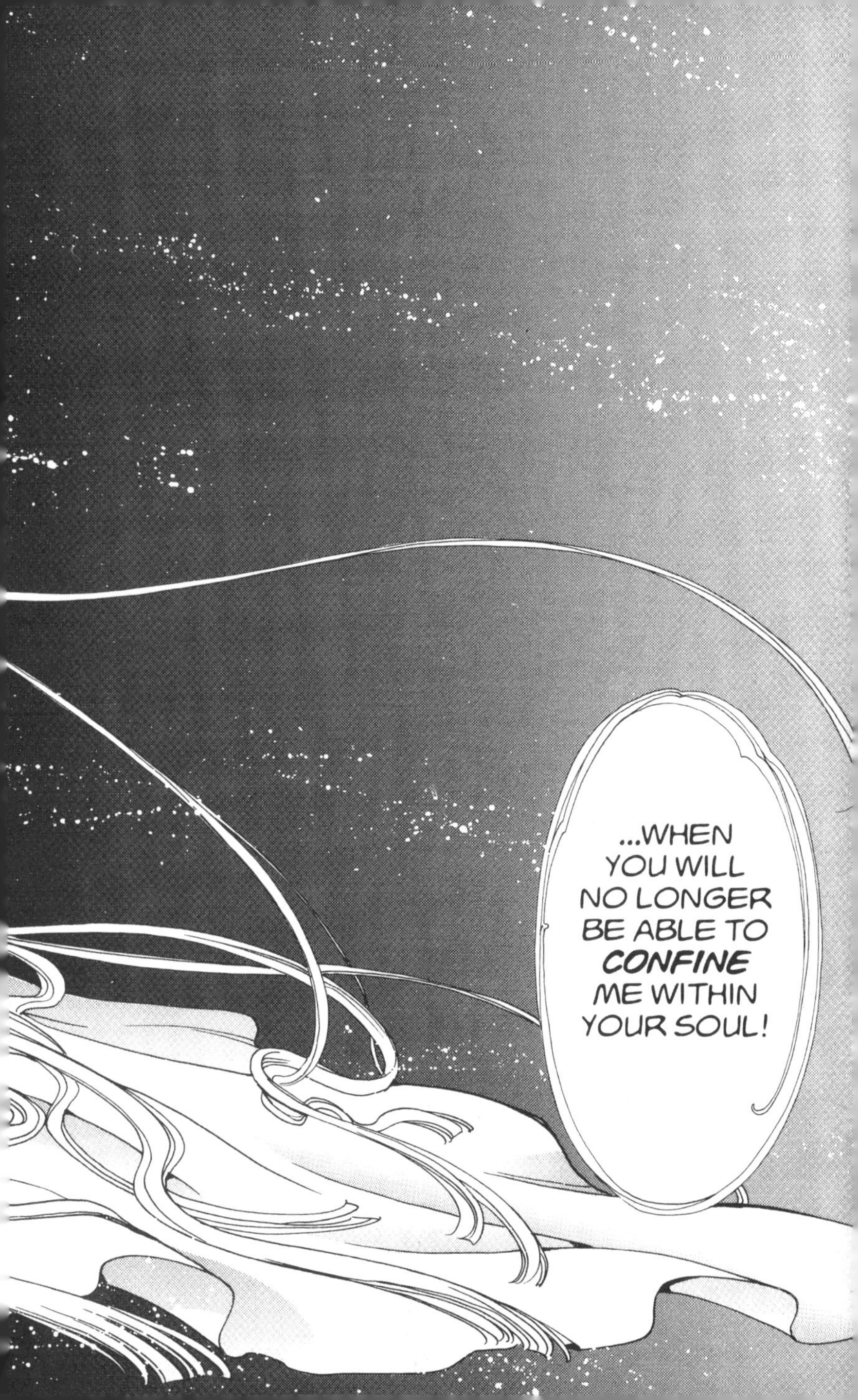
...WHEN YOU WILL NO LONGER BE ABLE TO *CONFINE* ME WITHIN YOUR SOUL!

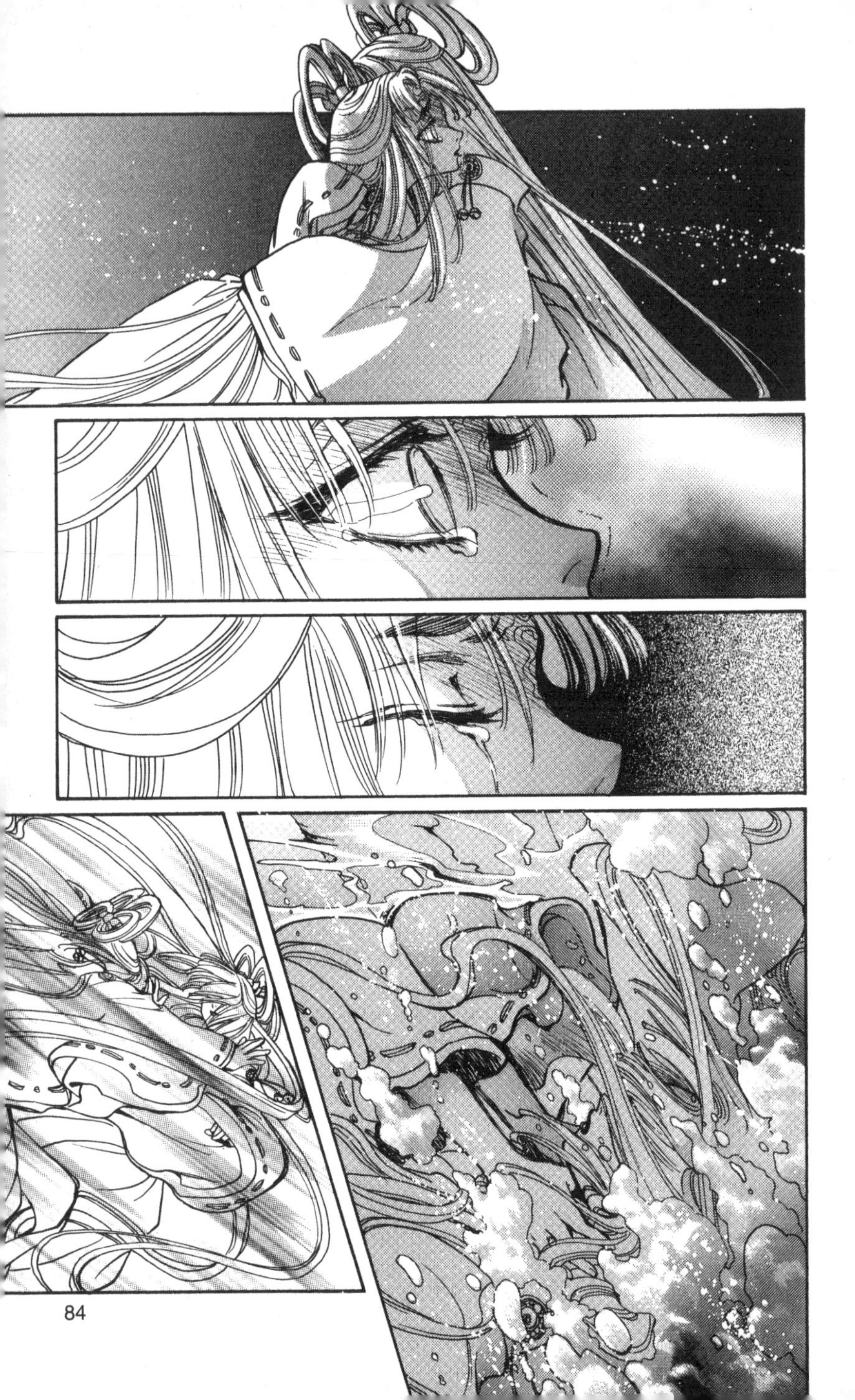

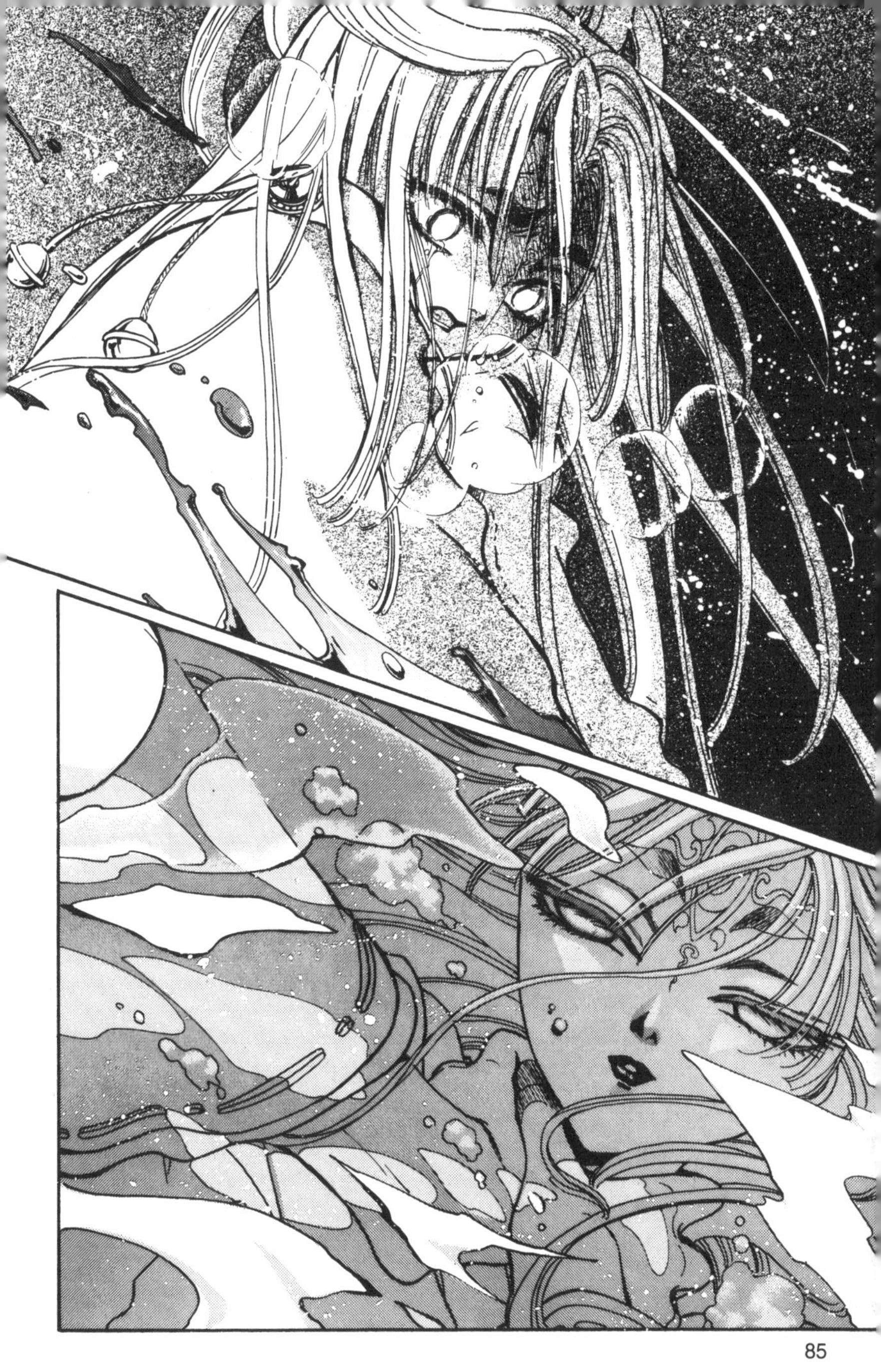

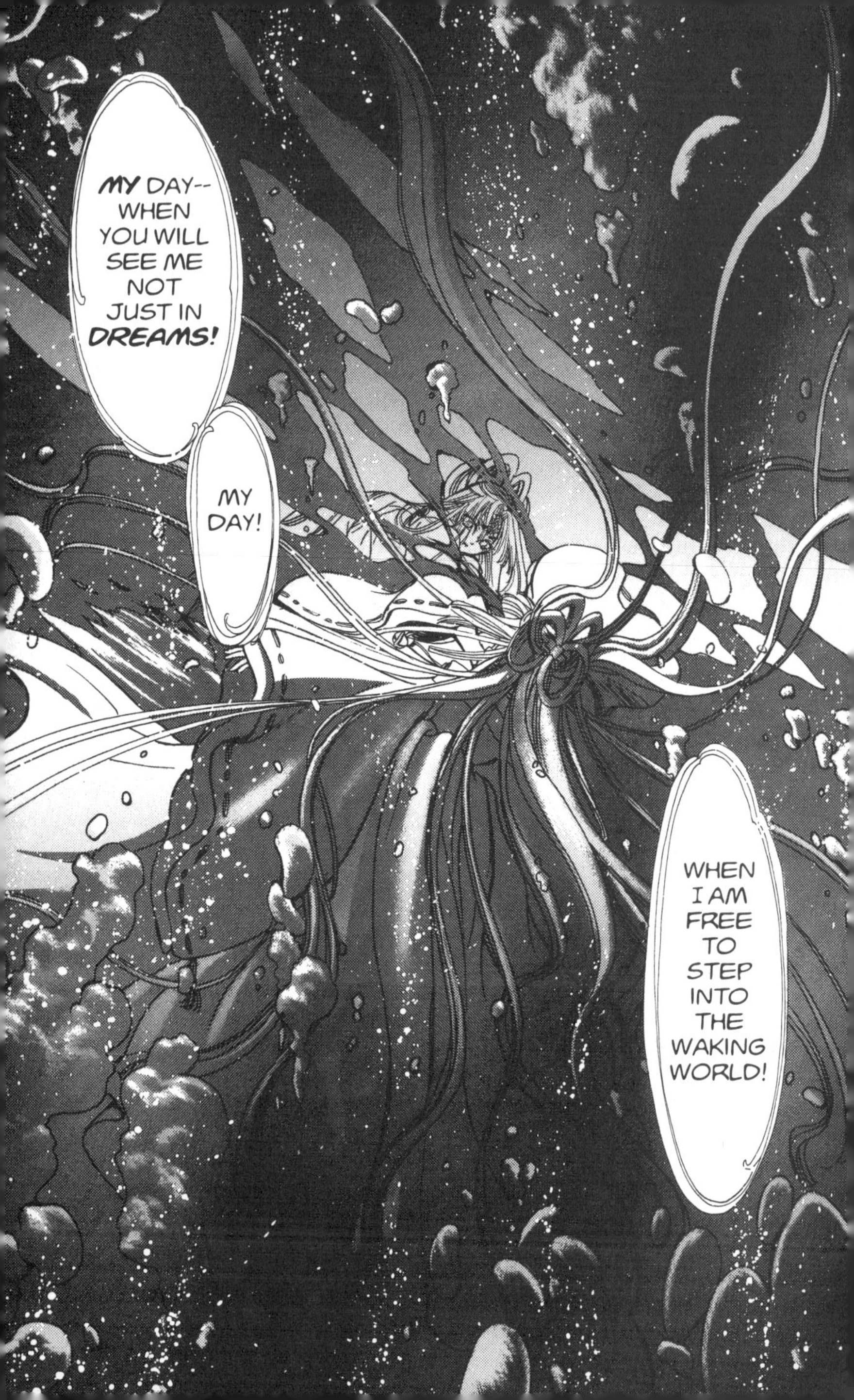
MY DAY-- WHEN YOU WILL SEE ME NOT JUST IN DREAMS!
MY DAY!
WHEN I AM FREE TO STEP INTO THE WAKING WORLD!

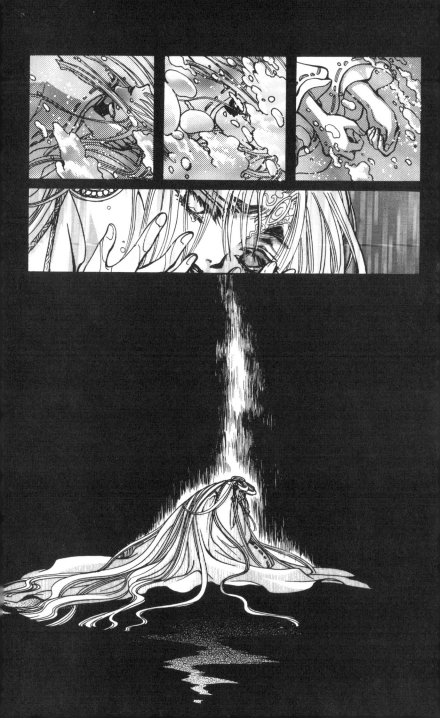

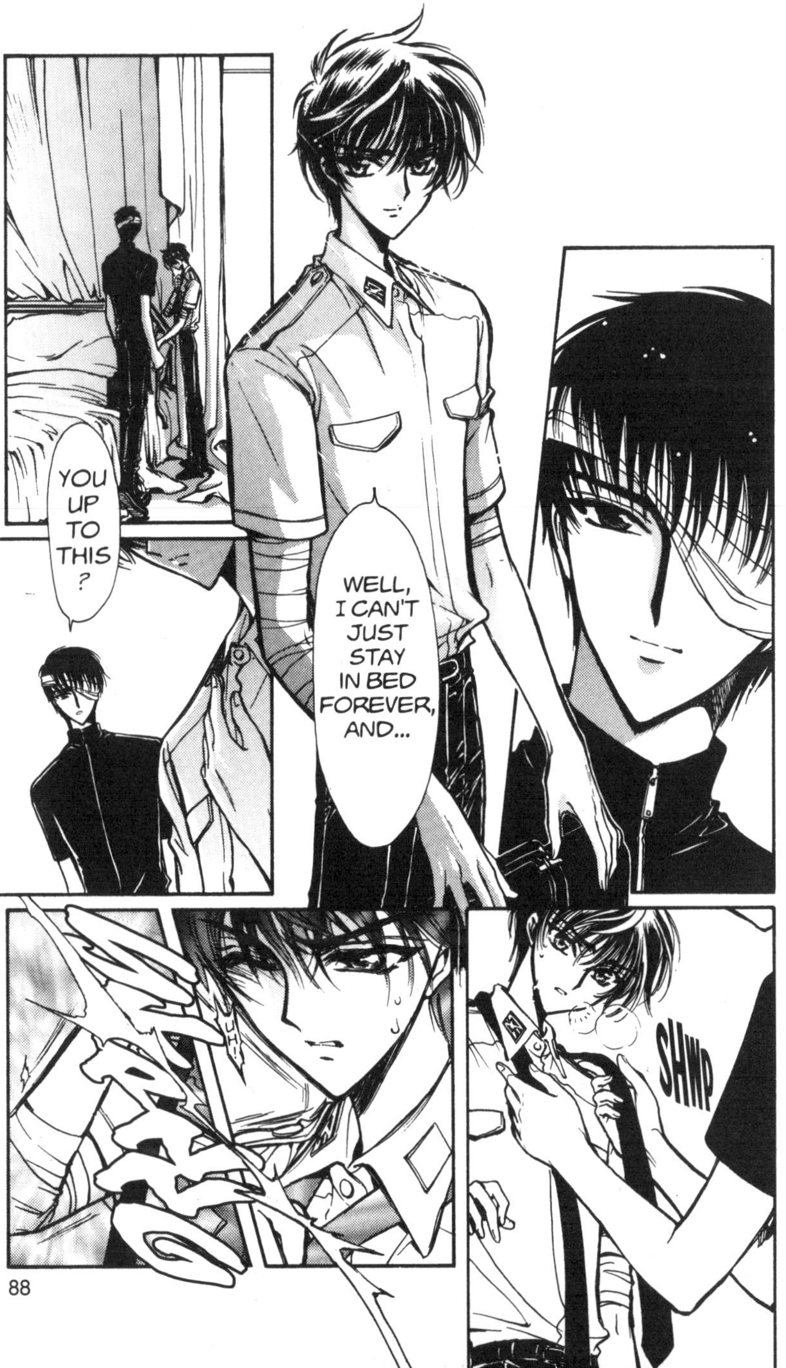
YOU UP TO THIS?
WELL, I CAN'T JUST STAY IN BED FOREVER, AND...
SHWP
UH!

SWSH

TH... THANK YOU.

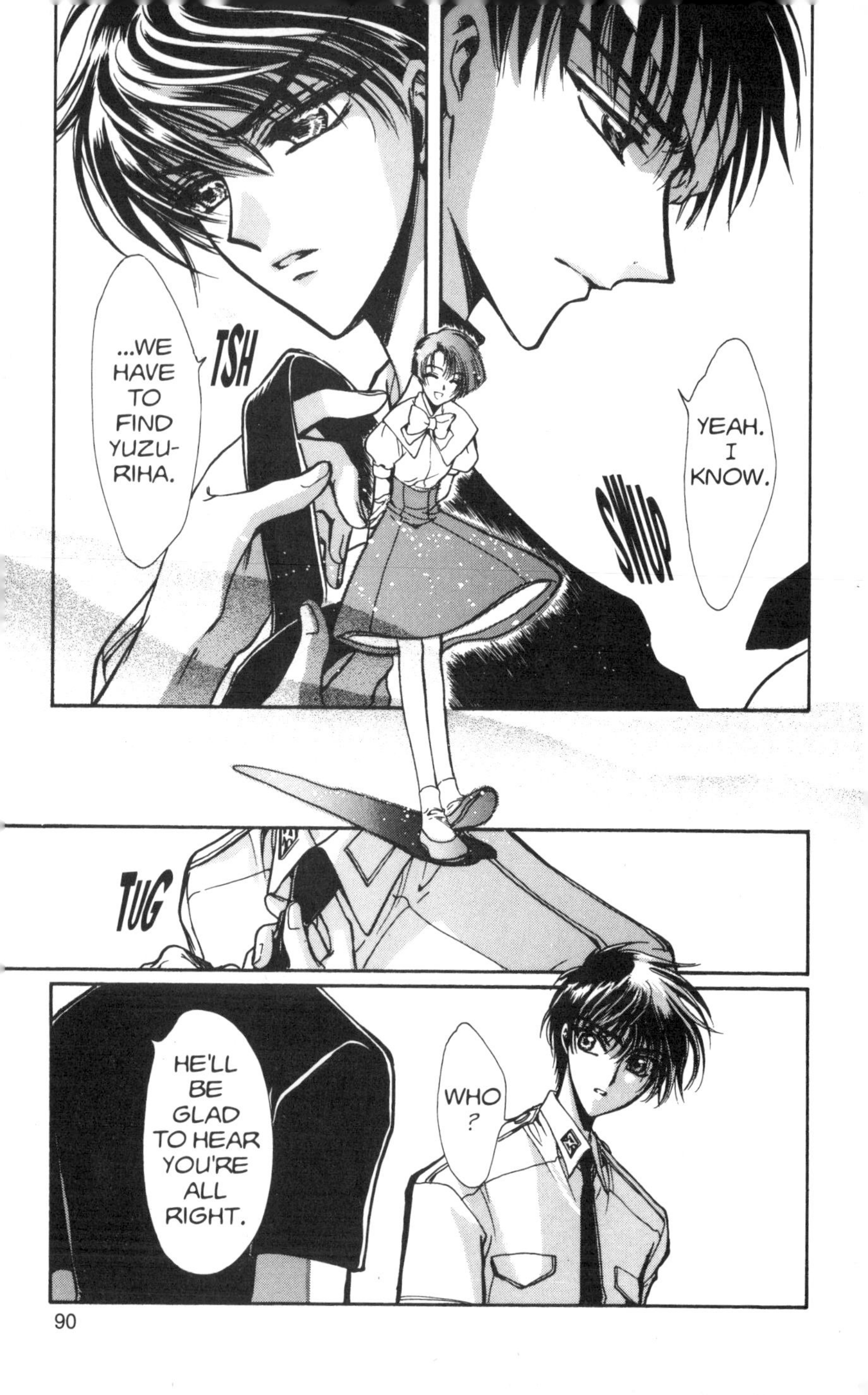
...WE HAVE TO FIND YUZURIHA.
TSH
YEAH. I KNOW.
SWIP
TUG
WHO?
HE'LL BE GLAD TO HEAR YOU'RE ALL RIGHT.

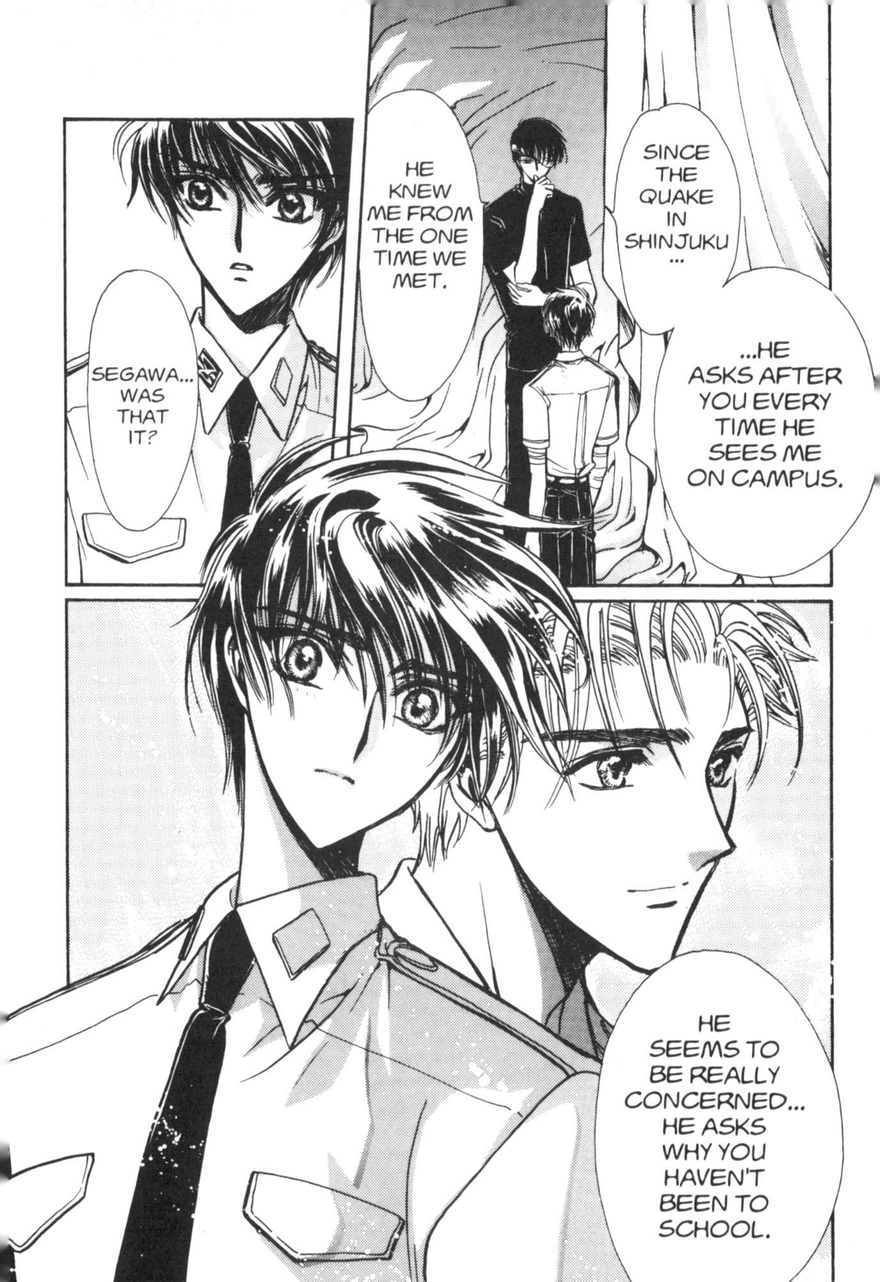
SINCE THE QUAKE IN SHINJUKU...
...HE ASKS AFTER YOU EVERY TIME HE SEES ME ON CAMPUS.
HE KNEW ME FROM THE ONE TIME WE MET.
SEGAWA... WAS THAT IT?
HE SEEMS TO BE REALLY CONCERNED... HE ASKS WHY YOU HAVEN'T BEEN TO SCHOOL.

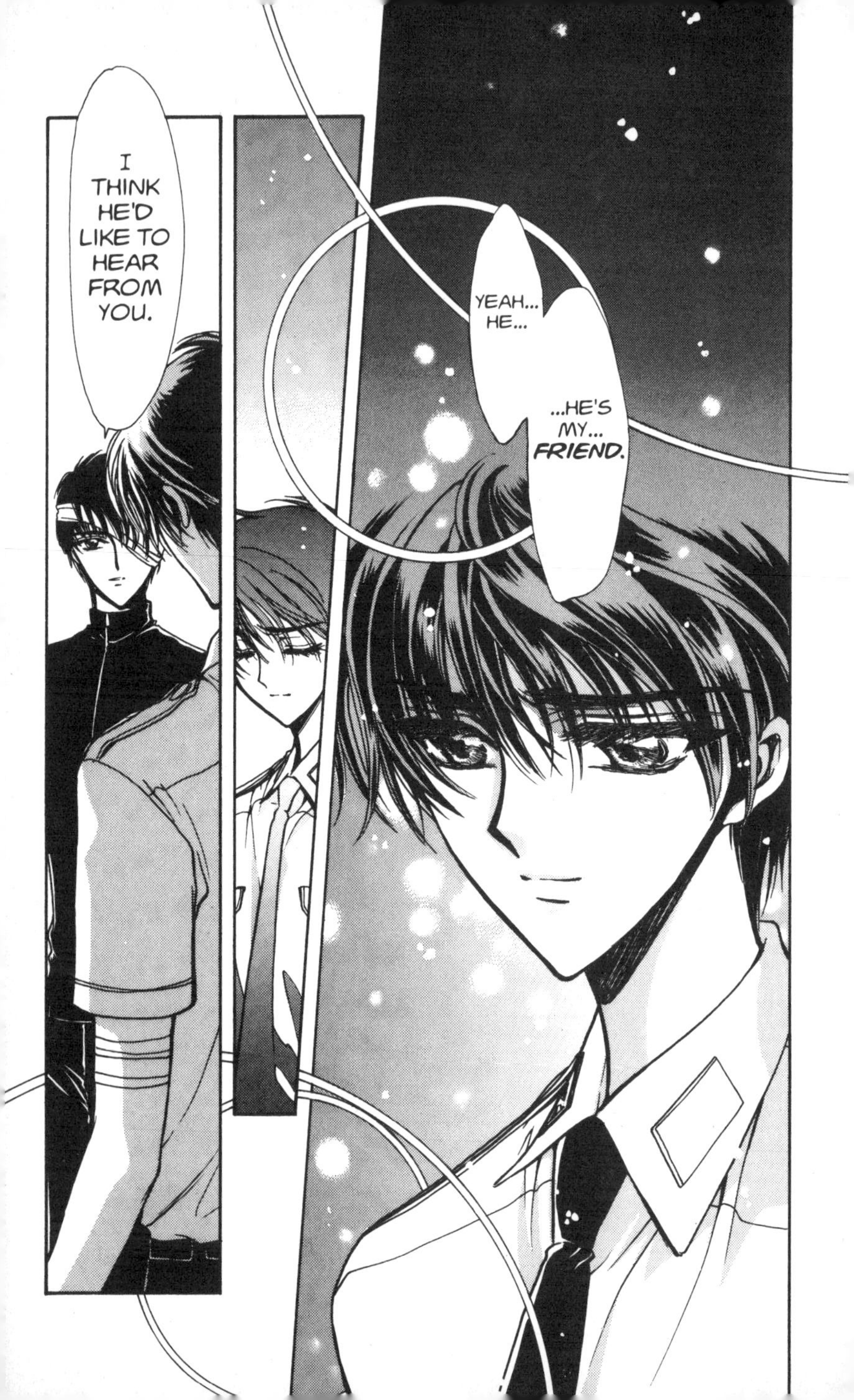
I THINK HE'D LIKE TO HEAR FROM YOU.
YEAH... HE...
...HE'S MY... **FRIEND.**

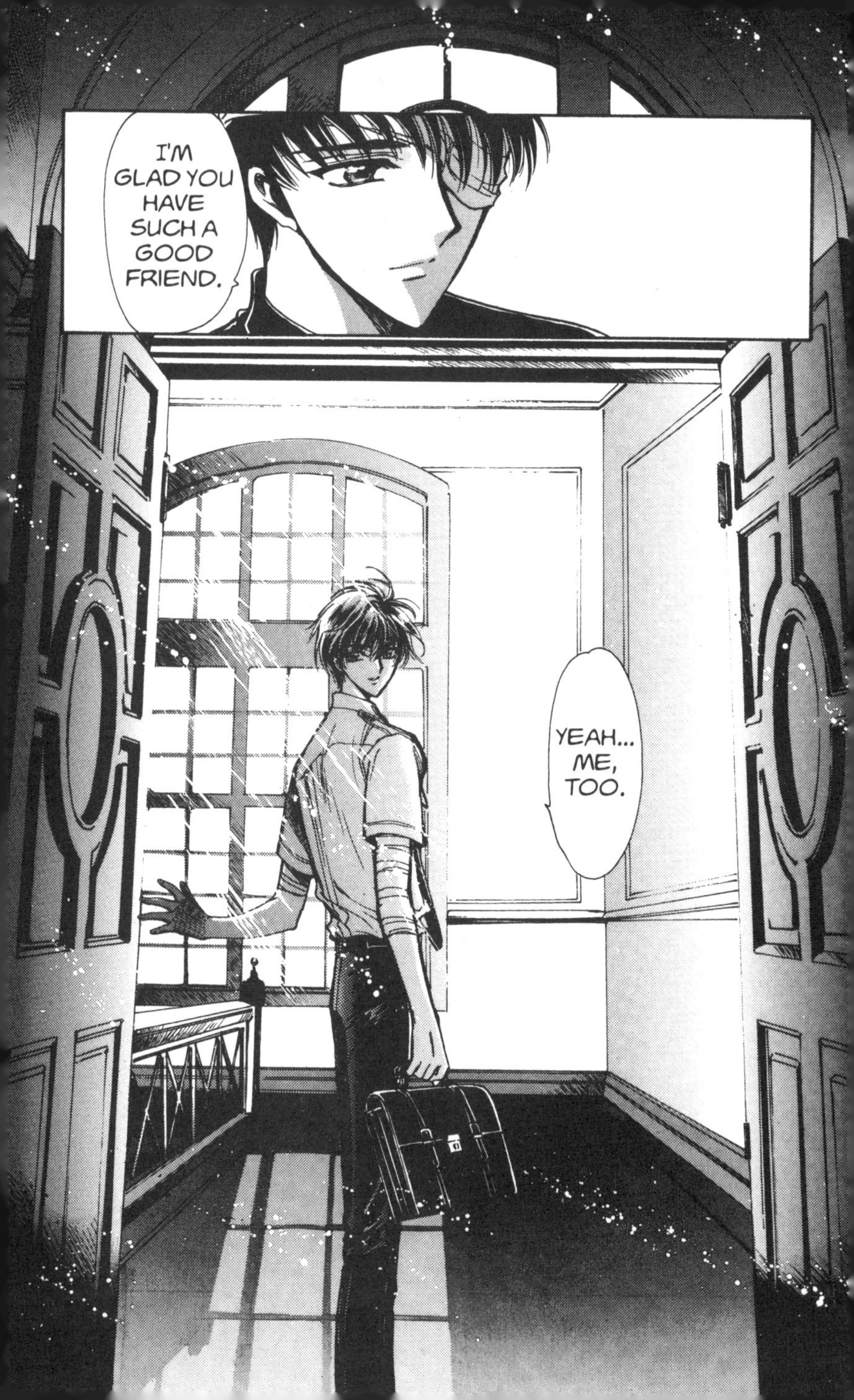
I'M GLAD YOU HAVE SUCH A GOOD FRIEND.
YEAH... ME, TOO.

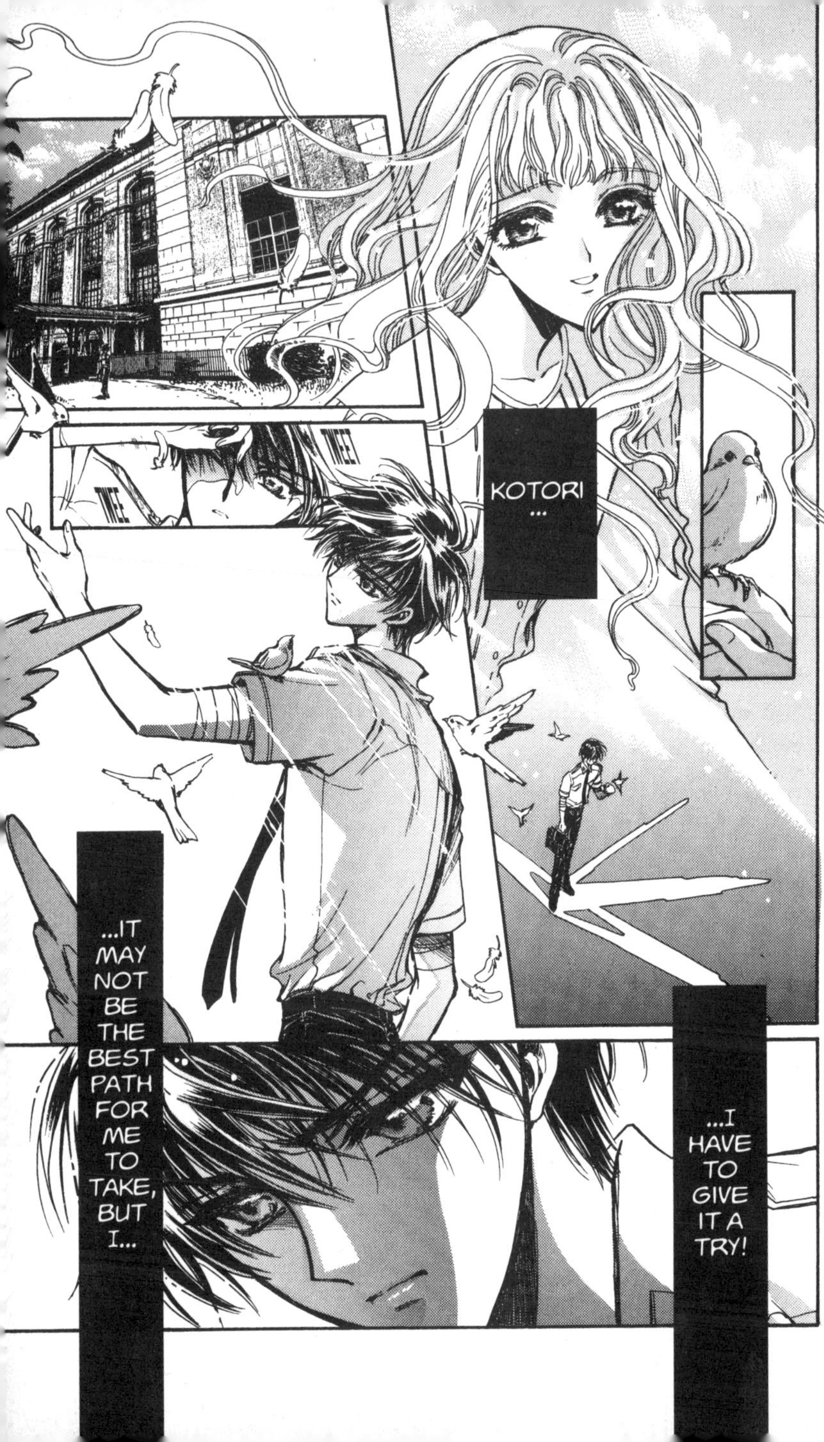
KOTORI ...
TWEET
...IT MAY NOT BE THE BEST PATH FOR ME TO TAKE, BUT I...
...I HAVE TO GIVE IT A TRY!

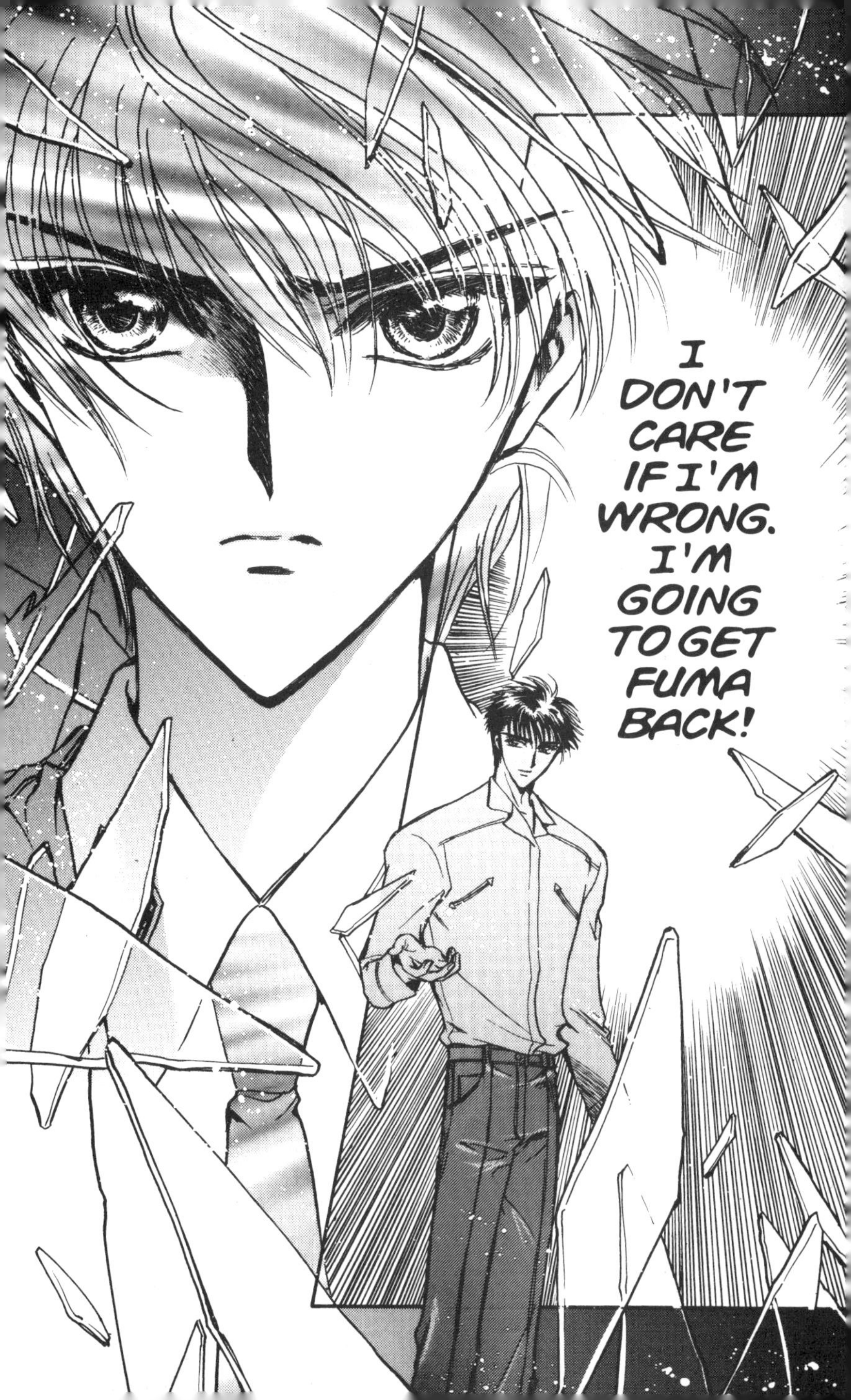
I DON'T CARE IF I'M WRONG. I'M GOING TO GET FUMA BACK!

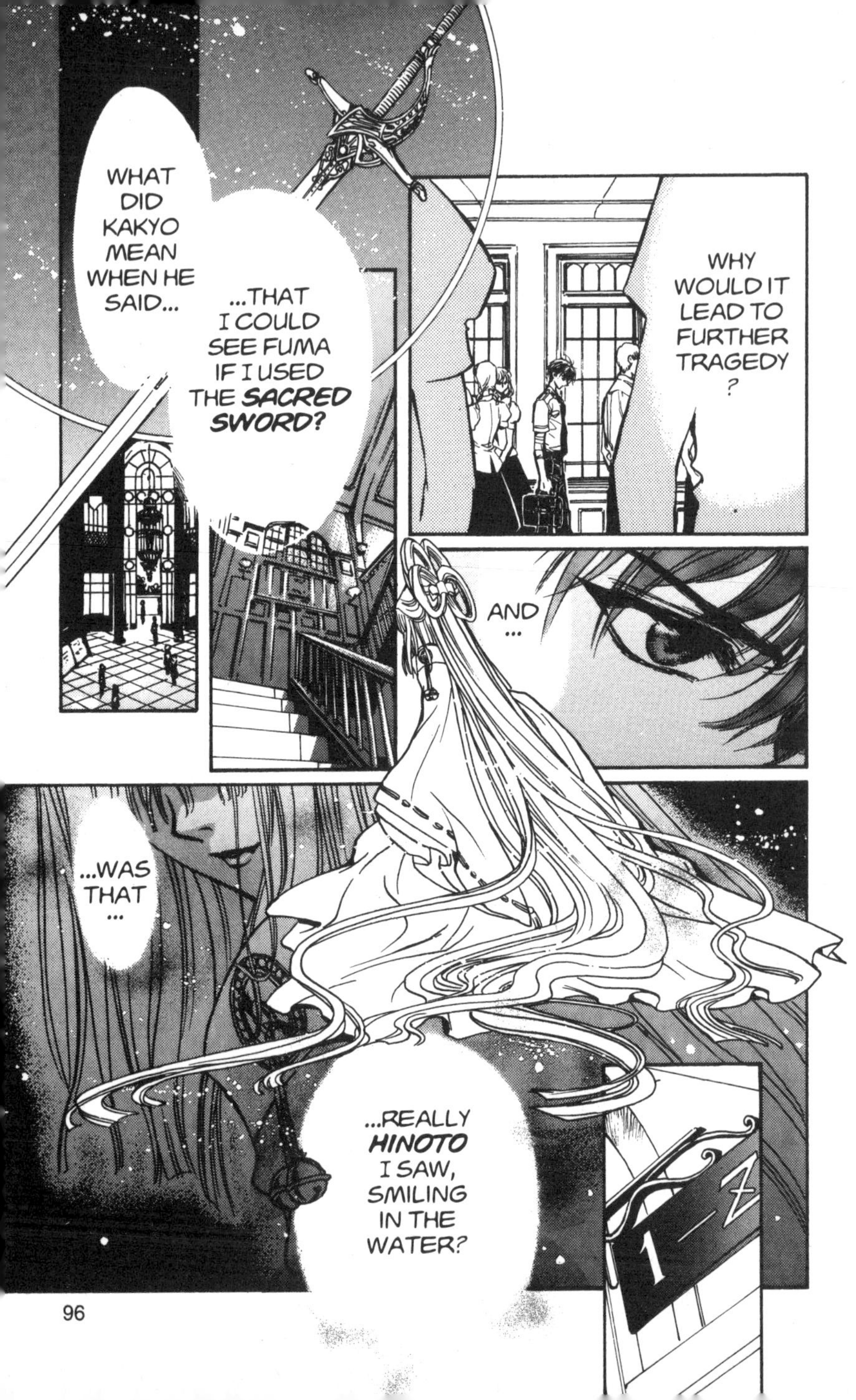
WHAT DID KAKYO MEAN WHEN HE SAID...
...THAT I COULD SEE FUMA IF I USED THE SACRED SWORD?
WHY WOULD IT LEAD TO FURTHER TRAGEDY?
AND ...
...WAS THAT ...
...REALLY HINOTO I SAW, SMILING IN THE WATER?
1-Z

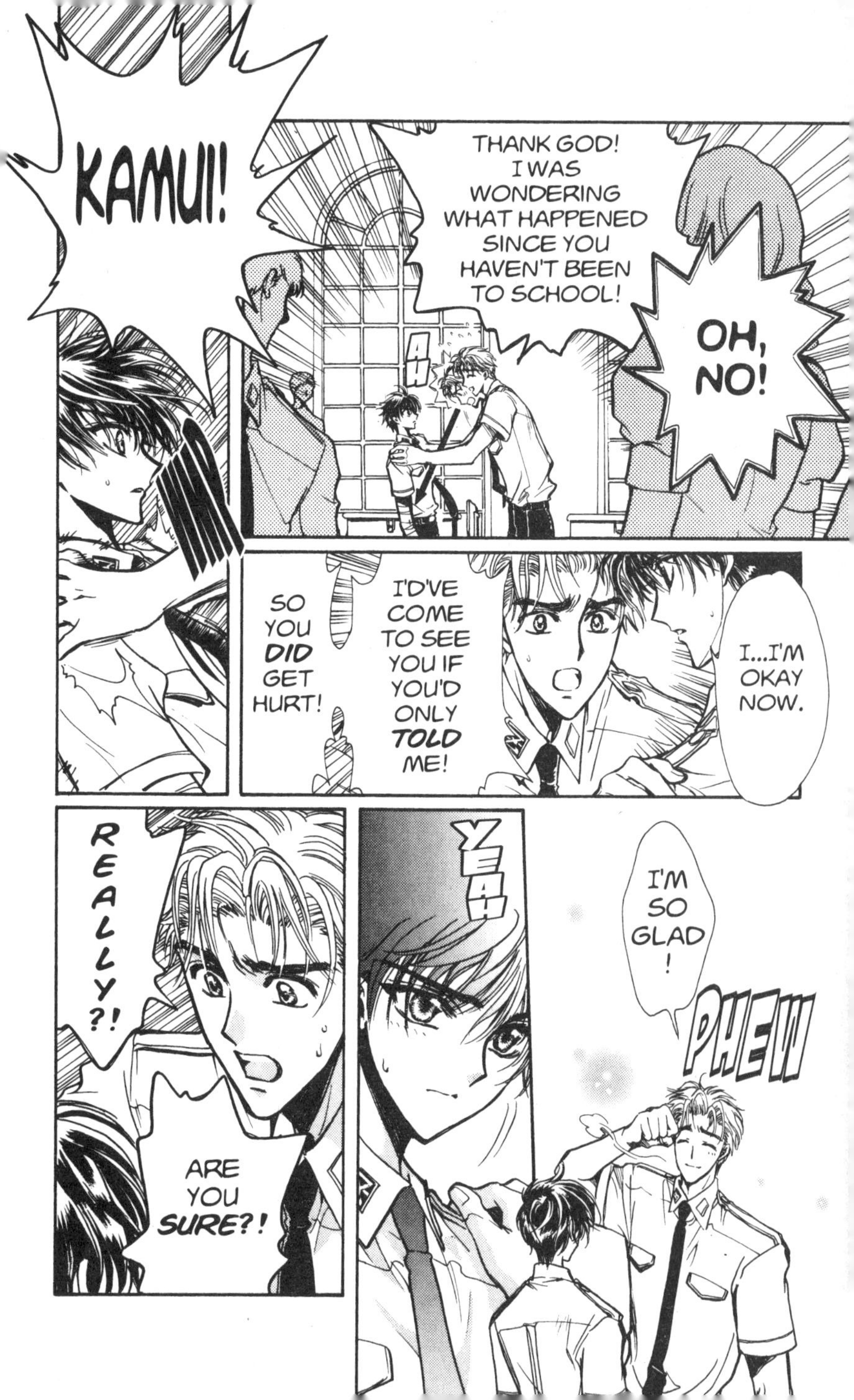
KAMUI!
THANK GOD! I WAS WONDERING WHAT HAPPENED SINCE YOU HAVEN'T BEEN TO SCHOOL!
OH, NO!
AH
I...I'M OKAY NOW.
I'D'VE COME TO SEE YOU IF YOU'D ONLY TOLD ME!
SO YOU DID GET HURT!
YEAH
I'M SO GLAD!
PHEW
REALLY?!
ARE YOU SURE?!

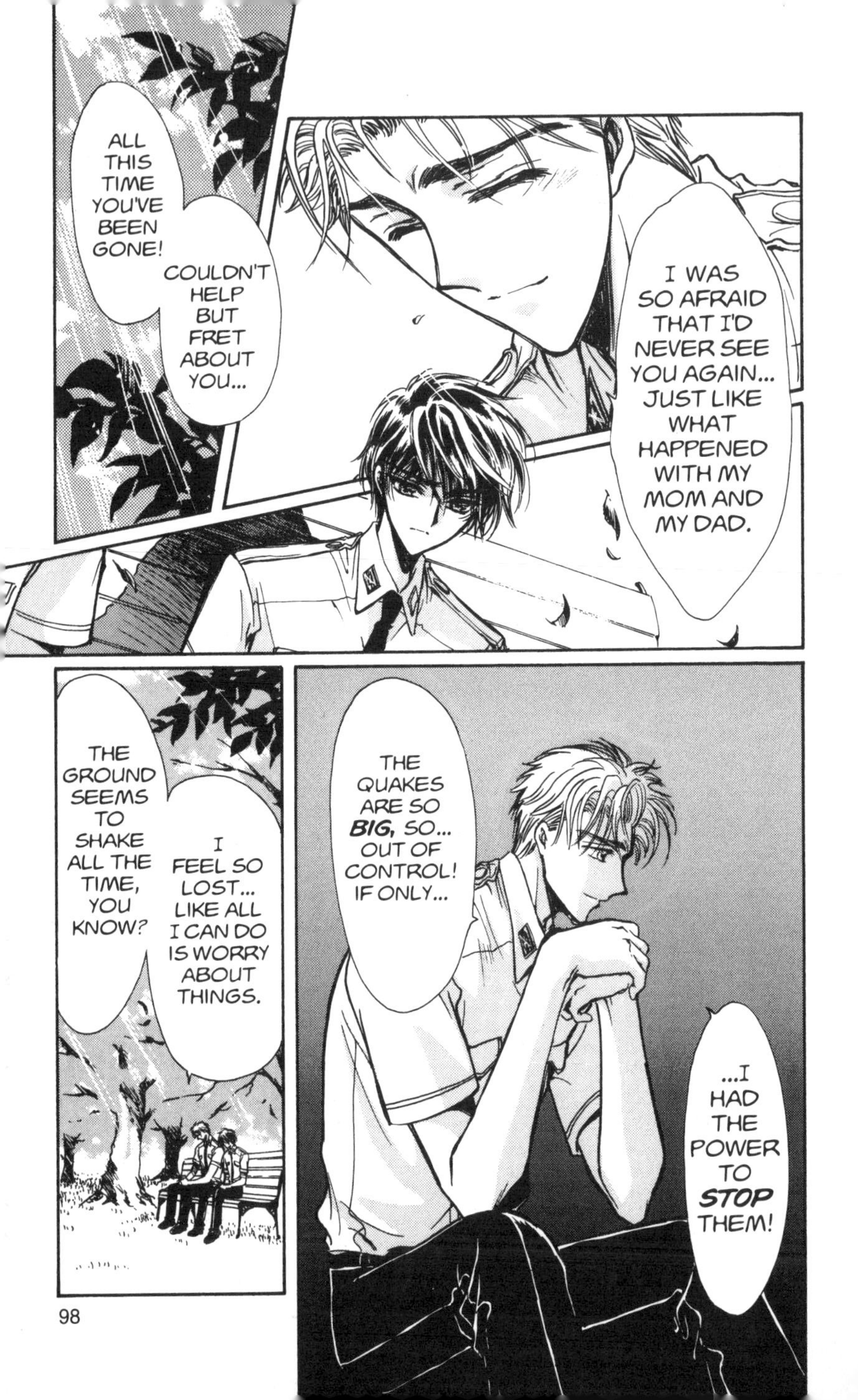
I WAS SO AFRAID THAT I'D NEVER SEE YOU AGAIN... JUST LIKE WHAT HAPPENED WITH MY MOM AND MY DAD.
ALL THIS TIME YOU'VE BEEN GONE!
COULDN'T HELP BUT FRET ABOUT YOU...
THE QUAKES ARE SO BIG, SO... OUT OF CONTROL! IF ONLY...
...I HAD THE POWER TO STOP THEM!
THE GROUND SEEMS TO SHAKE ALL THE TIME, YOU KNOW?
I FEEL SO LOST... LIKE ALL I CAN DO IS WORRY ABOUT THINGS.

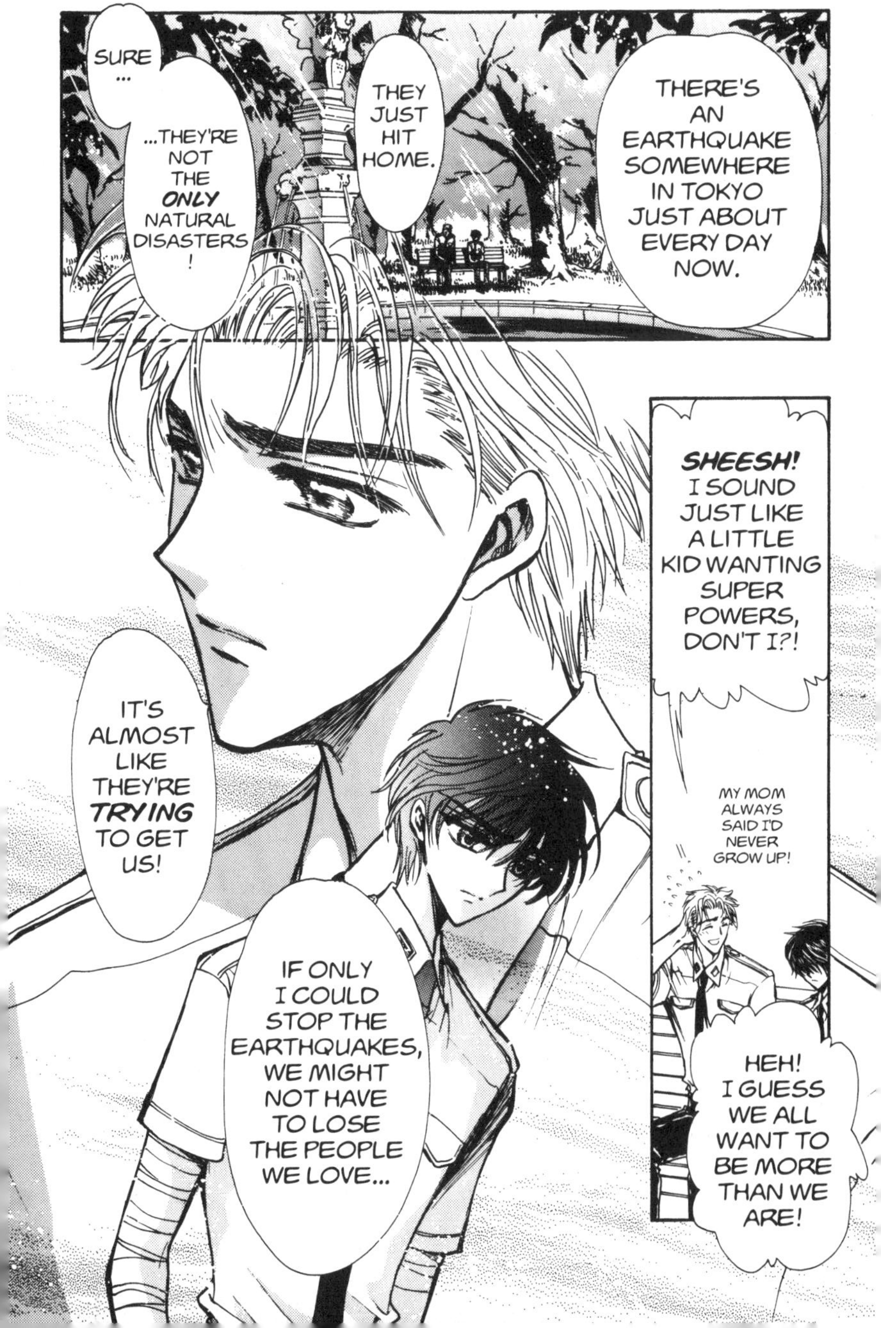
THERE'S AN EARTHQUAKE SOMEWHERE IN TOKYO JUST ABOUT EVERY DAY NOW.
THEY JUST HIT HOME.
SURE...
...THEY'RE NOT THE ONLY NATURAL DISASTERS!
IT'S ALMOST LIKE THEY'RE TRYING TO GET US!
IF ONLY I COULD STOP THE EARTHQUAKES, WE MIGHT NOT HAVE TO LOSE THE PEOPLE WE LOVE...
SHEESH! I SOUND JUST LIKE A LITTLE KID WANTING SUPER POWERS, DON'T I?!
MY MOM ALWAYS SAID I'D NEVER GROW UP!
HEH! I GUESS WE ALL WANT TO BE MORE THAN WE ARE!

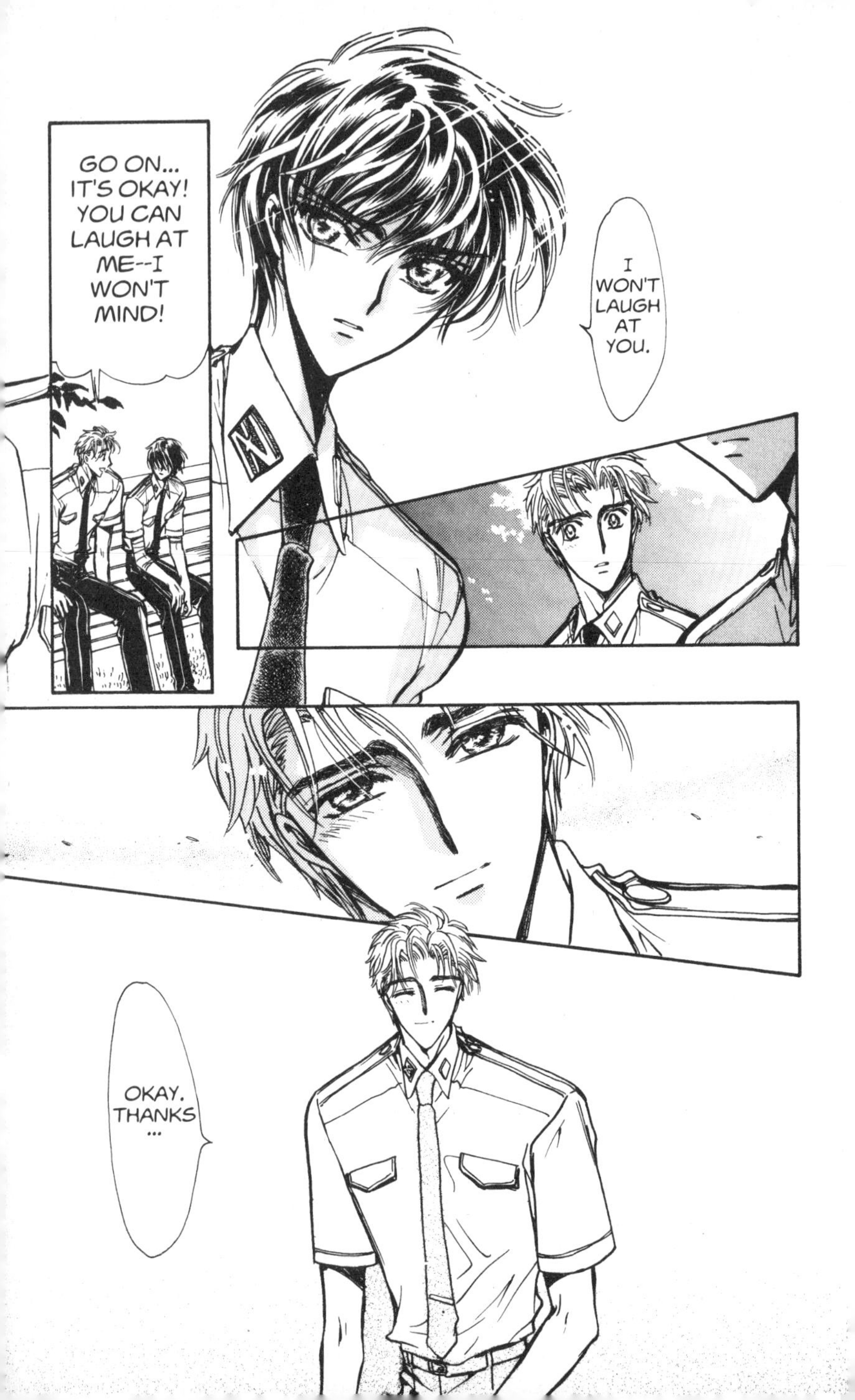
GO ON... IT'S OKAY! YOU CAN LAUGH AT ME--I WON'T MIND!
I WON'T LAUGH AT YOU.
OKAY. THANKS ...

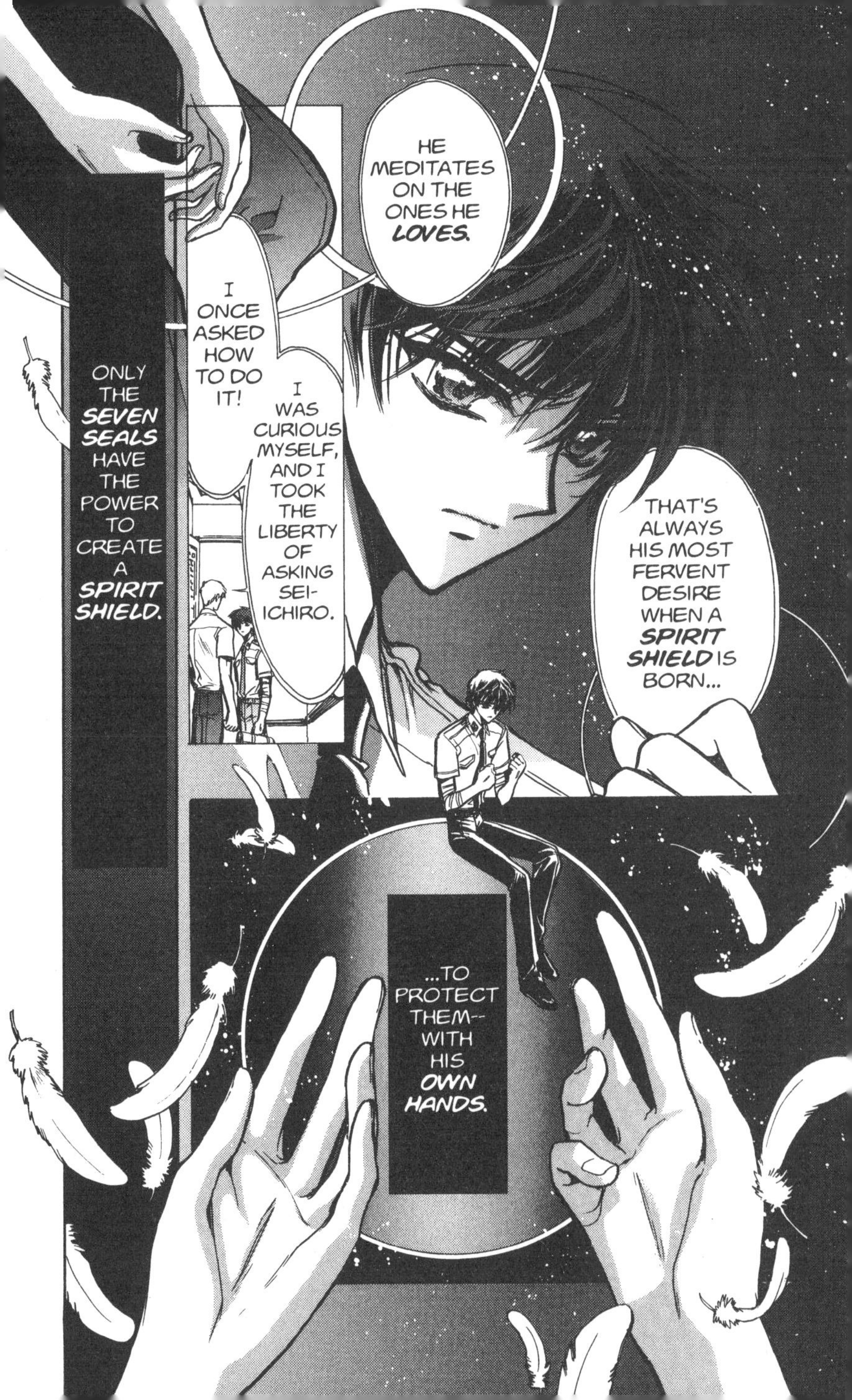
I ONCE ASKED HOW TO DO IT!
I WAS CURIOUS MYSELF, AND I TOOK THE LIBERTY OF ASKING SEI-ICHIRO.
HE MEDITATES ON THE ONES HE LOVES.
THAT'S ALWAYS HIS MOST FERVENT DESIRE WHEN A SPIRIT SHIELD IS BORN...
...TO PROTECT THEM-- WITH HIS OWN HANDS.
ONLY THE SEVEN SEALS HAVE THE POWER TO CREATE A SPIRIT SHIELD.

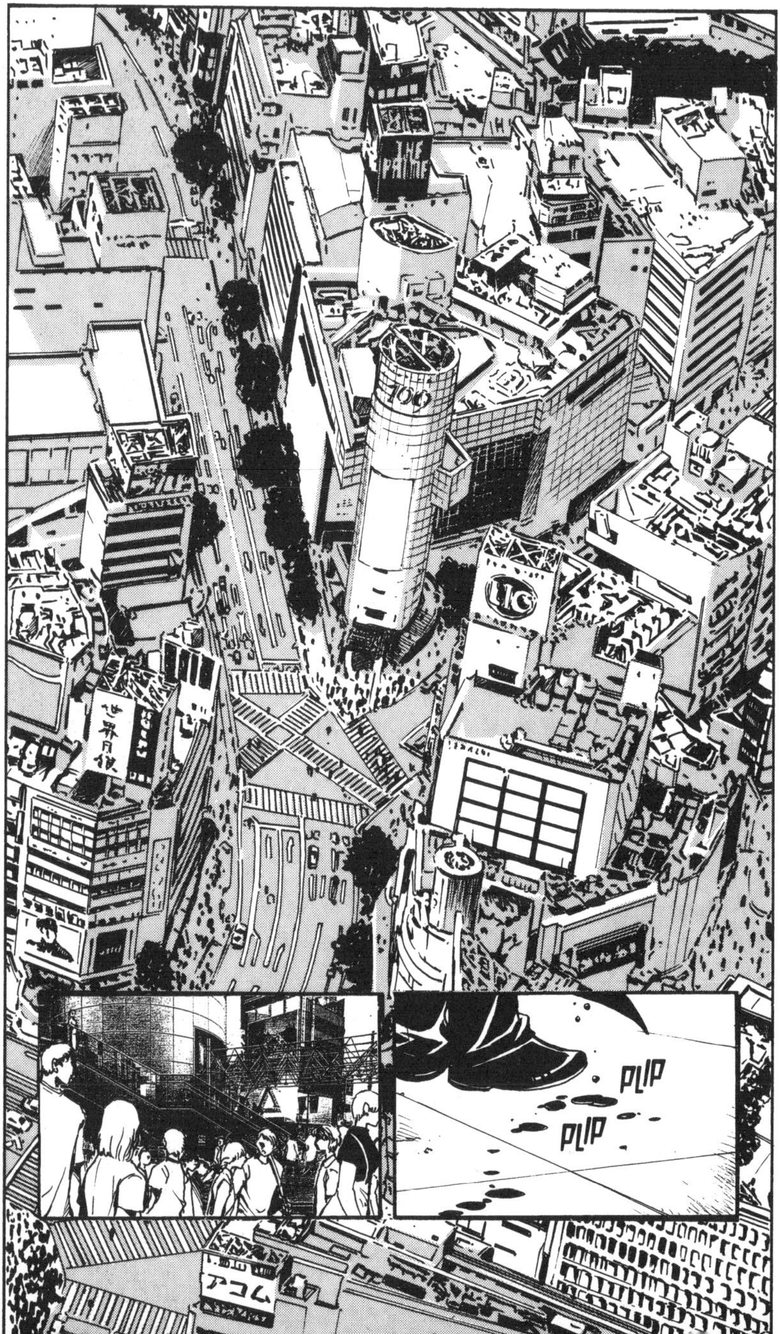
THE PRIME
PLIP
PLIP
アコム

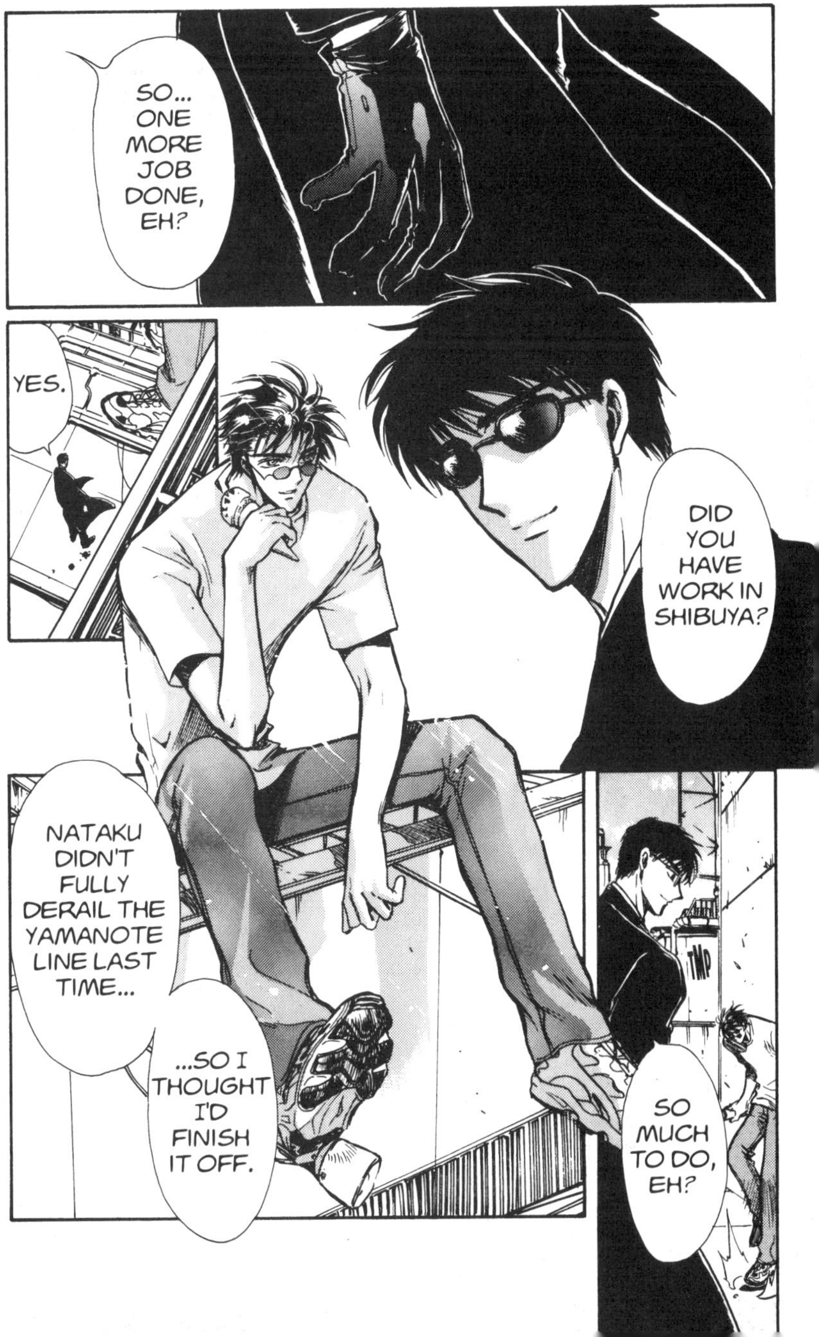
SO... ONE MORE JOB DONE, EH?
DID YOU HAVE WORK IN SHIBUYA?
YES.
SO MUCH TO DO, EH?
NATAKU DIDN'T FULLY DERAIL THE YAMANOTE LINE LAST TIME...
...SO I THOUGHT I'D FINISH IT OFF.

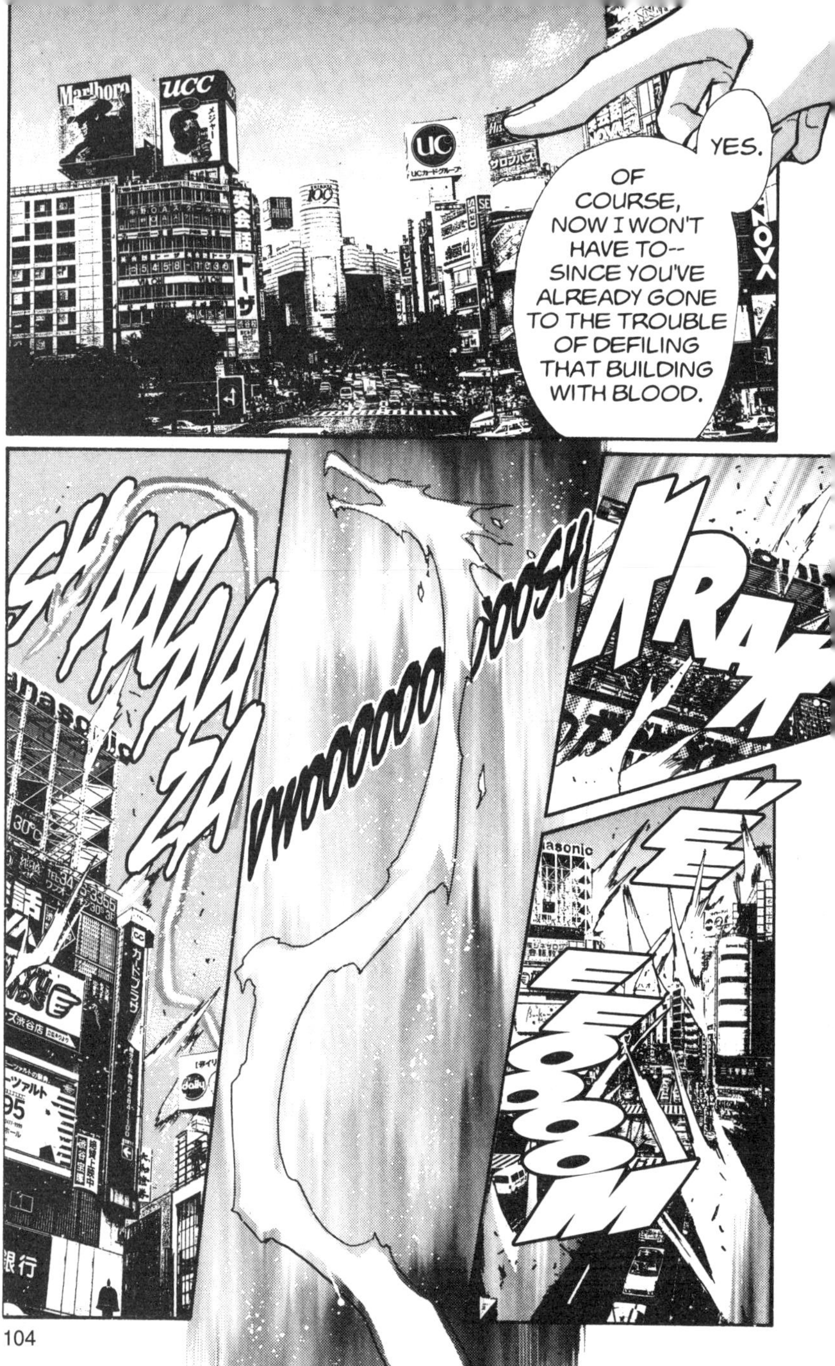
YES.
OF COURSE, NOW I WON'T HAVE TO-- SINCE YOU'VE ALREADY GONE TO THE TROUBLE OF DEFILING THAT BUILDING WITH BLOOD.
SHAAZAAZA
VWOOOOOOOOOSH

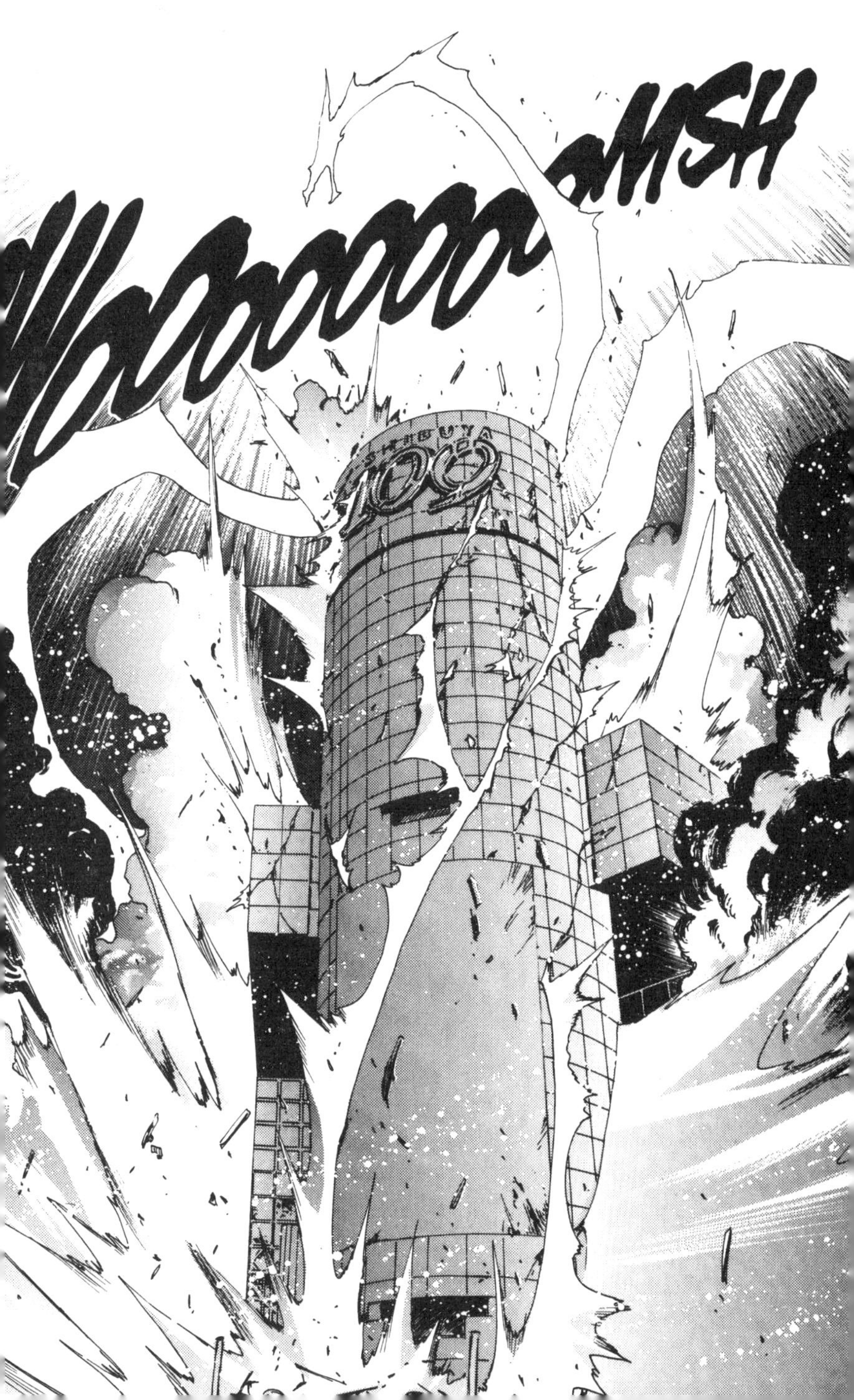
SHIBUYA
109

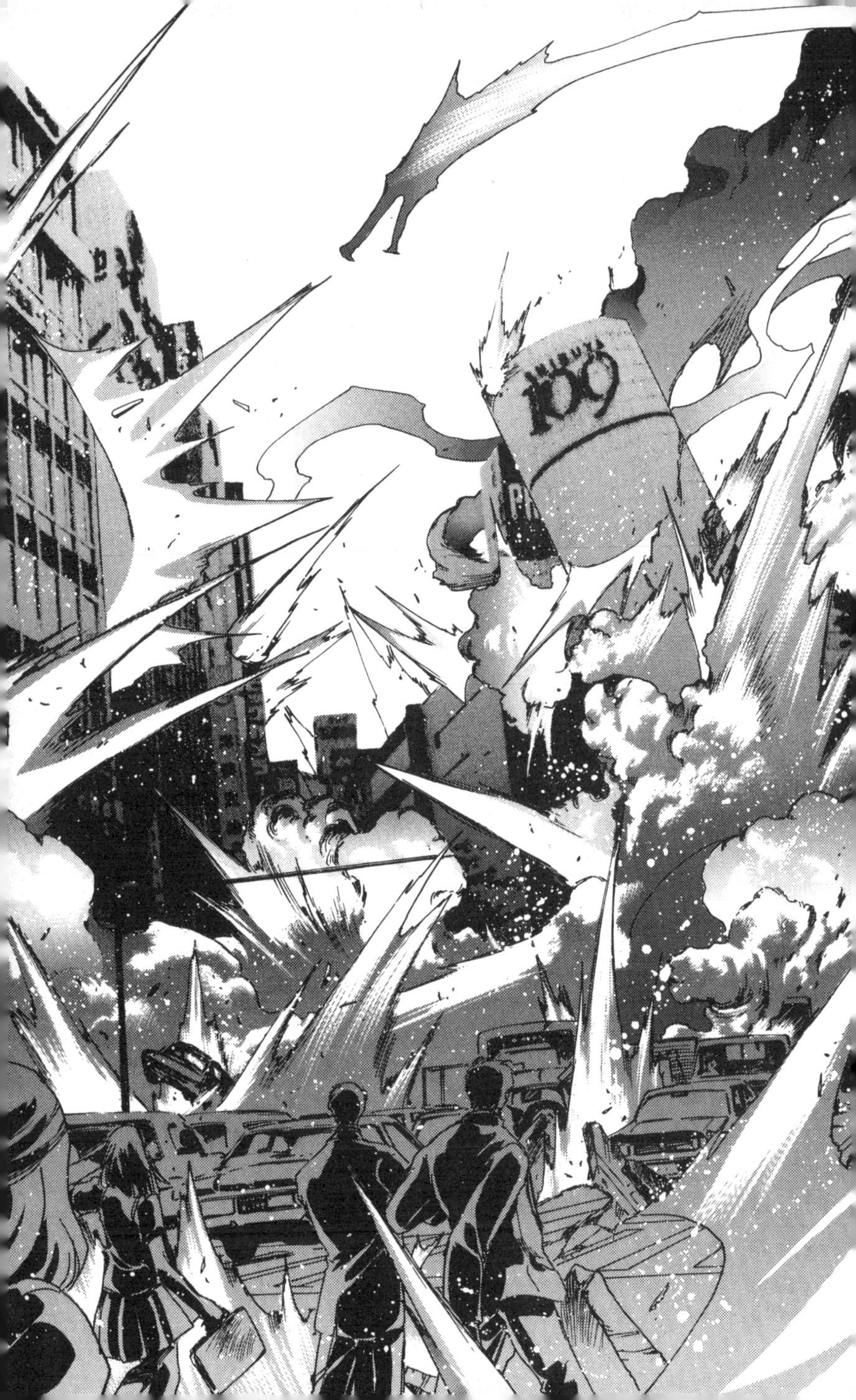
109

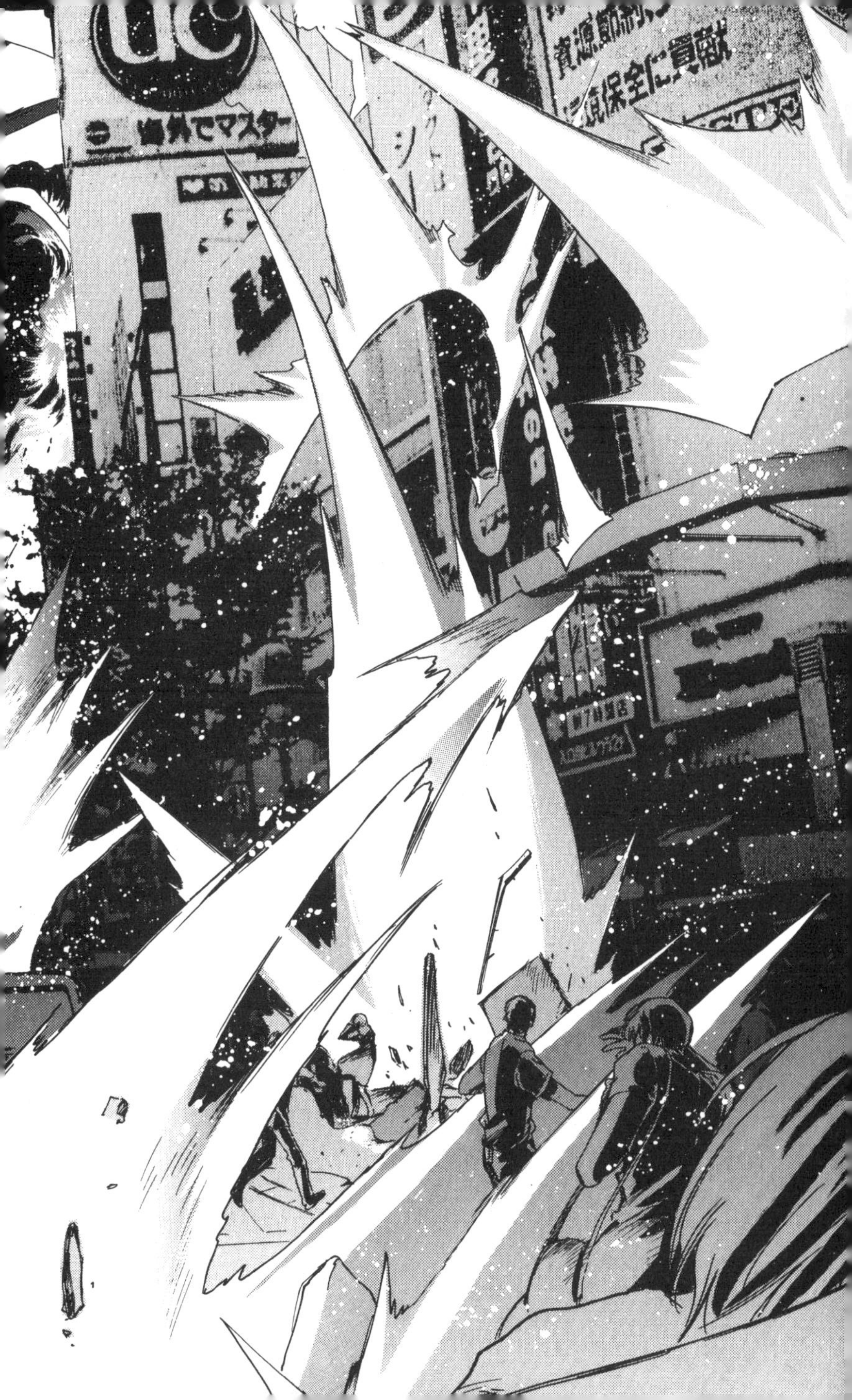
海外でマスター

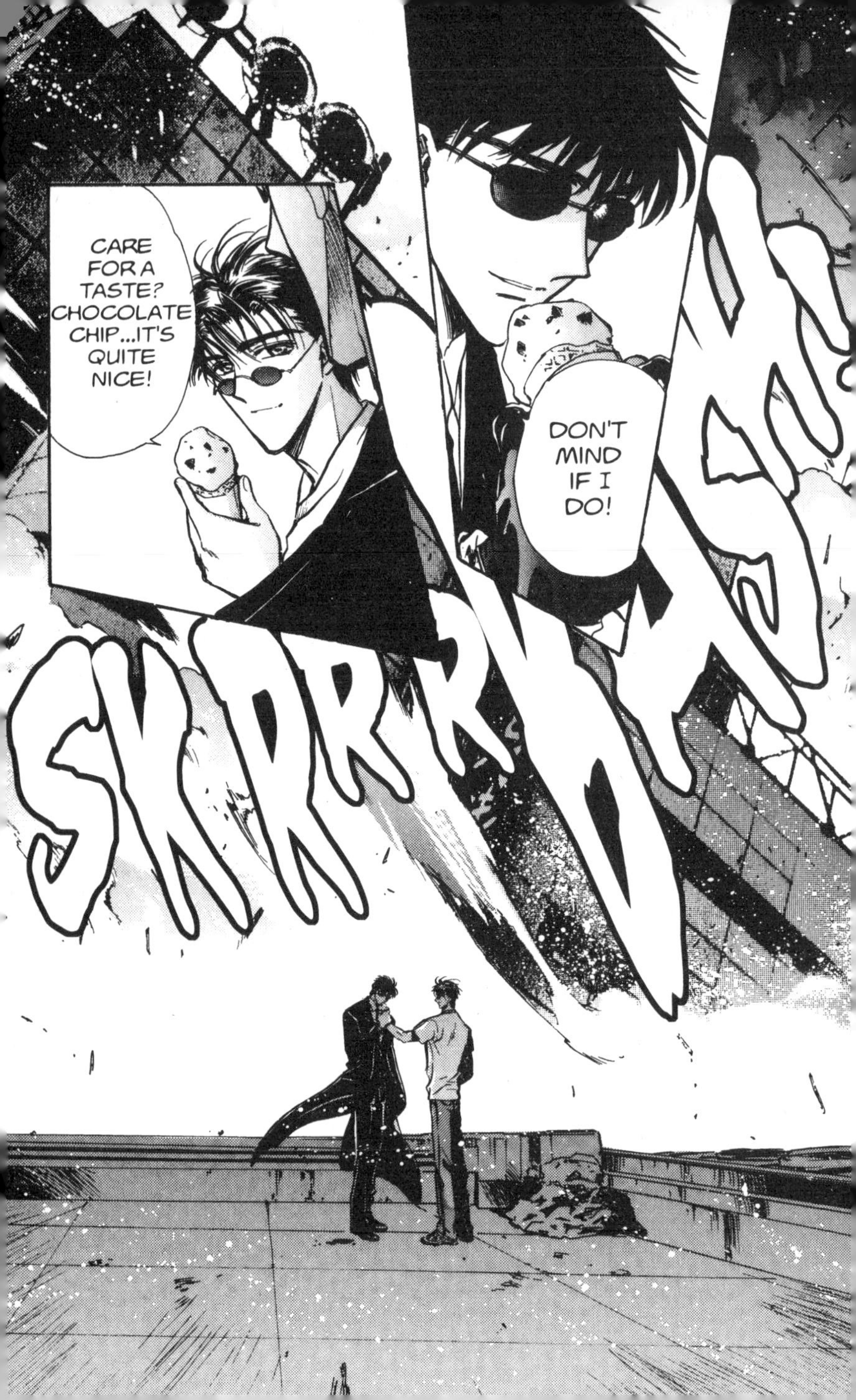
CARE FOR A TASTE? CHOCOLATE CHIP...IT'S QUITE NICE!
DON'T MIND IF I DO!

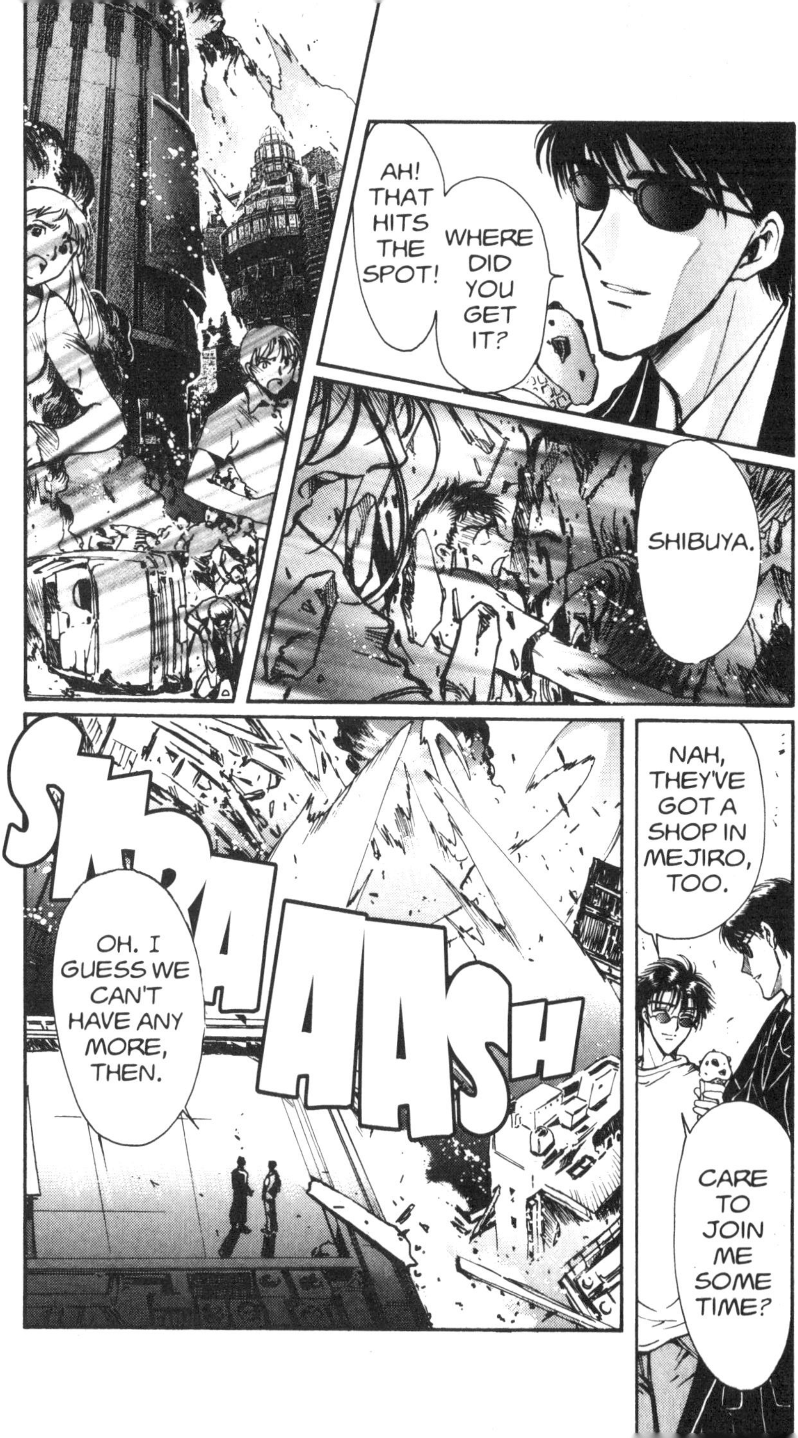
AH! THAT HITS THE SPOT!
WHERE DID YOU GET IT?
SHIBUYA.
NAH, THEY'VE GOT A SHOP IN MEJIRO, TOO.
CARE TO JOIN ME SOME TIME?
OH. I GUESS WE CAN'T HAVE ANY MORE, THEN.

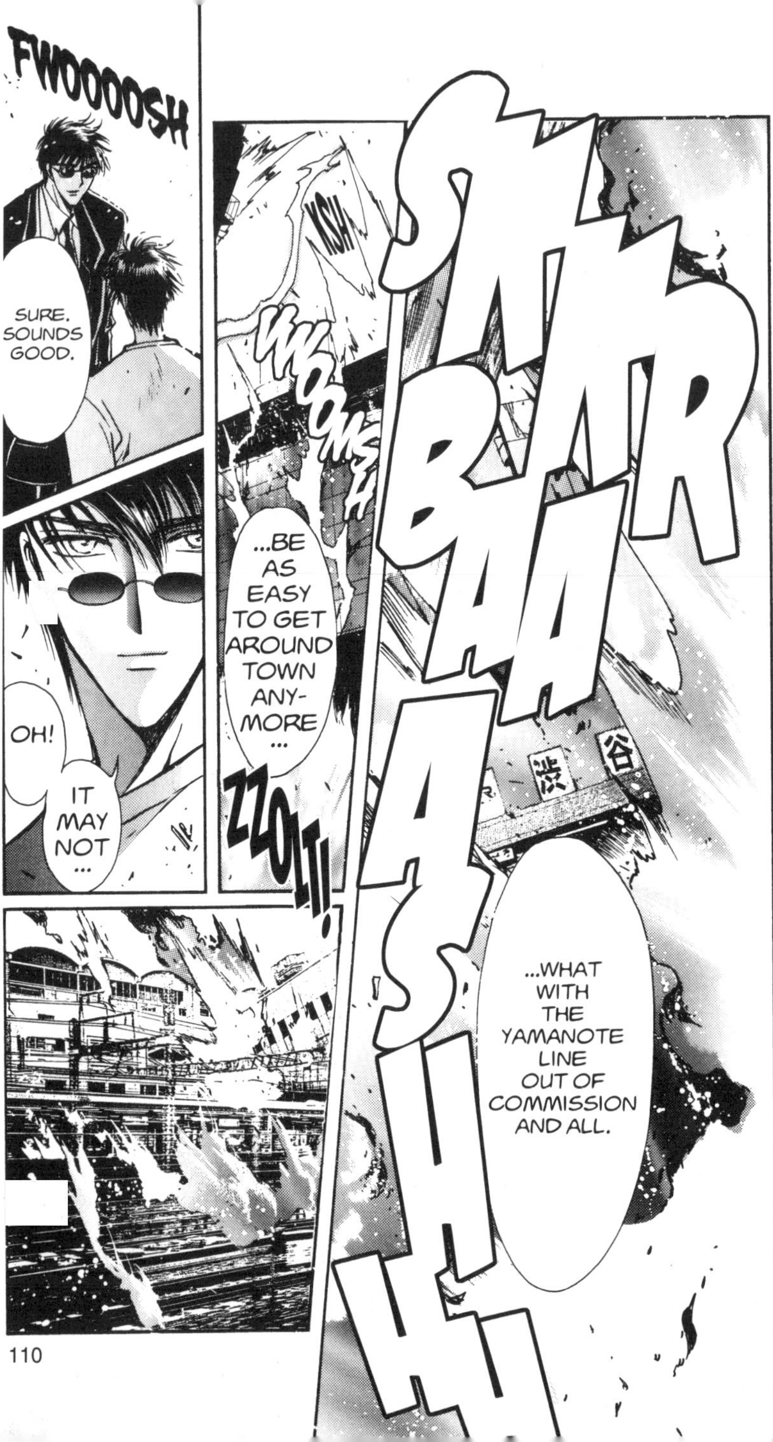
FWOOOOSH
SURE. SOUNDS GOOD.
OH!
IT MAY NOT...
KSH
WHOOMSH
...BE AS EASY TO GET AROUND TOWN ANY-MORE...
ZZOLT!!
渋谷
...WHAT WITH THE YAMANOTE LINE OUT OF COMMISSION AND ALL.

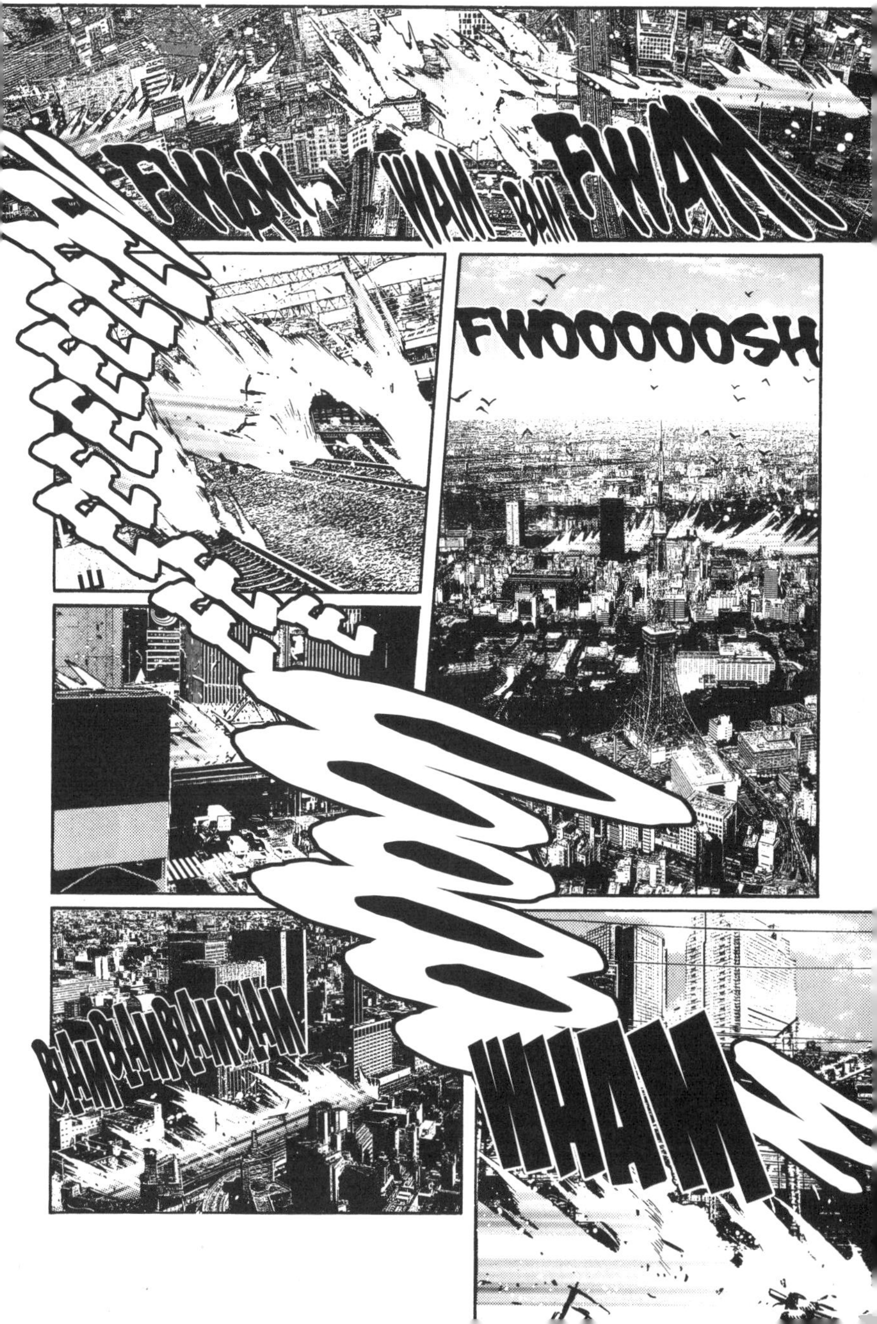
FWAM
BAM
WAM
FWAM
FWOOOOOSH
BLAM BLAM BLAM BLAM
WHAM

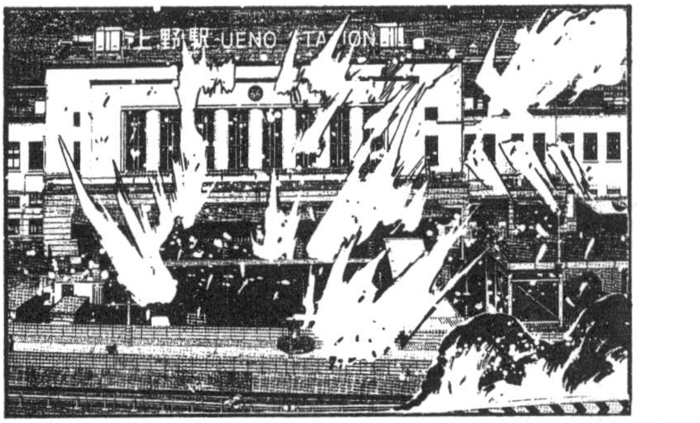
上野駅 UENO

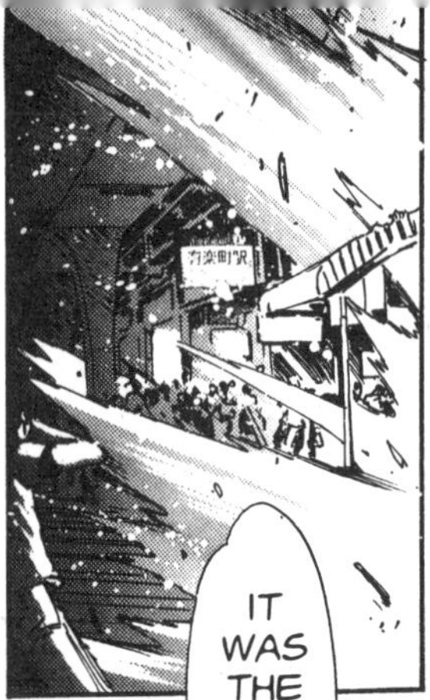
有楽町駅
IT WAS THE BEST!

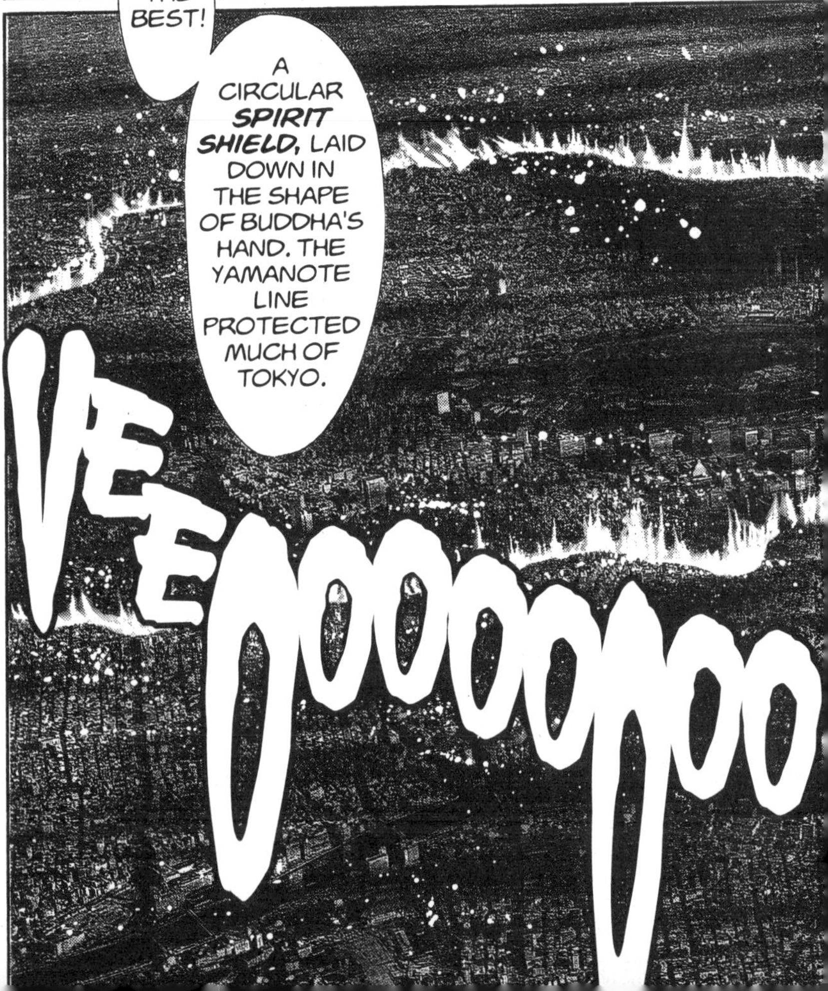
A CIRCULAR **SPIRIT SHIELD,** LAID DOWN IN THE SHAPE OF BUDDHA'S HAND. THE YAMANOTE LINE PROTECTED MUCH OF TOKYO.
VEEOOOOOOOOO

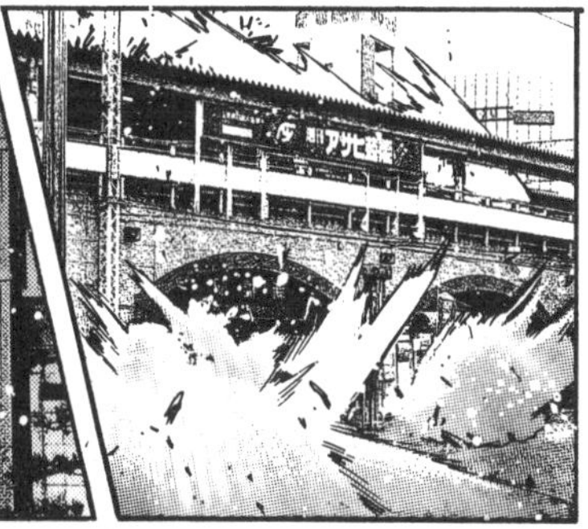

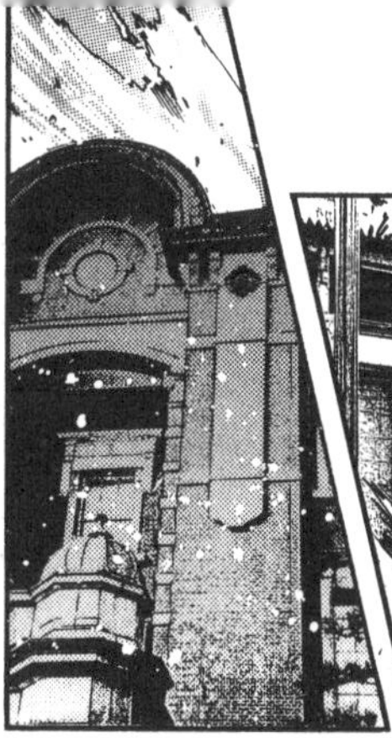

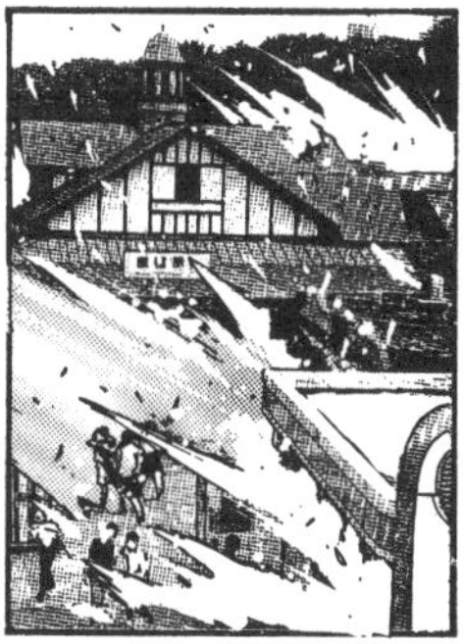

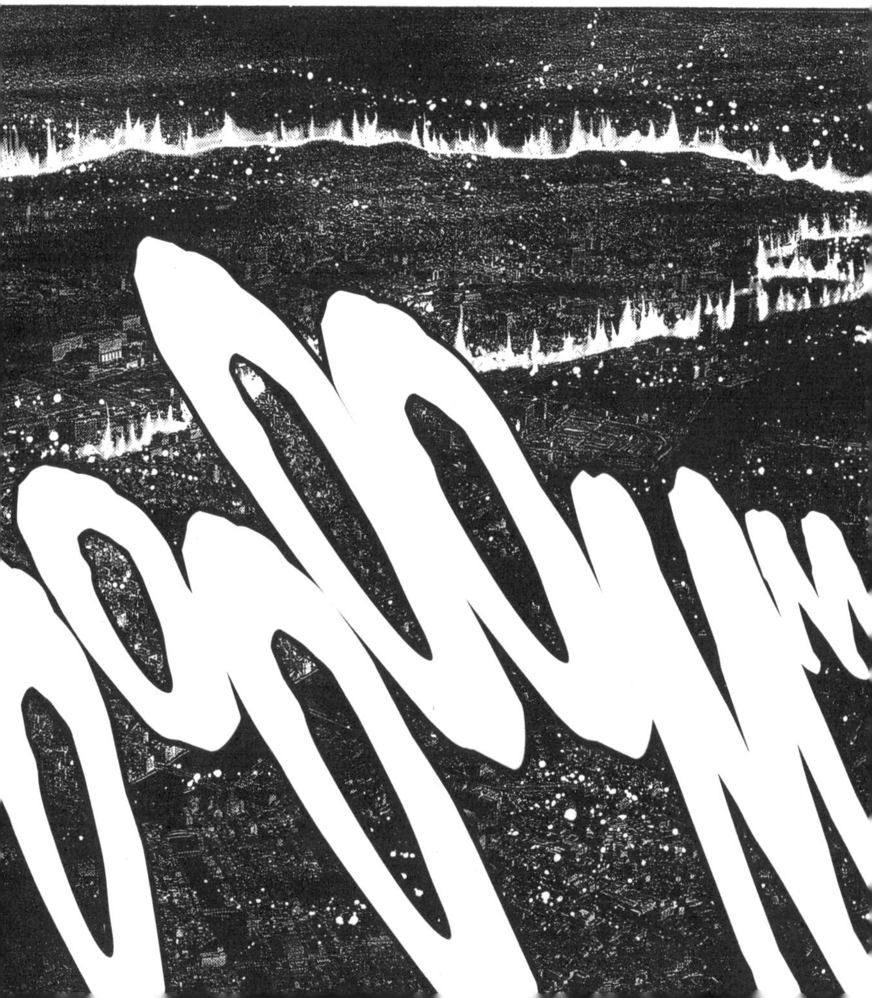

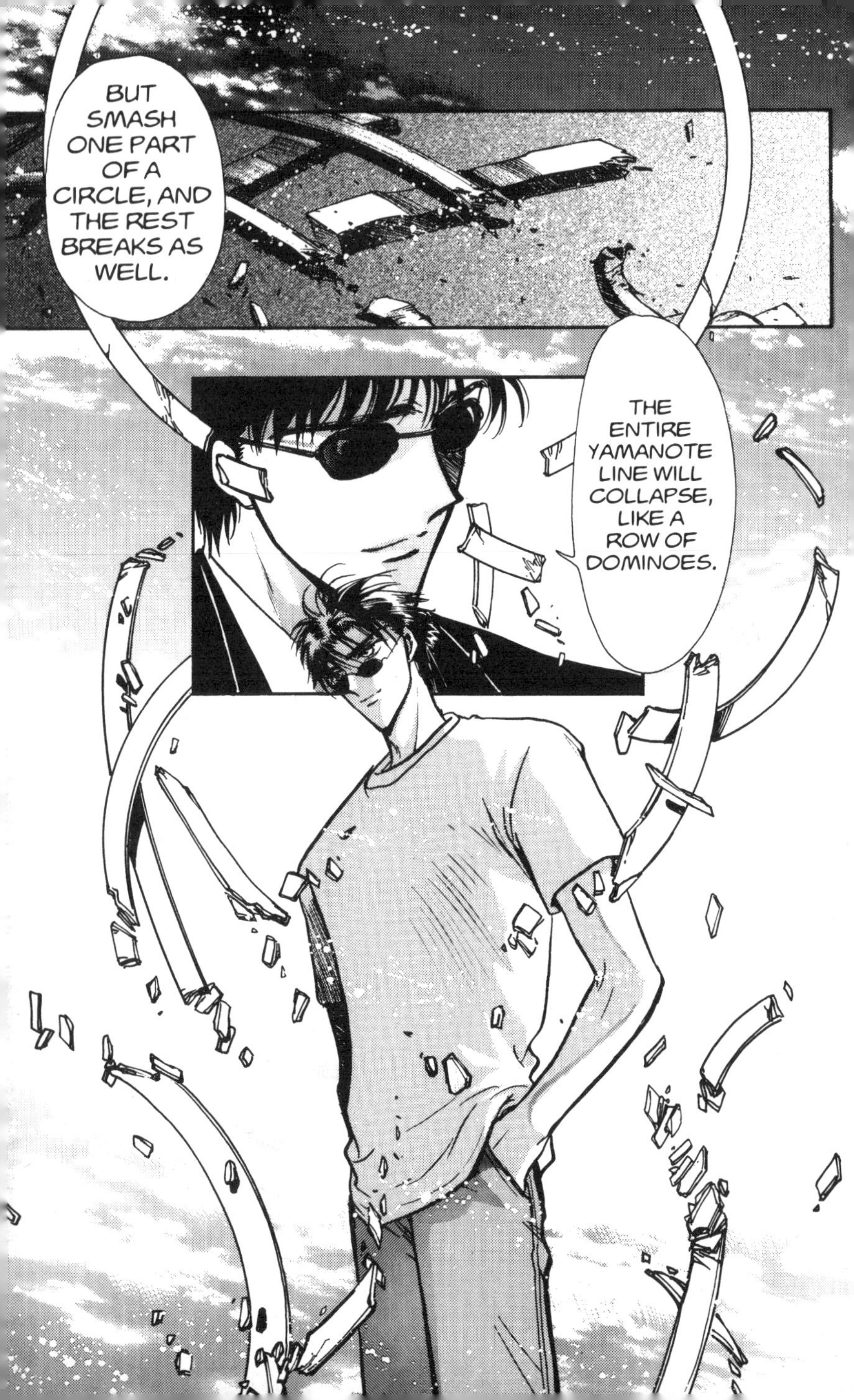
BUT SMASH ONE PART OF A CIRCLE, AND THE REST BREAKS AS WELL.
THE ENTIRE YAMANOTE LINE WILL COLLAPSE, LIKE A ROW OF DOMINOES.

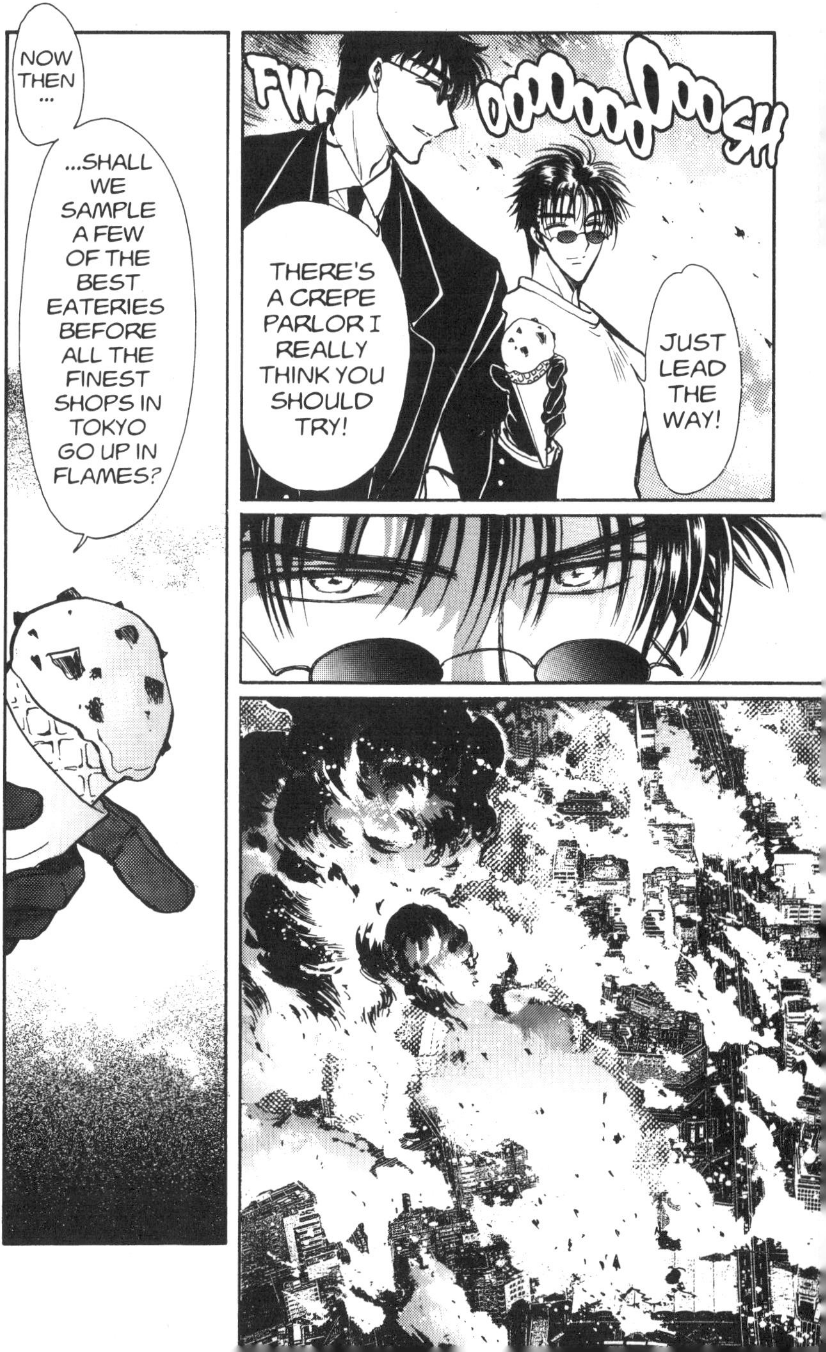
NOW THEN ...
...SHALL WE SAMPLE A FEW OF THE BEST EATERIES BEFORE ALL THE FINEST SHOPS IN TOKYO GO UP IN FLAMES?
FWOOOOOOOOOSH
THERE'S A CREPE PARLOR I REALLY THINK YOU SHOULD TRY!
JUST LEAD THE WAY!

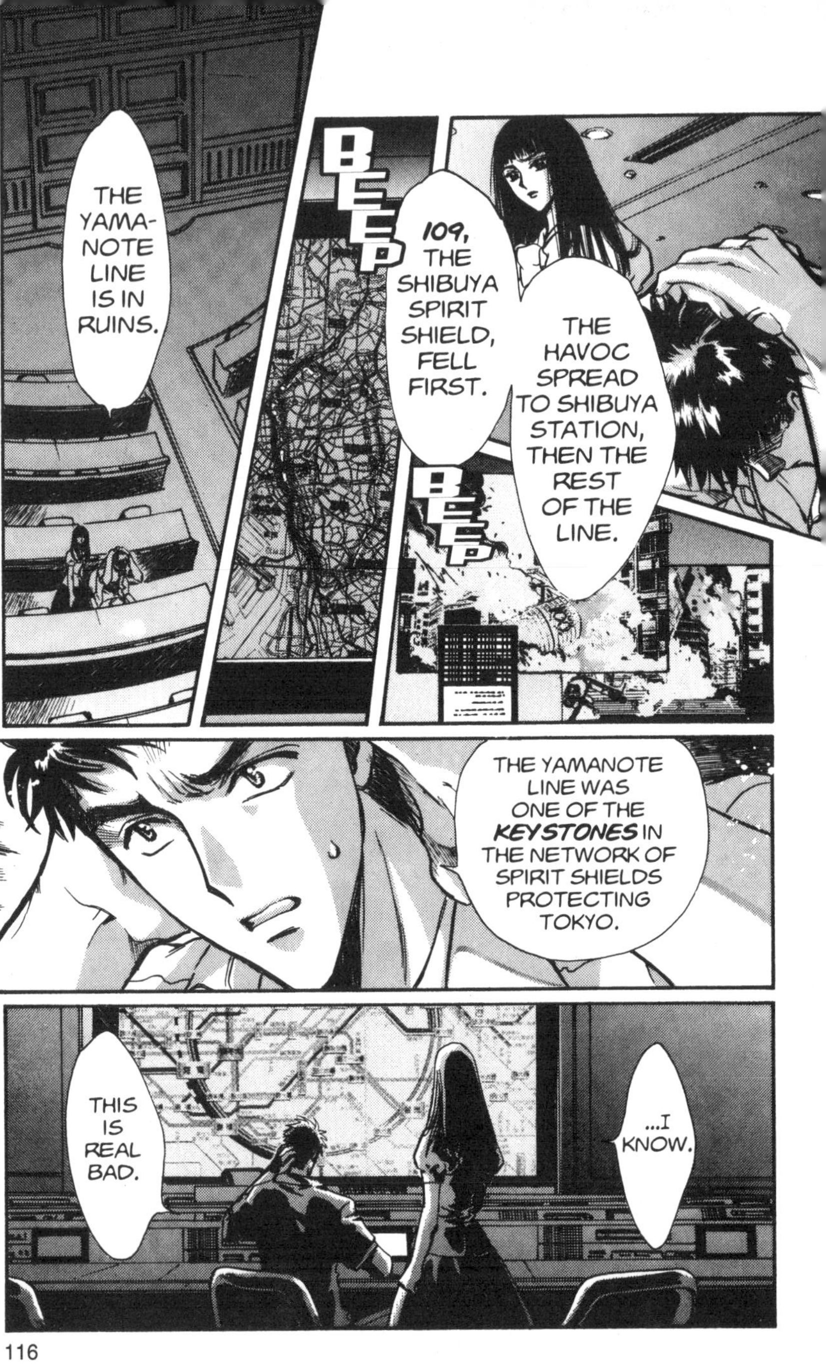
THE YAMANOTE LINE IS IN RUINS.
BEEP
109, THE SHIBUYA SPIRIT SHIELD, FELL FIRST.
THE HAVOC SPREAD TO SHIBUYA STATION, THEN THE REST OF THE LINE.
BEEP
THE YAMANOTE LINE WAS ONE OF THE ***KEYSTONES*** IN THE NETWORK OF SPIRIT SHIELDS PROTECTING TOKYO.
THIS IS REAL BAD.
...I KNOW.

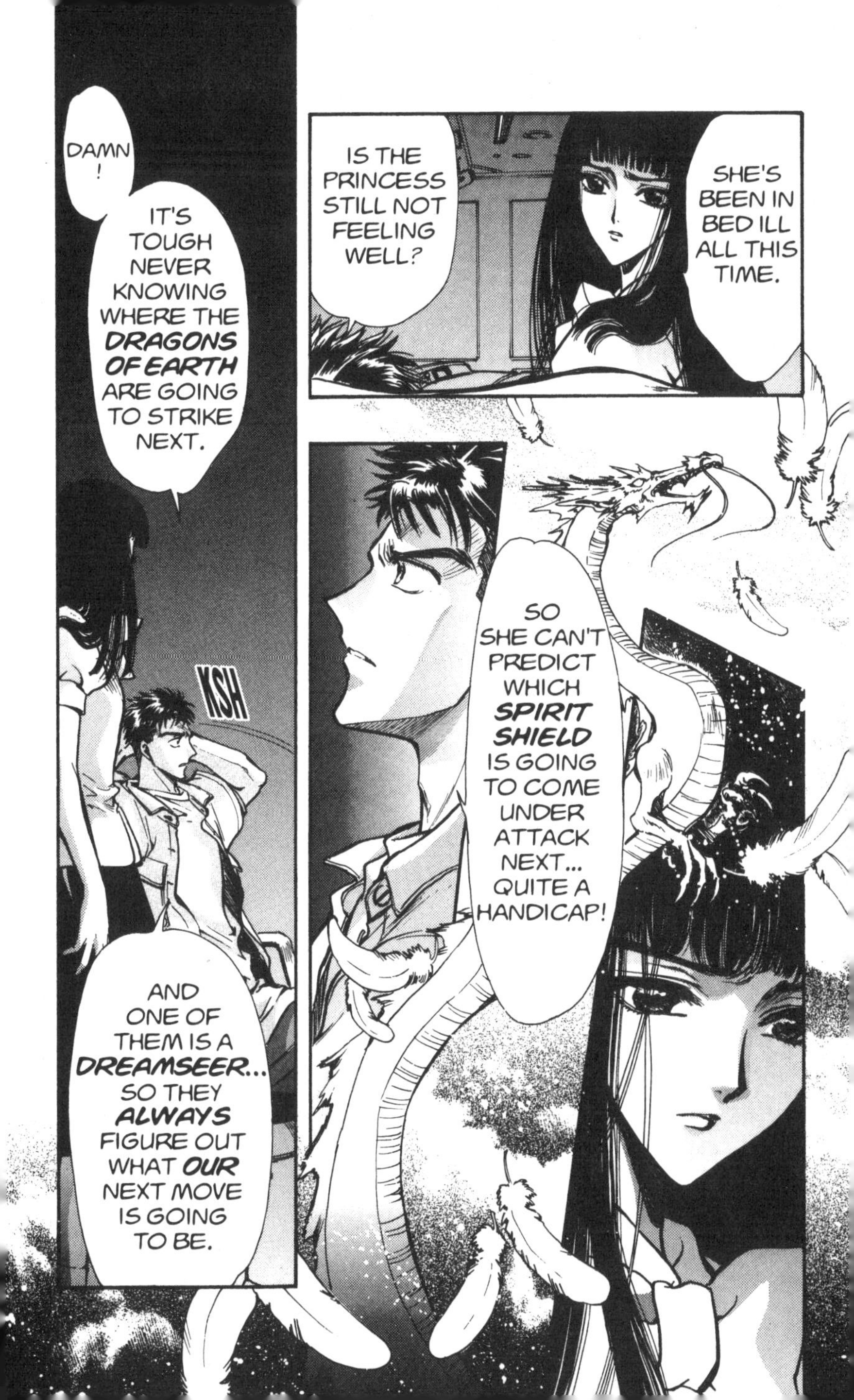
DAMN!
IT'S TOUGH NEVER KNOWING WHERE THE DRAGONS OF EARTH ARE GOING TO STRIKE NEXT.
KSH
AND ONE OF THEM IS A DREAMSEER... SO THEY ALWAYS FIGURE OUT WHAT OUR NEXT MOVE IS GOING TO BE.
IS THE PRINCESS STILL NOT FEELING WELL?
SHE'S BEEN IN BED ILL ALL THIS TIME.
SO SHE CAN'T PREDICT WHICH SPIRIT SHIELD IS GOING TO COME UNDER ATTACK NEXT... QUITE A HANDICAP!

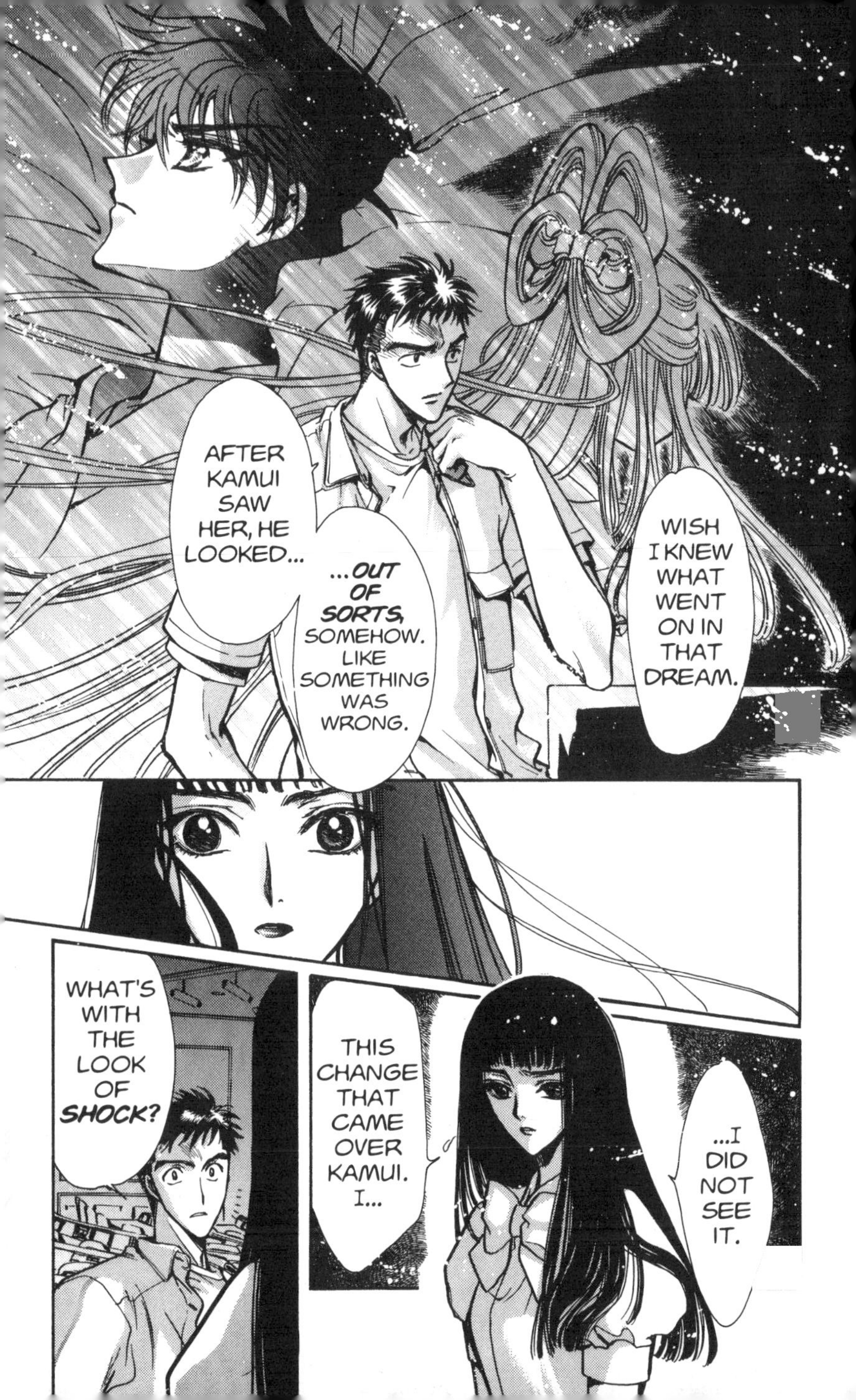
WISH I KNEW WHAT WENT ON IN THAT DREAM.
AFTER KAMUI SAW HER, HE LOOKED...
...*OUT OF SORTS*, SOMEHOW. LIKE SOMETHING WAS WRONG.
THIS CHANGE THAT CAME OVER KAMUI. I...
...I DID NOT SEE IT.
WHAT'S WITH THE LOOK OF *SHOCK*?

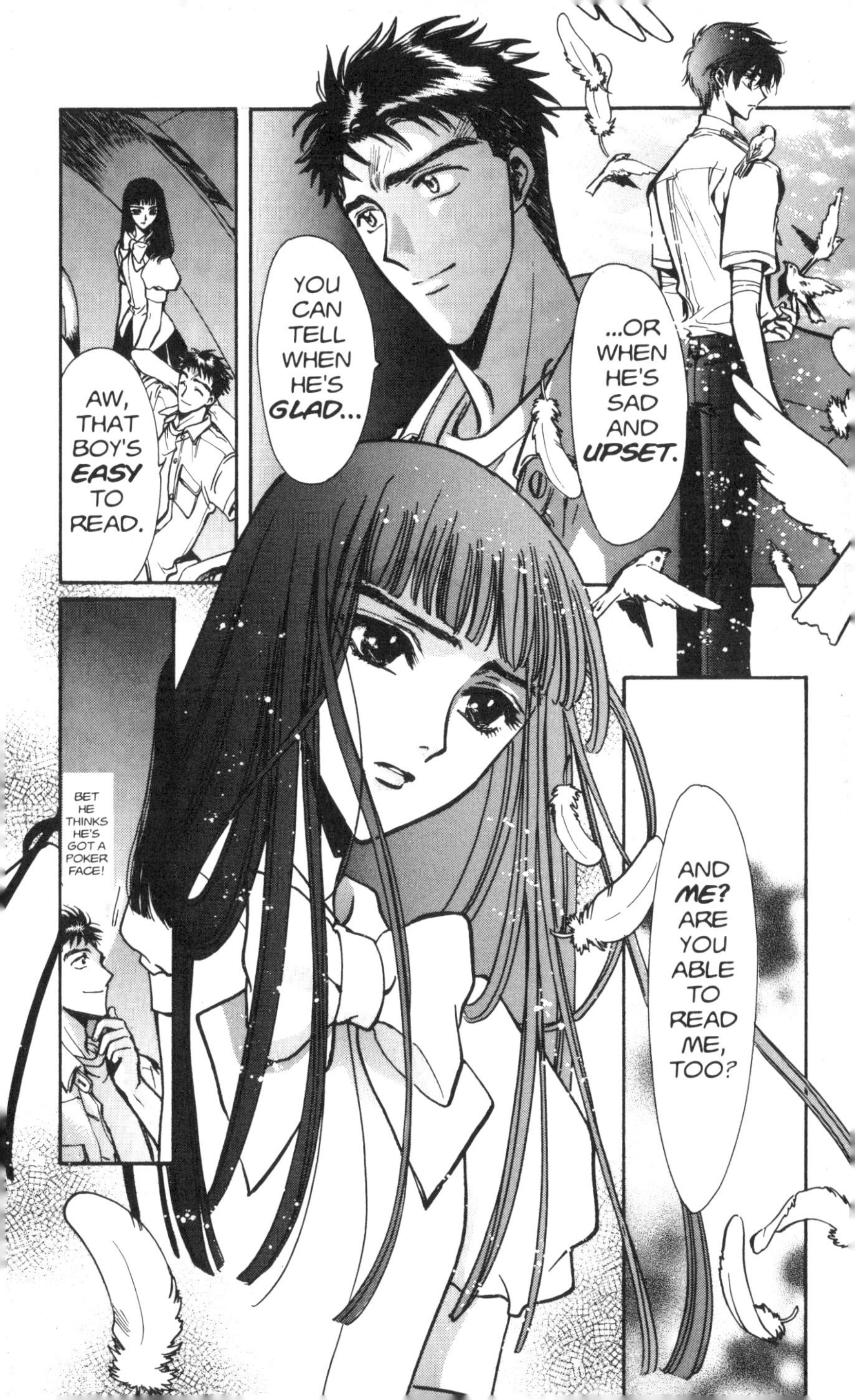
AW, THAT BOY'S EASY TO READ.
YOU CAN TELL WHEN HE'S GLAD...
...OR WHEN HE'S SAD AND UPSET.
BET HE THINKS HE'S GOT A POKER FACE!
AND ME? ARE YOU ABLE TO READ ME, TOO?

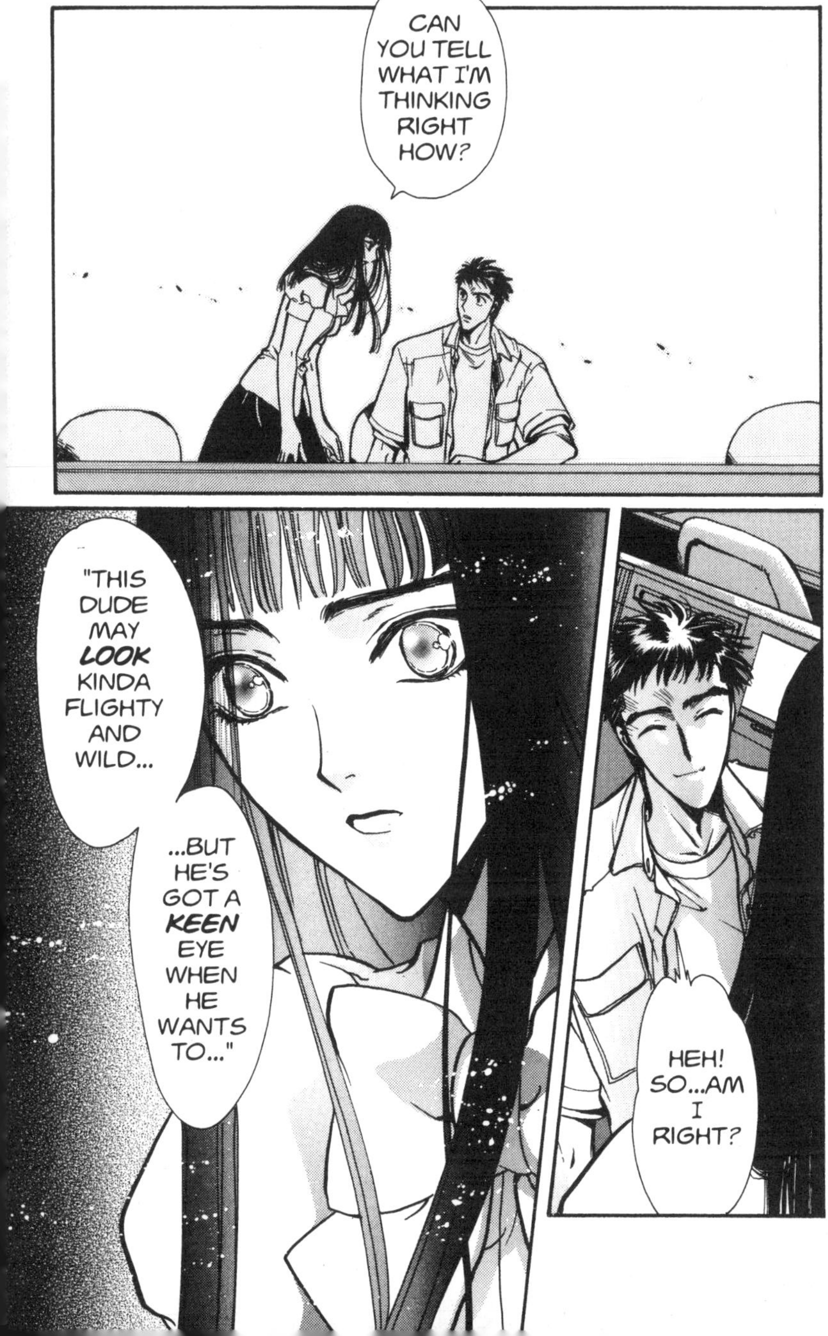
CAN YOU TELL WHAT I'M THINKING RIGHT HOW?
"THIS DUDE MAY ***LOOK*** KINDA FLIGHTY AND WILD...
...BUT HE'S GOT A ***KEEN*** EYE WHEN HE WANTS TO..."
HEH! SO...AM I RIGHT?

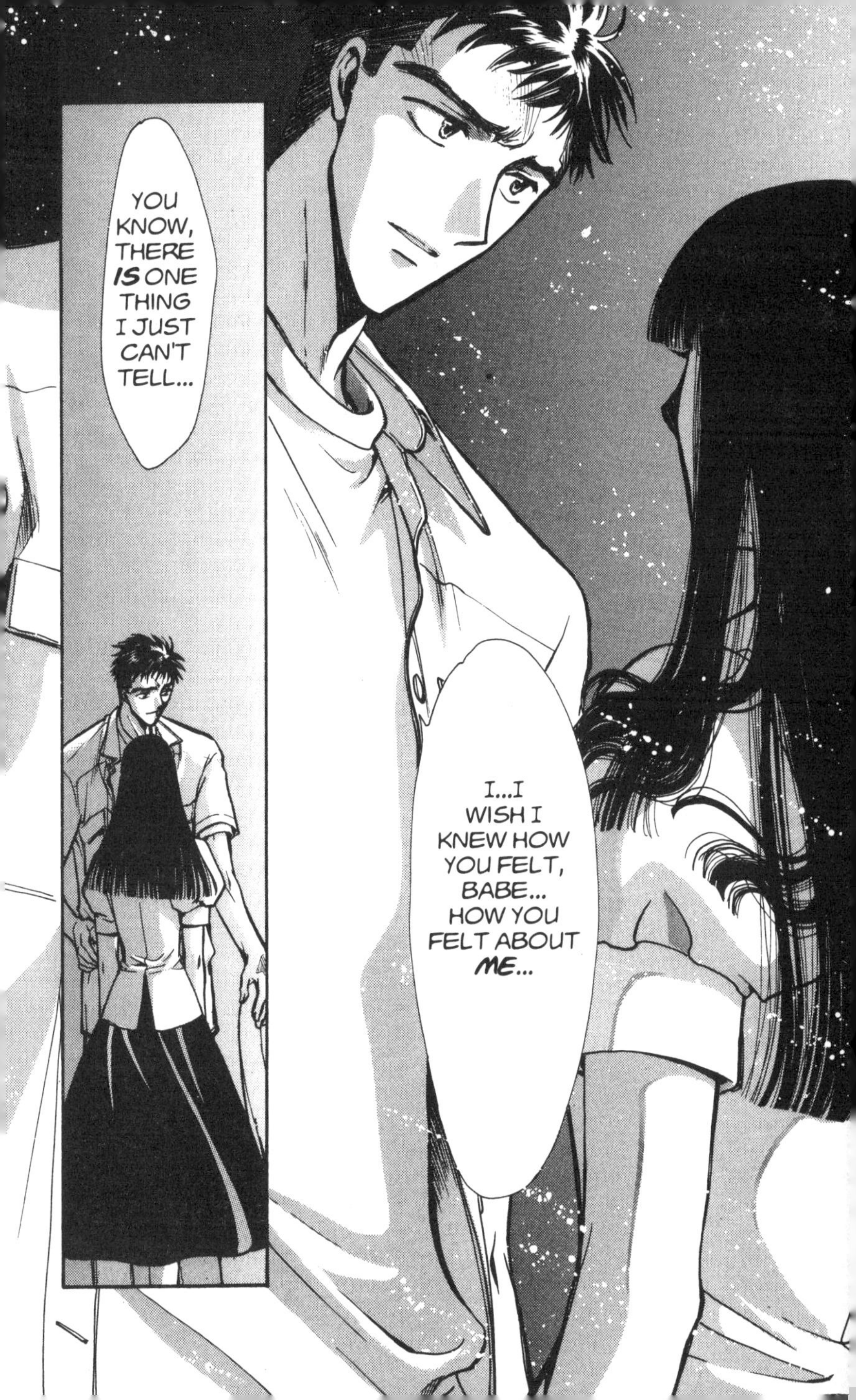
YOU KNOW, THERE IS ONE THING I JUST CAN'T TELL...
I...I WISH I KNEW HOW YOU FELT, BABE... HOW YOU FELT ABOUT ME...

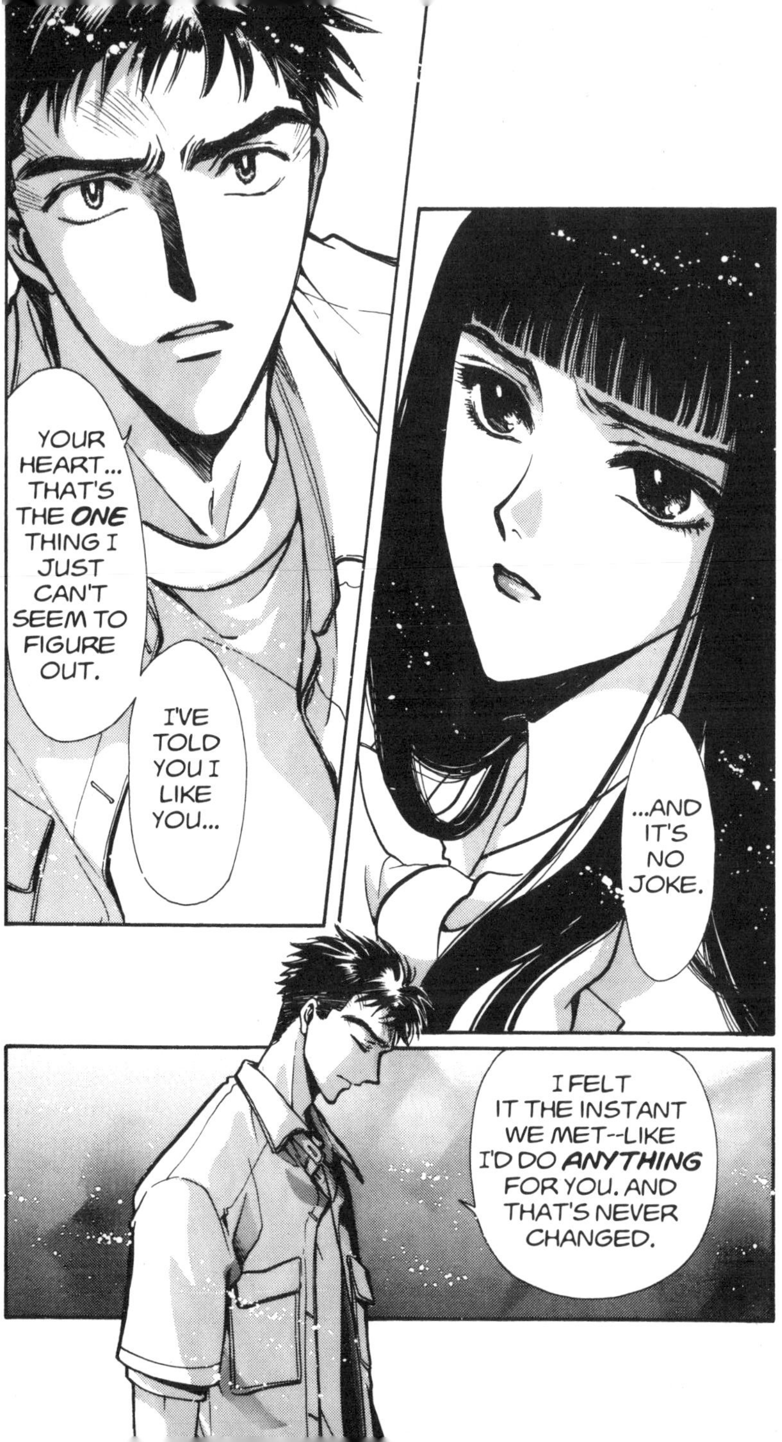
YOUR HEART... THAT'S THE *ONE* THING I JUST CAN'T SEEM TO FIGURE OUT.
I'VE TOLD YOU I LIKE YOU...
...AND IT'S NO JOKE.
I FELT IT THE INSTANT WE MET--LIKE I'D DO *ANYTHING* FOR YOU. AND THAT'S NEVER CHANGED.

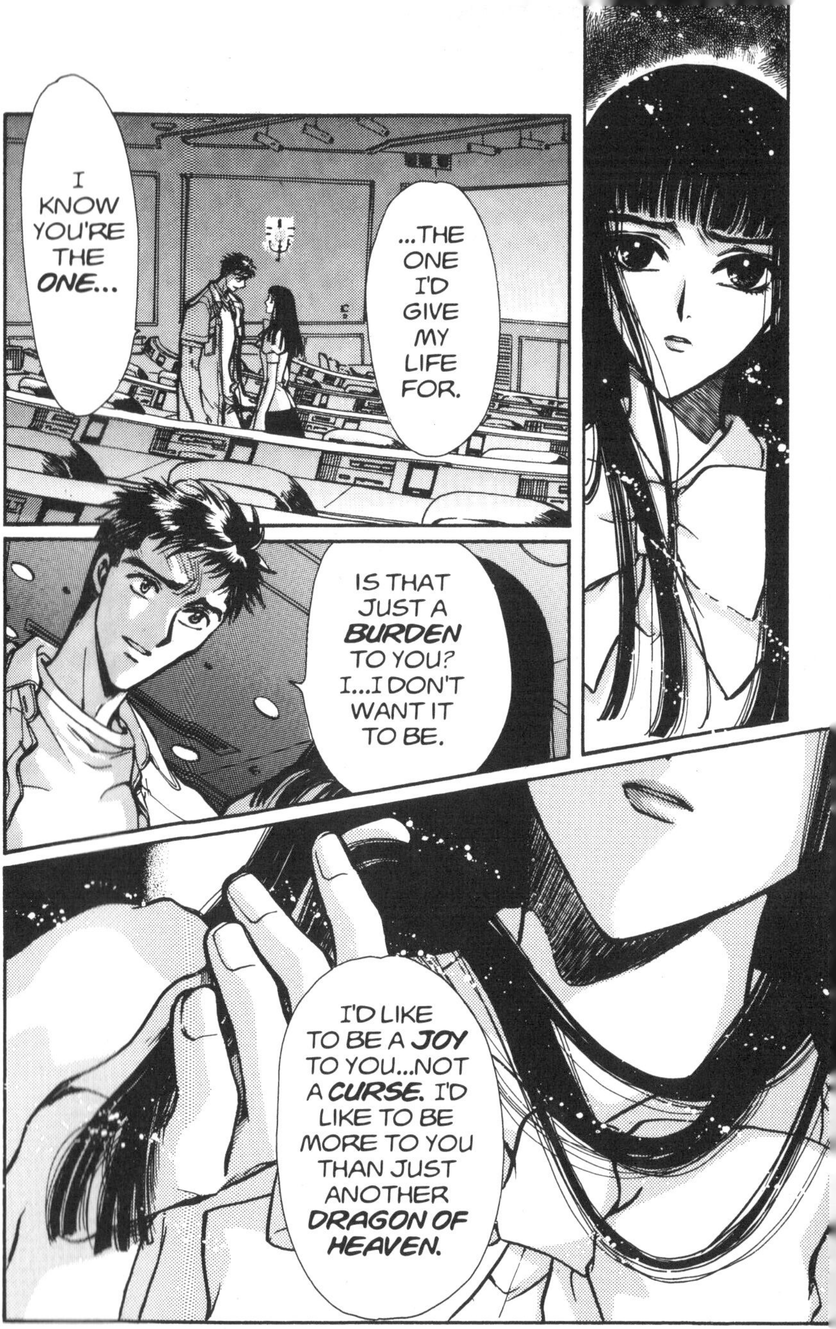
...THE ONE I'D GIVE MY LIFE FOR.
I KNOW YOU'RE THE ONE...
IS THAT JUST A BURDEN TO YOU? I...I DON'T WANT IT TO BE.
I'D LIKE TO BE A JOY TO YOU...NOT A CURSE. I'D LIKE TO BE MORE TO YOU THAN JUST ANOTHER DRAGON OF HEAVEN.

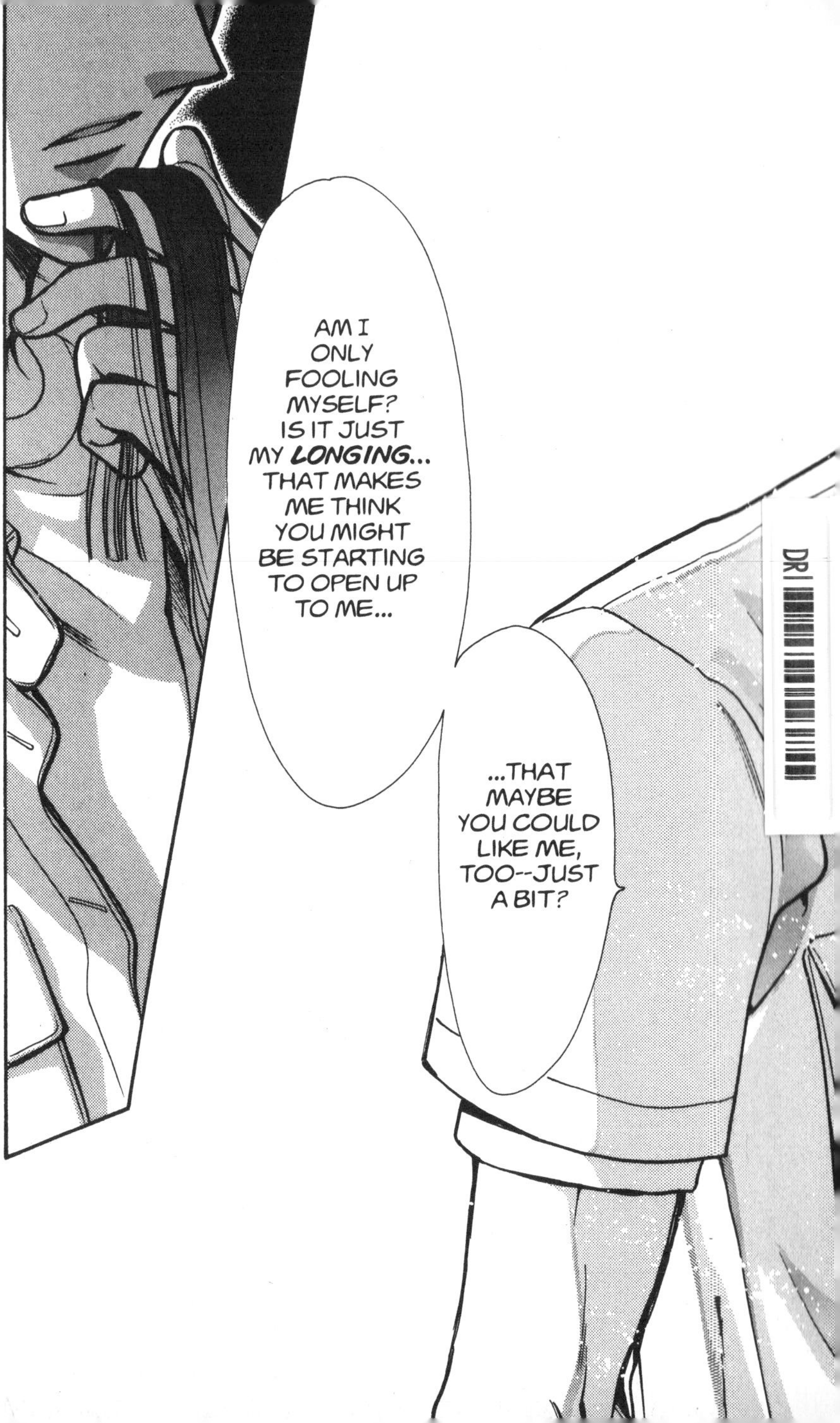
AM I ONLY FOOLING MYSELF? IS IT JUST MY LONGING... THAT MAKES ME THINK YOU MIGHT BE STARTING TO OPEN UP TO ME...
...THAT MAYBE YOU COULD LIKE ME, TOO--JUST A BIT?

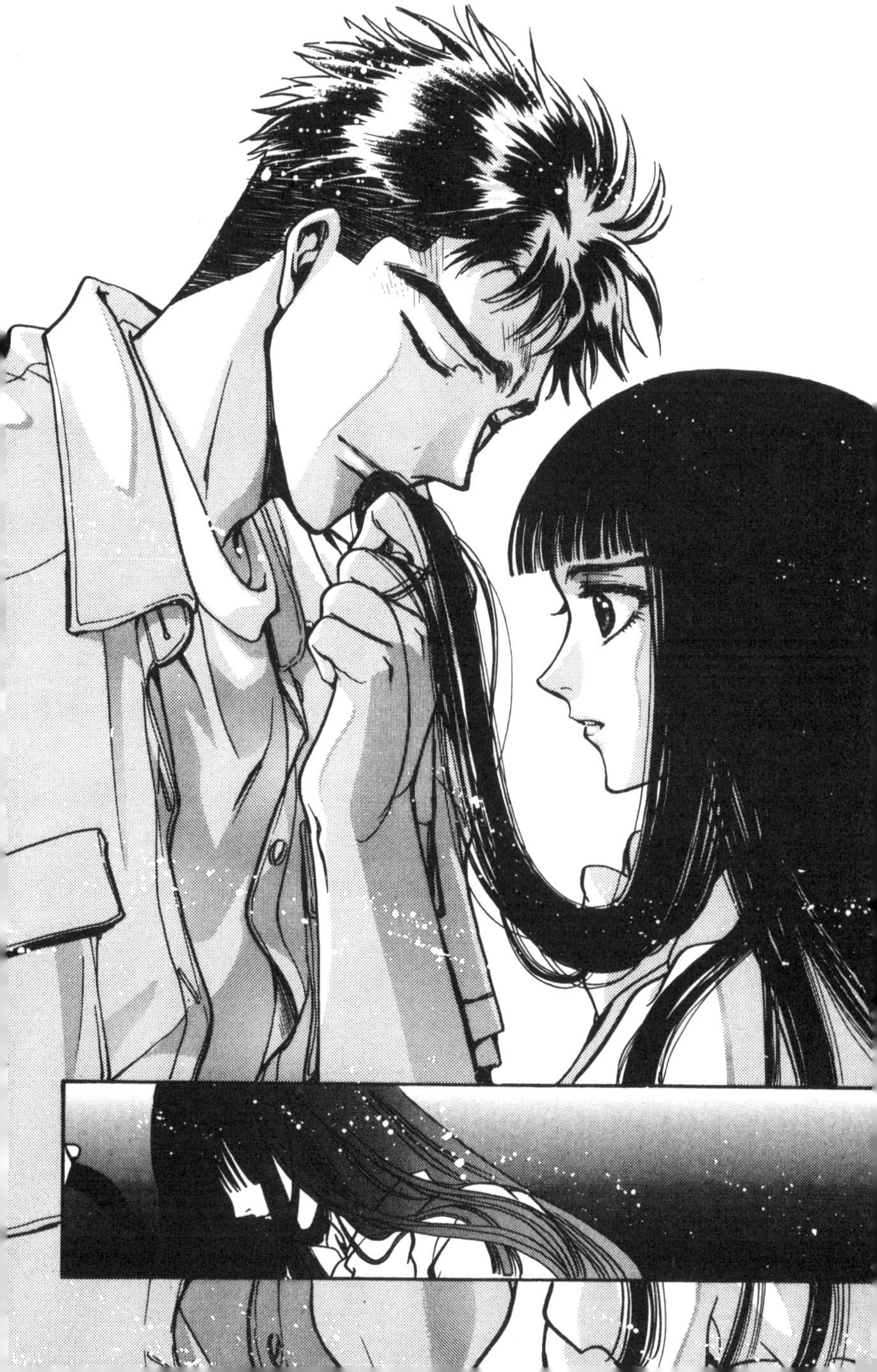

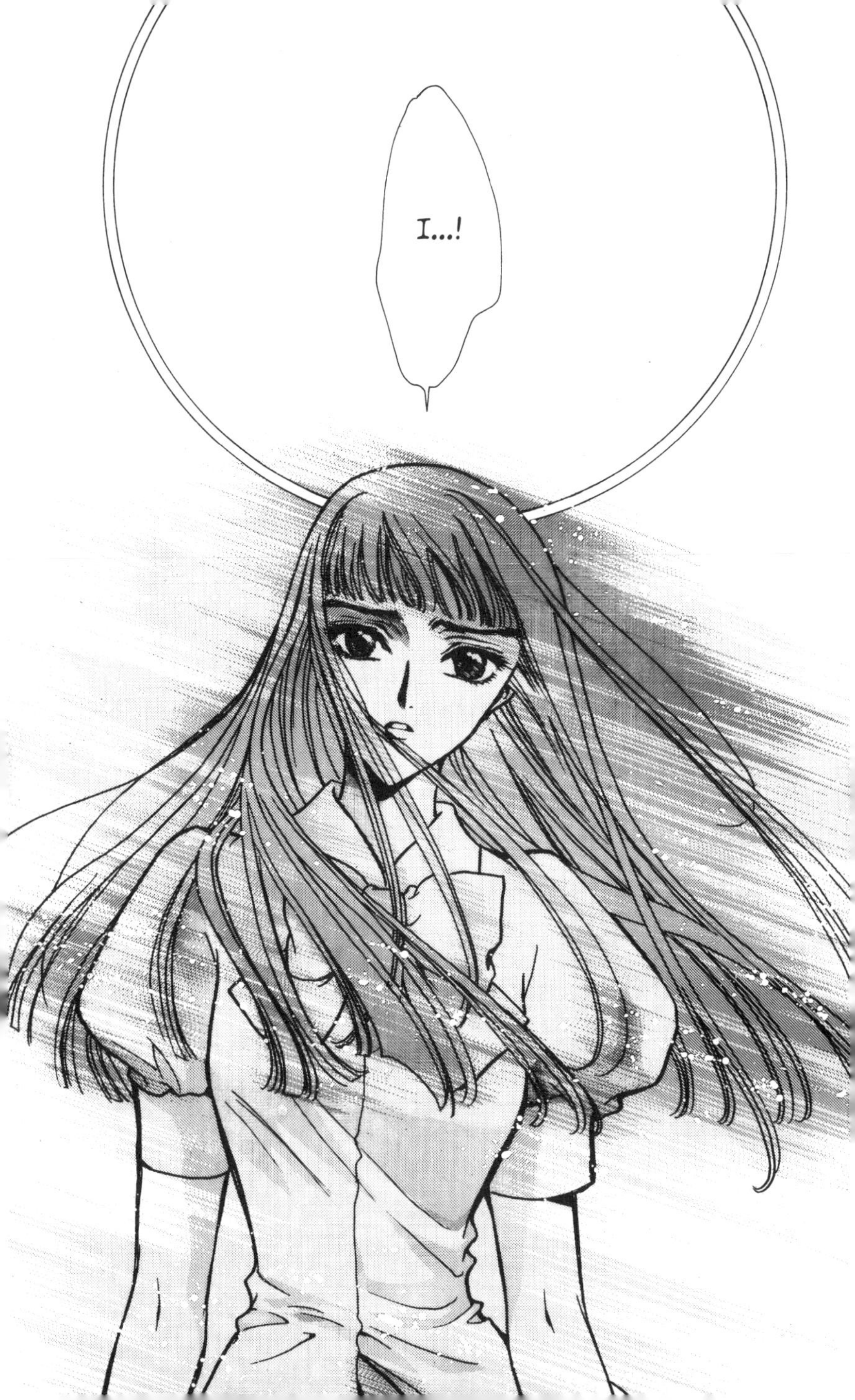
I...!

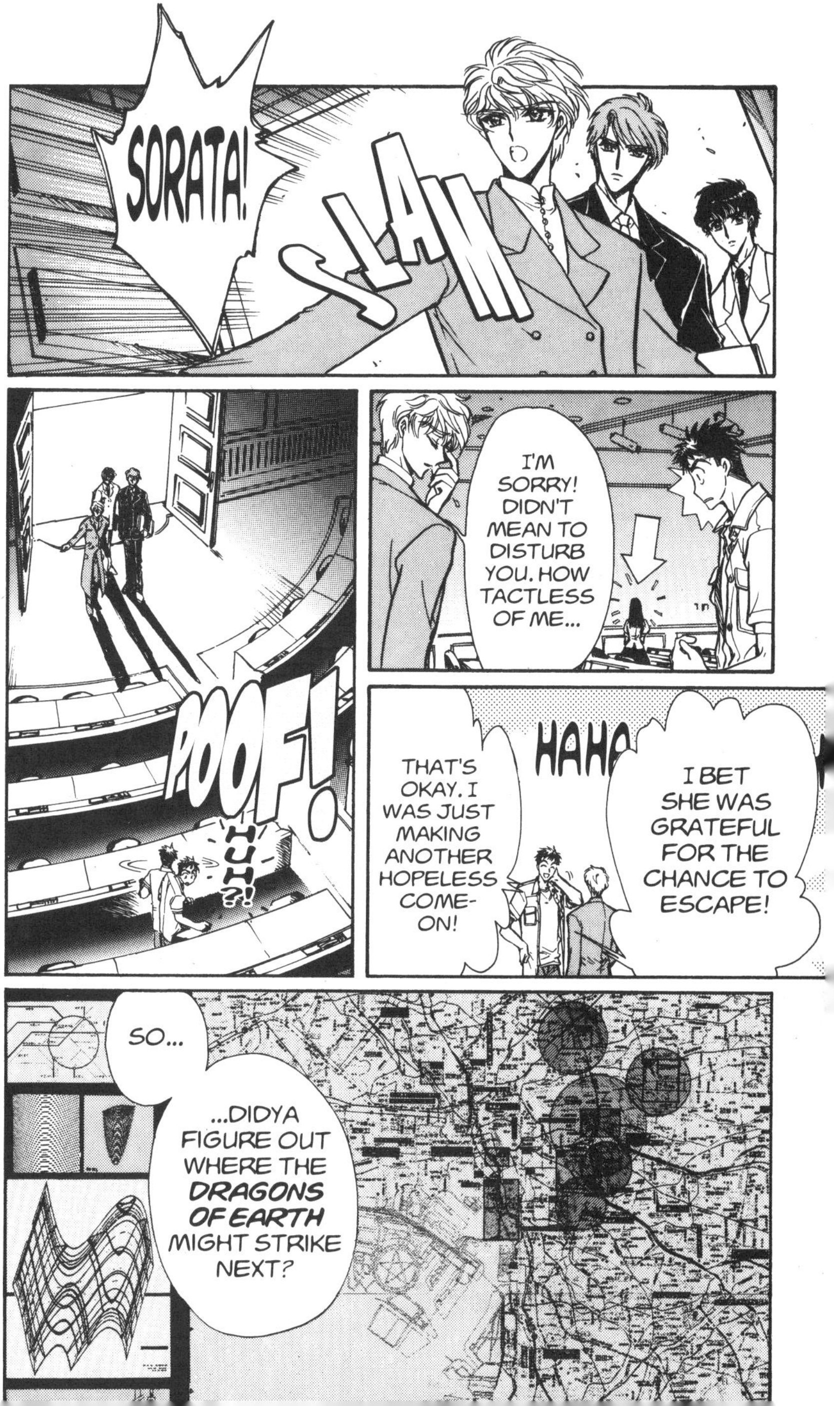
SORATA!
SLAM
POOF!
HUH?!
I'M SORRY! DIDN'T MEAN TO DISTURB YOU. HOW TACTLESS OF ME...
HAHA
THAT'S OKAY. I WAS JUST MAKING ANOTHER HOPELESS COME-ON!
I BET SHE WAS GRATEFUL FOR THE CHANCE TO ESCAPE!
SO...
...DIDYA FIGURE OUT WHERE THE *DRAGONS OF EARTH* MIGHT STRIKE NEXT?

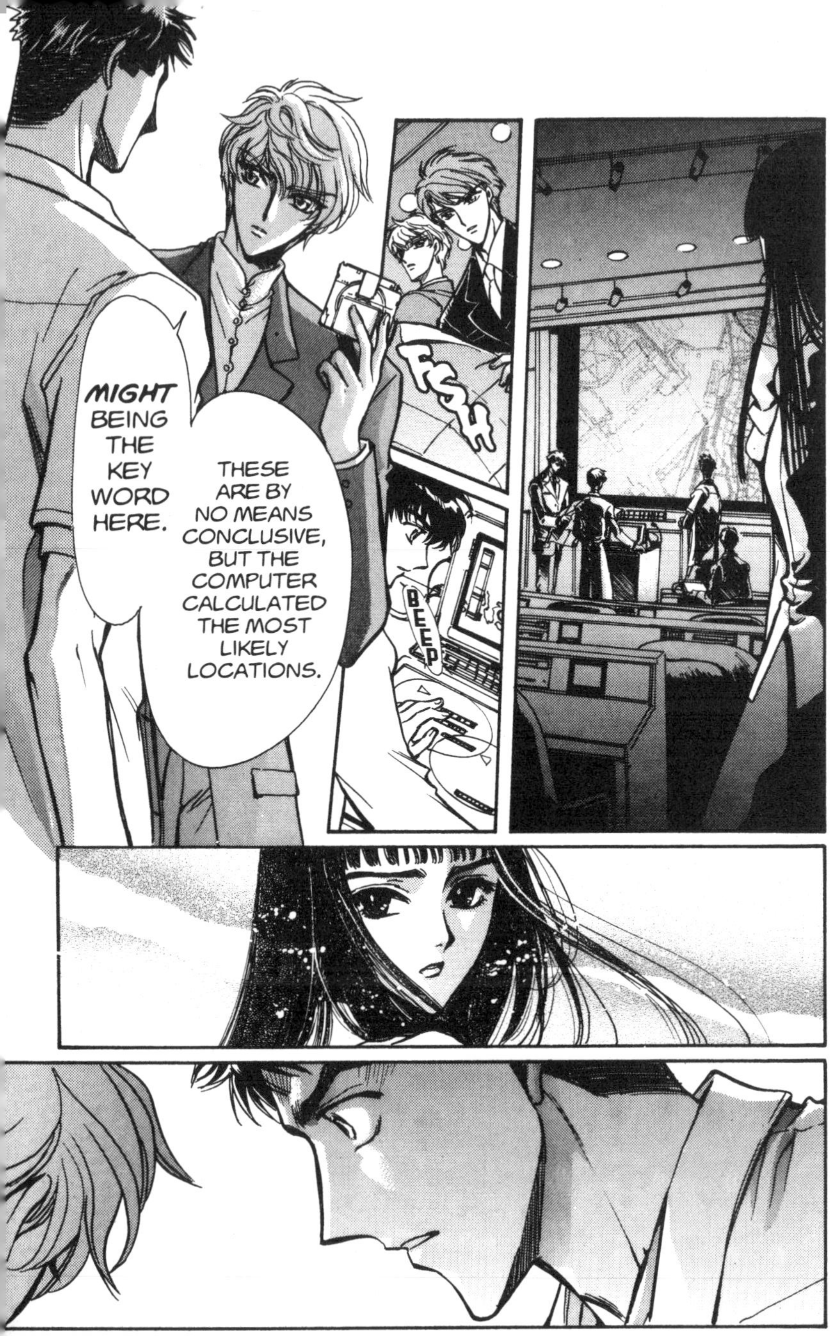
FSH
BEEP
THESE ARE BY NO MEANS CONCLUSIVE, BUT THE COMPUTER CALCULATED THE MOST LIKELY LOCATIONS.
MIGHT BEING THE KEY WORD HERE.

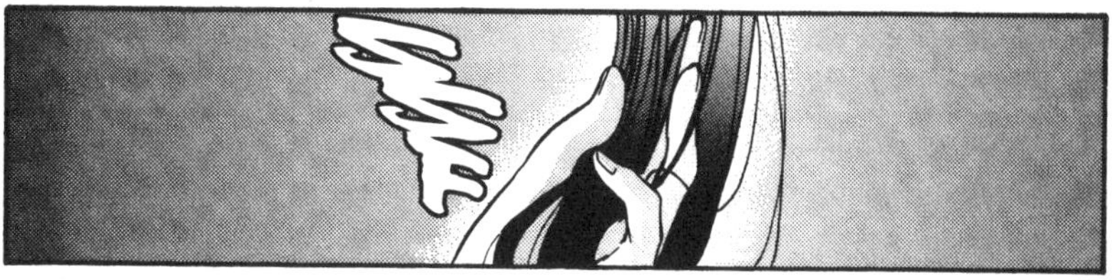
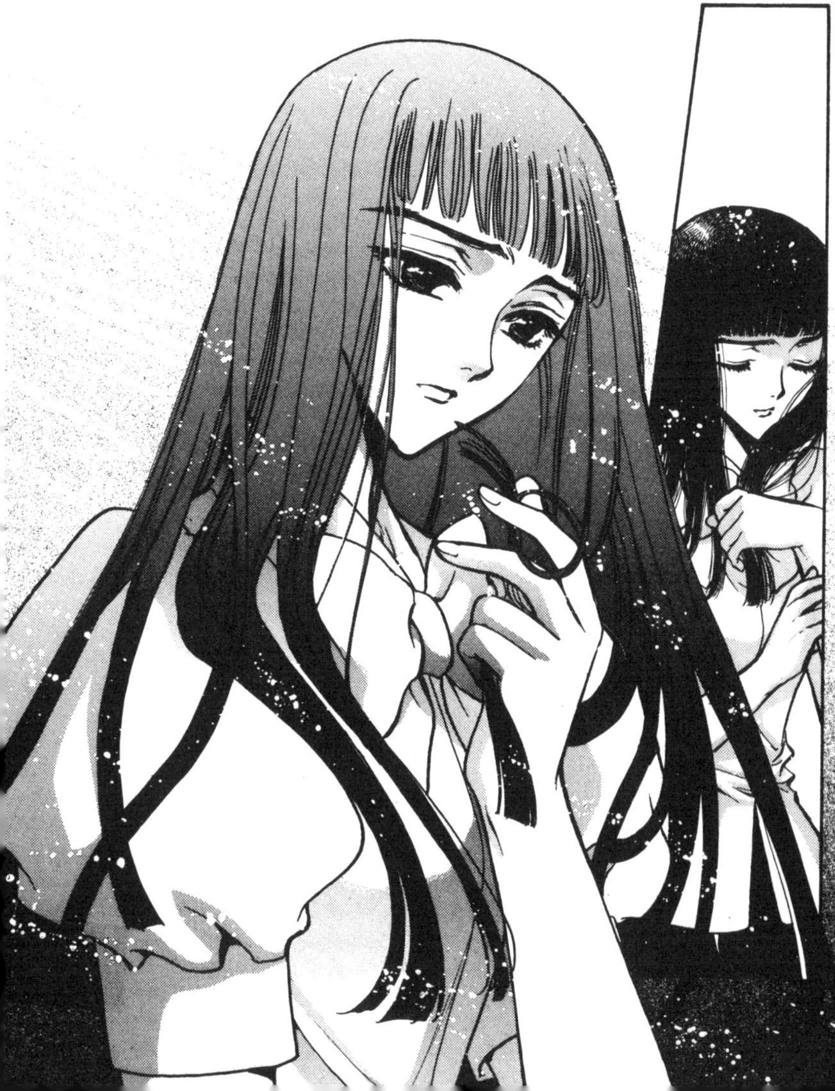

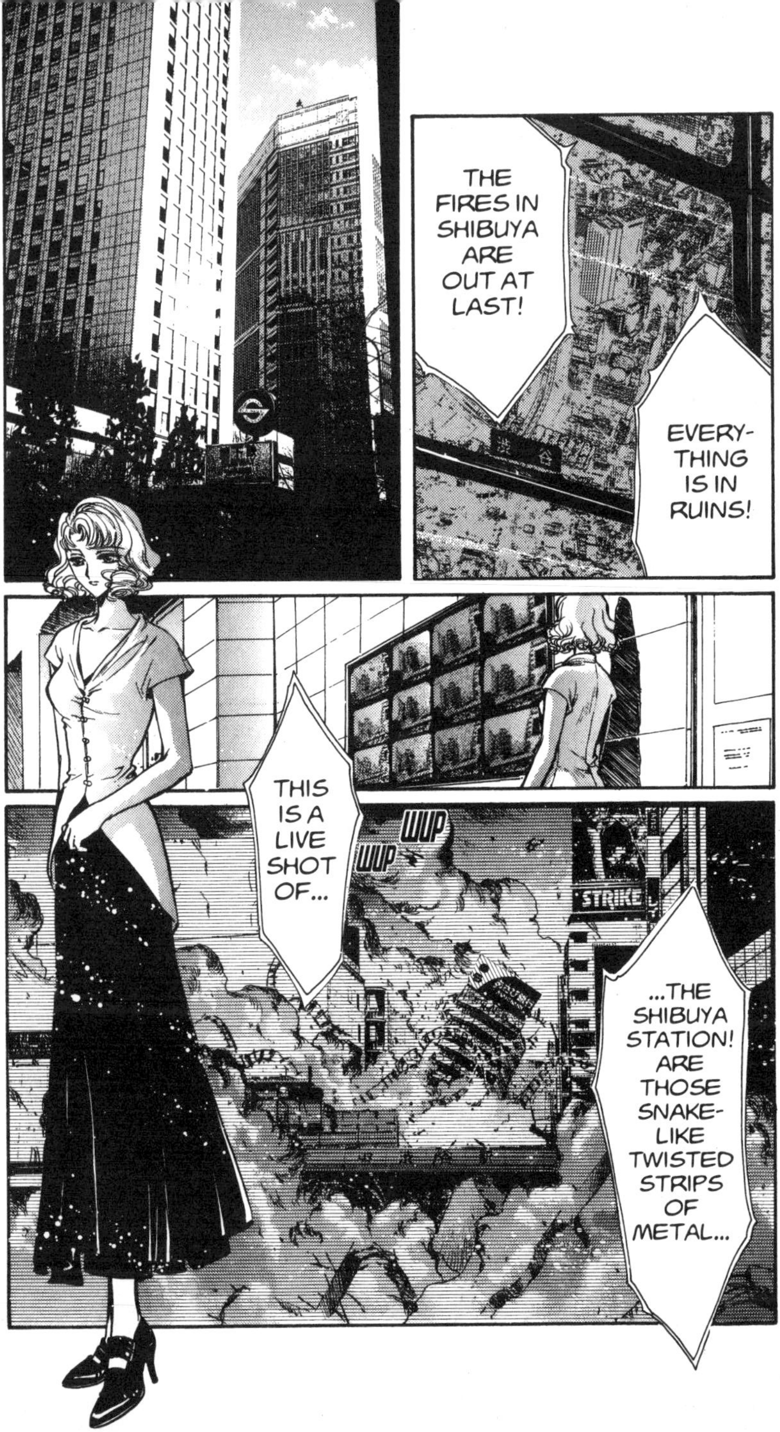
THE FIRES IN SHIBUYA ARE OUT AT LAST!
EVERYTHING IS IN RUINS!
THIS IS A LIVE SHOT OF...
WUP
WUP
STRIKE
...THE SHIBUYA STATION! ARE THOSE SNAKE-LIKE TWISTED STRIPS OF METAL...

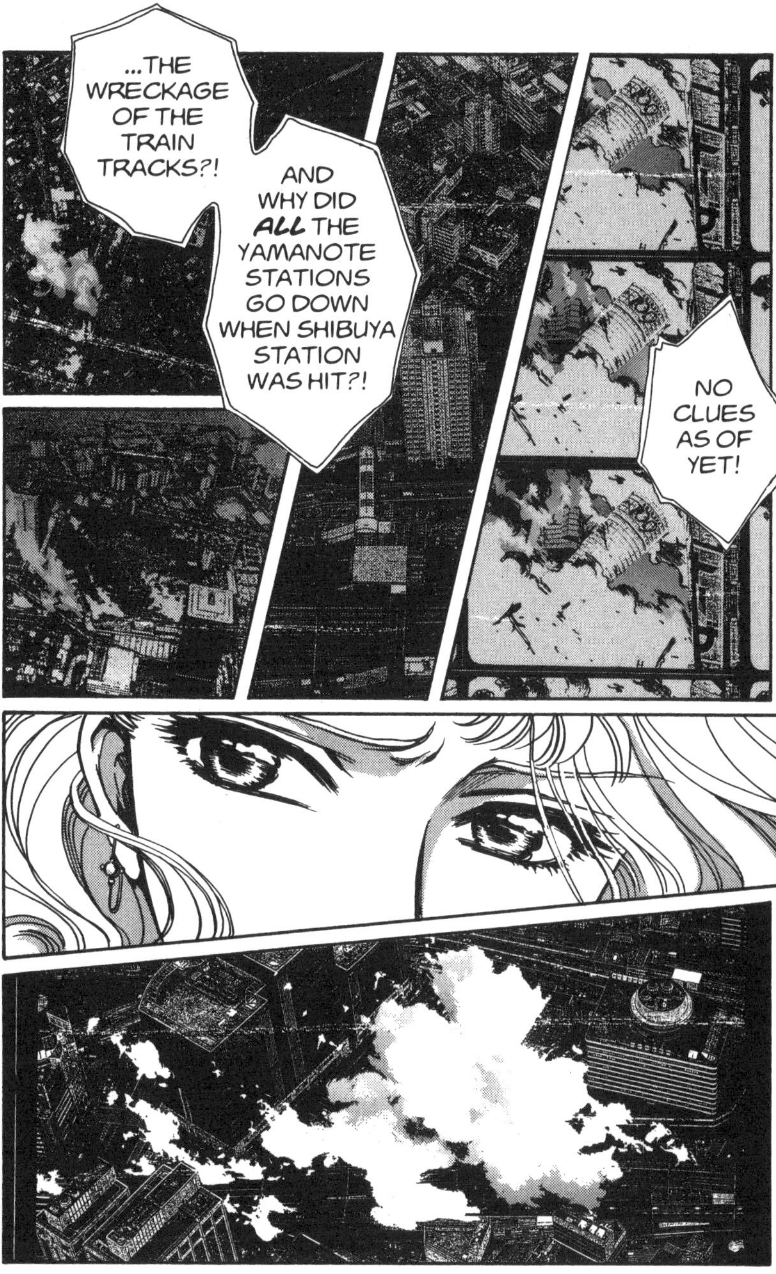
...THE WRECKAGE OF THE TRAIN TRACKS?!
AND WHY DID ALL THE YAMANOTE STATIONS GO DOWN WHEN SHIBUYA STATION WAS HIT?!
NO CLUES AS OF YET!

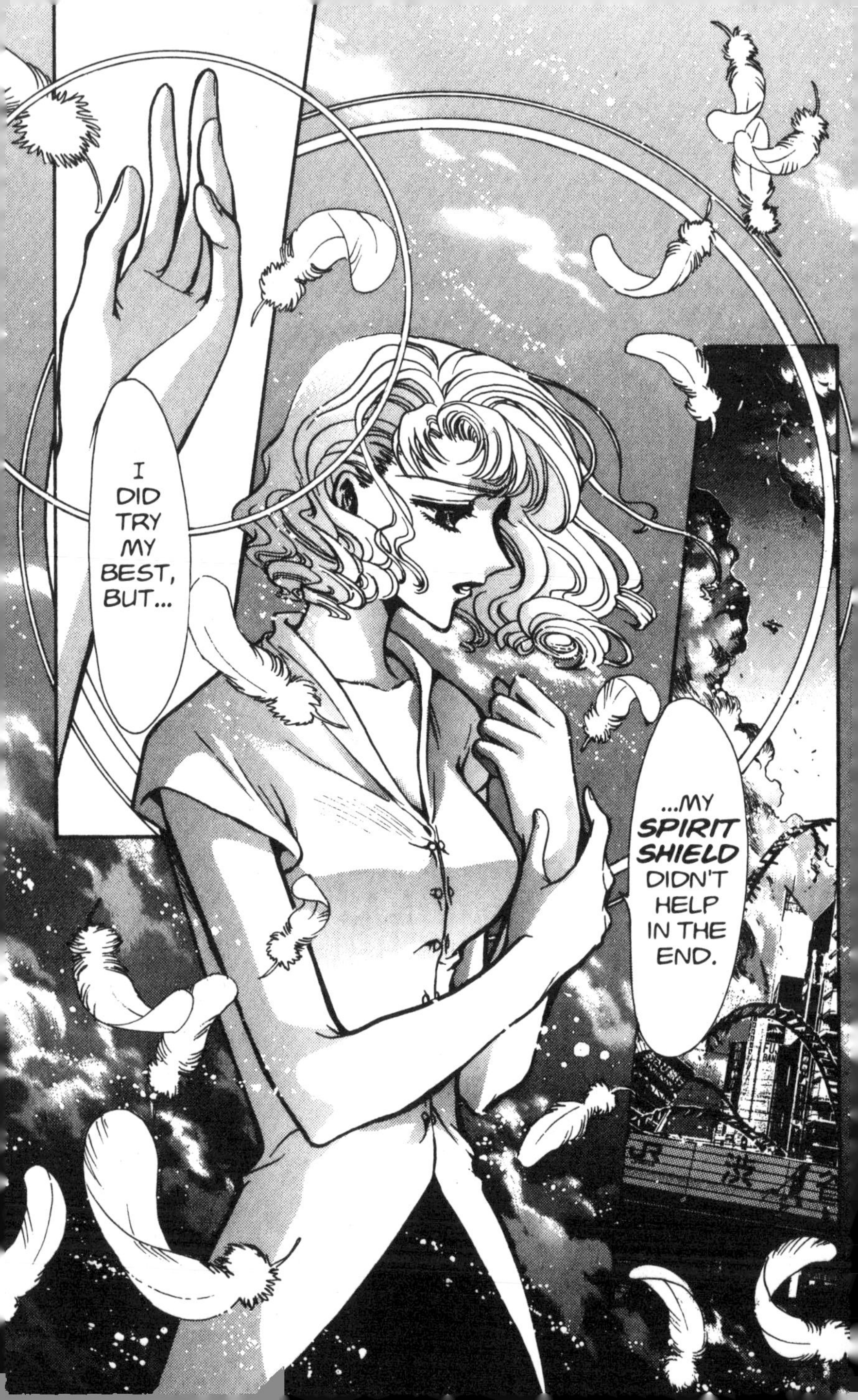
I DID TRY MY BEST, BUT...
...MY **SPIRIT SHIELD** DIDN'T HELP IN THE END.

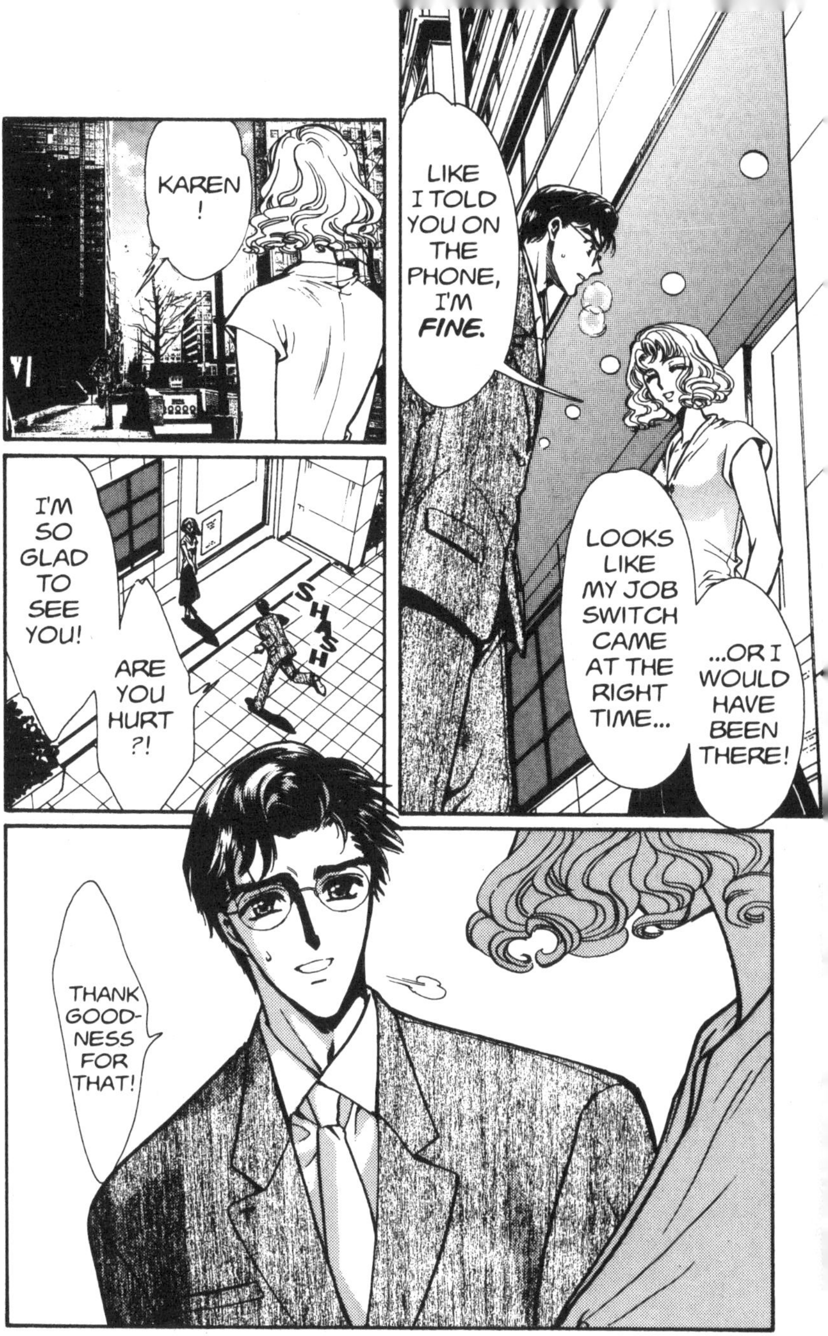
KAREN!
I'M SO GLAD TO SEE YOU!
SHASH
ARE YOU HURT?!
LIKE I TOLD YOU ON THE PHONE, I'M *FINE*.
LOOKS LIKE MY JOB SWITCH CAME AT THE RIGHT TIME...
...OR I WOULD HAVE BEEN THERE!
THANK GOODNESS FOR THAT!

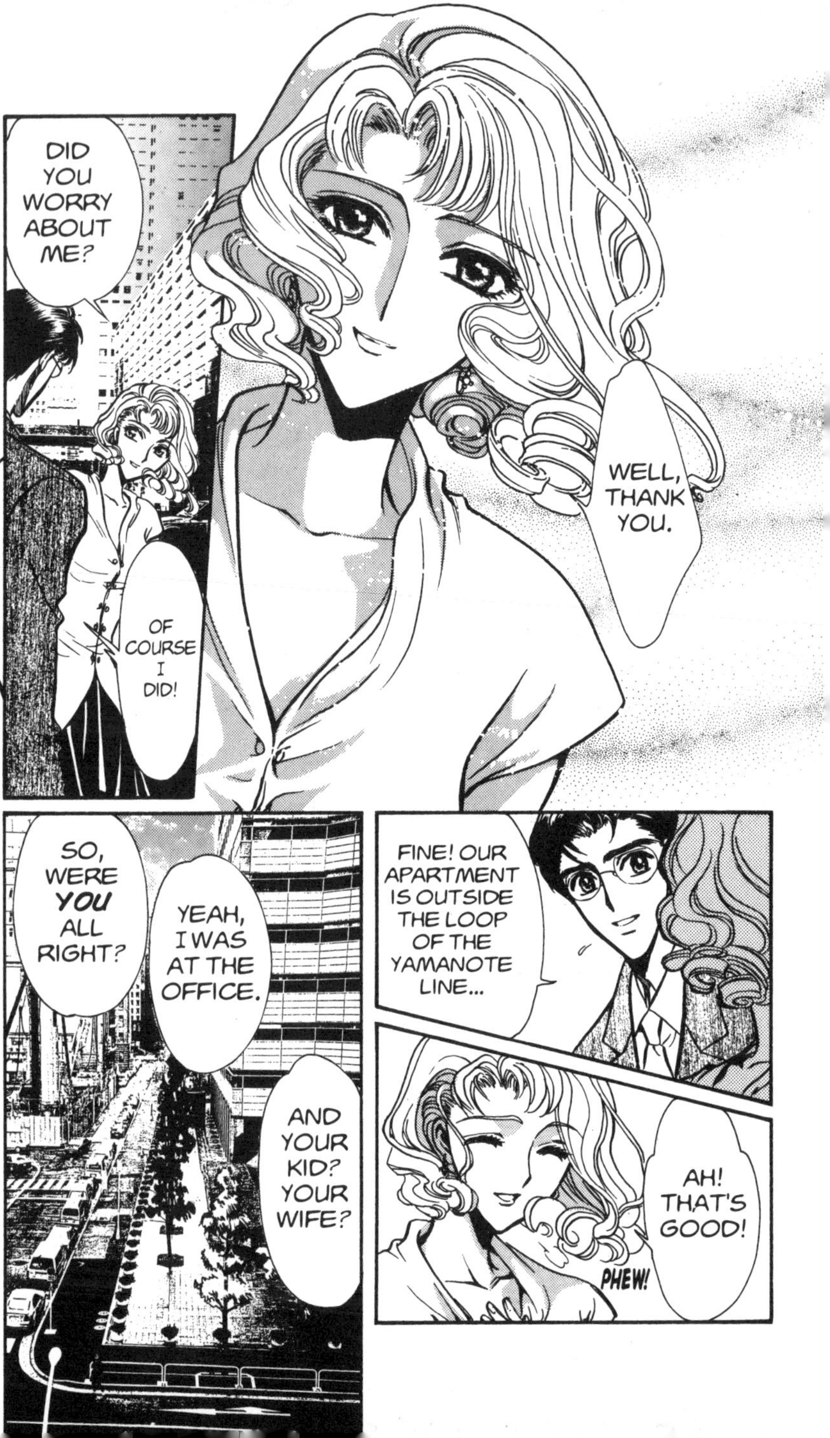
DID YOU WORRY ABOUT ME?
OF COURSE I DID!
WELL, THANK YOU.
SO, WERE YOU ALL RIGHT?
YEAH, I WAS AT THE OFFICE.
AND YOUR KID? YOUR WIFE?
FINE! OUR APARTMENT IS OUTSIDE THE LOOP OF THE YAMANOTE LINE...
AH! THAT'S GOOD!
PHEW!

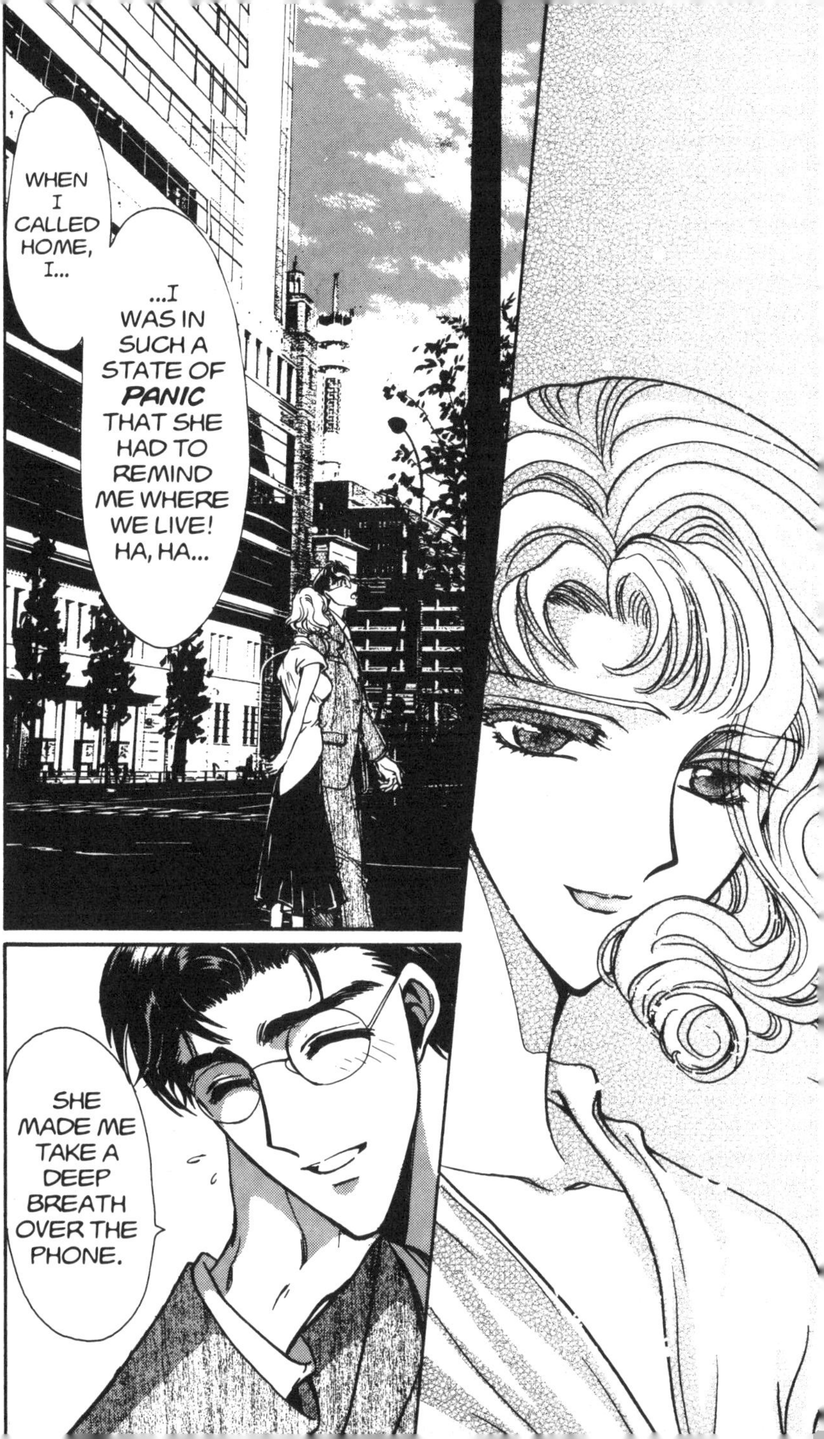
WHEN I CALLED HOME, I...
...I WAS IN SUCH A STATE OF PANIC THAT SHE HAD TO REMIND ME WHERE WE LIVE! HA, HA...
SHE MADE ME TAKE A DEEP BREATH OVER THE PHONE.

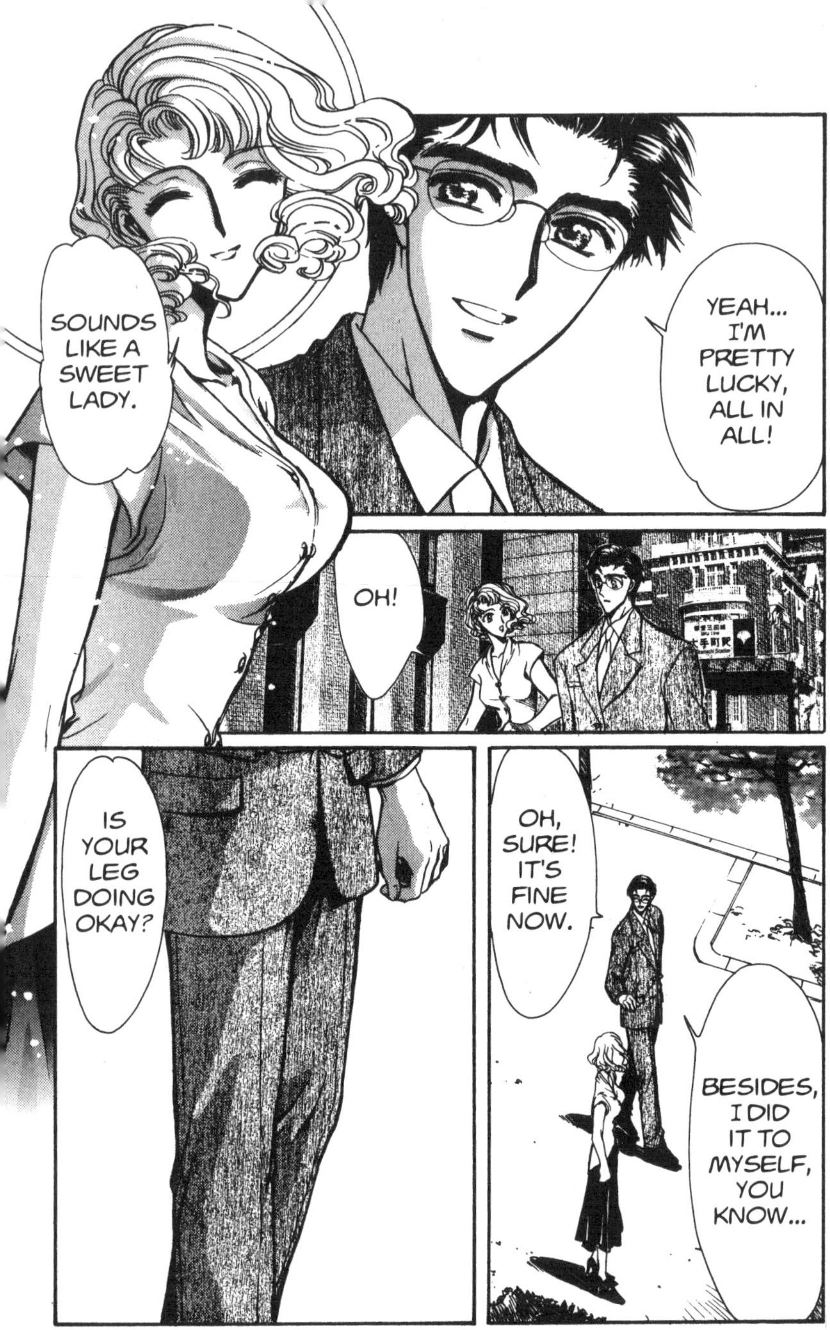
SOUNDS LIKE A SWEET LADY.
YEAH... I'M PRETTY LUCKY, ALL IN ALL!
OH!
IS YOUR LEG DOING OKAY?
OH, SURE! IT'S FINE NOW.
BESIDES, I DID IT TO MYSELF, YOU KNOW...

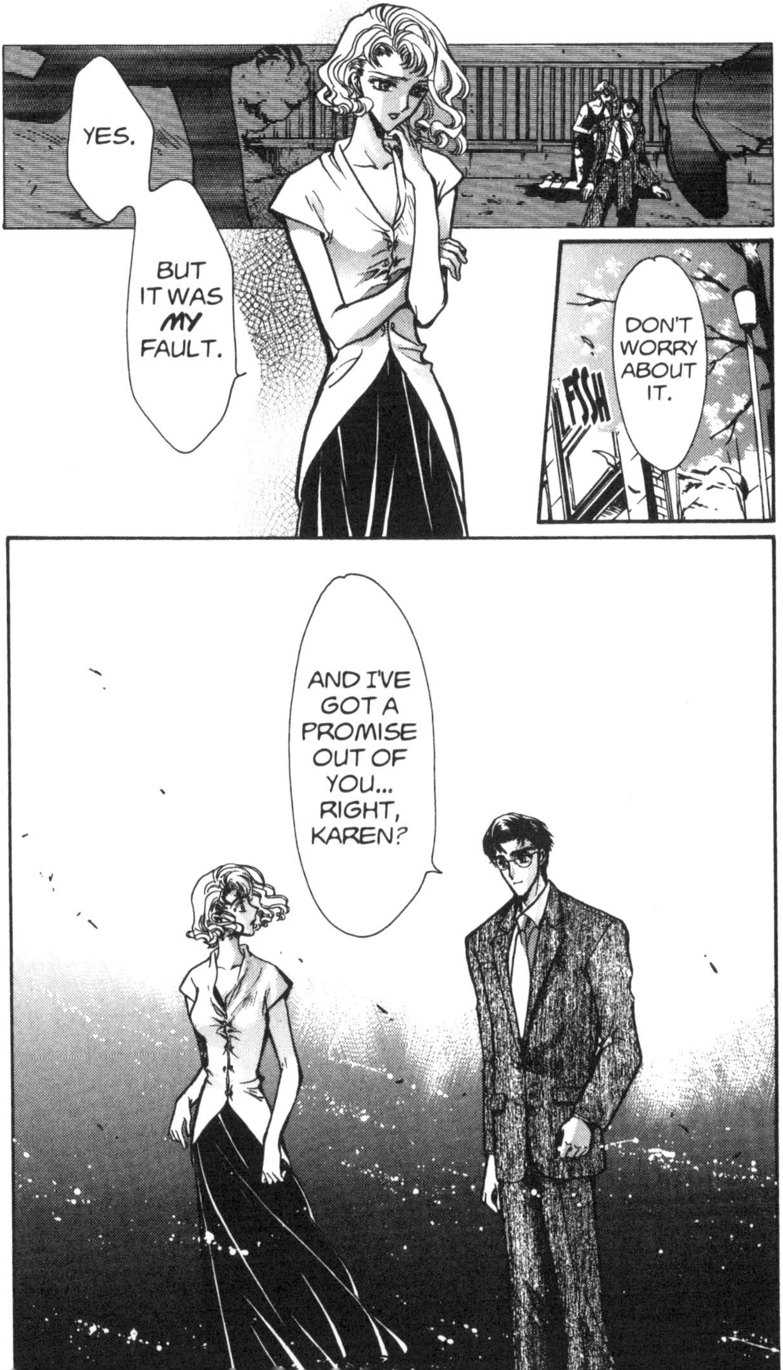
YES.
BUT IT WAS *MY* FAULT.
DON'T WORRY ABOUT IT.
FSSH
AND I'VE GOT A PROMISE OUT OF YOU... RIGHT, KAREN?

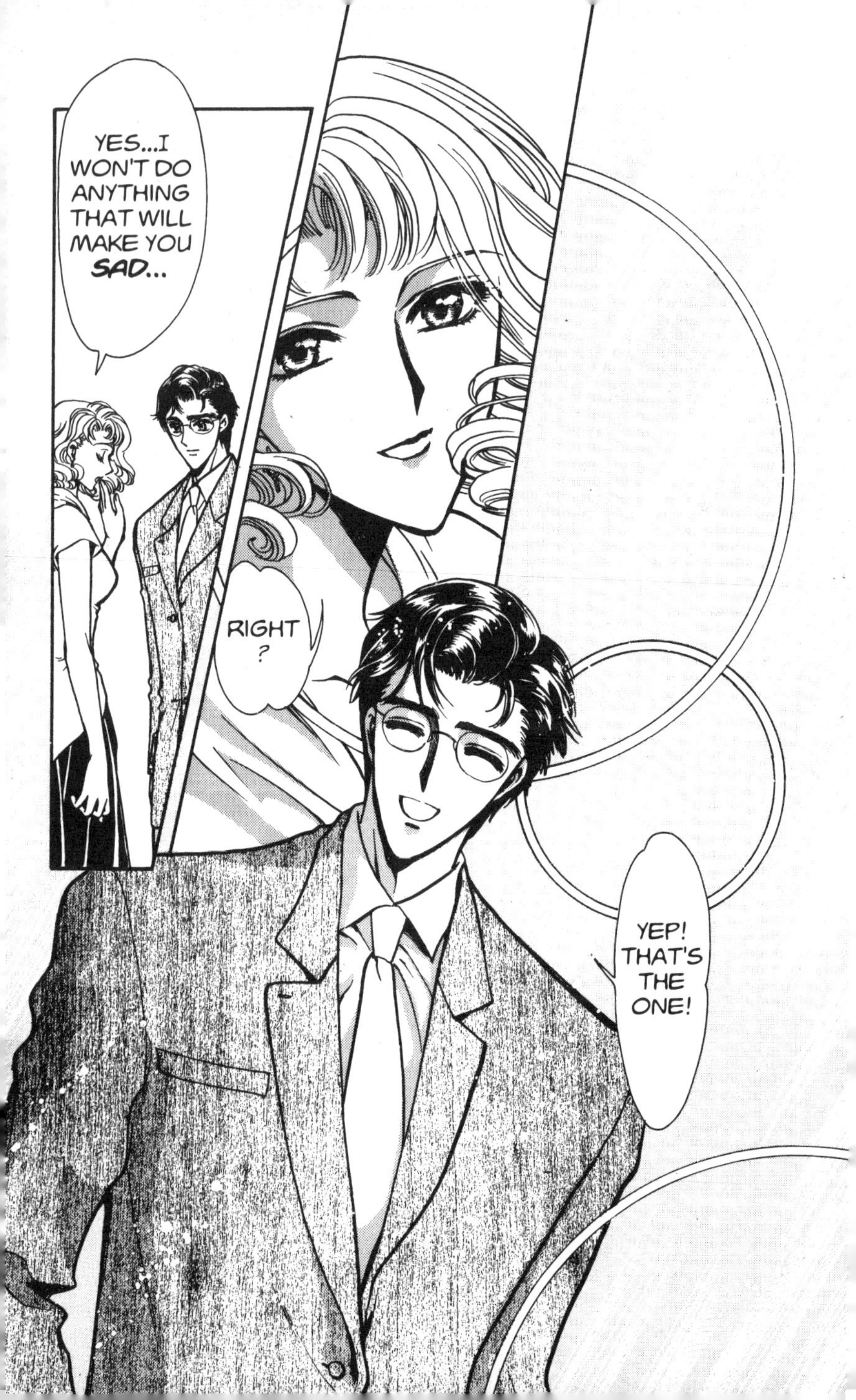
YES...I WON'T DO ANYTHING THAT WILL MAKE YOU **SAD**...
RIGHT?
YEP! THAT'S THE ONE!

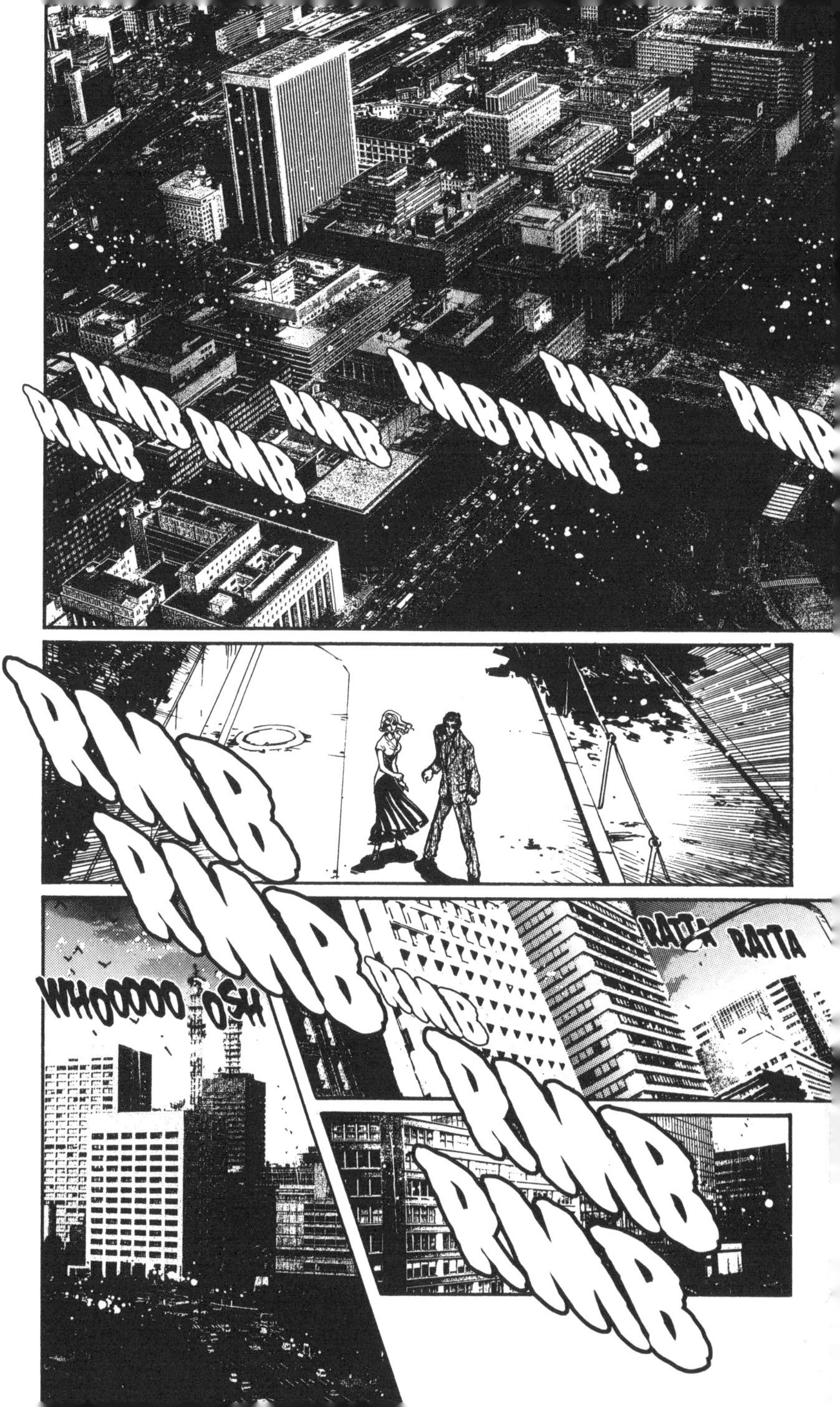
RMB
RMB
RMB
RMB
RMB
RMB
RMB
RMB
RMB
RMB
RATTA RATTA
RMB
WHOOOOO OSH
RMB
RMB

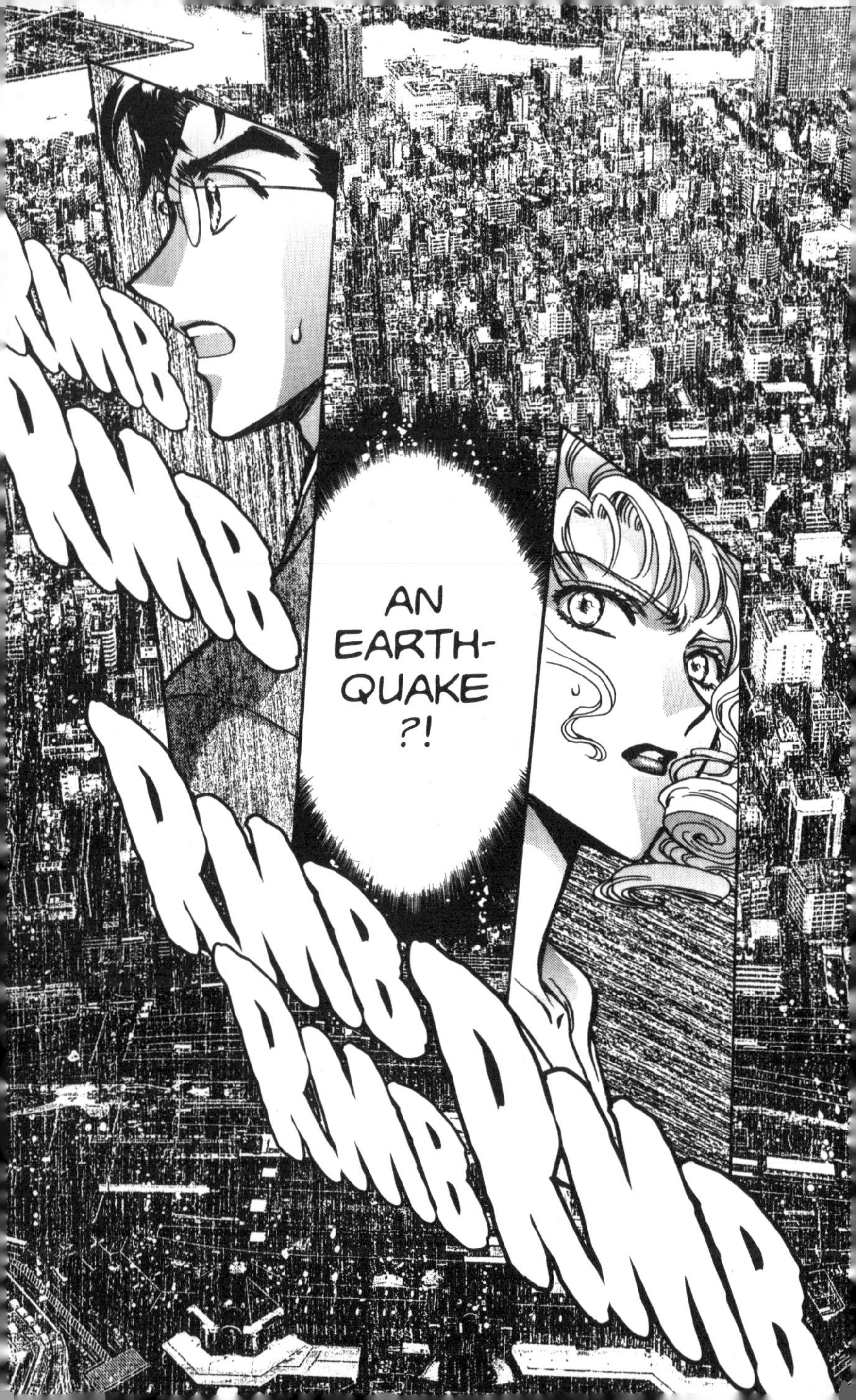
AN EARTH-QUAKE ?!

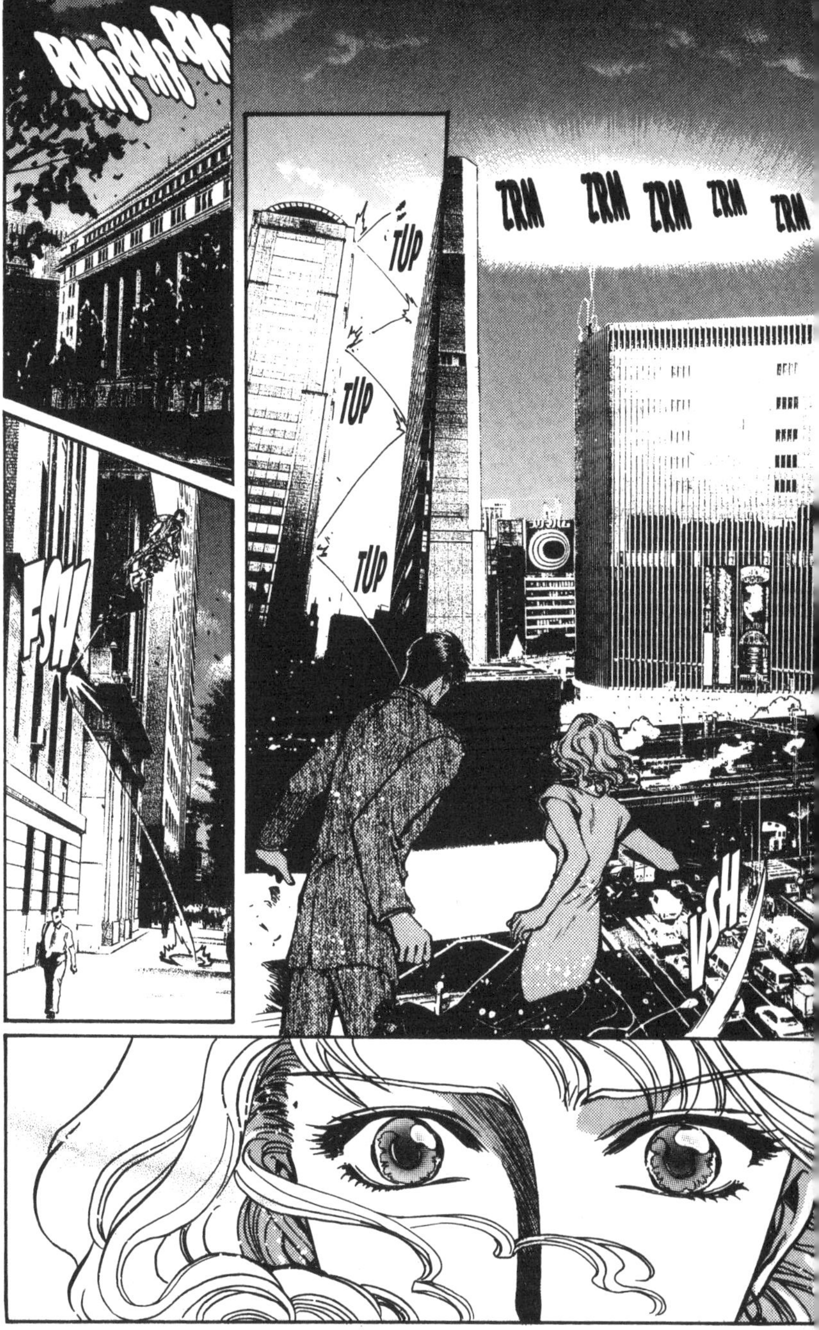
ZRM ZRM ZRM ZRM ZRM
TUP
TUP
TUP
VSH
FSH

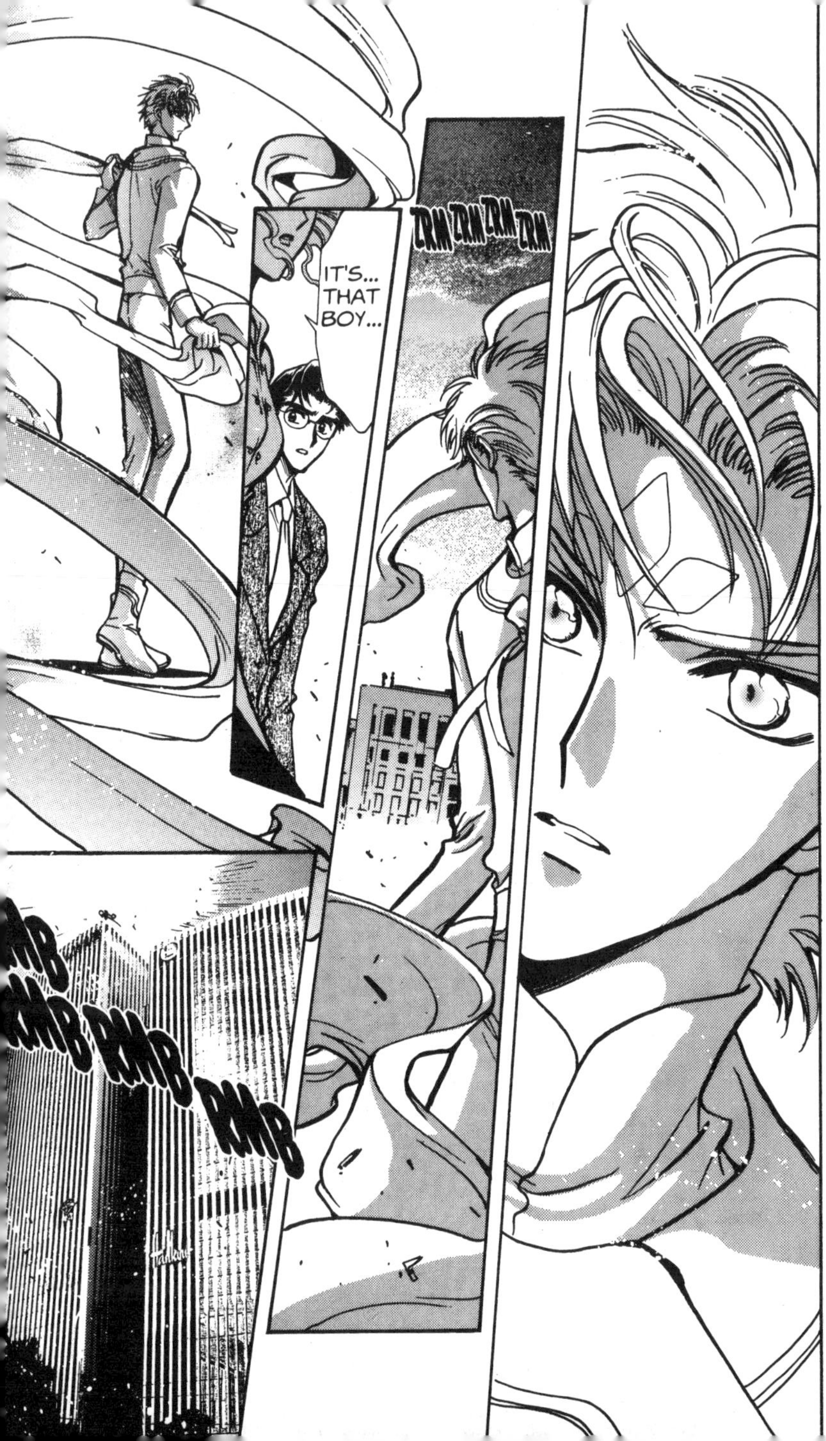
ZRM ZRM ZRM ZRM
IT'S... THAT BOY...
RMB RMB RMB RMB RMB

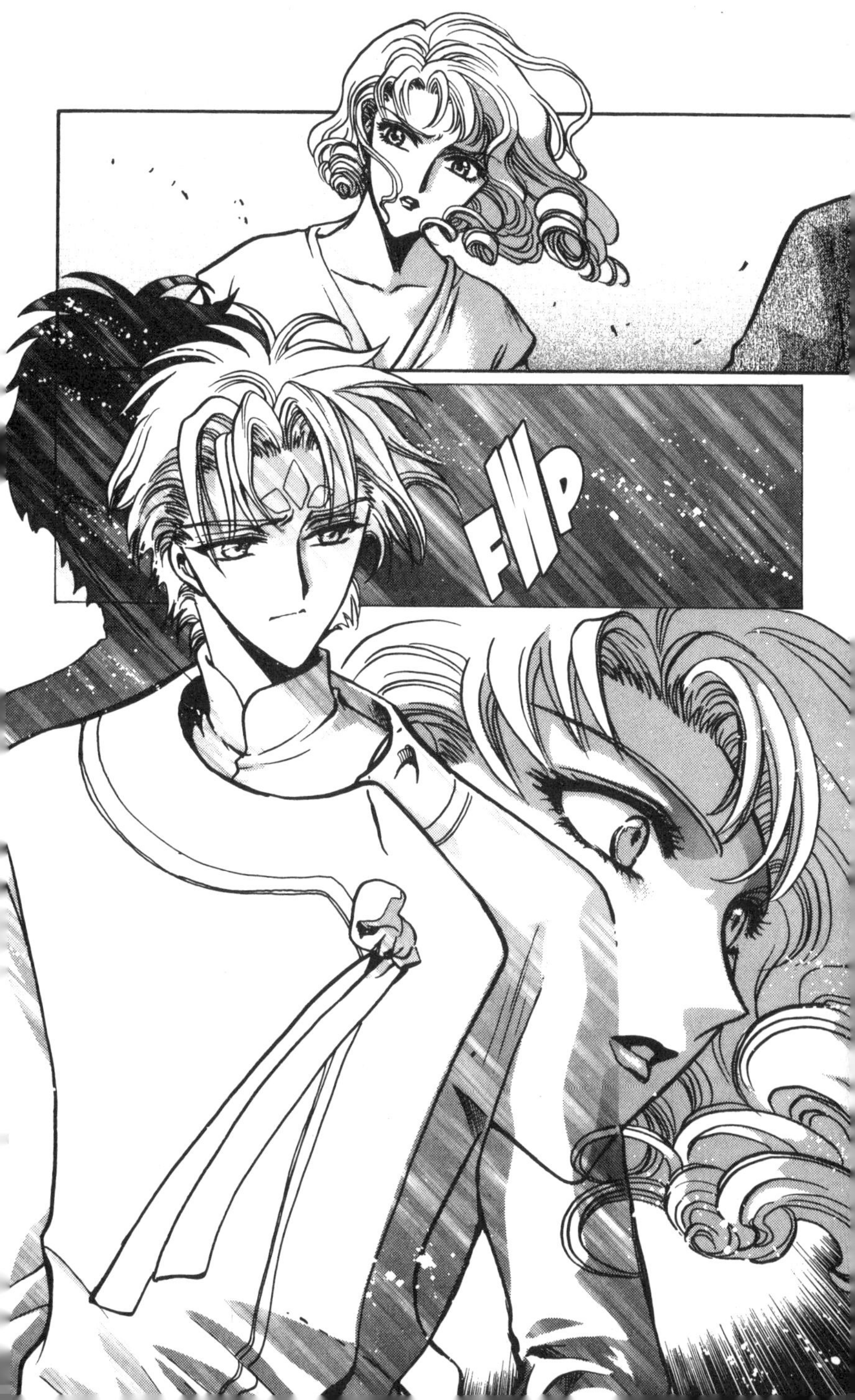
FWIP

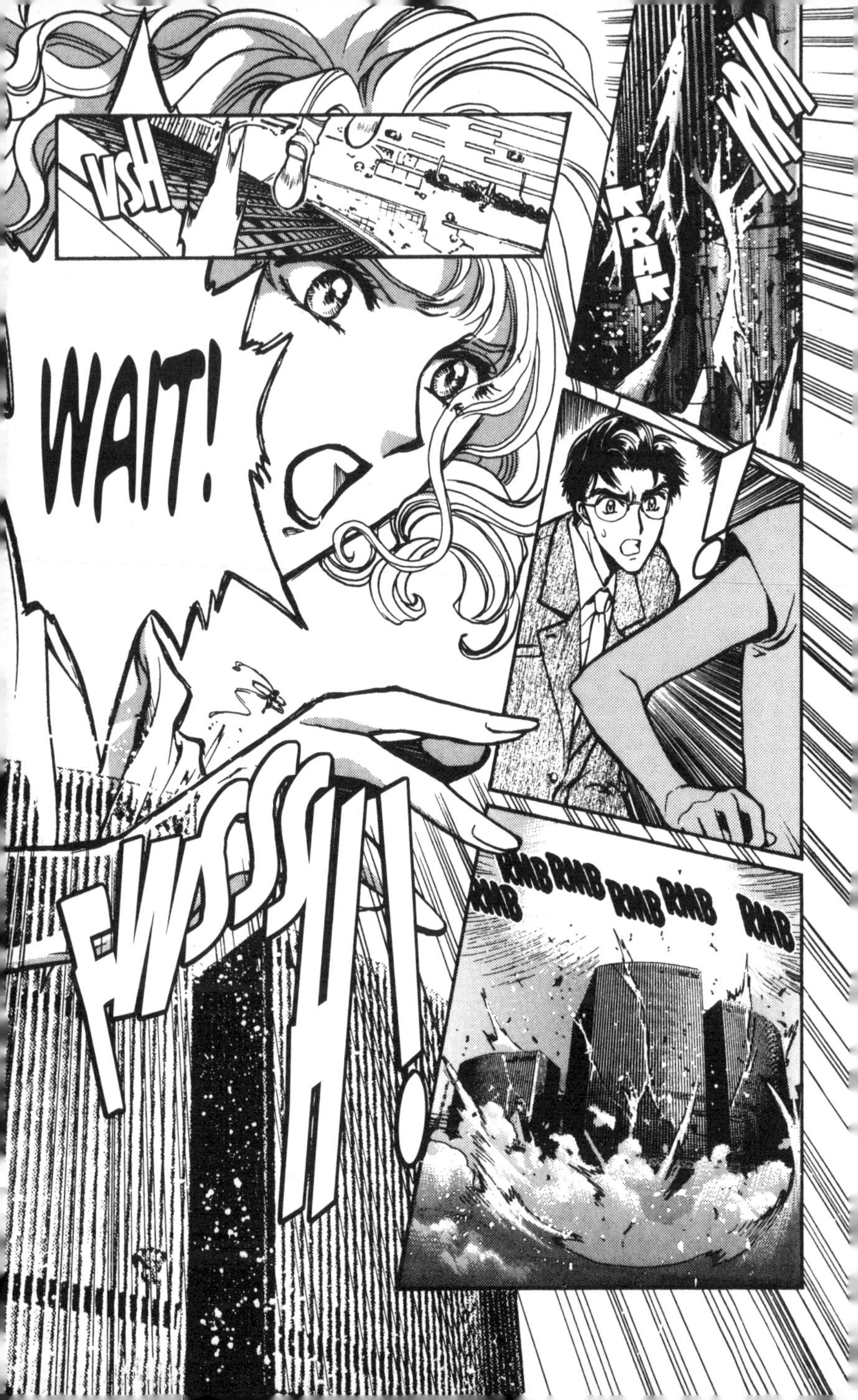
KRAK
VSH
WAIT!
FWSSH!!
RMB RMB RMB RMB RMB RMB RMB

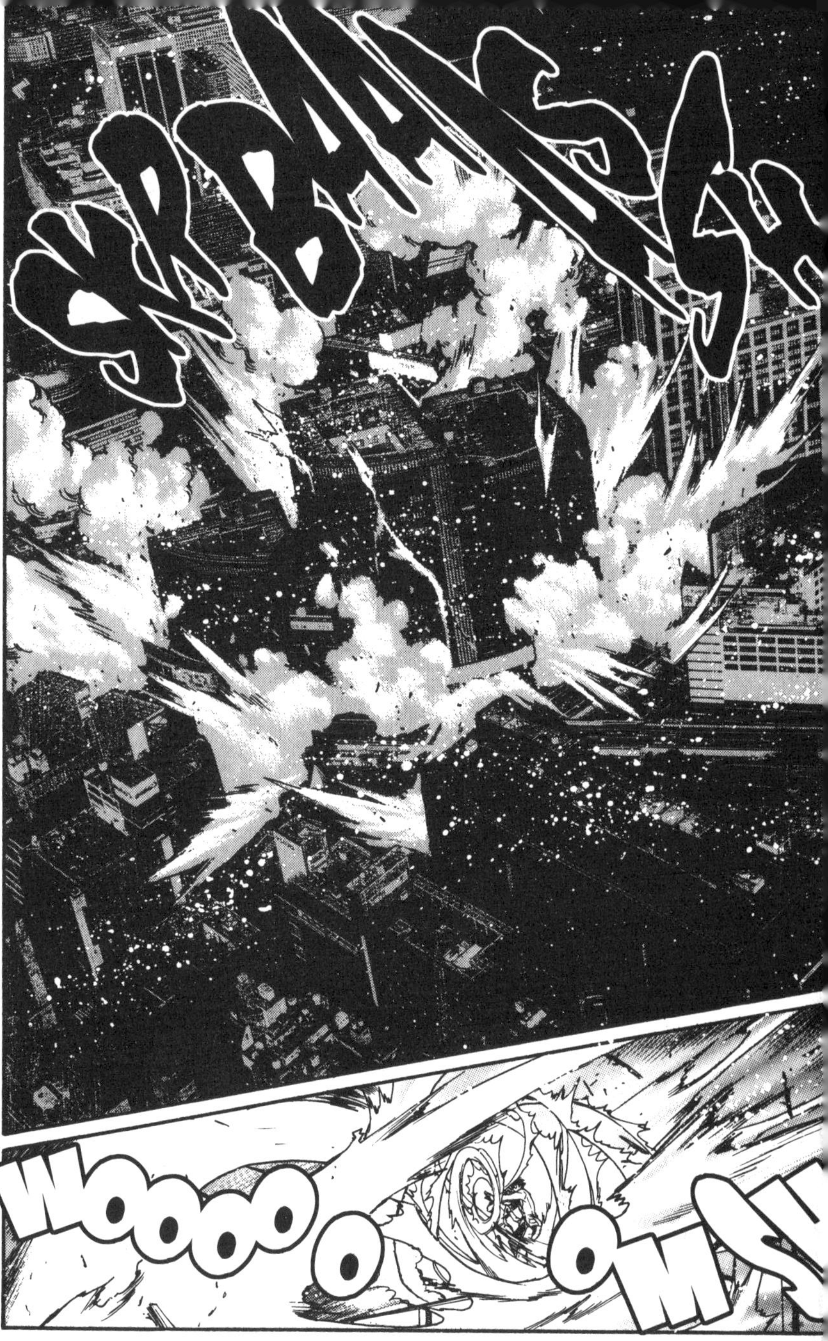

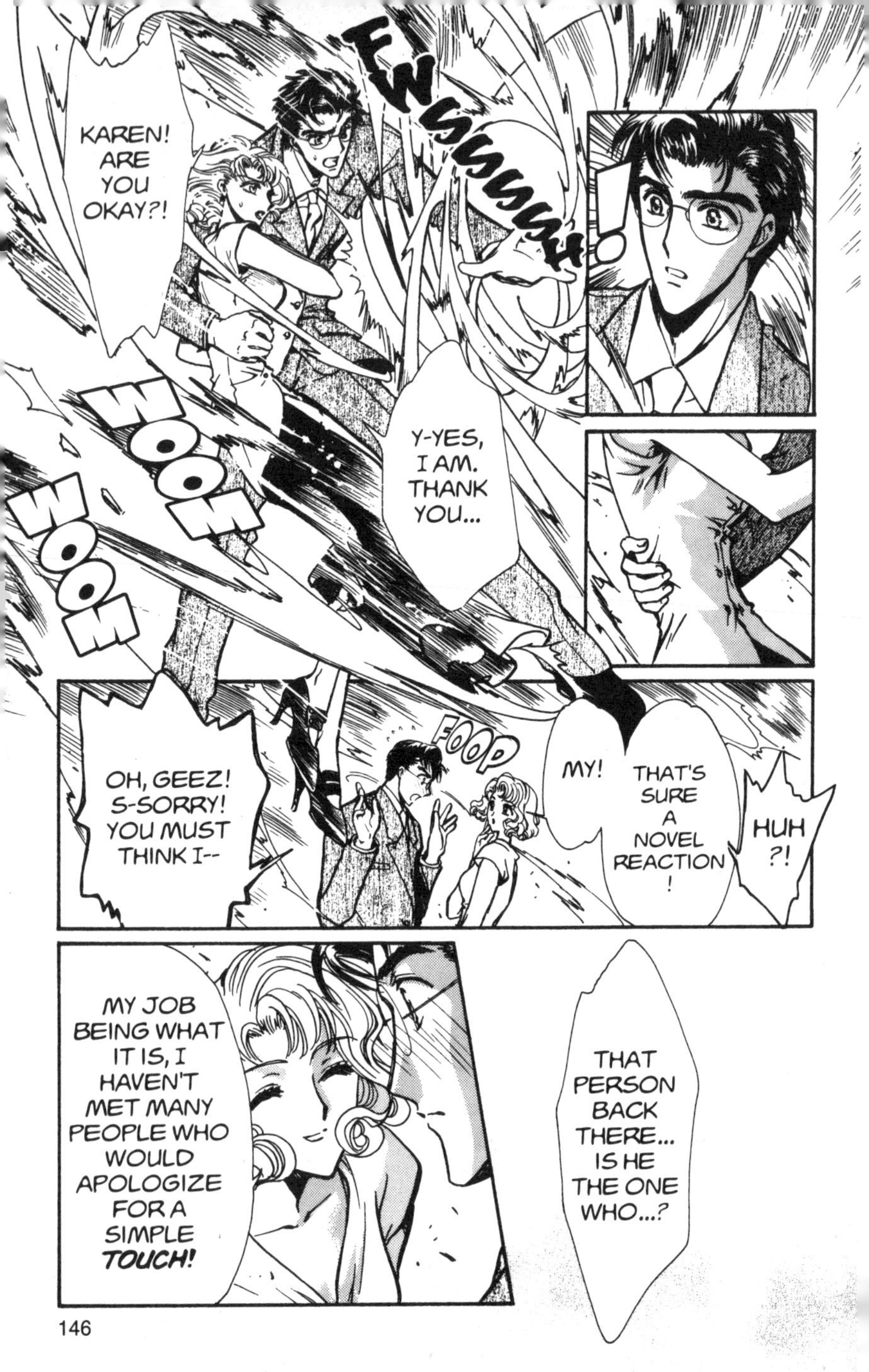
!
FWSSSSSH
KAREN! ARE YOU OKAY?!
WOOM WOOM
Y-YES, I AM. THANK YOU...
HUH?!
MY!
THAT'S SURE A NOVEL REACTION!
FOOP
OH, GEEZ! S-SORRY! YOU MUST THINK I--
THAT PERSON BACK THERE... IS HE THE ONE WHO...?
MY JOB BEING WHAT IT IS, I HAVEN'T MET MANY PEOPLE WHO WOULD APOLOGIZE FOR A SIMPLE TOUCH!

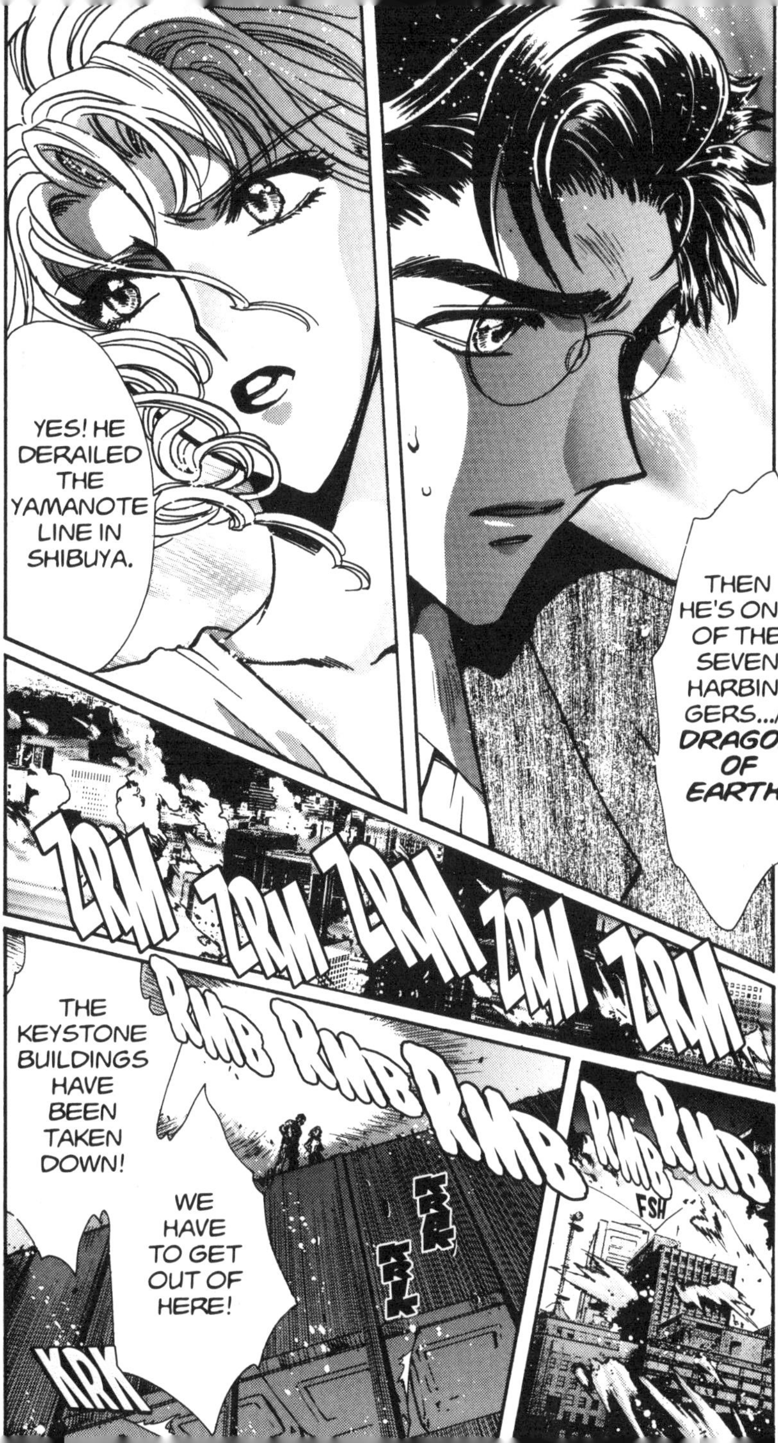
YES! HE DERAILED THE YAMANOTE LINE IN SHIBUYA.
THEN HE'S ONE OF THE SEVEN HARBINGERS...A *DRAGON OF EARTH.*
ZRRM ZRRM ZRRM ZRRM ZRRM
RMMB RMMB RMMB RMMB RMMB
THE KEYSTONE BUILDINGS HAVE BEEN TAKEN DOWN!
WE HAVE TO GET OUT OF HERE!
KRK KRK
KRK
FSH

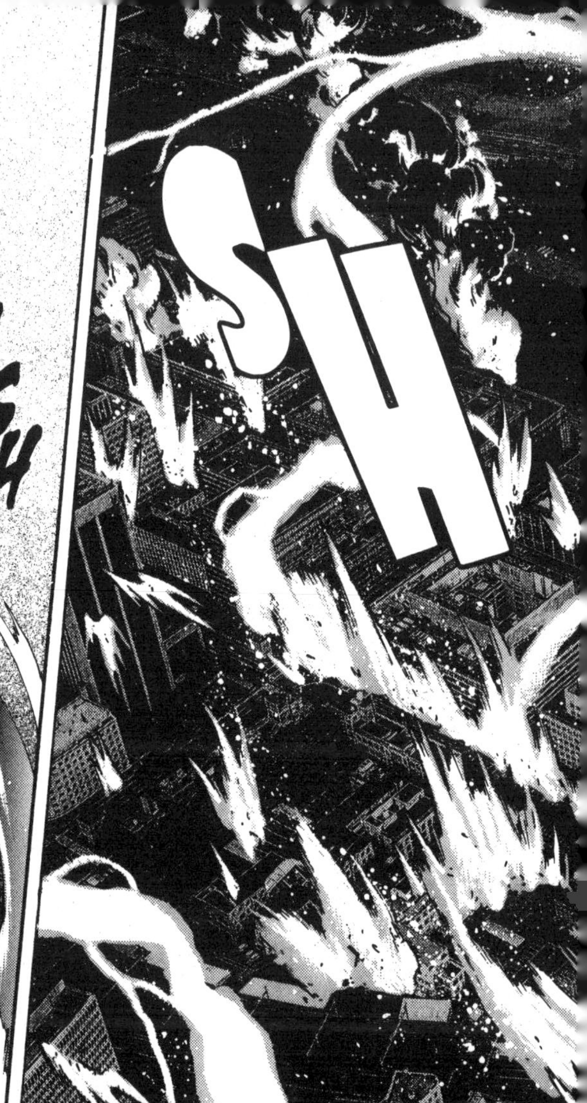
SHH
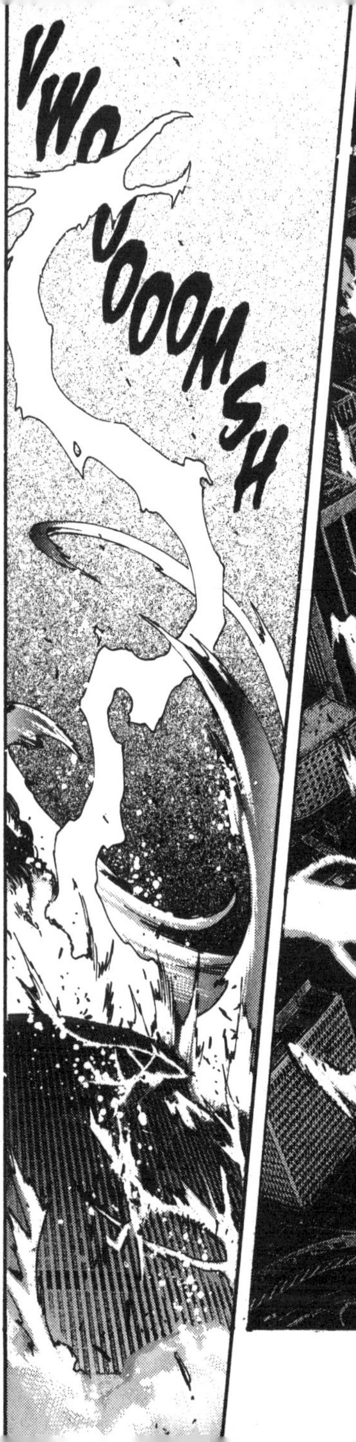
VWOOOOOMSH

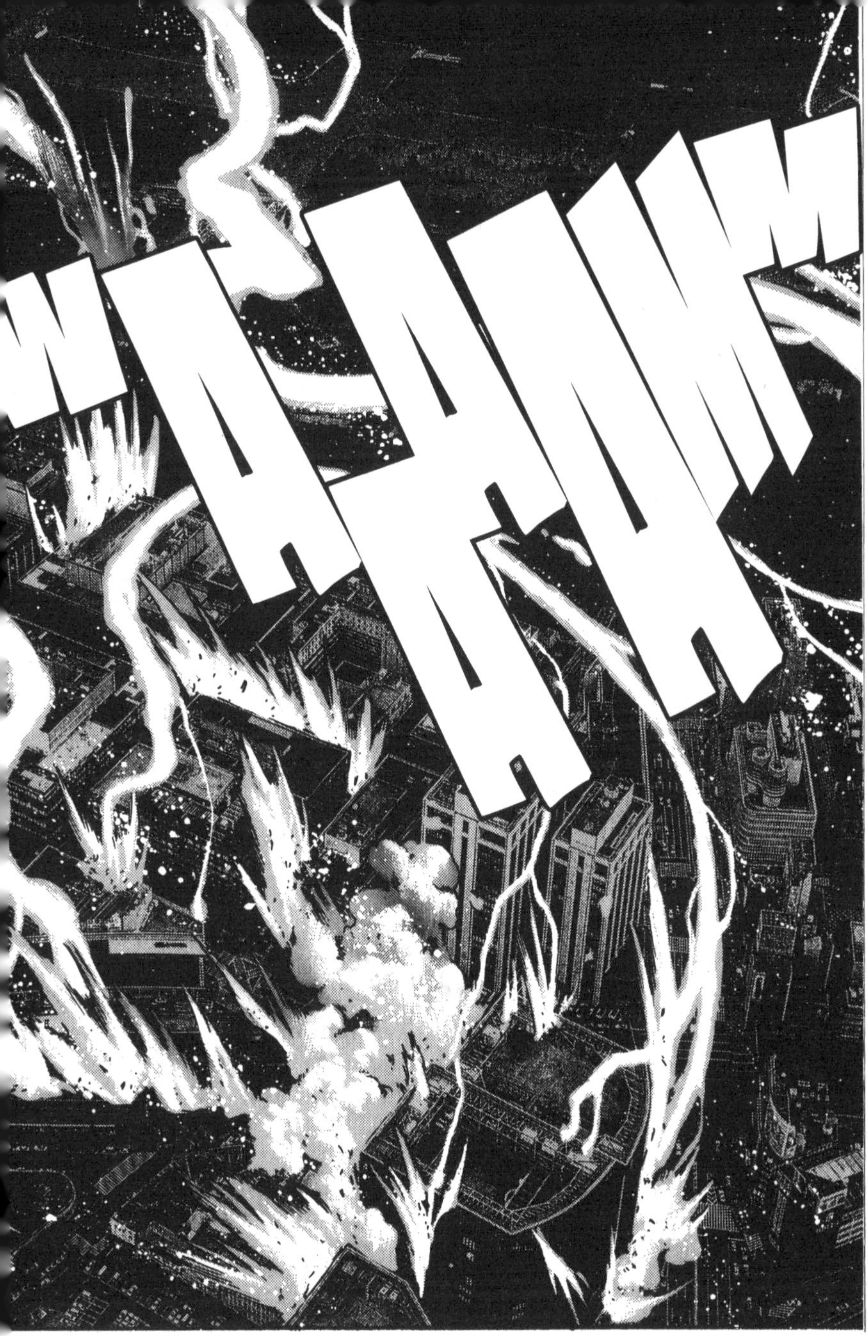

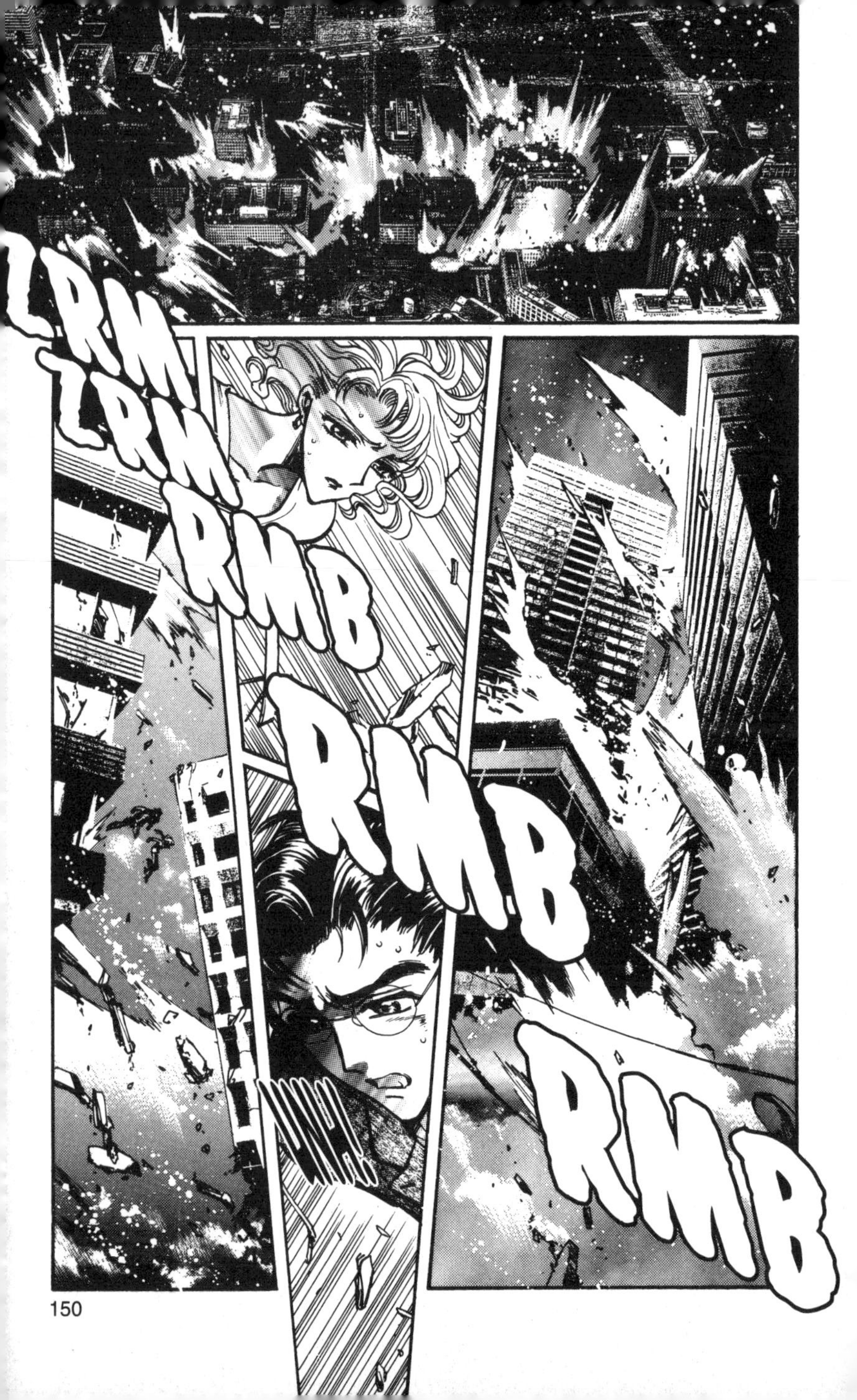
ZRM
ZRM
RMB
RMB
RMB

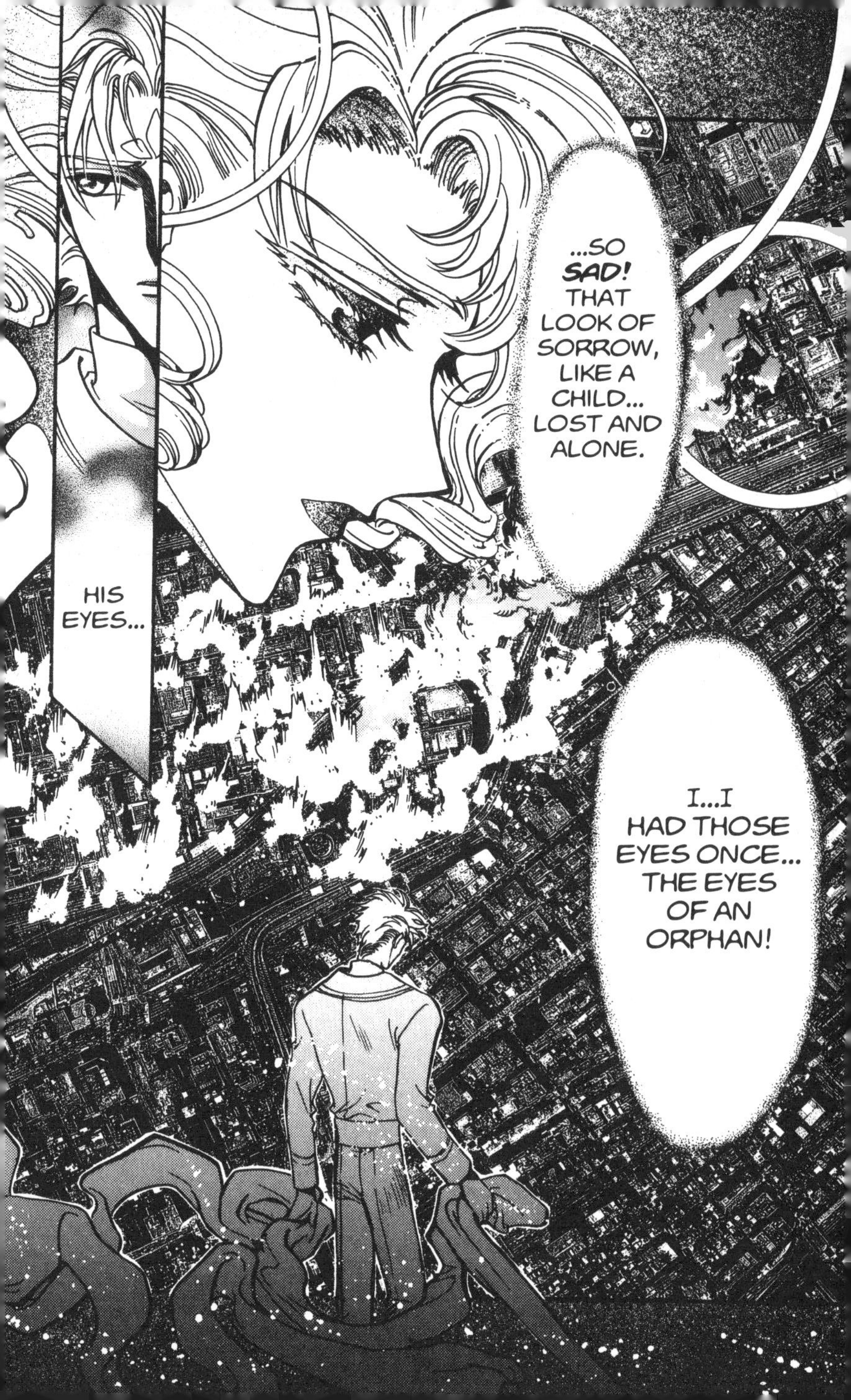

...SO SAD! THAT LOOK OF SORROW, LIKE A CHILD... LOST AND ALONE.
HIS EYES...
I...I HAD THOSE EYES ONCE... THE EYES OF AN ORPHAN!

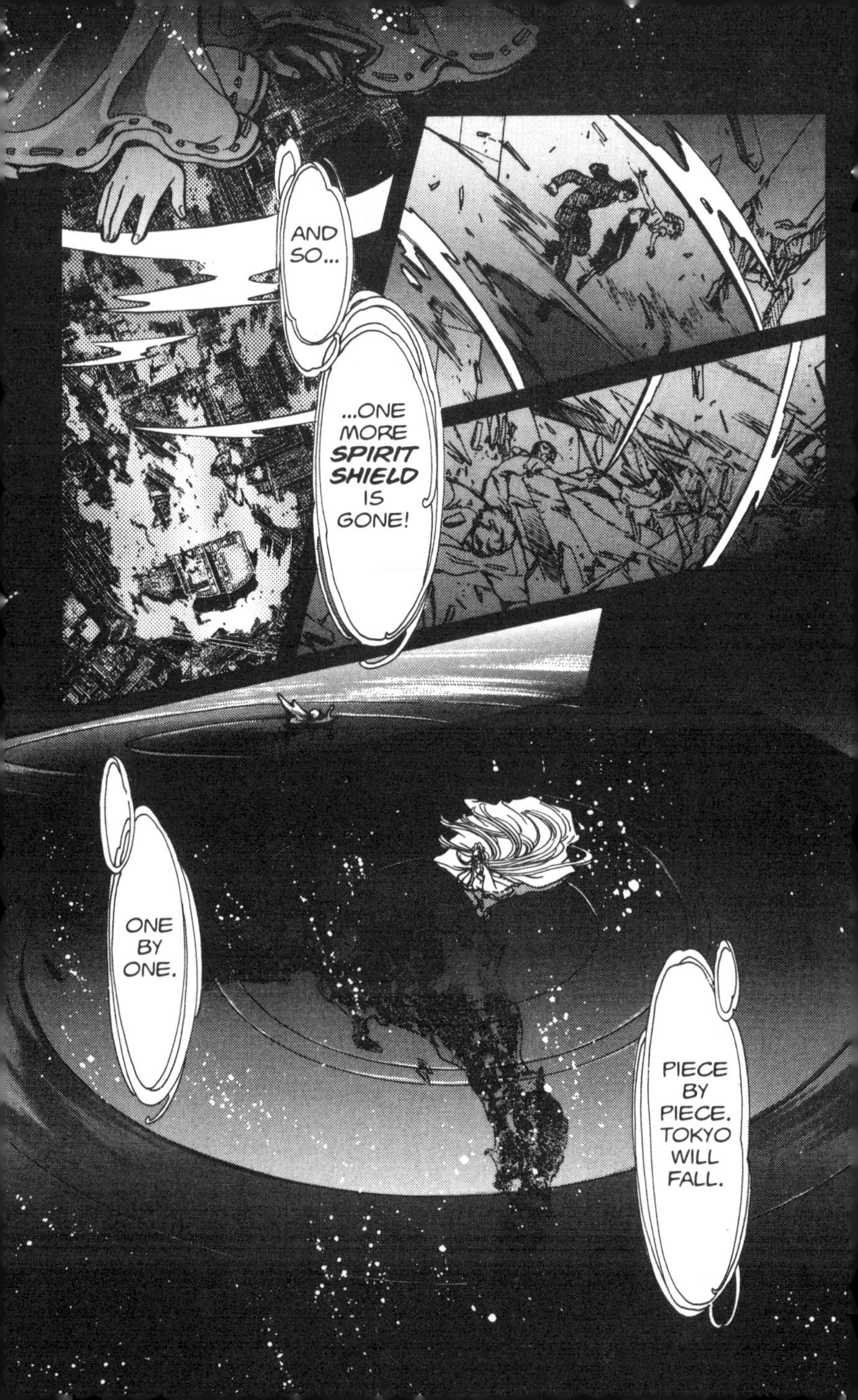
AND SO...
...ONE MORE SPIRIT SHIELD IS GONE!
PIECE BY PIECE. TOKYO WILL FALL.
ONE BY ONE.

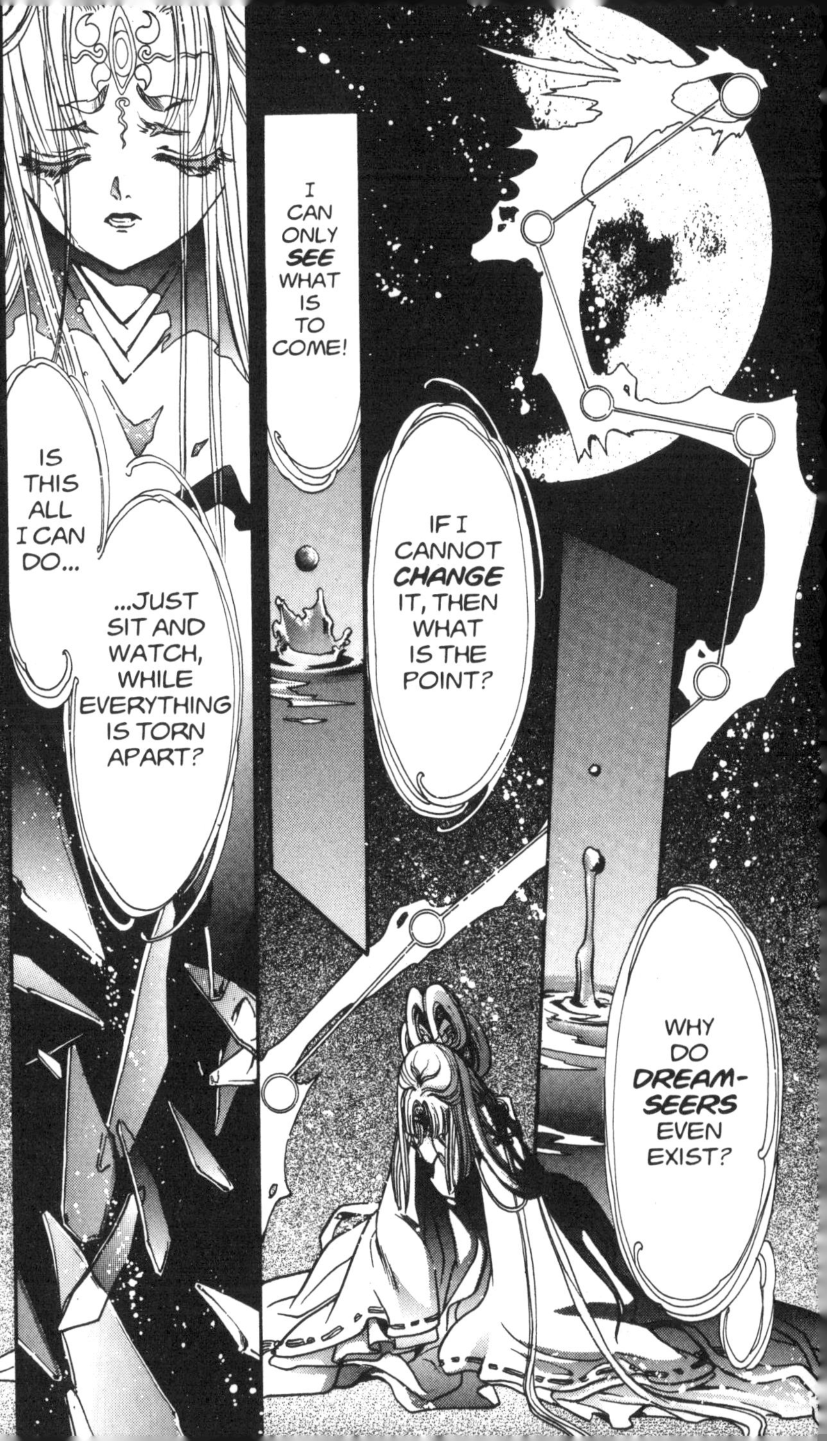

I CAN ONLY SEE WHAT IS TO COME!
IS THIS ALL I CAN DO...
...JUST SIT AND WATCH, WHILE EVERYTHING IS TORN APART?
IF I CANNOT CHANGE IT, THEN WHAT IS THE POINT?
WHY DO DREAM-SEERS EVEN EXIST?

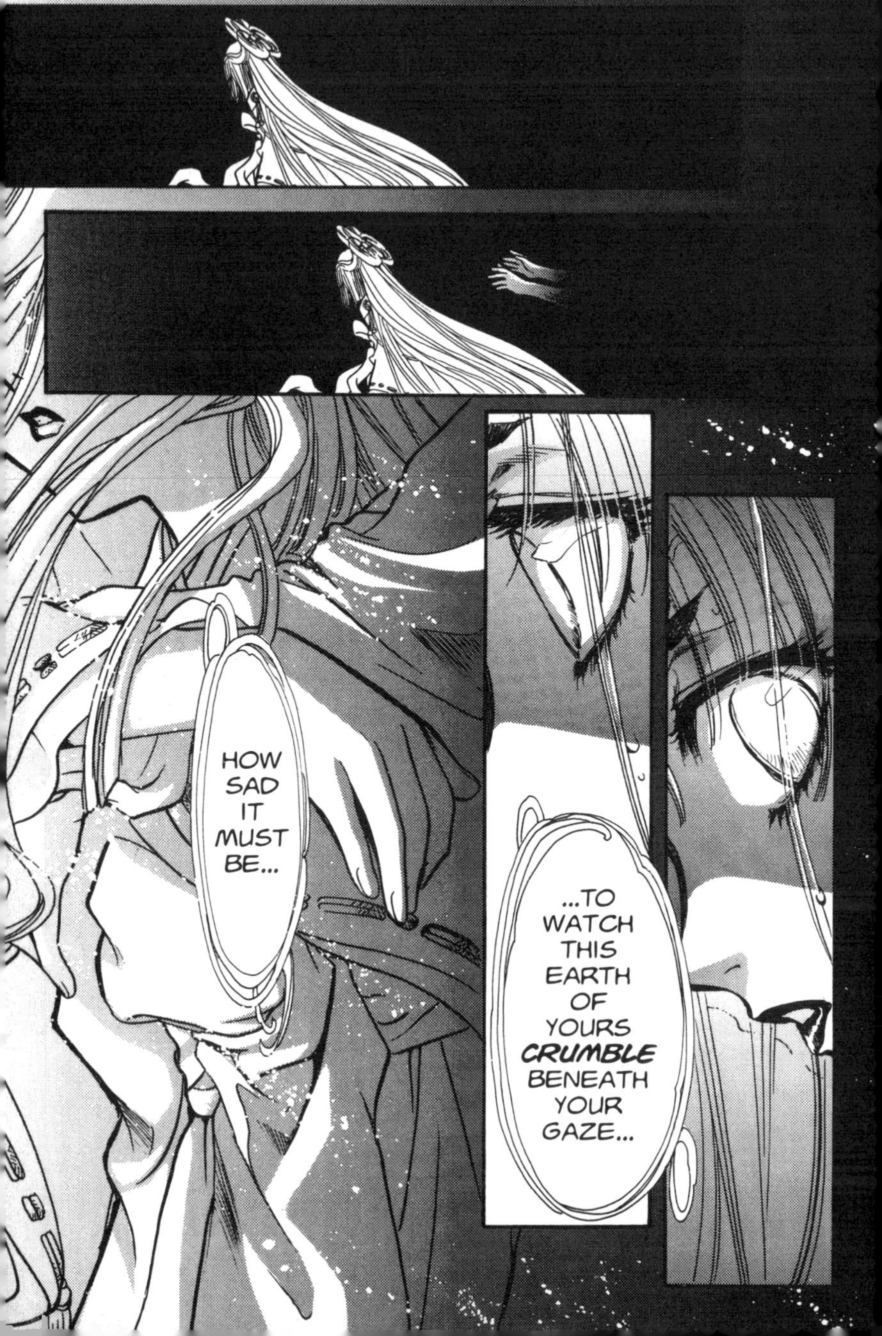
HOW SAD IT MUST BE...
...TO WATCH THIS EARTH OF YOURS CRUMBLE BENEATH YOUR GAZE...

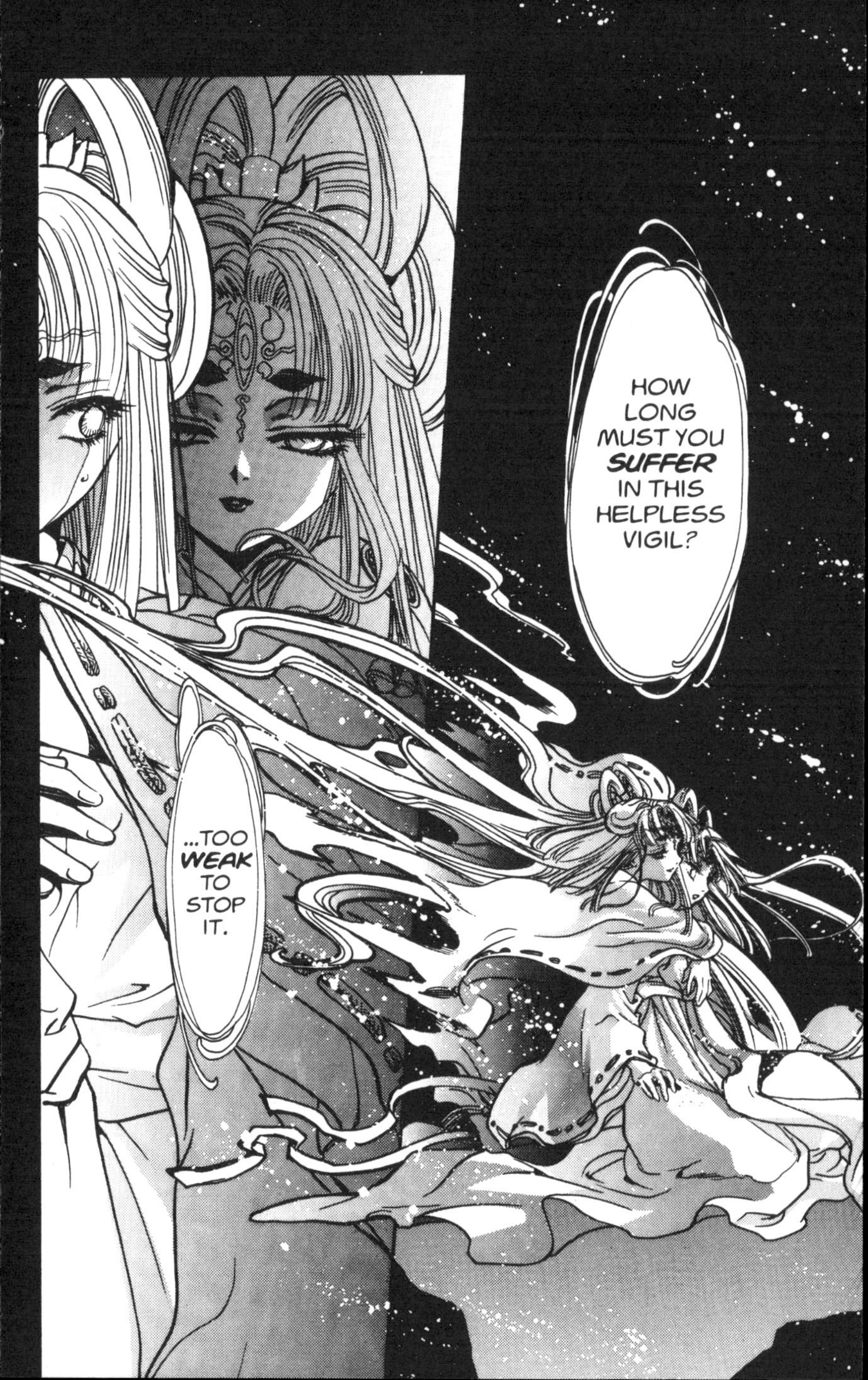
HOW LONG MUST YOU SUFFER IN THIS HELPLESS VIGIL?
...TOO WEAK TO STOP IT.

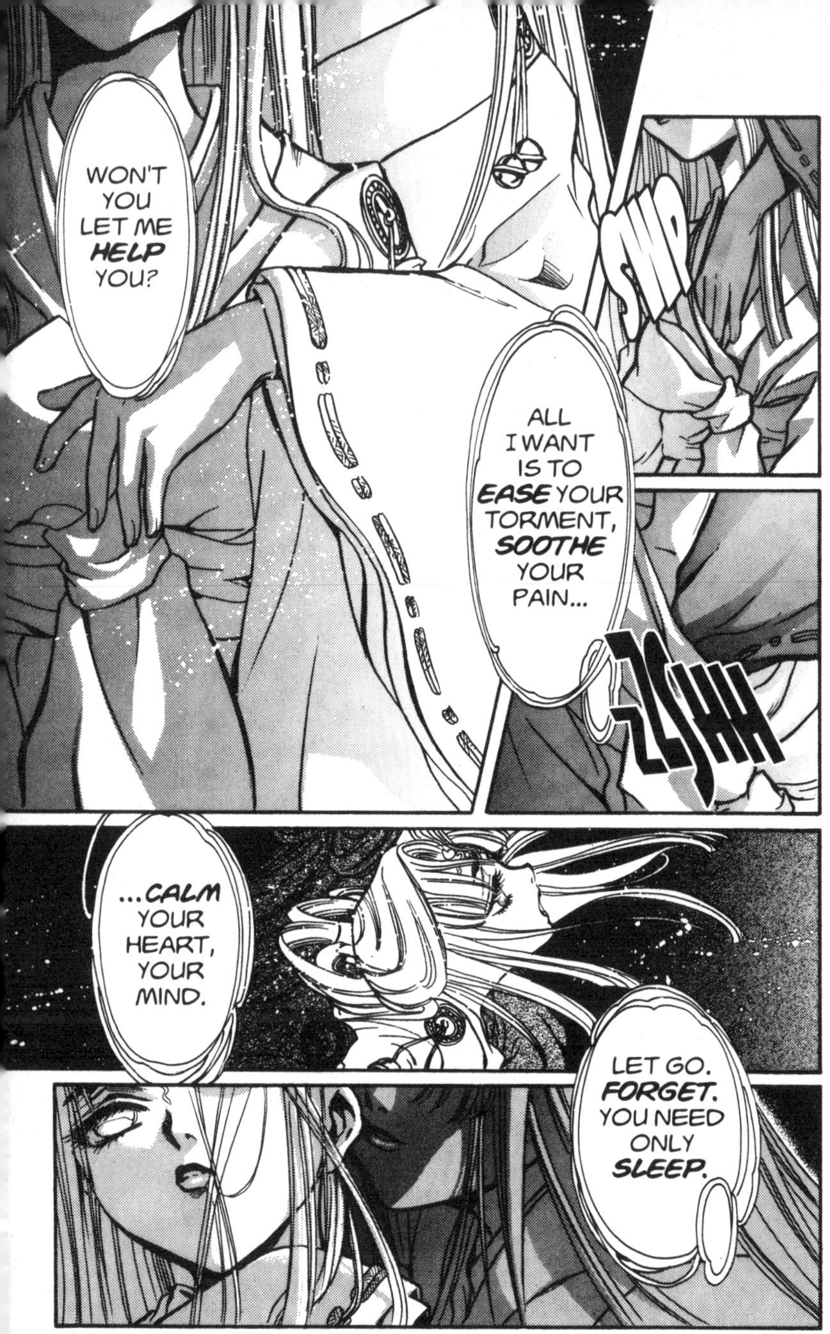
WON'T YOU LET ME **HELP** YOU?
ALL I WANT IS TO **EASE** YOUR TORMENT, **SOOTHE** YOUR PAIN...
...**CALM** YOUR HEART, YOUR MIND.
LET GO. **FORGET**. YOU NEED ONLY **SLEEP**.

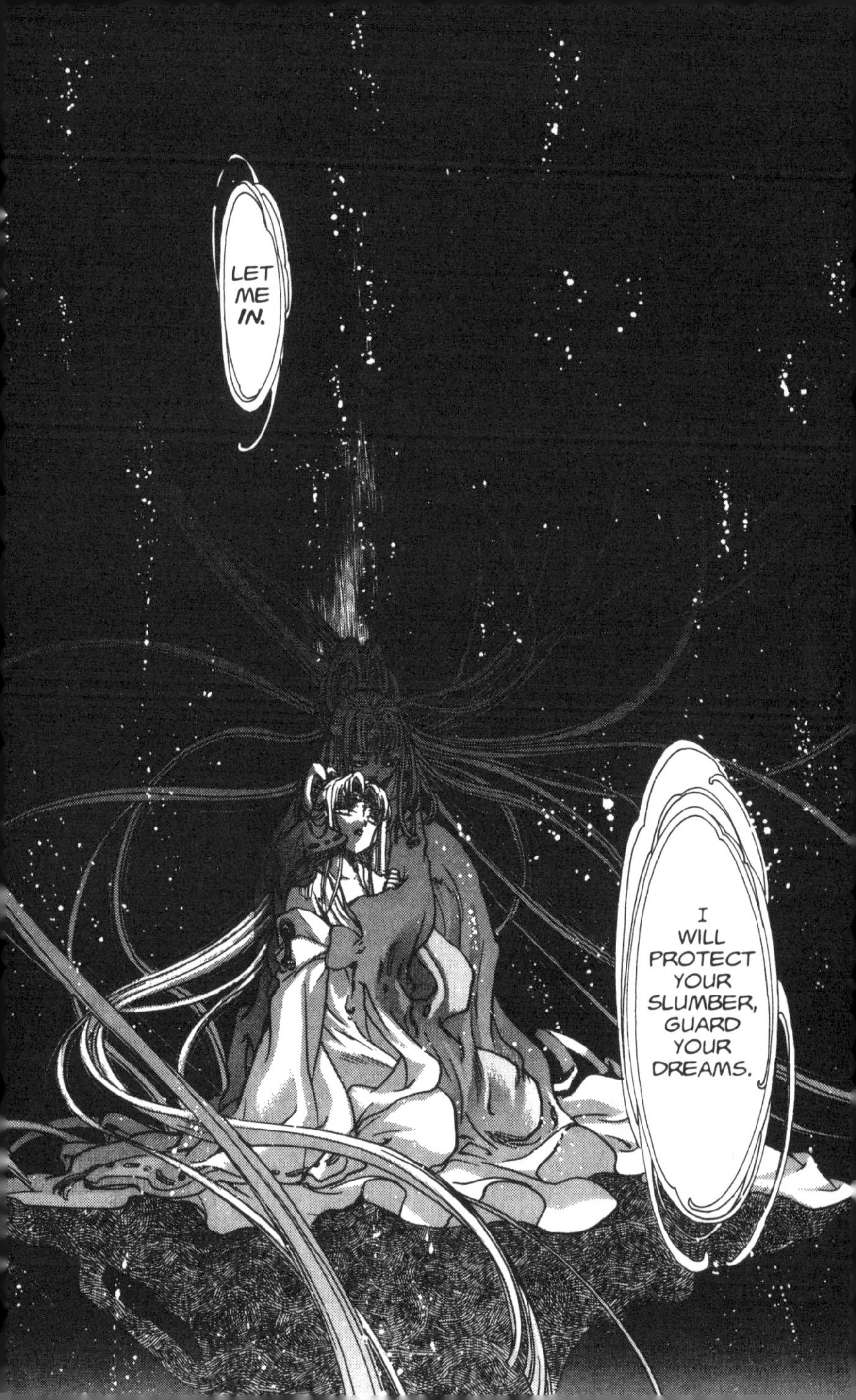
LET ME IN.
I WILL PROTECT YOUR SLUMBER, GUARD YOUR DREAMS.

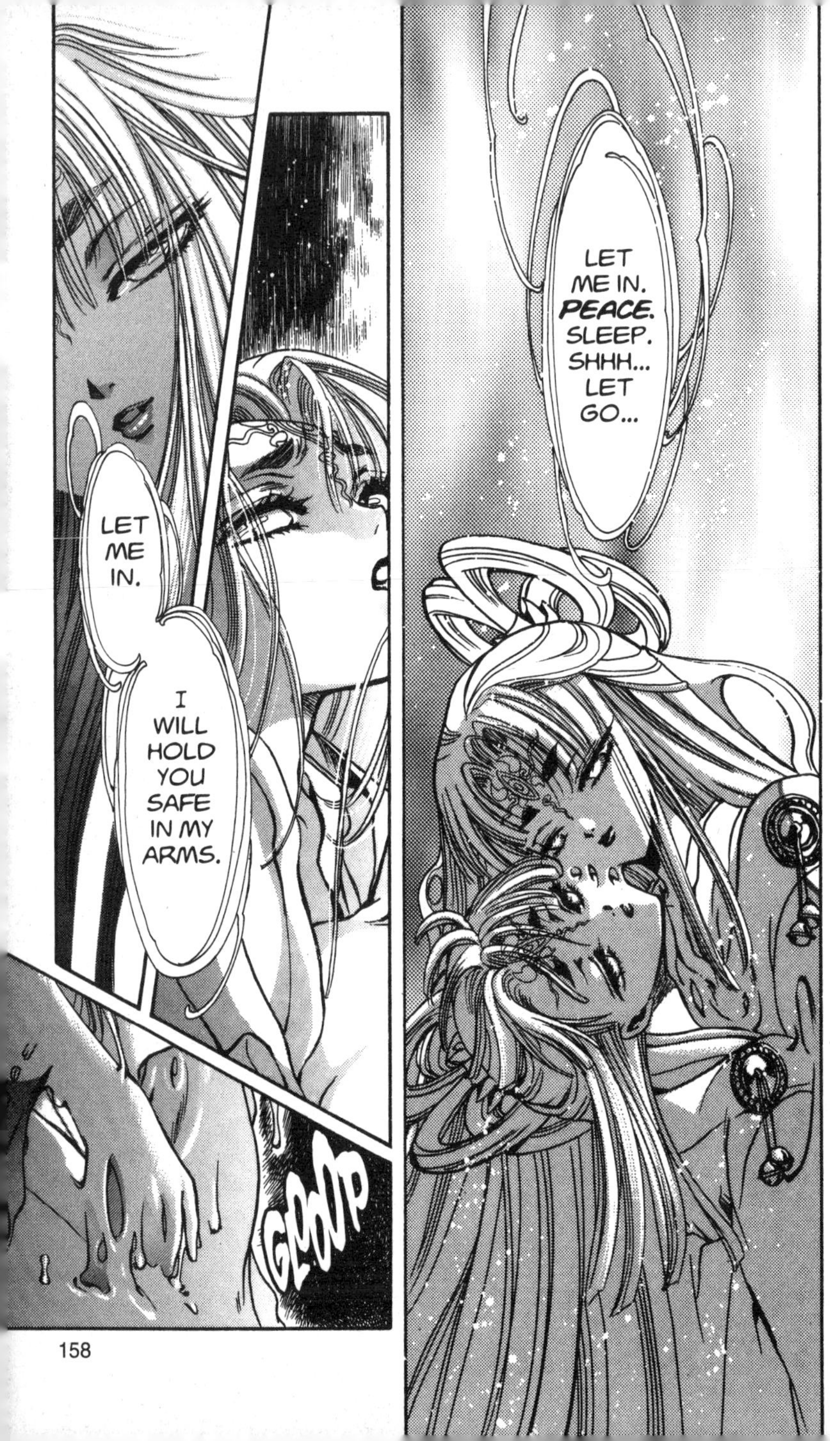
LET ME IN. **PEACE.** SLEEP. SHHH... LET GO...
LET ME IN.
I WILL HOLD YOU SAFE IN MY ARMS.
GLOOP

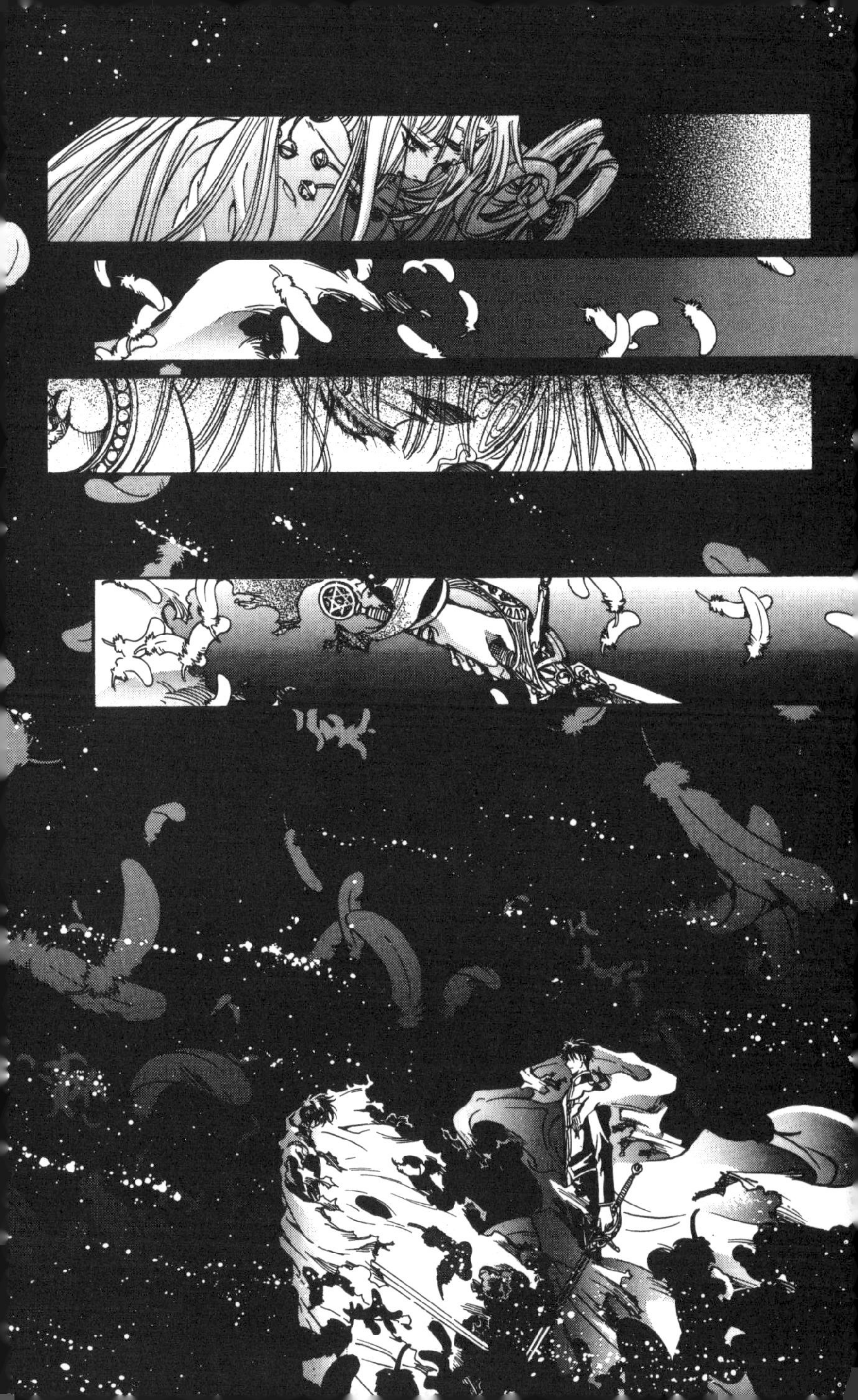

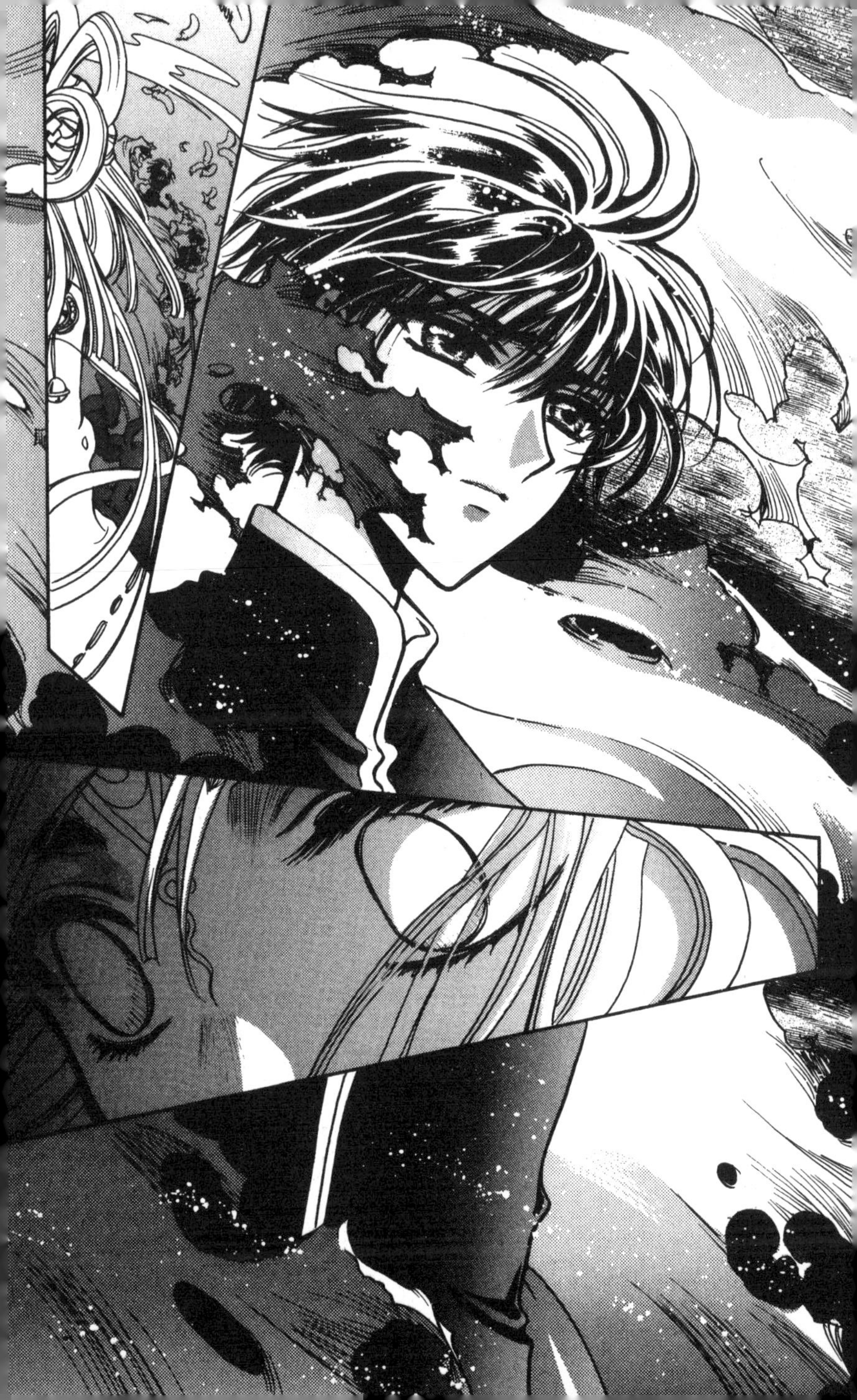

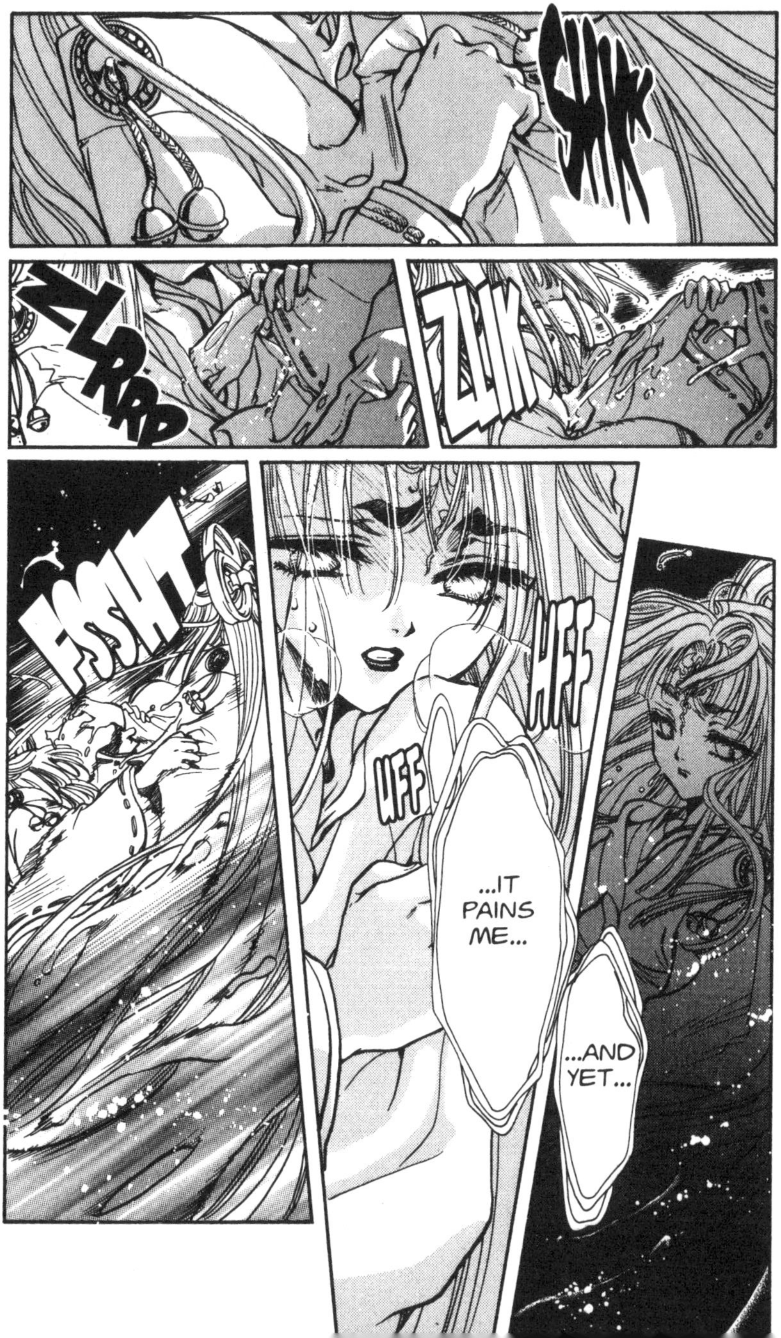
SHINK
ZUIK
ZLRRP
HFF
HFF
...IT PAINS ME...
...AND YET...
FSSHT

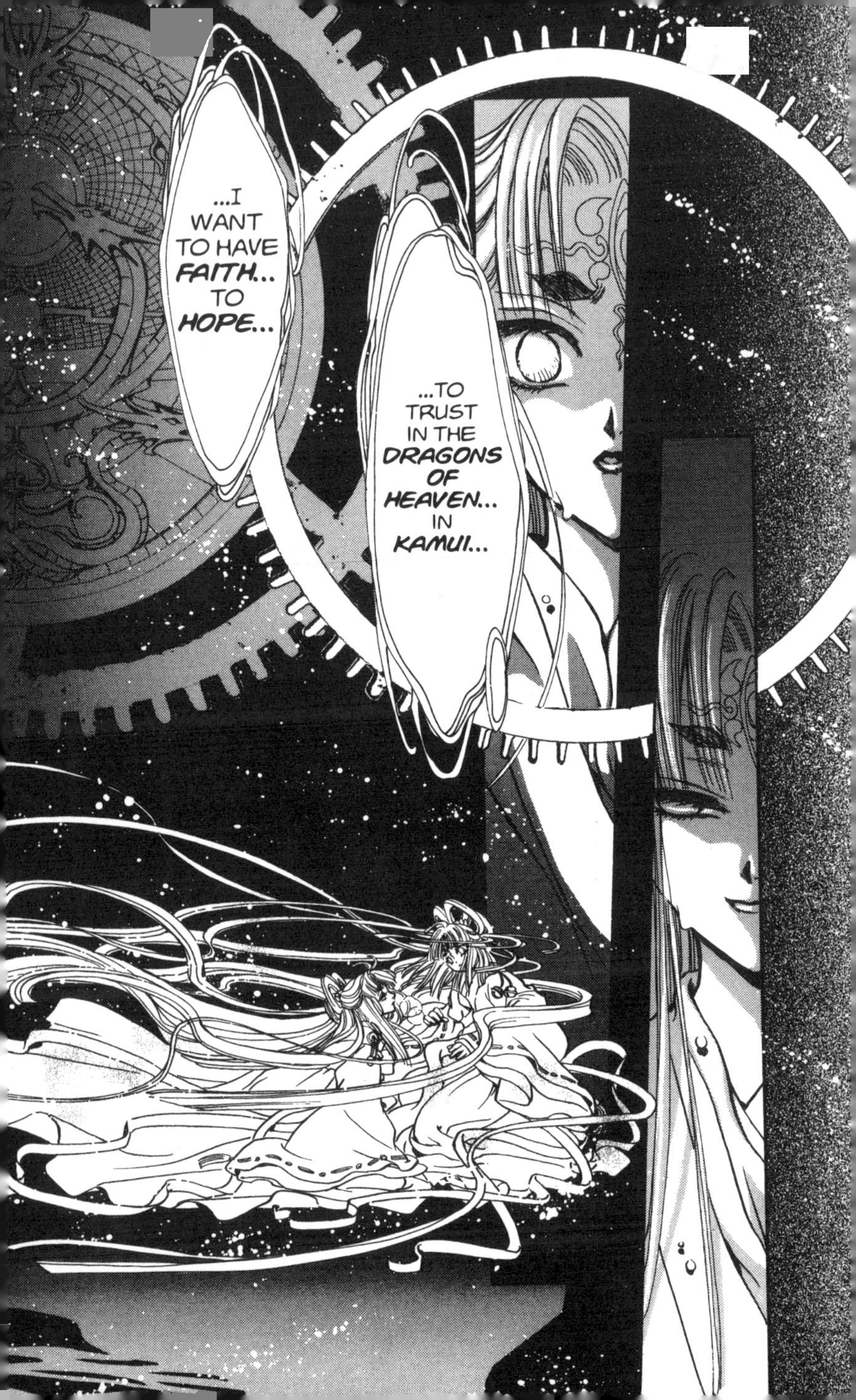
...TO TRUST IN THE DRAGONS OF HEAVEN... IN KAMUI...
...I WANT TO HAVE FAITH... TO HOPE...

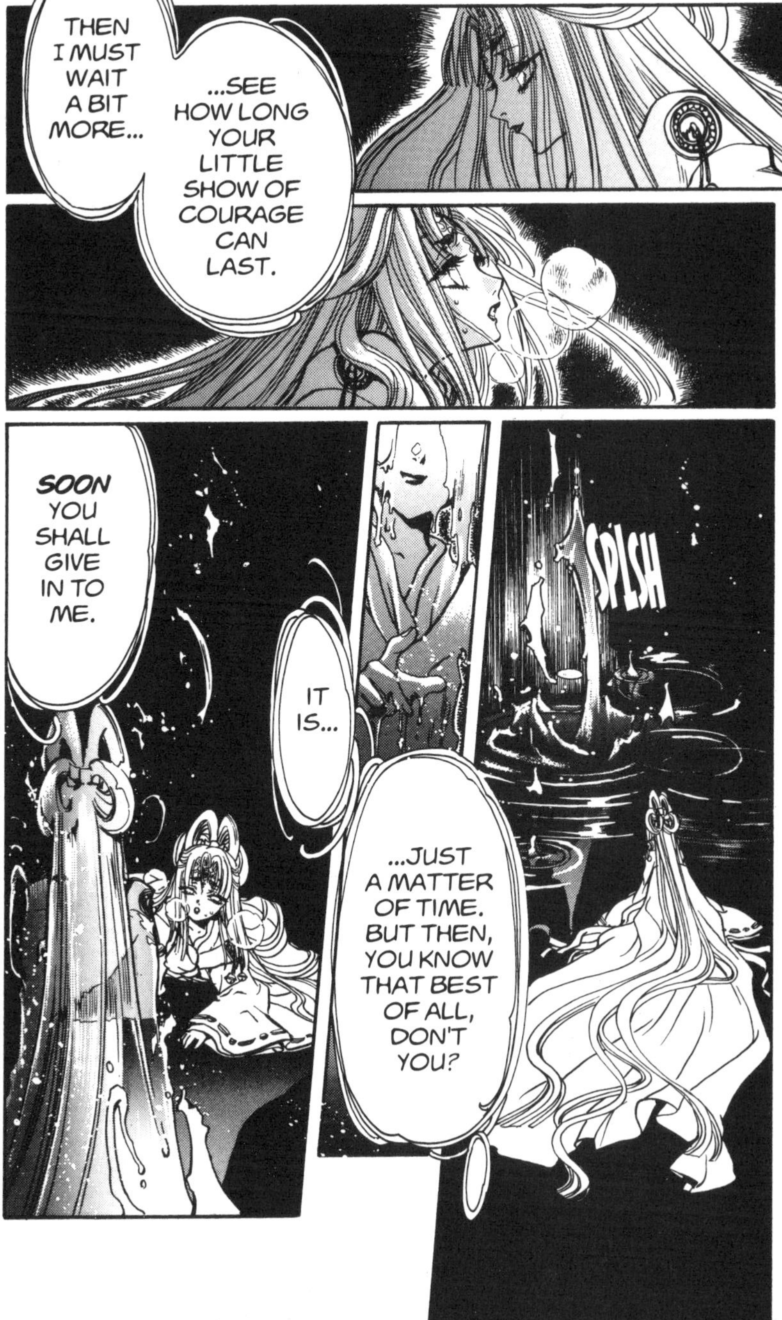
THEN I MUST WAIT A BIT MORE...
...SEE HOW LONG YOUR LITTLE SHOW OF COURAGE CAN LAST.
SPLSH
IT IS...
...JUST A MATTER OF TIME. BUT THEN, YOU KNOW THAT BEST OF ALL, DON'T YOU?
SOON YOU SHALL GIVE IN TO ME.

YES... I...

...I DO.

MY OTHER SELF... I DO NOT HAVE THE STRENGTH TO HOLD HER BACK AGAIN!

NEXT TIME WE MEET...

...I WILL SURELY SURRENDER MYSELF TO HER!

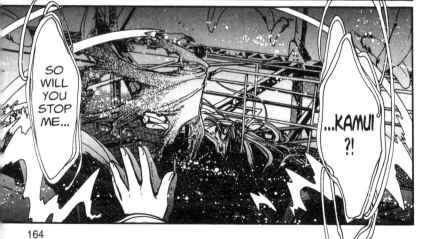

SO WILL YOU STOP ME...

...KAMUI?!

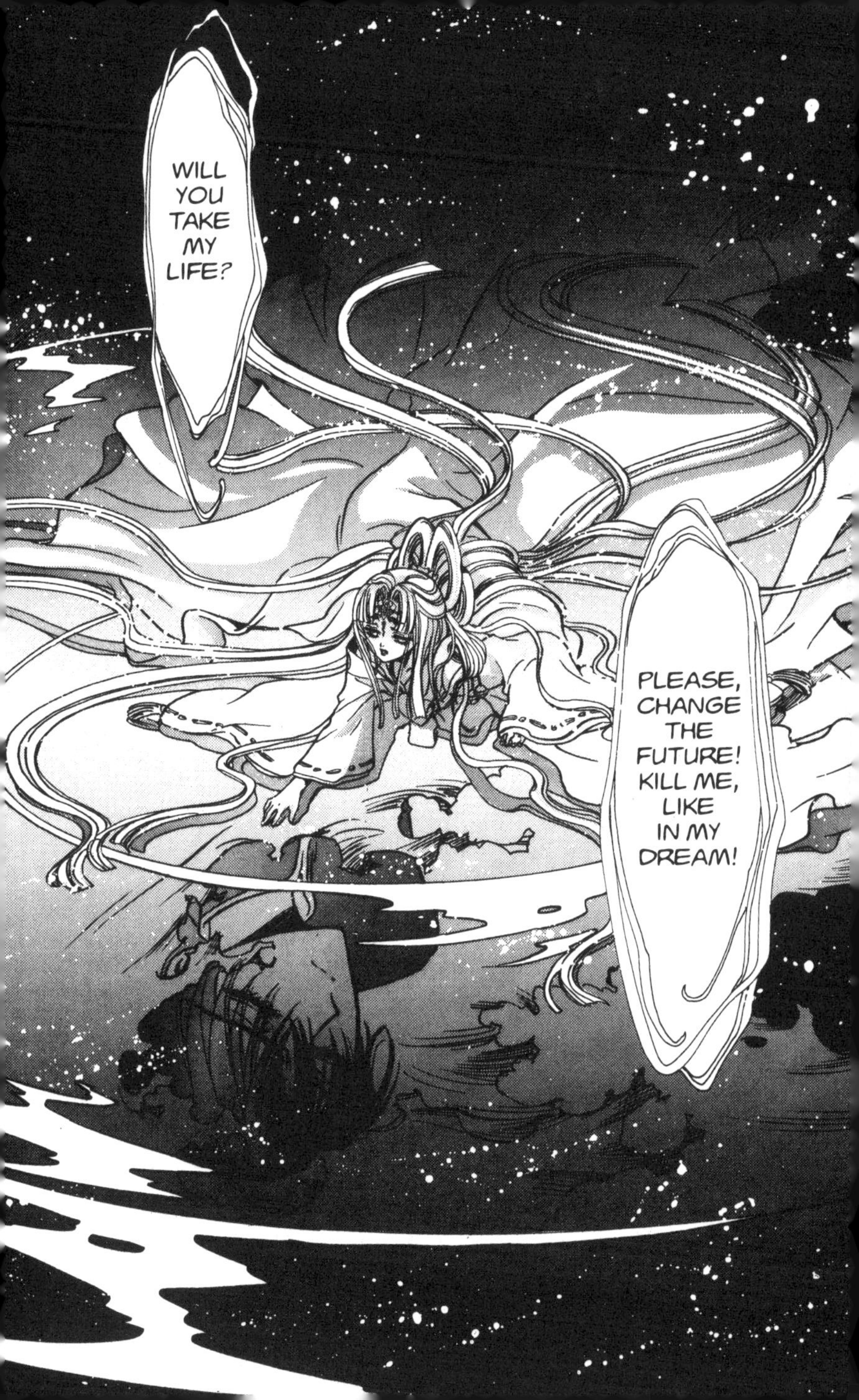
PLEASE, CHANGE THE FUTURE! KILL ME, LIKE IN MY DREAM!
WILL YOU TAKE MY LIFE?

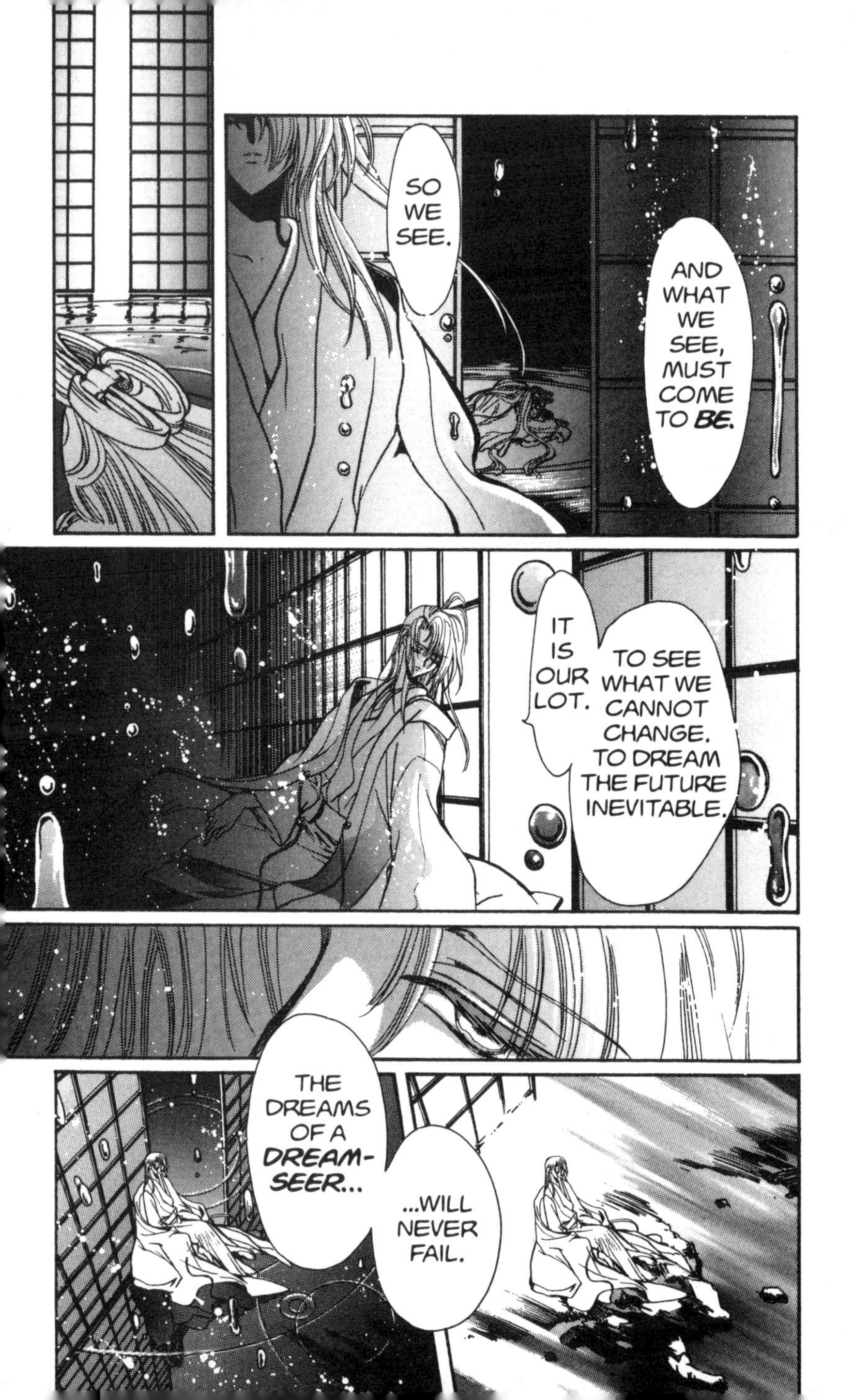
AND WHAT WE SEE, MUST COME TO **BE**.
SO WE SEE.
IT IS OUR LOT.
TO SEE WHAT WE CANNOT CHANGE. TO DREAM THE FUTURE INEVITABLE.
THE DREAMS OF A **DREAM-SEER**...
...WILL NEVER FAIL.

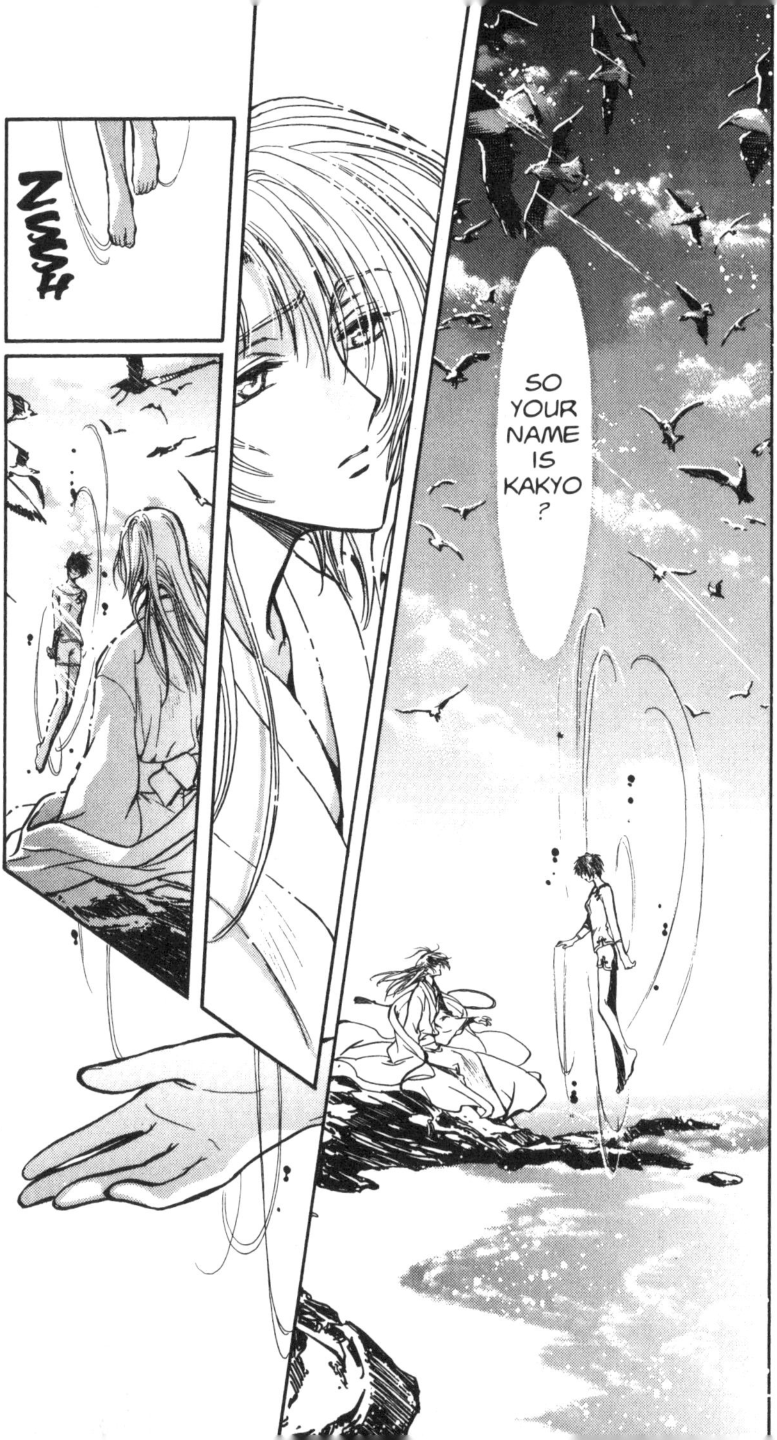
SO YOUR NAME IS KAKYO ?
NSSH

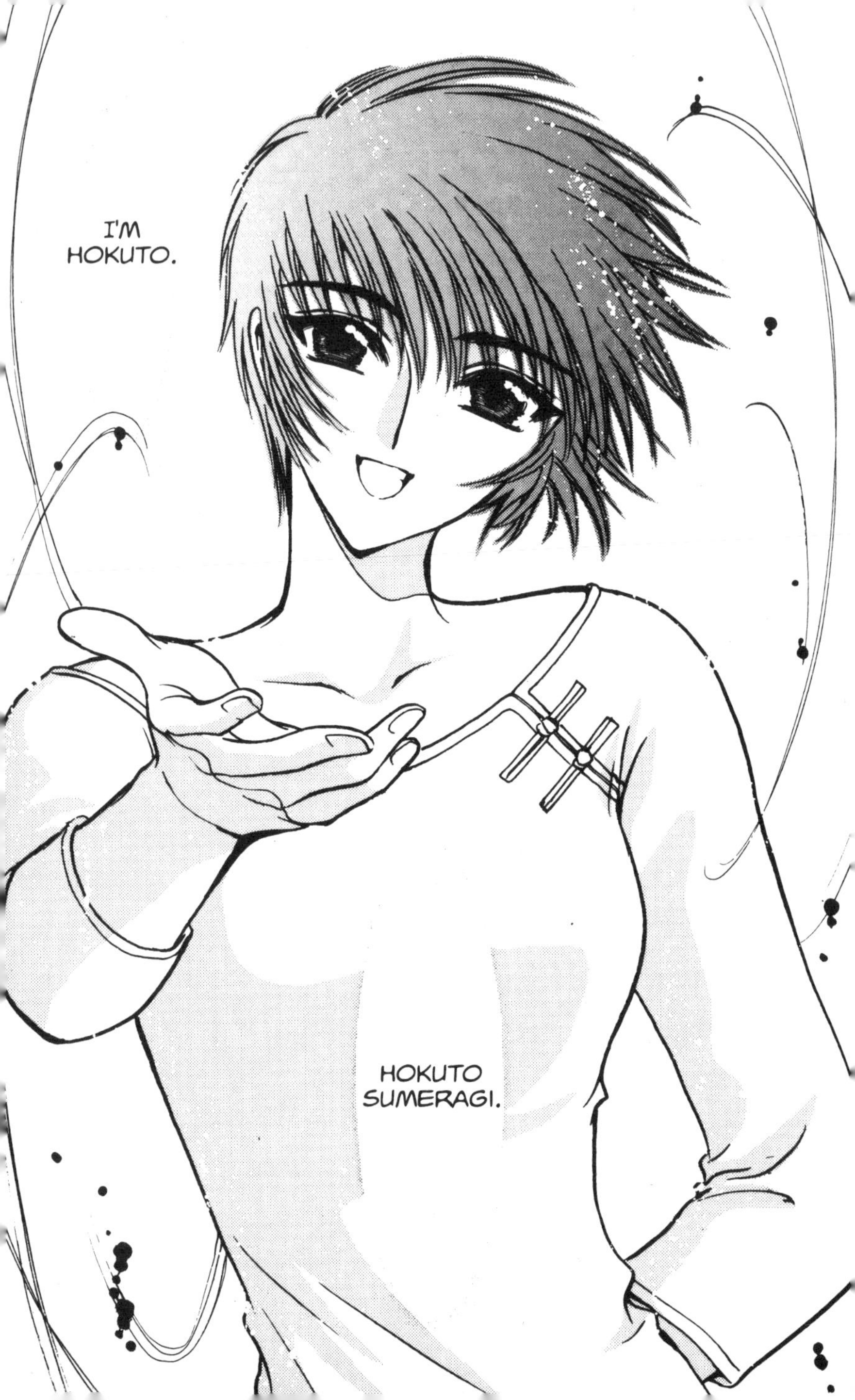
I'M HOKUTO.
HOKUTO SUMERAGI.

$$X$$ 14 END

X

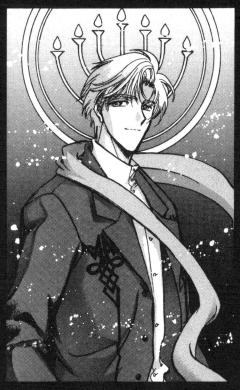

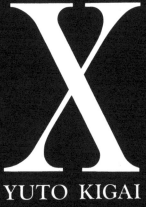

YUTO KIGAI

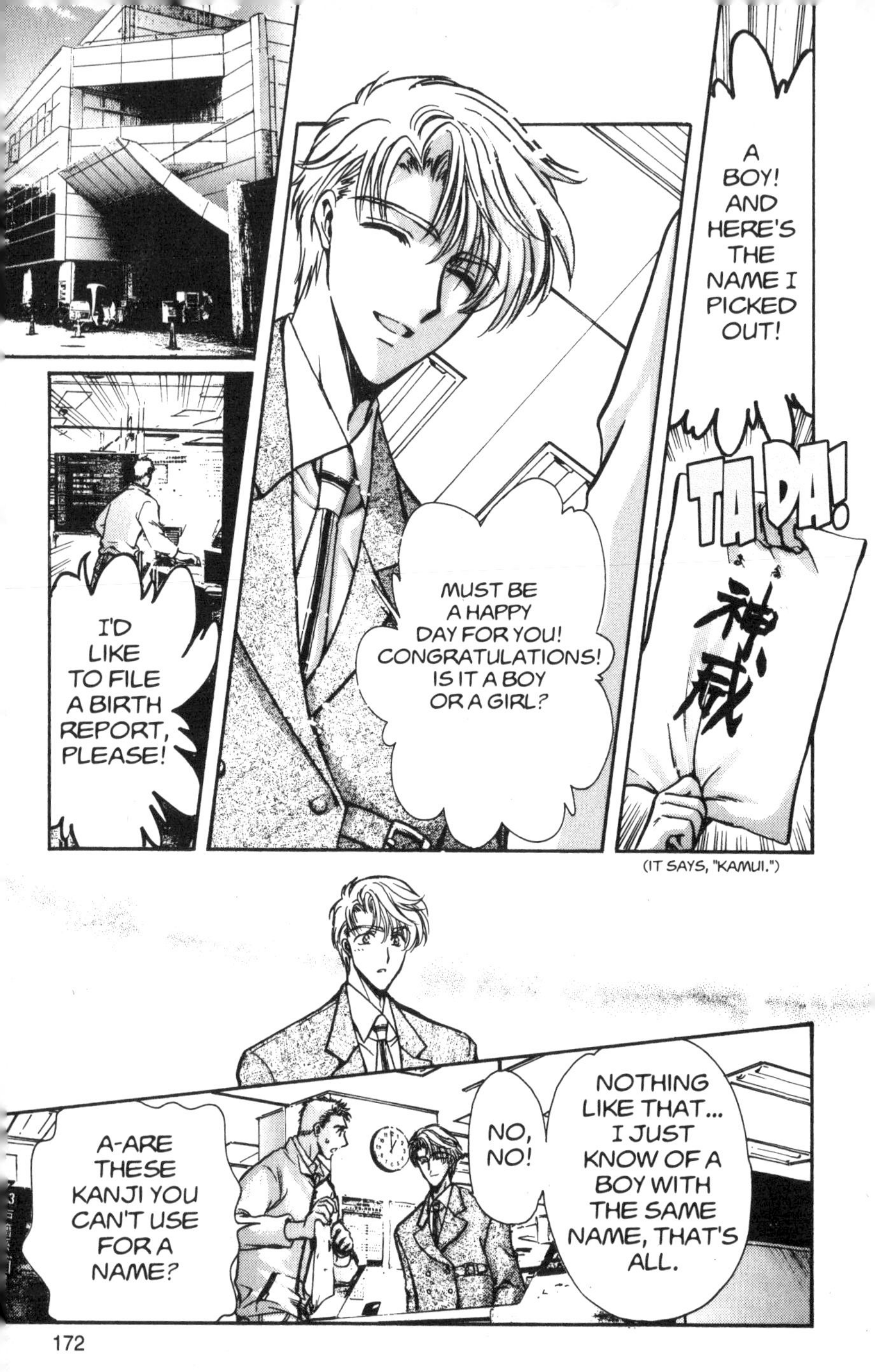
I'D LIKE TO FILE A BIRTH REPORT, PLEASE!
MUST BE A HAPPY DAY FOR YOU! CONGRATULATIONS! IS IT A BOY OR A GIRL?
A BOY! AND HERE'S THE NAME I PICKED OUT!
TA-DA!
神威
A-ARE THESE KANJI YOU CAN'T USE FOR A NAME?
NO, NO!
NOTHING LIKE THAT... I JUST KNOW OF A BOY WITH THE SAME NAME, THAT'S ALL.
(IT SAYS, "KAMUI.")

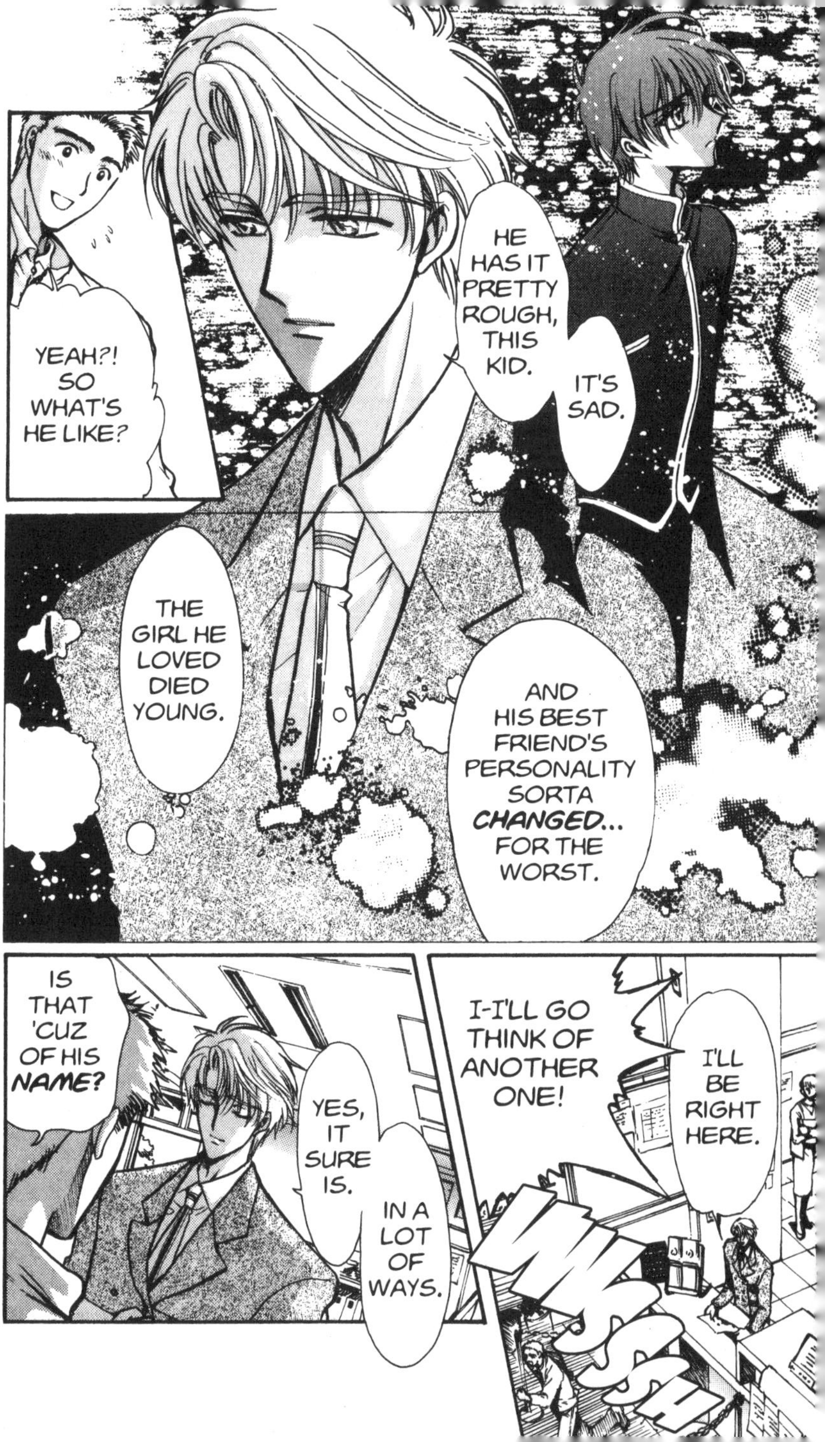
YEAH?! SO WHAT'S HE LIKE?
HE HAS IT PRETTY ROUGH, THIS KID.
IT'S SAD.
THE GIRL HE LOVED DIED YOUNG.
AND HIS BEST FRIEND'S PERSONALITY SORTA ***CHANGED***... FOR THE WORST.
IS THAT 'CUZ OF HIS ***NAME?***
YES, IT SURE IS.
IN A LOT OF WAYS.
I-I'LL GO THINK OF ANOTHER ONE!
I'LL BE RIGHT HERE.
WHSSH

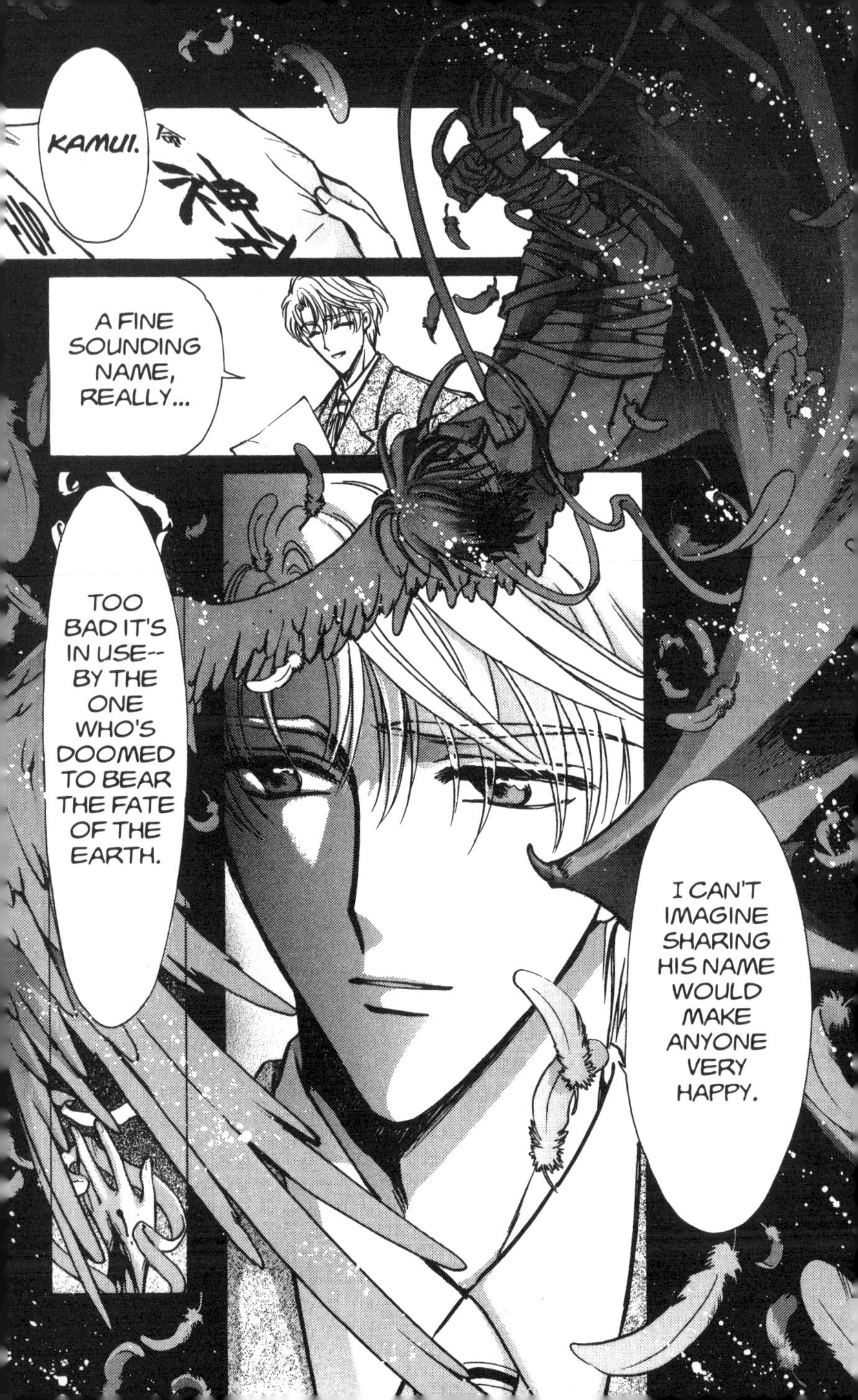
KAMUI.
A FINE SOUNDING NAME, REALLY...
TOO BAD IT'S IN USE-- BY THE ONE WHO'S DOOMED TO BEAR THE FATE OF THE EARTH.
I CAN'T IMAGINE SHARING HIS NAME WOULD MAKE ANYONE VERY HAPPY.

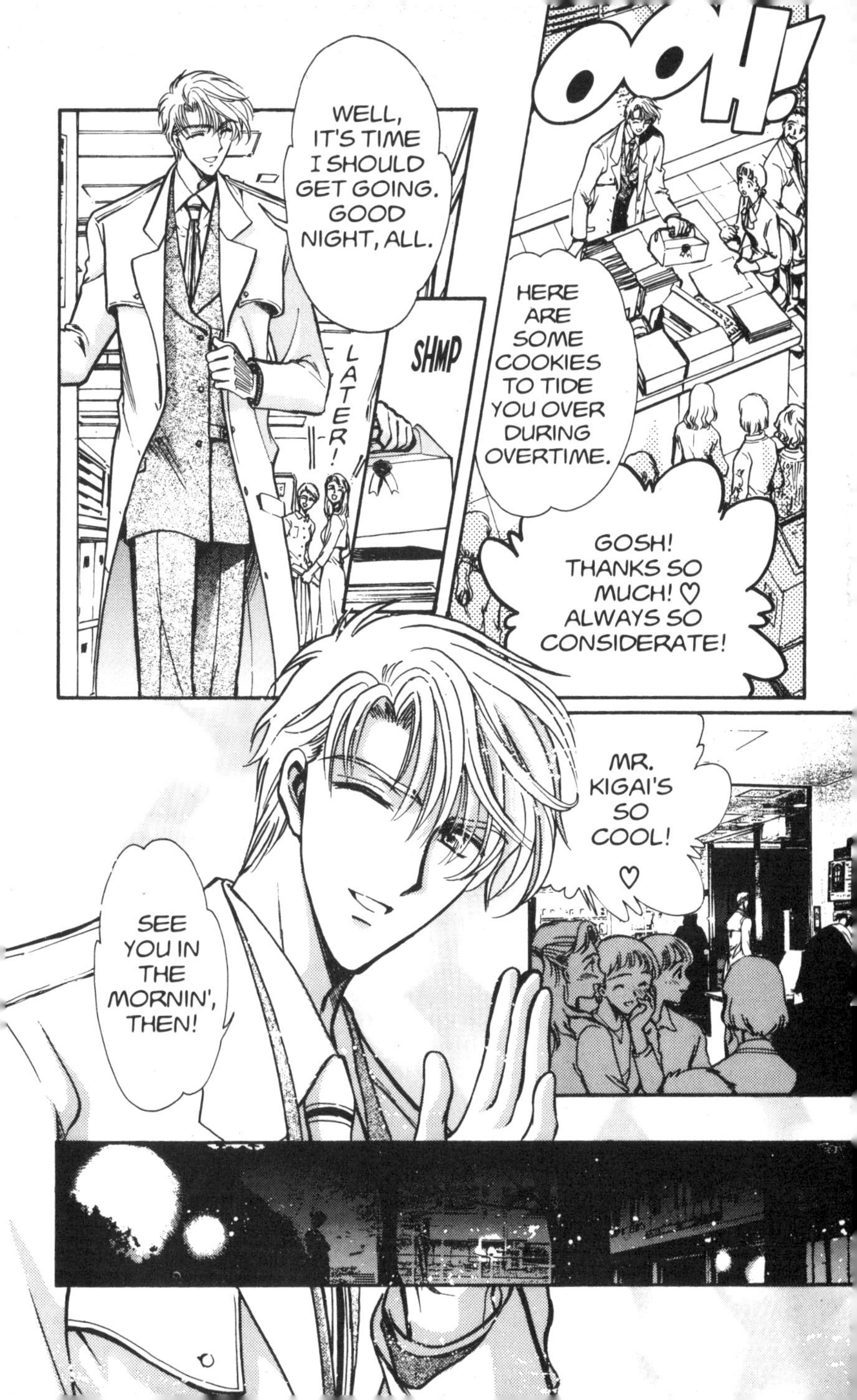
OOH!
HERE ARE SOME COOKIES TO TIDE YOU OVER DURING OVERTIME.
GOSH! THANKS SO MUCH! ♡ ALWAYS SO CONSIDERATE!
WELL, IT'S TIME I SHOULD GET GOING. GOOD NIGHT, ALL.
LATER!
SHMP
MR. KIGAI'S SO COOL! ♡
SEE YOU IN THE MORNIN', THEN!

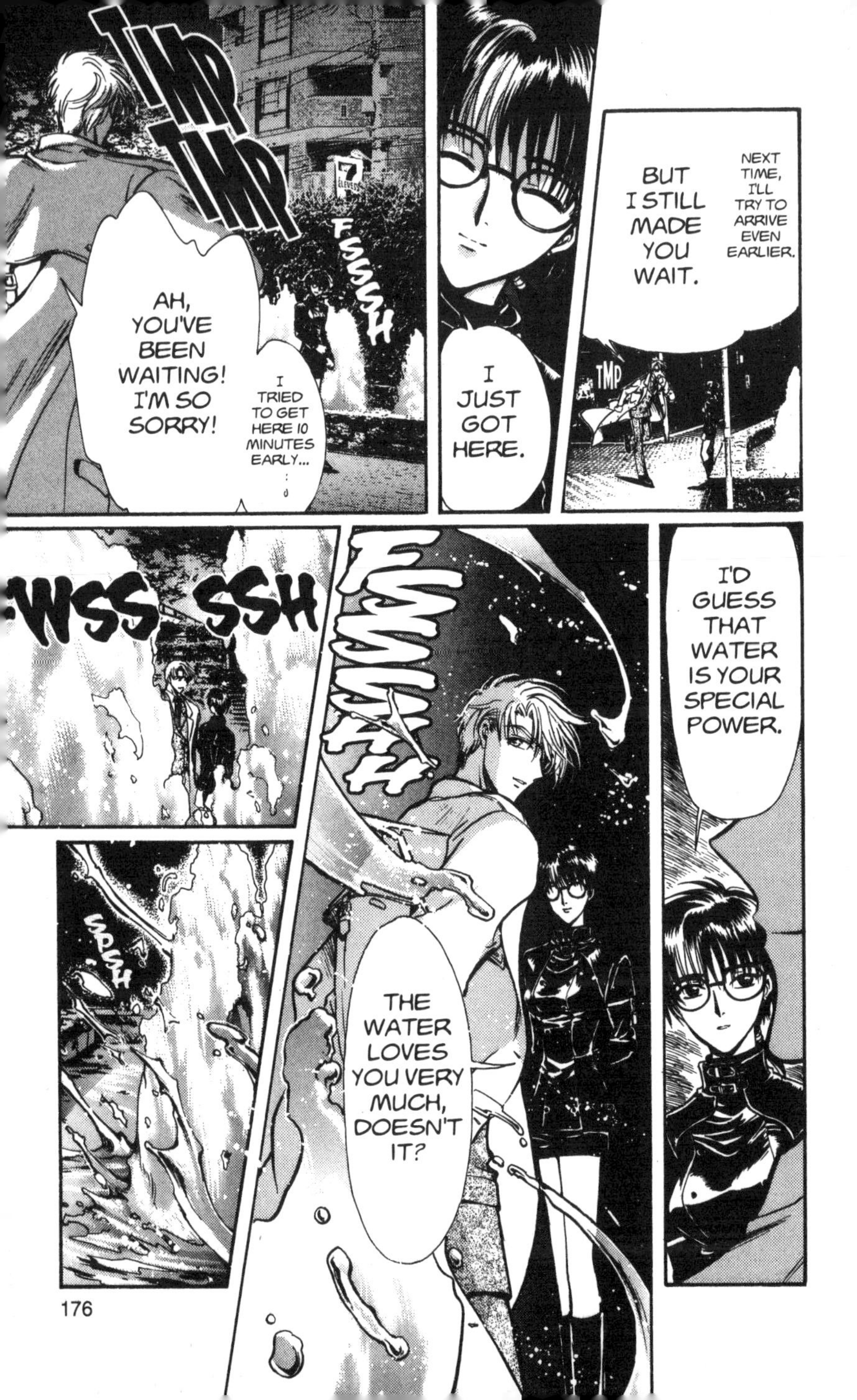
TMP TMP
FSSSSH
AH, YOU'VE BEEN WAITING! I'M SO SORRY!
I TRIED TO GET HERE 10 MINUTES EARLY...
I JUST GOT HERE.
BUT I STILL MADE YOU WAIT.
NEXT TIME, I'LL TRY TO ARRIVE EVEN EARLIER.
TMP
WSS SSH
THE WATER LOVES YOU VERY MUCH, DOESN'T IT?
I'D GUESS THAT WATER IS YOUR SPECIAL POWER.

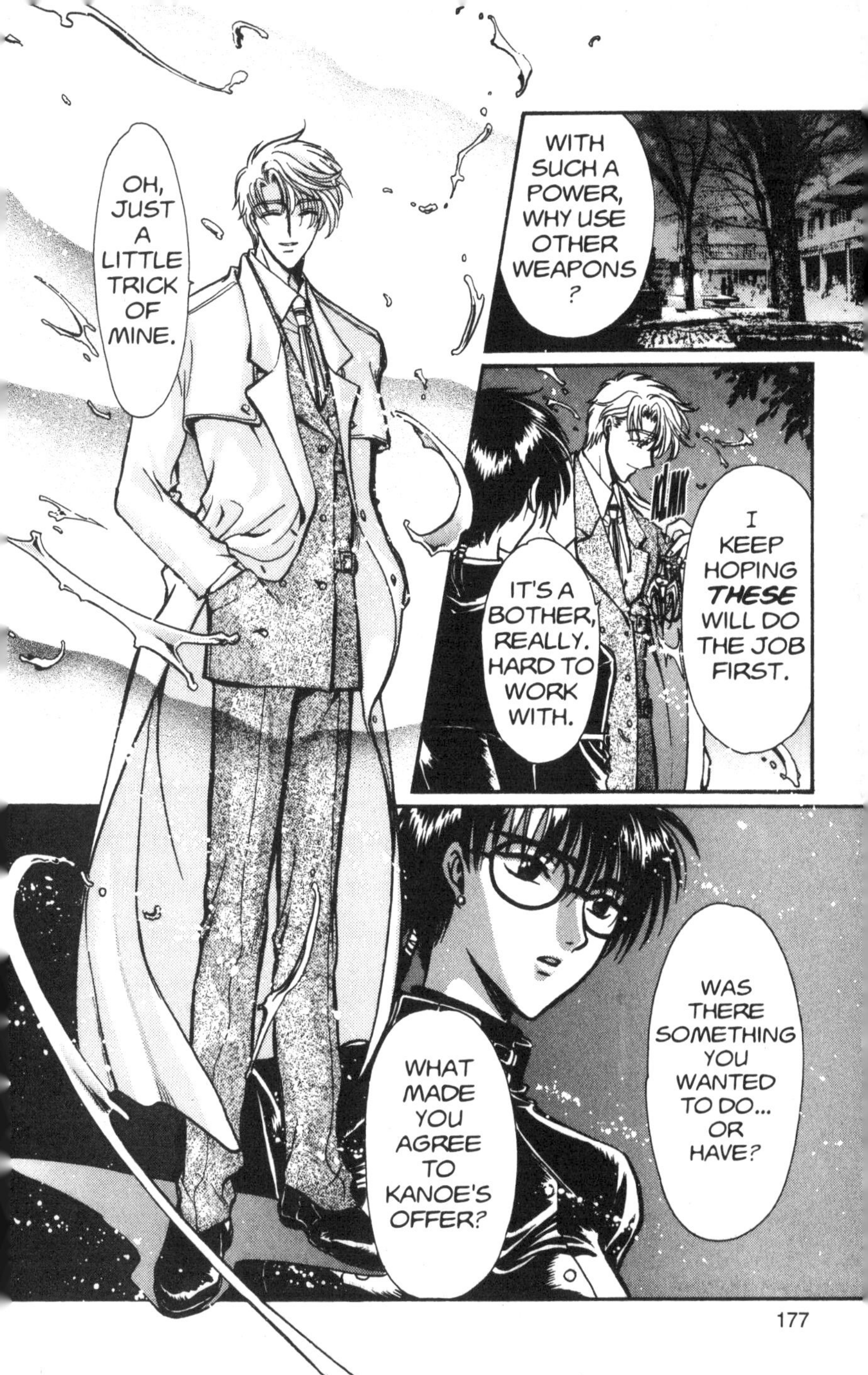
WITH SUCH A POWER, WHY USE OTHER WEAPONS?
I KEEP HOPING *THESE* WILL DO THE JOB FIRST.
IT'S A BOTHER, REALLY. HARD TO WORK WITH.
OH, JUST A LITTLE TRICK OF MINE.
WAS THERE SOMETHING YOU WANTED TO DO... OR HAVE?
WHAT MADE YOU AGREE TO KANOE'S OFFER?

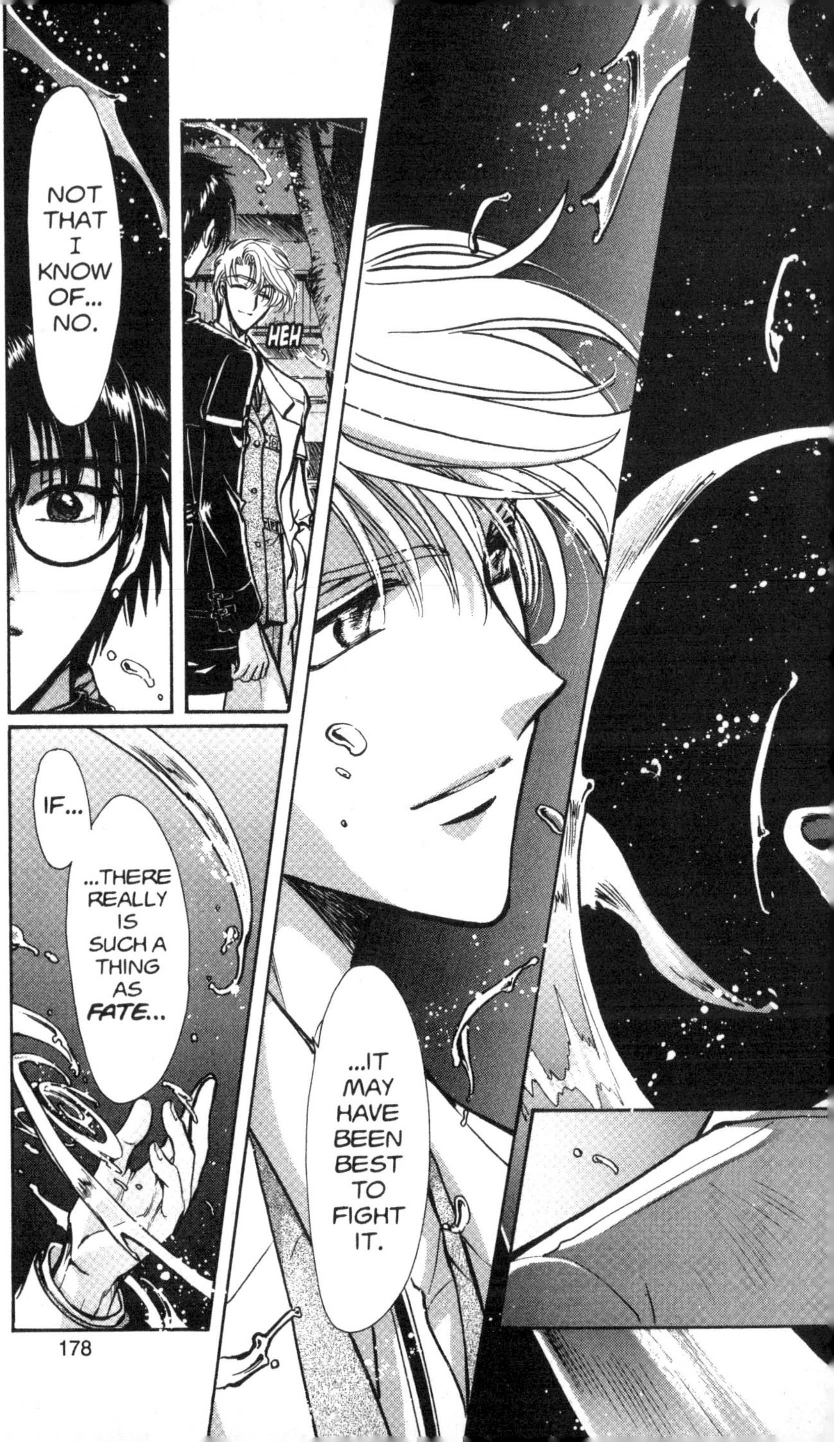
HEH
NOT THAT I KNOW OF... NO.
IF...
...THERE REALLY IS SUCH A THING AS *FATE*...
...IT MAY HAVE BEEN BEST TO FIGHT IT.

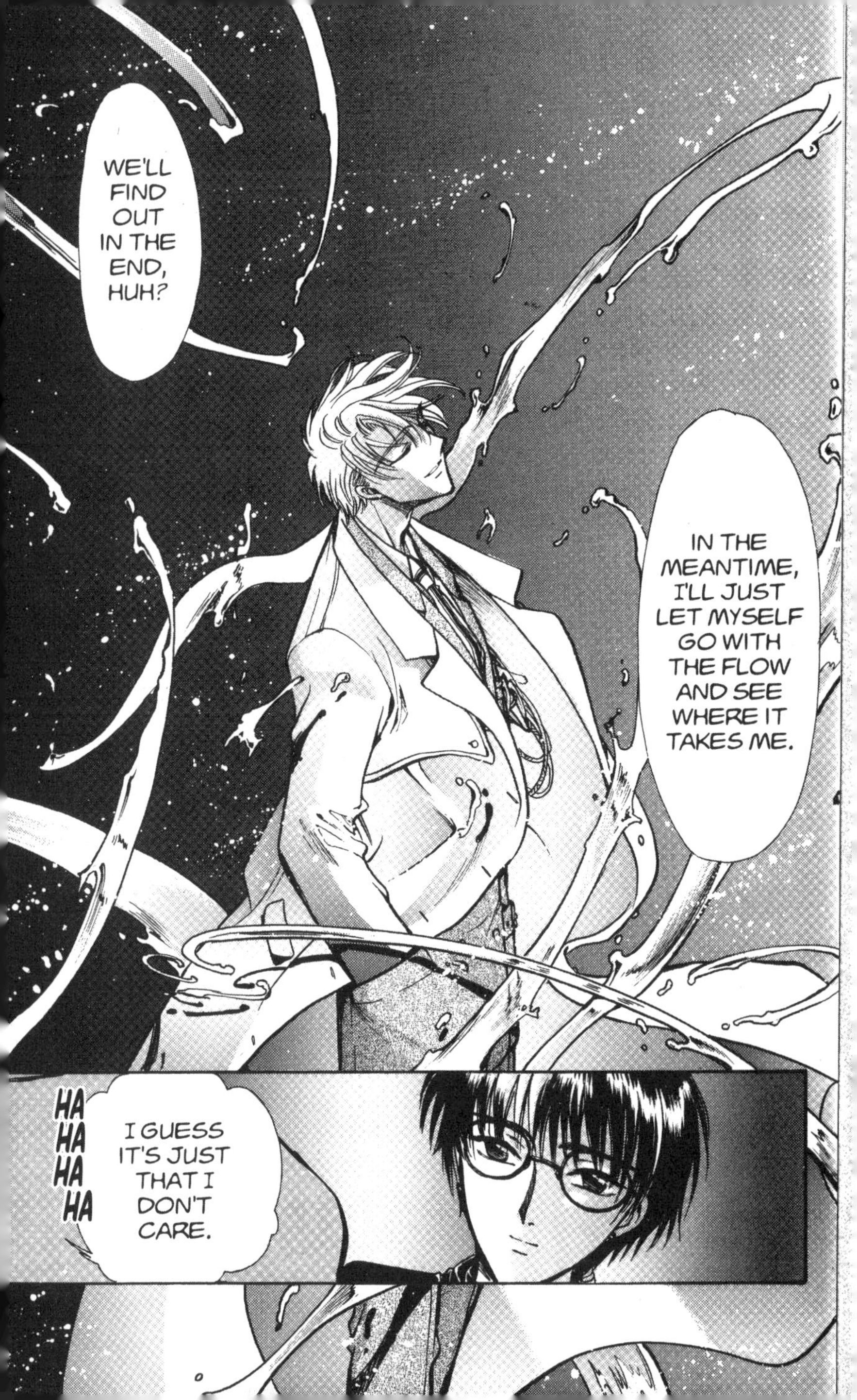
IN THE MEANTIME, I'LL JUST LET MYSELF GO WITH THE FLOW AND SEE WHERE IT TAKES ME.
WE'LL FIND OUT IN THE END, HUH?
I GUESS IT'S JUST THAT I DON'T CARE.
HA HA HA HA

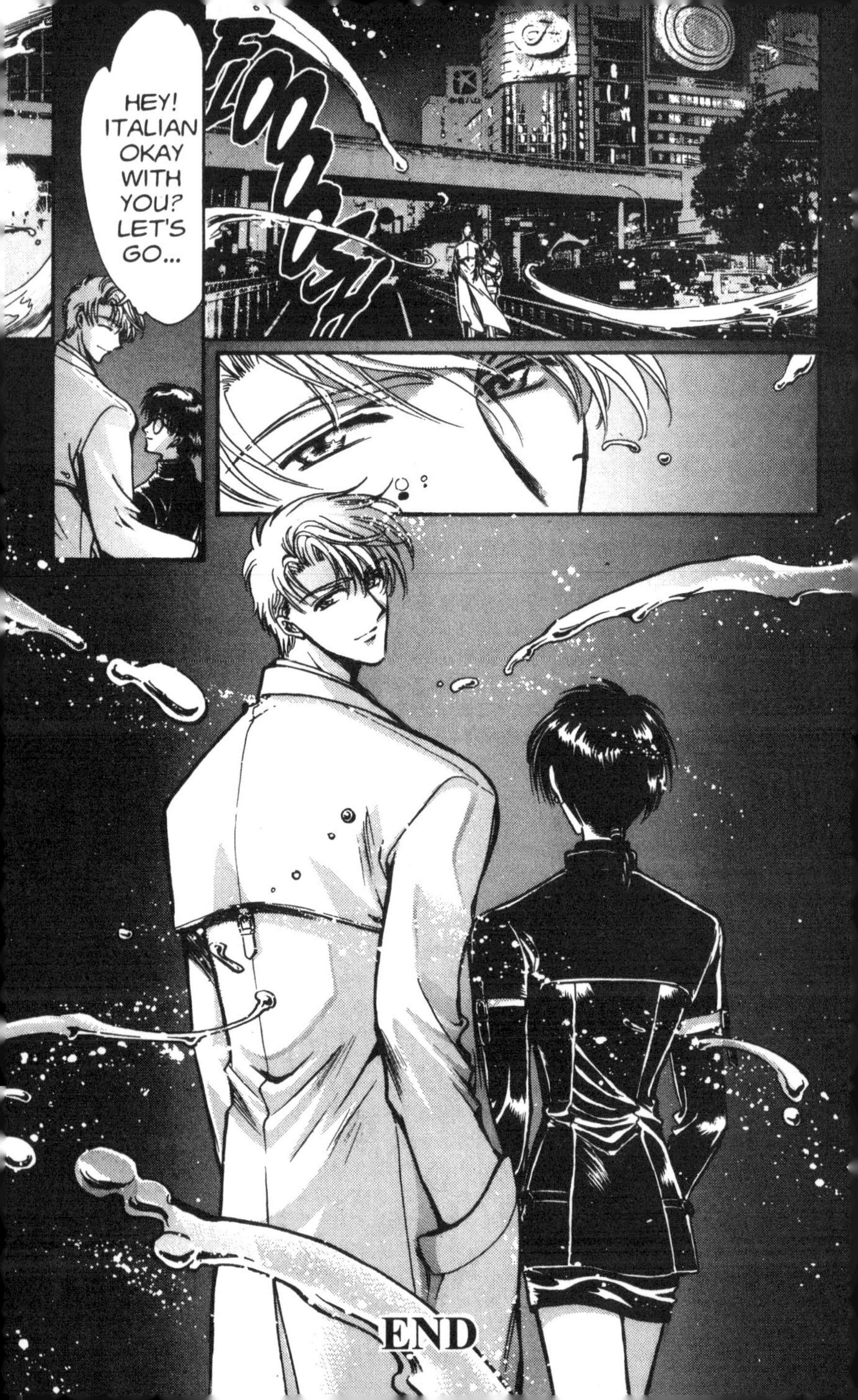
FOOOOSH
HEY! ITALIAN OKAY WITH YOU? LET'S GO...
END